FOUNDATIONS OF THE AMERICAN ECONOMY

THE AMERICAN COLONIES FROM INCEPTION TO INDEPENDENCE

VOLUME I

FOUNDATIONS OF THE AMERICAN ECONOMY

THE AMERICAN COLONIES FROM INCEPTION TO INDEPENDENCE

Edited by
Marianne Johnson
Steven G. Medema
Warren J. Samuels

VOLUME I

From Theocracy to Secular,
Materialist Commercial Society

LONDON AND NEW YORK

First published 2003 by Pickering & Chatto (Publishers) Limited

Published 2016 by Routledge
2 Park Square, Milton Park, Abingdon, Oxon OX14 4RN
711 Third Avenue, New York, NY 10017, USA

Routledge is an imprint of the Taylor & Francis Group, an informa business

BRITISH LIBRARY CATALOGUING IN PUBLICATION DATA

Foundations of the American economy : the American colonies from inception to
independence
    1. Economics – United States – Sources 2. United States – Economic conditions –
    Sources 3. United States – Economic policy – Sources
    I. Samuels, Warren J. (Warren Joseph), 1933– II. Johnson, Marianne III. Medema,
    Steven G. IV. From theocracy to secular, materialist commercial society V. Individu-
    alism and the structure of power VI. Colonial money, credit and debt VII. Mercantil-
    ism and colonialism, part I VIII. Mercantilism and colonialism, part II
    330.9'73

LIBRARY OF CONGRESS CATALOGING-IN-PUBLICATION DATA

Foundations of the American economy. 1. The American colonies from inception to
independence / edited by Marianne Johnson, Warren J. Samuels, and Steven G. Medema
    p.cm
    Includes index.
    Contents: v.1. From theocracy to secular, materialist commercial society – v.2. Indi-
    vidualism and the structure of power – v.3. Colonial money, credit and debt – v.4.
    Mercantilism and colonialism, pt. 1 – v.5. Mercantilism and colonialism, pt.2.
    1. Economics – United States – History. 2. United States – Economic conditions – To
    1865. I. Johnson, Marianne. II. Samuels, Warren J., 1933- III. Medema, Steven G.

HB119 .E17 2001
330'.0973'09032-dc21

    2001036917

ISBN-13: 978-1-85196-727-8 (set)

New material typeset by
P&C

CONTENTS

GENERAL INTRODUCTION

FROM THE SEVENTEENTH CENTURY TO 1888

These volumes constitute a selection of early American economic writing. The collection as a whole is composed of fifteen volumes, containing complete works and excerpts from writings dating between 1616 and 1888. It is important to define what we mean by the phrase 'early American economic thought'. In this collection 'early' concludes with economists active before the end of the nineteenth century. This means, for example, that the later volumes include Amasa Walker, Simon Newcomb and Henry George, as well as Richard T. Ely and John Bates Clark. The end date of the collection was chosen to include the founding of the American Economic Association in 1885, an event that can be seen as a conspicuous step in the professionalisation of American economics. After that point, economic thought in America became largely that of professional university and college economists.

The collection is broken into three chronological groups. The first group (of five volumes) contains economic works from the seventeenth and eighteenth centuries, prior to the American Revolution, the second group (of six volumes) covers the period from American Independence to the Civil War and the third group (of four volumes) contains works from the post-Civil War period until 1888. As the volume of economic literature increased steadily, greater selectivity was required as we progressed through time. The relative emphasis on the earlier period is deliberate, as these are the writings least known to historians of economics. For the later periods we attempt to provide a representative sample of contemporary works. However, due to constraints of space, there were, inevitably, some important texts which we were unable to include.

But how much should be included from before the end of the nineteenth century? The collection includes representative works from the beginning of the colonial period, the earliest of which is John Smith's *A Description of New England* (1616). The topics for the colonial period include wealth, money, trade, slavery and taxation. This literature certainly is part of the story of American economic thought. It provided the basis for the practical and day-to-day policy-making of the period and laid the groundwork for later economic theory. The selections chosen display the variety and transformation of religious views on economic subjects and dispel common myths about American economic thought during that period (for example, that it was politically motivated and derivative of European thought).

'American' means English-speaking, as economic thought from Central and South America are not included. Those born in Europe or elsewhere, but who immigrated to the United States are included as Americans; for example, John Cotton, William Penn, John Smith and Roger Williams. This is also true for individuals in later volumes, such as Thomas Cooper, Albert Gallatin, Alexander Hamilton, Francis Lieber, Friedrich List, Thomas Paine, John Rae and George Tucker. Needless to say, individuals educated in Europe – primarily England, Scotland, Germany, and France – but of American origin, are also included. It was common for Americans to study in Germany during the 1880s and 1890s. Such German-trained scholars included Richard T. Ely, H. C. Adams, John Bates Clark, Arthur Hadley, Simon Patten, Edmund J. James and E.R.A. Seligman. Cotton Mather is notable as the first author in this collection solely educated in America; he received his undergraduate and master's degrees from Harvard University in 1678 and 1681, respectively.

Europeans writing on 'American' topics are not generally included – an obvious example would be Adam Smith's discussion of colonial economic policy in the *Wealth of Nations* (1776). However, one exception is the inclusion of *The Fundamental Constitutions of Carolina* (1698) that has been attributed to John Locke. This piece provides an excellent example of the legal-economic rights of colonists granted by the King of England.

'Economic' means more than 'professional academic economists', and the approach taken is to reflect what Joseph Dorfman, in his five magisterial volumes, called the economic mind of American civilisation.[1] Accordingly, the story of early economic thought must encompass contributions and ideas emanating from people who were not academic economists. But to what extent should we adhere to Dorfman's definition? No collection can attempt to present a truly comprehensive record of the volume of writings on economics, broadly defined. No matter what else can and must be said, the collection is a sample. Yet, the issues are, how representative a sample, and representative of what? Sufficient diversity of topics, authors and positions have been included to demonstrate the vastness and diversity of economic thought which was both cause and consequence of the evolving American economy during the three centuries covered by this collection.

'Thought', means writings pertaining to the major economic themes/topics that arose. This means, for example, the moral basis of the economy,

---

[1] Joseph Dorfman, *The Economic Mind in American Civilization* (New York: VikingPress, 1946).

protectionism, paper currency, debt, growth policy (Hamiltonian 'industrial policy'), public improvements, population, rent theory, taxation, the economic role of government, property, class structure, socialism, critique and reform of regnant economic system, slavery/slave system, the banking system and so on. This implies, therefore, a wide conception of 'economic' and of 'economic thought'.

II

The scope of 'economic thought' is but one historiographical issue on which the editors have had to take a position. A second issue is the question of multiplicity, which arises in several ways. First, multiple and different positions were taken on all issues. Space constraints do not permit inclusion of writings representative of every side of every issue. Second, individual writings can be and indeed have been interpreted in multiple and different ways by later writers. Over two hundred years of interpretive writings – for example, on the meaning of various works of Thomas Jefferson, John Adams, and James Madison – have shown that the meaning of individual writings and authors can vary with interpretive standpoint and perceptions of context. Here we can provide only the original works – and only a sample of these – but not the interpretive writings. Hopefully, careful and unbiased study of these works will help either dispel and/or place in perspective various mythic views of what early Americans stood for, with regard to, for example, the place of religion, the nature of freedom, the economic role of government and so on – though one person's myth is another's definition of reality. Consequently, many of the issues debated remain contested in the early twenty-first century.

A third historiographical issue is also an epistemological one. The overwhelming majority of writers whose works are included in this collection were not objective scholars attempting to describe and explain the world around then in a non-normative manner. True, many, if not most, writings do include descriptions and explanations. But these are typically incidental to, or involved in, making a case for some policy. For the overriding character of these writings is their social constructivist orientation. These – and later – authors were aware that they were actively engaged in working out the type and structure of society that would come to exist in North America. The same is true, it should be said, of the later interpreters of these early works and authors.

American economic thought reflects a variety of factors and forces, from the challenges of a newly forming society in the seventeenth century through the much disputed issues of banking and trade policy in the eighteenth century to the debates over method that marked the stabilisation of an intellectual, scientific discipline at the end of the nineteenth century. This collection reflects the economic thinking to be found in America as that thought evolved. Judging by the canons of modern economics, the picture is broad, diffuse and very mixed. There is some dilettantism and amateurism, but there are also, and from the beginning, many serious and penetratingly deep writings on important questions. Such work not only contributed to contemporary dialogues but also anticipated and set the stage for later work.

Prior to the late nineteenth century, there were professors of economics who described and interpreted economic affairs, promulgated economic theory and proposed schemes of economic policy. They did not write primarily for each other; they wrote to influence public opinion on economic issues. They were, however, only some of the authors from whom issued the economic mind of American civilisation. Concurrent with these professional writings were those of many other groups in the country with an interest in economic affairs. In this collection, there is a variety of professions, beyond that of professional or academic economist – doctors, lawyers, farmers, politicians, merchants, religious leaders, journalists, adventurers and speculators. There is also a variety of mediums, beyond books and academic journals – newspapers, privately published pamphlets, speeches, governmental policies and reports, sermons, private letters, autobiographies and popular magazines. Accordingly, the story of early economic thought must encompass the contributions and ideas emanating from people who were not academic economists. Propagandists some of them may have been, but the distinction between propaganda and work with analytical content and intent is not a sharp one. This is evident in the pre-Civil War literature on slavery, as well as in discussions of population, money and banking, and protection. Of course, this diversity and plurality diminishes as we move to the close of the nineteenth century, and professionally trained economists dominate the discussion in books and academic journals.

III

With this understanding of who is relevant to a meaningful account of the history of early thought on economic topics, the question arises as to the political and institutional context within which that history is to be understood as taking place.

A number of features of American economic thought are particularly evident in this collection. First, there is the close interweaving of economics and politics. Indeed, our periods and groupings are themselves defined by major political events: the colonisation of America, the Revolutionary

War, and the Civil War and its aftermath. This is further evident in that many of the 'economists' in this collection were also politicians: Benjamin Franklin, Alexander Hamilton, John Jay, Thomas Jefferson, George Logan, Albert Gallatin, Henry Clay and John C. Calhoun, among others. The earliest writers in our collection were both political and religious leaders in their communities: men like John Cotton, Cotton Mather, William Penn, Roger Williams and John Winthrop.

Second, the literature clearly reflects the gradual building of commercial and national economic institutions in America. In the earlier years American economic writings express the struggles over and transformation from a theocratic to a secular, materialist commercial society. Corresponding writings relate to the correlative establishment and transformation of the legal foundations and framework of the new economic order. Clearly related are writings expressive of conflicts over individualism, democracy and the structure of political and economic power amongst the colonists, as well as between the colonists and Great Britain. Writings address important, controversial and technical problems of colonial money, credit and debt, including the chronic currency shortages suffered by the colonists. Lastly, writings relate the colonial perspective on mercantilism, British colonial policy and free trade.

Within the period from the American Revolution to the US Civil War, the writings of primary importance express concerns over how to construct a national economy and which economic interests the federal government should promote and protect. This includes the discussion of agriculture versus manufacturing, protectionism versus free-trade, and slavery. Writings address taxation and national-infrastructure investment, the expansion of the frontiers of the United States and theories of population growth. The selections include the highly political and caustic discussions on the formation of a national bank, as well as monetary policy, credit and debt. Writings begin to express the self-conscious development of the study of political economy and economic theory in America.

In the period from the Civil War to the end of the nineteenth century writings consider the national debt and supply of money, protection versus free trade, railroad regulation, poverty in relation to institutions, competition versus monopoly, social structure in relation to economic policy, monetary theory, the socioeconomic role of religion, the 'labour question' and the organisation of labour, as well as government regulation versus ownership. Writings address the controversy over the Single Tax, as well as several other efforts at social reform and applied policy topics such as taxation, tariffs, antitrust, unionisation and strikes, immigration, imperialism.

Third, the collection displays the gradual professionalisation of economics in a number of ways: in the early efforts to present systematised textbook statements of political economy, in writings treating issues of the appropriate scope and methodology of economics as an academic discipline, in the organisation of the American Economic Association and in the early attempts to write the history of American economic thought. Also included are evermore esoteric but important issues of theory such as income distribution, monetary standards and questions of evolutionary and dynamic economics.

IV

The people in every society formulate over time both their conceptions of the economic system – what it is and what it should be – and the actual institutionalised economy in which they live. These formulations are not undertaken once and for all time; neither are they undertaken entirely consciously. They are, basically, worked out over time through political, theological, cultural and social processes. The economic system of a society is but one subprocess of the multifaceted total social process. There is an evident interaction between actual arrangements and experiences, on the one hand, and the belief systems through which those arrangements and experiences are pursued and interpreted. The 'arrangements' are institutions which form and operate through the economy; to the extent that the economy is a market economy, institutions – governments, firms, and so on – structure and operate through the actual markets in which economic actors operate. Power of all kinds and belief systems – or ideologies – operate in a process marked by mutual interaction and cumulative causation.

Every society/economy has to work out, not once and for all time but continuously in a never-ending process, the temporary, problematic ongoing solutions to what Joseph J. Spengler called the problem of order.[1] This is the need to work out resolutions of a multitude of conflicts between continuity and change, between freedom (or autonomy) and control, between hierarchy and egalitarianism. The process of working all this out is further complicated not only because of interdependencies between each of the three sets of conflicts but because what is taken to constitute continuity, change, freedom, control, hierarchy and egalitarianism varies among subgroups and over time (e.g., the nature of the status quo). What is taken, subjectively and selectively, as 'order' is some more or less ambiguous and more or less realised and more or less problematic set of resolutions of these conflicts. Further complications arise because of different conceptions of what is given by the nature of things, what is possible and what is desirable.

---

[1] Joseph J. Spengler, 'The Problem of Order in Economic Affairs' in *Southern Economic Journal*, 15 (July 1948), pp. 1–29.

Another way of looking at the foregoing is to say that society has to work out – adopt, adapt and change – the institutions which structure the economy, the institutions which determine who can make what decisions and when, who can do what to whom and when not, and so on. Much of these, ultimately, are matters of belief, always subject to change of nuance and of application; but much is a matter of what John R. Commons called an institution, namely, collective action both in control and liberation of individual action.

One of the most important yet most obscure and unappreciated domains of collective action is the common law, the law promulgated incrementally by the state and federal courts. From the seventeenth through to the twentieth century what had commenced as the legal system of an essentially agrarian, rural, landed-property system became trans-formed into the legal system of an increasingly urban, commercial, eventually industrial, non-landed-property system. This transformation involved enormous changes in the meaning of property, contract and lib-erty, and the social system and structure in which economic activity took place. The interests protected as property, and their corresponding social groupings or classes, changed enormously. Yet, compared to issues of money and banking, tariff protection and internal improvements, for example, much of this change took place quietly and unappreciated by many of the interests affected by them.

Take the construction of the system of money and banking. This is the most dominant topic of this collection, comprising four of the fifteen vol-umes and covering the entire period from the early seventeenth to the end of the nineteenth century. Numerous economists, notably including Carl Menger and Friedrich A. von Hayek, have pointed to the history of money as one in which the systemic consequences of various decisions and actions have been unintended and unexpected, with the implication that monetary systems cannot be planned. This has not, however, prevented both econo-mists and non-economists, especially parties with directly affected material interests, from proposing and lobbying for their own schemes of monetary reform. One fact of the matter is that, in the United States, as elsewhere, policy with respect to money – or, more accurately, monetary and banking policy, inasmuch as the promulgation of a large part of the money supply comes through the banking system, something which took people centu-ries to appreciate – has, like most legislation, emanated from the lobbying of various interest groups, notably those with an immediate interest in reshaping the law governing their affairs. Such should not be surprising in a democracy, especially a plutocratic one; as John R. Commons showed with respect, in principle, to all the legal foundations of capitalism, it is the normal state of affairs that out of the political-legal and economic actions and interactions of legislatures, courts and interested parties emerge the institutions, like money, within which we conduct our affairs and define our interests.[1] Such is the legal-economic nexus. Out of all this emerges, through a process of working things out, what may, or may not be called 'the public interest'.

Throughout our history a number of issues in monetary economics were unsettled and controversial – as some, or many, remain. These include the definition of money as between specie and paper and as between currency and bank credit, the relation of debt to money both in general and in relation to demand deposit balances, the nature and role of reserves, the multiple expansion and contraction process, the definition of money supply, the nature and role of commercial banks and (when present) of the central bank in the creation and management of money, the respective roles of money substitutes and of non-bank financial intermediaries and other institutions, the fact and the goals of monetary policy and, *inter alia*, the relation of the monetary and banking system to the larger polity and society.

Legislators and judges, as well as the lay public, may have used some more or less inchoate definitions of relevant terms, but whatever the meanings, the statutes and the decisions which they produced influenced the monetary, or monetary and banking, system. Like the other institutions of a market economy, they are fundamentally legal in character, the law thereof is an object of control and use, and institutions change in response to what might be called the market for institutional change – in which market various interests contend to advance and protect their interests, both within existing institutions and with regard to potential changes therein.

Accordingly, it is hardly surprising that the term 'money interest' has been one of opprobrium over the years, referring to nefarious, greedy manipulators of the system with only their interest in mind, often clothed in the rhetoric of 'the public interest', defining the public interest along lines favourable to their interests and not that of the masses of workers, consumers and citizens. Given the nature of our system, coupled with the widespread propensities to invoke some notion of rights, public interest and/or the natural order of things, i.e., invocation of transcendent authority, it is not surprising that we find both eloquent justifications for the pursuit of self-interest and the use of terms like 'the money interest' in a pejorative way. For many people over the years, it was difficult to accept the idea of bank credit as money in the same sense as gold or, for that matter, paper money (itself a form of debt). For many people, too, it came as something of a shock to appreciate that in our monetary and banking system (1) the power to issue money, given in the Constitution to the national government (specifically the Congress), had effectively been delegated to

---

[1] John R. Commons, *Legal Foundations of Capitalism* (New York: Macmillan, 1934).

private profit-seeking banks and (2) that the banking system creates money, in the form of credits to demand deposit accounts, in the act of a bank lending money to a borrower.

As for the juxtaposition of the private money interest and the public interest, one problem or complication is that there often are conflicting private interests with regard to money; 'the money interest' is heterogeneous. Another, and presently more interpretively serious, problem is the generic, non-specific nature of the term 'public interest'. One can comprehend private interests in monetary arrangements centring on what will increase, or maximise, profits. But what is the 'public interest' – in a world in which (1) markets (however institutionalised) are deemed by many to regulate buying and selling in the public interest; (2) different notions of the public interest will merge with different notions of private interest; (3) no economists' stone exists by which to identify the public interest, especially in institutional or structural matters; and (4) the basic theory of democracy is widely held to contemplate the public interest as something to be worked out in the crucible of the legal-economic nexus and not something which can be conclusively stipulated in advance – if only because of such phenomena as uncertainty, the destruction of some values in the process of creating others, and the operation of the principle of unintended and unexpected consequences, as well as one or another dialectical approach to the meaning of events – all of which also affect perceptions of private interest. In the terminology of the comedian Arte Johnson, all this is 'verrry interesting' – and laden with interpretive difficulty. The concept of the 'public interest' is both a hortatory device and a mode of discourse, a conceptual tool, not, or not necessarily, a definition of reality.

Two related important themes should be noted. One is the enormous diversity of ideas on every subject, in part because of the different economic interests both forming and formed by the economy, and the different standpoints from which different and often seriously conflicting perspectives issued. The other is that throughout the history covered in this collection the form that the economy should take was in dispute. From the vantage point of the present day, it may seem inevitable that the economy of the United States would become not only an industrial market economy but also a capitalist economic system. Yet these were contested issues. Questions arose concerning what type of economy we were making and of the type we should be making. Not everyone supported urbanisation, commercialisation, industrialisation, the formation of a 'banking interest', the construction of a 'corporate system', the erection of a social structure on top of which stood the owners of old landed property, the owners of commercial and industrial property and the professional managers of property of all types, but especially that in the hands of corporations. Even, and perhaps especially, among these elite groups, conflicts of interest and ideas, as well as mutually beneficial accommodations of interest, were to be observed. But, especially in the nineteenth and early twentieth centuries, people of various types were more or less aware that decisions were being made which would transform the economy from one of individual entrepreneurs to one of vast corporate entities and from an agricultural system supported by manufacturing to an industrial system with agriculture in some respects a group of poor relation (especially the family farmer) and in other respects a group of industrial corporations ('agribusiness'). The Jeffersonian ideals of local businesses, local markets and problems for local government, with 'all' people property owners, came into conflict with the growth of regional and then national markets, national (and international) business and problems for national government.

V

It is commonplace but nonetheless true that history does not write itself and that history is a seamless web. As to the first, the facts of history (slavery, the American Revolution, the Civil War, industrialisation) and the documents of intellectual history/the history of ideas (pamphlets, columns, essays, books, journal articles, political and religious documents) are relatively straightforward. Not straightforward are (1) which facts and which documents are important and (2) how they are to be understood. Every possible topic of US history, from the meaning of Puritanism to the meaning of freedom to the meaning of the modern corporation to the meaning of 'reform', has been given variegated interpretation. Each generation of historians and others has tended to interpret the past on its own terms; and every topic has been viewed and interpreted from different, often contradictory, perspectives.

History is thus socially constructed in two different senses. First, the individuals who live, act, think and work out ideas and programs for themselves and thereby make that which later people think of as history. For example, what Puritanism was to become was an object of debate, as were the institutions of money and banking, slavery, business, the welfare state and so on. Second, both contemporary and later thinkers socially construct the meaning of what actually or putatively happened. History is made by both those who live it and those who later interpret it; the latter, in part, as they live and make it in their own time. Such considerations are evident in the selections such as John Woolman's *Considerations on Keeping Negroes* (1754) and James Swan's *A Dissuasion…from the Slave Trade* (1772). Both works provide early criticisms of slavery based on economic arguments and stand out from their contemporaries. However, economic justifications or rationalisations of slavery are not included.

As to the second, history can be comprehended and written as political history, social history, economic history, intellectual history and so on. Sometimes and in some respects these divisions are clear and meaningful. The history of money and banking, the development of agriculture, the evolution of technology, and so on, are reasonably delimitable topics. But the history of economic thought (for example) is more than a narrow rendition of production, exchange and distribution. It is part and parcel of a larger conception of the economy. This conception envisions the economic system as part of a larger social whole and as, in part, an emanation of a legal-economic nexus. The economy, in a certain sense, therefore, takes on the hue and tenor of the larger culture. Religion and law, for example, influence the structure, belief system and operation of economic life; and economic life influences the conduct of religion and law. It is not only a Constitution that the courts are helping to make by issuing decisions. It is also the economy and the operative system of religious beliefs and institutions that are made by people in the ordinary business of life. What Dorfman called the economic mind of American civilisation therefore focused on economic life and thought, and yet it was wide ranging, precisely because the economic system, as an aspect of civilisation/society, was itself both an object of social construction and part of a seamless web of life.

William J. Barber, Marianne Johnson, Steven G. Medema,
Malcolm Rutherford, and Warren J. Samuels

INTRODUCTION

THE SEVENTEENTH AND EIGHTEENTH CENTURIES (TO 1776)

I

These five volumes trace the evolution of economic thinking in North America, from John Smith's description of the economic riches of the continent in 1616 to the economic motivations of the desire for independence from Great Britain that arose in the mid-1700s.

The history of the economic thought of this period is largely – but by no means completely – omitted from the purview of the field and texts of the subdiscipline of the history of economic thought. One notable exception is, of course, Joseph Dorfman's *Economic Mind in American Civilization*.[1] This exclusion is partly because the economic thought of this period is generally considered politically motivated and partly because the developing technical sophistication of English and continental writers eventually dwarfed American contributions. Nevertheless, some of the most creative and insightful criticisms of the early English classical school could be found emanating from the colonies and their rapidly deteriorating relationship with Great Britain. The collection includes selected representative works from the American colonial period on a variety of topics, including wealth, money, trade, slavery, taxation and the variety and transformation of religious views on economic subjects. This literature certainly is part of the story of American economic thought. It lays the groundwork for both later economic theory and the practical day-to-day policy-making endeavours of this period. The materials are efforts both to construct and to interpret economic, or political-economic, life in North America from 1616 to the start of the Revolutionary War. In the seventeenth and early eighteenth centuries the writings were initially and even primarily political or religious. In all cases, the writings dealt with specific contemporary problems of society and contributed to the larger project of making a new society in the New World.

As large as this collection has become, we must emphasise that it is only a representative sample. No such collection can attempt to either preserve

[1] Joseph Dorfman, *The Economic Mind in American Civilization* (New York: Viking Press, 1946).

or present a truly comprehensive record of the volume of relevant newspaper articles, editorials, pamphlets, speeches, sermons, lectures, letters and books. Sufficient diversity of topics, authors and positions are included to be indicative, even if only suggestive, of the vastness and diversity of economic thought which was both cause and consequence of the social construction of the economy during the roughly two centuries covered by this part of the collection.

This first part of the larger collection is organised into five volumes. Each volume is ordered chronically and the volumes differ as to the broad themes that connect the works. The first volume includes writings expressive of the struggles over and the transformation from a theocratic to a secular, materialist commercial society. The second volume contains writings that relate to the correlative establishment and transformation of the legal foundations and framework of the new economic order. Clearly related to these themes were writings expressive of the several conflicts over individualism, democracy, and the structure of political and economic power amongst the colonists. Writings that address important, controversial and technical problems of colonial money, credit and debt are included in the third volume. Volumes four and five contain writings that relate the colonial perspective of mercantilism, the structure of political and economic power between the colonists and Great Britain, British colonial policy and free trade. These themes are also prevalent in the first three volumes, though often of secondary consideration in the selected writings.

II

In the American colonies, the new society borrowed facets of previous economic systems and forged new economic institutions and relationships based on the different geographic, climatic, cultural, social, political and religious conditions found in, brought to, and/or sought in America. The people in every society formulate, over time, both their conception(s) of that economic system – what it is and what it should be – and the actual institutionalised economy in which they live. This is readily apparent in the American colonial literature. These formulations are not undertaken once and for all time; neither are they undertaken entirely consciously. They are, basically, worked out over time through political, theological, cultural, and social processes, as belief systems influence institutions and institutions influence belief systems.

From 1616 to 1776, the American colonial society underwent dramatic changes in the organisation and control of the economic system – changes in access to markets, international trading partners, monetary systems, property rights, internal and external taxation and attitudes toward slavery.

By the dawn of the American Revolution, economic activity ranged from subsistence farming to increasingly sophisticated and, for that period, large-scale manufacturing in the major cities. At the same time, America was still an economy in which some eighty-five per cent of people (other than slaves or indentures) worked for themselves and a comparable percentage of output was either consumed by the producing family or bartered with neighbours. Further, most individuals were directly or indirectly engaged in agriculture.

Several different stages of economic development, organisation, and orientation existed simultaneously in the American colonies, leading to conflicting interests and views on various issues. Although the colonists began with what was essentially the structure of the British economy of the 1600s – in terms of property rights, economic organisation, distribution systems and British mercantilist policies – the fundamental structure of the colonial economy evolved and changed in the face of the different conditions and constraints in America. By the time of John Smith's landing in America, the first wave of the British enclosure movement was complete. This had led to the removal of a significant portion of the population from the land and the increased urbanisation of England. Manufacturing and wage-labour became increasingly prevalent and by the mid 1700s, Great Britain was the leading manufacturing nation in the world.

In contrast, the American colonies faced seemingly limitless land and natural resources and developed industries that centred on agriculture, mining, forestry and fishing. Farming was by far the dominant trade/profession. However, farms ranged from subsistence frontier farms, to small family farms in the northern coastal colonies, to the large slave-based plantations in the southern colonies. Westward expansion was constant during this period as the frontiers of America were extended into northern New York and west from Pennsylvania to the Ohio River Valley. Yet, while land was cheaply available, labour was scarce and expensive. Benjamin Franklin's *Interest of Great Britain Considered…* (1760) illustrated the connections between land, population growth and density, and occupational choice in America.[1]

The affordability of land made it difficult for employers in the cities to maintain wage labourers for long, undermining the cost-effectiveness of domestic manufactures, even on a small scale. The shortage of labour helps to explain the widespread adoption of indentured servitude in the northern colonies and slavery in the southern colonies. These institutions had a sig-

---

[1] Benjamin Franklin, *The Interest of Great Britain Considered with Regard to her Colonies and the Acquisitions of Canada and Guadalupe to which are added Observations Concerning the Increase of Mankind, Peopling of Countries* (Boston: B. Mecom, 1760).

nificant impact on perceptions of individual rights and individual versus collective economic decision-making.

During the eighteenth century, an increasing divergence between the interests of Great Britain and the American colonies took place. By the middle of that century, the wide apparatus of British mercantilist policies were in place and were beginning to constrain colonial development. In 1764 and 1765 respectively, the Sugar and Stamp Acts were imposed on the colonists in an attempt to raise funds to pay the British expenses from the French and Indian War. John Dickinson's *The Late Regulations Respecting the British Colonies...Considered* (1765) illustrated the changing economic views of such regulations.

> However under all these restraints and some others that have been imposed on us, we have not till lately been unhappy...But the modern regulations are in every circumstance afflicting. The remittances we have been able to make to Great-Britain, with all the license hitherto granted or taken, and all the money brought among us in the course of the late war, have not been sufficient to pay her what we owe; but there remains due, according to a late calculation made by the English merchants, the sum of four millions sterling. Besides this, we are and have been for many years heavily taxed, for the payment of the debts contracted by our efforts against the common enemy. These seem to be difficulties severe enough for young colonies to contend with. [1]

The colonial anti-mercantilist literature contained a growing demand for separation from Great Britain. The economic writings in this collection are therefore part of wider social and political writings that evidence the changes in America leading up to the American declaration of independence and Revolutionary War. The initial perceptions of the separateness of America evident in John Smith's and William Penn's writings in the first volume become more pronounced, culminating in Dickinson's statement in the fifth volume:

> What can we expect, when the exhausted colonies shall feel the Stamp Act drawing off, as it were, the last drops of their blood...Great Britain gives us an example to guide us. She teaches us to make a distinction between her interests and our own. Teaches! She requires—commands—insists upon it—threatens—compels—and even distresses us into it. [2]

The status of 'colony' and the relationship between the American colonies and Great Britain defined and gave context to various themes of the economic thought of this period – individual rights, taxation, property, money and so on. How the colonists were constrained by their status and

[1] John Dickinson, *The Late Regulations Respecting the British Colonies* (Philadelphia: William Bradford, 1765), pp. 7–8.
[2] *Ibid.*, pp. 19, 25.

the subordination of their interests to those of Great Britain are evident in nearly every work of these first five volumes.

III

As already stated, the volumes of this collection have been ordered by major themes: (1) theocracy and materialist society, (2) individual and society, (3) money and (4 and 5) mercantilism and free trade. Within those groupings are a number of other themes. Emphases on defining individual and property rights and on the rights and duties of countries to one another is found throughout all five volumes. One economic manifestation of these broader issues is seen in writings that address the right of an individual to set prices based on market rather than moral conditions. Another is the right of the colonies to choose their own trading partners. Additional themes of seventeenth- and eighteenth-century economic thought are identified below.

FROM THEOCRACY TO A SECULAR, MATERIALIST COMMERCIAL SOCIETY

Many of the selections included in this volume are political and religious, as well as economic; many of the earliest American economic writings expressed the struggles over, and transformation from, a theocratic to a secular, materialist commercial society. The writings address the complex, variegated and kaleidoscopic relations of religion and government, of individual and collective action, and of theological and secular views and interests. Some of these pieces can stand alone and some are most effective in conjunction with others. In all cases, they provide a sample of the writings on religious-economic topics that covers the first two centuries of life in America. Everything from pricing and taxes to monetary policy was governed in part by religious interpretations of society; this is apparent in Cotton Mather's *Some Considerations on the Bills of Credit, Now Passing in New England* (1691), included in the volume on monetary economics. Several early pieces of the first volume discuss the maintenance of the clergy and the connection between taxation by the state and governmental financial support of religion. These writings evidence the working out of a culture in which religion continued to be important, if transformed, and in which commercial and eventually manufacturing activity and ends came to dominate everyday life.

The complex relationship between religion, government and economics was evident from the start of the American colonies. The Northern Vir-

ginia Colony was founded as a joint-stock company with the twin
expressed goals of the religious conversion of the Native Americans and
profits for the shareholders. John Smith's *A Description of New England*
(1616) set an optimistic tone for America, lauding the extensive God-given
natural resources of the continent. Smith promised that those who settled
and worked hard would quickly become wealthy. While *A Description of
New England* is part travel guide, part economic history, and part economic
geography, it also evidenced the puritan belief that God rewards hard work
with earthly riches. Smith's work is the first in a series of propaganda pieces
encouraging immigration to America. Several other such writings are
included in this volume, including John Cotton's *God's Promise to his Plantations* (1634) and the two *Account(s) of Pennsylvania* (1681 and 1685) by
William Penn. In a similar vein, Thomas Budd's *Good Order Established*
(1685) is a good example of how economics was broadly defined in the
seventeenth century in America. His piece not only falls under the purview
of the theme of the first volume – the transformation from a religious to
commercial society – but also deals with highly practical economic concerns of money, banking and debt.

Many of the early writings in this volume originate in the Puritan society
of New England. Puritanism was a complex social, religious, political and
economic system. While what constituted Puritanism is certainly subject to
debate, there are several major puritanical themes that clearly influenced
the development of economic thought in America. These themes include
individualism and the complex relationship between the individual and the
community. One complaint common in the colonies was that of the exces-
sive self-interest of individuals, which the Puritans considered a sin. This
led to the Puritan condemnations of price gouging and the charging of
high rates of interest. In addition, as Dorfman noted, the attempts at wage
regulation in Massachusetts relied on the philosophy that an individual
should not take advantage of market conditions at the expense of the community.[1] Several of the writings in this volume – Cotton Mather's
Bonifacius (1710), for example – address conceptions of the social good
and ideas of the individual's responsibility to society.

In addition, Puritanism emphasised serving God through one's calling
to labour in a particular occupation.[2] Hard work and frugality were hall-
marks of the Puritan mindset and these attributes spread far beyond the
Puritan communities in New England to become characteristic of the
American colonies. The theme of economic gain through labour and frugality is prevalent in nearly all of the works of the first two volumes,

[1] Dorfman, *op. cit.*, pp. 44–5.
[2] Max Weber, *The Protestant Ethic and the Spirit of Capitalism*, trans. Talcott Parsons
(New York: Scribners, 1950).

engendered by both religious doctrine and the circumstances of material existence.

These early Puritan societies were highly socially stratified; laws designed to preserve the Puritan religious hierarchy were generally intolerant of different religious interpretations. Political control by the religious elders helped to maintain the hierarchy over time.

Puritanism held considerable influence in the early American colonies, in particular with regard to intellectual life. Boston was the centre for learning during this period; Puritans controlled the curriculum at Harvard University under the influence of the Puritan preacher Increase Mather.

However, throughout the colonial period, the Puritan influence waned, and, in addition to greater religious freedom and tolerance, the colonies also saw the increasing secularisation of individual choices and the concurrent transformation of society, from one based on religion to one based on trade and wealth accumulation. The secular philosophy of upward mobility and financial success through hard work, frugality and intelligence reached its pinnacle in Benjamin Franklin's *Autobiography* (1794). Yet the Puritan ethic does not entirely disappear from American economics or philosophy, as will be seen in the writings of Daniel Raymond and Francis Wayland.

INDIVIDUALISM AND THE STRUCTURE OF POWER

Writings in the second volume thus relate to the correlative establishment and transformation of the legal foundations and framework of the new economic order. Clearly related to the themes of the first volume were writings expressive of conflicts over individualism, democracy and the structures of political and economic power amongst the colonists, as well as between the colonists and Great Britain.

The definition of individual and property rights was an on-going process in the American colonies, evident in a number of the writings in this volume, including those of John Cotton, Thomas Pownall and Joel Barlow. The writing by William Berkeley addressed the trading rights of the colonists and whether different colonies should have different rights.

Also related to the themes of individual rights and the establishment of property was the issue of slavery and indentured servitude. Two anti-slavery writings are included that use very different rationales for their opposition to slavery. These writings manifest the beginning of the debate over slavery. The slavery debate would continue long after American Independence and dominated much of the economics, either explicitly or implicitly, until the Civil War.

COLONIAL MONEY, CREDIT AND DEBT

Writings also addressed important, controversial and technical problems of colonial money, credit and debt, including the chronic currency shortages suffered by the colonists. This volume includes fascinating discussions of the nature of money and the role of paper currency, suggested as early as 1688 (see Blackwell's *Bank of Credit*) to relieve the currency shortage. The present collection cannot but suggest the vast quantity of writings and schemes regarding money and speculation in the American colonies before the Revolutionary War, not to mention the debate that was to arise over a national bank, money, credit and debt following the Revolution. The four volumes of *Colonial Currency Reprints, 1682–1751* edited by Andrew McFarland Davis provide a much more complete collection of monetary theory in the American colonies, including reprints of pamphlets and newspaper editorials, even though almost exclusively from Massachusetts.[1] The present collection would benefit being read in conjunction with Davis's detailed history of money and bills of credit in Massachusetts in the introduction to his collection. Further, in the introduction to the Augustus M. Kelley 1970 edition, Joseph Dorfman provides an excellent, if brief, summary of the origins of monetary controversy in America. Given Davis's collection, we attempt to provide only a sample of the more important writings on money in this collection.

Specie was in chronic shortage in the American colonies – a problem created and compounded by British mercantilist policies designed to channel specie out of the colonies and into English coffers. Discussions on what constitutes money and how to create and manage paper money thus occurred very early. Paper money, sometimes-called 'bills of credit', was first used in Massachusetts and was issued privately. One interesting aspect of the debate is the fact that there was no overriding presumption that government should issue paper money instead of private banks. This was a subject of intense debate.

Most of the men writing on paper money were generally politically conservative and were well versed in the English monetary theory of the time, including the theories of John Locke, William Petty and William Potter. Unlike writings in the first two volumes, their writings are highly technical and detail oriented, traits that were to increasingly characterise monetary thought. The pieces by Benjamin Franklin and Hugh Vans explicate relatively sophisticated value theories as a basis for arguing for paper money; these are generally considered the first use of value theory

---

[1] *Colonial Currency Reprints, 1682–1751*, ed. Andrew McFarland Davis, 4 vols (Boston: Publications of the Prince Society, 22–5, 1910–11, reprinted by Augustus M. Kelley, 1964).

in America.[1] Arguments are made that a greater money supply would increase trade, promote economic growth and investment and encourage more people to move to America. The American experiments with banks and paper money, in many of the different colonies, played an important role in the development of monetary economics, as the first bank of credit in America preceded the bank of England by nearly four years.

MERCANTILISM AND COLONIALISM

Numerous writings in the preceding volumes – in addition to dealing with the variety of themes related to economics, religion, individual rights, property rights, money and the continuing working out of societal organisation along the lines of Spengler's problem of order – also presented colonial perspectives on mercantilism, British colonial policy and free trade. Certainly, the issues of mercantilism and free trade dominate the colonial discussion of economic issues of the time. The writings in volumes four and five present the changing colonial view of Great Britain and mercantilist policy from 1600 to 1776. Often they were written by the leading political figures of colonial America, evidencing, once again, the close connection between economics and politics that existed in the seventeenth and eighteenth centuries.

Mercantilism and free trade were closely related to other economic issues that were important to the colonies, including the evolving role for government in the economy – issues of legal rights of economic significance and of the basic economic institutions – and the transformation of society from religious to secular and from subsistence farming to commercial tradable activity. Hence, there was deliberate attention to promotion of agriculture, trade and manufacture, as well as to issues of taxation and public expenditure (e.g. poor relief). Some writings discuss the initial stages of the legal transformation from a landed-capital to a non-landed-capital system, with explicit attention to institutional change through government as both cause and consequence of economic development. Last, and importantly for the historian of economic thought, there is the initial attention to theories of price, value and production.

---

[1] Joseph Dorfman, 'On the Origins of Monetary Controversy in the United States' in Davis (ed.), *Colonial Currency Reprints* (1964). Incidentally, in this introduction, as well as his *Economic Mind in American Civilization* (1946), Dorfman refers to a work, titled 'An Inquiry into the Nature and Uses of Money', by Hugh Vance. In the original of this writing, included in this collection, the author's name is 'Vans', although 'Vance' could be an alternative spelling.

IV

The first five volumes of this collection trace the varied uses of economic ideas, even of what may be called economic theory, in America from 1616 to the eve of the American Revolution. Many of the works included in these volumes are important in their own right as contributions to economic thought, although often overlooked. Thomas Pownall's *A Letter to Adam Smith* (1776) provided a very insightful critique of Smith's economic analysis of colonies and labour theory of value. Benjamin Franklin, whose works were cited by Robert Malthus and Karl Marx, was one of the few early Americans mentioned by Joseph Schumpeter in his *History of Economic Analysis*.[1] Many of the works are included because of their respective contributions to understanding 'the economic mind in American civilization', which was in many ways very different from the economic mindset of the Europeans, and in particular the English, during this period.

These works also contribute to our understanding of later American economic thought. Many of the later and more famous American economists pick up the themes of their forebears. Few of the tensions in American economic life were resolved by victory in the American Revolution. In many ways, the economics of America became more difficult as the colonies sought to establish a single country and a single economic policy – issues of trading partners, tariffs, taxes and money had to be resolved, not to mention whether the government was going to promote manufacturing or agriculture. The discussion over the latter issue reached its peak in the Jefferson–Hamilton debates. The economic issues and themes presented in the first five volumes set the stage for later work in economics.

Marianne Johnson and Warren J. Samuels

---

[1] Thomas Malthus, *Essay on the Principle of Population* (Ann Arbor: University of Michigan Press, 1959); Karl Marx, *Capital: Volume One* (New York: Vintage, 1977); Joseph A. Schumpeter, *History of Economic Analysis* (New York: Oxford University Press, 1954).

NOTE ON COPY-TEXTS

The following texts are reproduced in facsimile; however, exceptions occur where the quality of the original text was poor and therefore would not reproduce well.

In order to fit texts comfortably onto the pages of this edition, certain liberties have been taken with the format of the originals: occasionally right-hand pages have become left-hand pages (and vice-versa) and texts from consecutive pages have been fitted onto a single page.

For permission to reproduce the texts included in this edition, we would like to thank the American Antiquarian Society, Baker-Kress Library, the British Library, The Boston Athenaeum, the University of Glasgow Library, Harvard Houghton University Library, The Huntingdon Library, The Library Company of Philadelphia, the University of London Library, Michigan State University Library, the New York Public Library, the Union Theological Seminary, and The Watkinson Library.

EXCERPTS FROM
A DESCRIPTION OF NEW ENGLAND

John Smith, *A Description of New England: or The Observations, and Discoueries, of Captain John Smith (Admirall of that Country) in the North of America, in the year of our Lord 1614: with the successe of sixe Ships, that went the next yeare 1615; and the accidents befell him among the French men of warre: With the proofe of the present benefit this Countrey affoords: whither this present yeare, 1616, eight voluntary Ships are gone to make further tryall* (London, 1616), pp. 1–3, 10–14, 16–23 and 31–40.

John Smith (1579–1631) made his reputation as an adventurer and a mercenary soldier in Europe (1597–1604), after which he promoted and organised the Virginia Company of London, a joint-stock company, formed in 1606 with a charter from King James I, with the aim of settling in Virginia. Arriving in Jamestown in 1607, he served as a member of the governing council. However, on an exploration in search of food, Smith was taken prisoner by local Indians. According to legend, he was sentenced to death but saved by Pocahontas, an Indian princess, whom he later married. Smith spent the rest of his life attending to governing the turbulent colony, both in North America and in England.

Smith wrote a series of books on conditions in New England to aid settlers, based on his explorations of the Potomac and Rappahannock Rivers and the Chesapeake Bay. His *Description of New England* set an optimistic tone for America, lauding the extensive god-given natural resources of the continent. Smith promised that those who settled and worked hard would quickly become wealthy. While the *Description of New England* is part travel guide, part economic history and part economic geography, this piece is also evidence of the Puritan belief that God would reward work with earthly riches. This theme remains prominent in many of the other pieces in this volume, culminating in the excerpt from Benjamin Franklin's *Autobiography* (1794).

Another of Smith's themes involves the difficulty in balancing the multiple and competing objectives of colonial charters. The colony of Jamestown, founded as it was by a joint-stock company, was formed with the twin expressed goals of the religious conversion of the Native Americans and financial profits. As one of the Virginia Company's leaders, Smith was forced to attempt to reconcile these competing claims, and the complex relationship between religion, government, and economics in American colonial life are borne out in his writings.

Smith's work should also be viewed in part as propaganda, as he had a vested interest in the economic success of the Northern Virginia colony, later called the New England Council. *A Description of New England* was the first in a long series of pieces encouraging immigration to America, with promises of religious freedom and wealth. Several other such works reproduced in this volume are John Cotton's *God's Promise to his Plantations* (1634) and Thomas Budd's *Good Order Established* (1685), as well as several of William Penn's writings.

A DESCRIPTION

of *New England:*

OR

THE OBSERVATIONS, AND

discoueries, of Captain *Iohn Smith* (Admirall
of that Country) in the North of *America*, in the yeare
of our *Lord* 1614: *with the successe of sixe Ships,
that went the next yeare* 1615; *and the
accidents befell him among the
French men of warre:*

With the proofe of the present benefit this
Countrey affoords: whither this present yeare,
1616, *eight voluntary Ships are gone
to make further tryall.*

At LONDON
Printed by *Humfrey Lownes,* for *Robert Clerke*; and
are to be sould at his house called the Lodge,
in Chancery lane, ouer againft Lin-
colnes Inne. 1616.

A DESCRIPTION OF
New-England, by Captaine
Iohn Smith.

N the moneth of Aprill, 1614.
with two Ships from *London*, of
a few Marchants, I chanced to arriue in *New-England*, a parte of
Ameryca, at the Ile of *Monahig-
gan*, in 43½ of Northerly lati-
tude : our plot was there to take Whales and make
tryalls of a Myne of Gold and Copper. If thofe failed, Fifh and Furres was then our refuge, to make
our felues fauers how focuer : we found this Whale-
fifhing a coftly conclufion: we faw many, and fpent
much time in chafing them ; but could not kill any :
They beeing a kinde of Iubartes, and not the
Whale that yeeldes Finnes and Oyle as wee expected. For our Golde, it was rather the Mafters deuice to get a voyage that proiected it, then any
knowledge hee had at all of any fuch matter. Fifh
& Furres was now our guard: & by our late arriual,
and long lingring about the Whale, the prime of
both thofe feafons were paft ere wee perceiued it ;
we thinking that their feafons ferued at all times:
but

but wee found it otherwife; for, by the midft of Iune, the fifhing failed. Yet in Iuly and Auguft fome was taken, but not fufficient to defray fo great a charge as our ftay required. Of dry fifh we made about 40000. of Cor fifh about 7000. Whileft the failers fifhed, my felfe with eight or nine others of them might beft bee fpared; Ranging the coaft in a fmall boat, wee got for trifles neer 1100 Beuer skinnes, 100 Martins, and neer as many Otters; and the moft of them within the diftance of twenty leagues. We ranged the Coaft both Eaft and Weft much furder; but Eaftwards our commodities were not efteemed, they were fo neare the French who affords them better: and right againft vs in the Main was a Ship of Sir *Frances Popphames*, that had there fuch acquaintance, hauing many yeares vfed onely that porte, that the moft parte there was had by him. And 40 leagues weftwards were two French Ships, that had made there a great voyage by trade, during the time wee tryed thofe conclufions, not knowing the Coaft, nor Saluages habitation. With thefe Furres, the Traine, and Cor-fifh I returned for *England* in the Bark: where within fix monthes after our departure from the *Downes*, we fafe arriued back. The beft of this fifh was folde for fiue pound the hundreth, the reft by ill vfage betwixt three pound and fifty fhillings. The other Ship ftaied to fit herfelfe for *Spaine* with the dry fifh which was fould, by the Sailers reporte that returned, at forty ryalls the quintall, each hundred weighing two quintalls and a halfe.

New-

New England is that part of *America* in the O-
cean Sea oppofite to *Noua Albion* in the South
Sea; difcouered by the moft memorable Sir *Francis Drake* in his voyage about the worlde. In re-
garde whereto this is ftiled *New England*, beeing
in the fame latitude. *New France*, off it, is North-
ward: Southwardes is *Virginia*, and all the ad-
ioyning Continent, with *New Granado, New Spain,
New Andolofia* and the *Weft Indies.*

And furely by reafon of thofe fandy cliffes and
cliffes of rocks, both which we faw fo planted with
Gardens and Corne fields, and fo well inhabited
with a goodly, ftrong and well proportioned people, befides the greatneffe of the Timber growing
on them, the greatneffe of the fifh and the moderate temper of the ayre (for of twentie fiue, not a-
ny was ficke, but two that were many yeares dif-
eafed before they went, notwithftanding our bad
lodging and accidentall diet) who can but ap-
prooue this a moft excellent place, both for health
& fertility? And of all the foure parts of the world
that I haue yet feene not inhabited, could I haue
but meanes to tranfport a Colonie, I would rather
hue here then any where: and if it did not maintaine if felfe, were wee but once indifferently well
fitted, let vs ftarue.

The maine Staple, from hence to bee extracted
for the prefent to produce the reft, is fifh; which
howeuer it may feeme a mean and a bafe commoditie: yet who who will but truely take the pains
and confider the fequell, I thinke will allow it well
worth the labour. It is ftrange to fee what great
aduen

aduentures the hopes of fetting forth men of war
to rob the induftrious innocent, would procure;
or fuch mafsie promifes in groffe : though more
are choked then well fedde with fuch haftie hopes.
But who doth not know that the poore Hollanders, chiefly by fifhing, at a great charge and labour in all weathers in the open Sea, are made a
people fo hardy, and induftrious ? and by the
venting this poore commodity to the Eafterlings
for as meane, which is Wood, Flax, Pitch, Tarre,
Rofin, Cordage, and fuch like (which they exchange againe, to the French, Spaniards, Portu-
gales, and Englifh, &c. for what they want) are
made fo mighty, ftrong and rich, as no State
but *Venice*, of twice their magnitude, is fo
well furnifhed with fo many faire Cities, goodly
Townes, ftrong Fortreffes, & that aboundance of
fhipping and all forts of marchandize, as well of
Golde, Siluer, Pearles, Diamonds, Pretious ftones,
Silkes, Veluets, and Cloth of golde; as Fifh, Pitch,
Wood, or fuch groffe commodities? What Voy-
ages and Difcoueries, Eaft and Weft, North and
South, yea about the world, make they? What
an Army by Sea and Land, haue they long maintained in defpite of one of the greateft Princes of
the world? And neuer could the Spaniard with
all his Mynes of golde and Siluer, pay his debts,
his friends, & army, halfe fo truly, as the Hollanders ftil haue done by this contemptible trade of
fifh. Diuers (I know) may alledge, many other afsi-
ftances : But this is their Myne; and the Sea the
fource

source of those siluered streames of all their vertue; which hath made them now the very mira-
cle of induftrie, the pattern of perfection for thefe
affaires: and the benefit of fishing is that *Primum
mobile* that turnes all their *Spheres* to this height of
plentie, strength, honour and admiration.

Herring, Cod, and Ling, is that triplicitie that
makes their wealth & shippings multiplicities, such
as it is, and from which (few would thinke it) they
yearly draw at leaft one million & a halfe of pounds
ftarling; yet it is moft certaine (if records be true);
and in this faculty they are fo naturalized, and of
their vents fo certainely acquainted, as there is no
likelihood they will euer bee paralleld, hauing 2
or 3000 Buffes, Flat bottomes, Sword pinks,
Todes, and fuch like, that breedes them Saylers,
Mariners, Souldiers and Marchants, neuer to be
wrought out of that trade, and fit for any other.
I will not deny but others may gaine as well as
they, that will vfe it, though not fo certainely, nor
fo much in quantity; for want of experience. And
this Herring they take vpon the Coaft of *Scotland*
and *England*; their Cod and Ling, vpon the Coaft
of *Ireland* and in the North Seas.

Hamborough, & the *Eaft Countries*, for Sturgion
and Cauiare, gets many thoufands of pounds from
England, and the *Straites*: *Portugale*, the *Biskaines*,
and the *Spaniards*, make 40 or 50 Saile yearely
to *Cape-blank*, to hooke for Porgos, Mullet, and
make *Pattardo*: and *New found Land*, doth yearely
fraught neere 800 fayle of Ships with a fillie leane
skinny

skinny Poore-Iohn, and Corfifh, which at leaft
yearely amounts to 3 or 400000 pound. If from
all thofe parts fuch paines is taken for this poore
gaines of fifh, and by them hath neither meate,
drinke, nor clothes, wood, iron, nor fteele, pitch,
tarre, nets, leades, falt, hookes, nor lines, for
fhipping, fifhing, nor prouifion, but at the fecond,
third, fourth, or fift hand, drawne from fo many
feuerall parts of the world ere they come together
to be vfed in this voyage : If thefe I fay can gaine,
and the Saylers liue going for fhares, leffe then
the third part of their labours, and yet fpend as
much time in going and comming, as in ftaying
there , fo fhort is the feafon of fifhing; why
fhould wee more doubt, then *Holland*, *Portugale*,
Spaniard, *French*, or other, but to doe much better then they, where there is victuall to feede vs,
wood of all forts, to build Boats, Ships, or Barks;
the fifh at our doores, pitch, tarre, mafts, yards,
and moft of other neceffaries onely for making?
And here are no hard Landlords to racke vs with
high rents, or extorted fines to confume vs, no tedious pleas in faw to confume vs with their many
years difputations for Iuftice : no multitudes to
occafion fuch impediments to good orders, as in
popular States. So freely hath God & his Maiefty
beftowed thofe blefsings on the that will attempt
to obtaine them, as here euery man may be mafter
and owner of his owne labour and land ; or the
greateft part in a fmall time. If hee haue nothing
but his hands, he may fet vp this trade; and by induftry

duſtrie quickly grow rich ; ſpending but halfe that
time wel, wch in *England* we abuſe in idlenes, worſe
or as ill. Here is ground alſo as good as any lyeth in
the height of forty one, forty two, forty three, &c.
which is as temperate and as fruitfull as any other
paralell in the world. As for example, on this ſide
the line Weſt of it in the South Sea, is *Noua Albion*, diſcouered as is ſaid, by Sir *Francis Drake.*
Eaſt from it, is the moſt temperate part of *Portugale*, the ancient kingdomes of *Galazia*, *Biskey*,
Nauarre, *Arragon*, *Catalonia*, *Caſtilia* the olde,
and the moſt moderateſt of *Caſtilia* the new, and
Valentia, which is the greateſt part of *Spain*: which
if the *Spaniſh* Hiſtories bee true, in the *Romanes*
time abounded no leſſe with golde and ſiluer
Mines, then now the *Weſt Indies*; The *Romanes*
then vſing the *Spaniards* to work in thoſe Mines,
as now the *Spaniard* doth the *Indians.*

    Firſt, the ground is ſo fertill, that queſtionleſſ it
is capable of producing any Grain, Fruits, or Seeds
you will ſow or plant, growing in the Regions
afore named: But it may be, not euery kinde to
that perfection of delicacy ; or ſome tender plants
may miſcarie, becauſe the Summer is not ſo hot,
and the winter is more colde in thoſe parts wee
haue yet tryed neere the Sea ſide, then we finde in
the ſame height in *Europe* or *Aſia*; Yet I made
a Garden vpon the top of a Rockie Ile in 43. ꞊, 4
leagues from the Main, in May, that grew ſo well,
as it ſerued vs for ſallets in Iune and Iuly. All ſorts
of

of cattell may here be bred and fed in the Iles, or *Peninsulaes*, fecurely for nothing. In the *Interim* till they encreafe if need be (obferuing the feafons) I durft vndertake to haue corne enough from the Saluages for 300 men, for a few trifles; and if they fhould bee vntoward (as it is moft certaine they are) thirty or forty good men will be fuffici- ent to bring them all in fubie&ion, and make this prouifion; if they vnderftand what they doe: 200 whereof may nine monethes in the yeare be imployed in making marchandable fifh, till the reft prouide other neceffaries, fit to furnifh vs with other commodities.

In March, Aprill, May, and halfe Iune, here is Cod in abundance; in May, Iune, Iuly, and Au- guft Mullet and Sturgion; whofe roes doe make Cauiare and Puttargo. Herring, if any defire them, I haue taken many out of the bellies of Cods, fome in nets; but the Saluages compare their ftore in the Sea, to the haires of their heads: and furely there are an incredible abundance vpon this Coaft. In the end of Auguft, September, Oc- tober, and Nouember, you haue Cod againe, to make Cor fifh, or Poore Iohn : and each hundred is as good as two or three hundred in the *New- found Land*. So that halfe the labour in hooking, fplitting, and turning, is faued : and you may haue your fifh at what Market you will, before they can haue any in *New-found Land*; where their fifhing is chiefly but in Iune and Iuly: whereas it is heere in March, Aprill, May, September, October, and

Nouem-

Nouember, as is faid. So that by reafon of this plantation, the Marchants may haue fraught both out and home: which yeelds an aduantage worth confideration.

Your Cor-fifh you may in like manner tranfport as you fee caufe, to ferue the Ports in *Portugale* (as *Lisbon, Auera, Portaport*, and diuers others, or what market you pleafe) before your *Ilanders* returne: They being tyed to the feafon in the open Sea; you hauing a double feafon, and fifhing before your doors, may euery night fleep quietly a fhore with good cheare and what fires you will, or when you pleafe with your wiues and familie: they onely, their fhips in the maine Ocean.

The Mullets heere are in that abundance, you may take them with nets, fometimes by hundreds, where at *Cape blank* they hooke them; yet thofe but one foot and a halfe in length; thefe two, three, or foure, as oft I haue meafured: much Salmon fome haue found vp the Riuers, as they haue paffed: and heer the ayre is fo temperate, as all thefe at any time may well be preferued.

Now, young boyes and girles Saluages, or any other, be they neuer fuch idlers, may turne, carry, and return fifh, without either fhame, or any great paine: hee is very idle that is paft twelue yeares of age and cannot doe fo much: and fhe is very olde, that cannot fpin a thred to make engines to catch them.

For their tranfportation, the fhips that go there to fifh may tranfport the firft: who for their paffage

sage will spare the charge of double manning their ships, which they must doe in the *New-found Land*, to get their fraught; but one third part of that companie are onely but proper to serue a stage, carry a barrow, and turne Poor Iohn: notwith-standing, they must haue meate, drinke, clothes, & passage, as well as the rest. Now all I desire, is but this; That those that voluntarily will send ship-ping, should make here the best choise they can, or accept such as are presented them, to serue them at that rate: and their ships returning leaue such with me, with the value of that they should re-ceiue comming home, in such prouisions and ne-cessarie tooles, armes, bedding and apparell, salt, hookes, nets, lines, and such like as they spare of the remainings; who till the next returne may keepe their boates and doe them many other pro-fitable offices: prouided I haue men of ability to teach them their functions, and a company fit for Souldiers to be ready vpon an occasion; becausse of the abuses which haue beene offered the poore Saluages, and the liberty both French, or any that will, hath to deale with them as they please: whose disorders will be hard to reforme; and the longer the worse. Now such order with facilitie might be taken, with euery port Towne or Citie, to obserue but this order, With free power to con-uert the benefits of their fraughts to what aduan-tage they please, and increase their numbers as they see occasion; who euer as they are able to subsist of themselues, may beginne the new Townes in

New

New England in memory of their olde : which freedome being confined but to the necefsity of the generall good, the euent (with Gods helpe) might produce an honeft, a noble, and a profitable emulation.

Salt vpon falt may affuredly be made; if not at the firft in ponds, yet till they bee prouided this may be vfed: then the Ships may tranfport Kine, Horfe, Goates, courfe Cloath, and fuch commodities as we want; by whofe arriuall may be made that prouifion of fifh to fraught the Ships that they ftay not: and then if the failers goe for wages, it matters not. It is hard if this returne defray not the charge: but care muft be had, they arriue in the Spring, or elfe prouifion be made for them againft the Winter.

Of certaine red berries called Alkermes which is worth ten fhillings a pound, but of thefe hath been fould for thirty or forty fhillings the pound, may yearely be gathered a good quantitie.

Of the Musk Rat may bee weil raifed gaines, well worth their labour, that will endeuor to make tryall of their goodnefle.

Of Beuers, Otters, Martins, Blacke Foxes, and Furres of price, may yearely be had 6 or 7000: and if the trade of the *French* were preuented, many more: 25000 this yeare were brought from thofe Northren parts into *France*; of which trade we may haue as good part as the *French*, if we take good courfes.

Of Mynes of Golde and Siluer, Copper, and
proba-

probabilities of Lead, Chriftall and Allom, I could fay much if relations were good affurances. It is true indeed, I made many trials according to thofe inftructions I had, which doe perfwade mee I need not defpaire, but there are metalls in the Countrey : but I am no Alchymift, nor will promife more then I know : which is, Who will vndertake the rectifying of an Iron forge, if thofe that buy meate, drinke, coals, ore, and all neceffaries at a deer rate gaine; where all thefe things are to be had for the taking vp, in my opinion cannot lofe.

Of woods feeing there is fuch plenty of all forts, if thofe that build fhips and boates, buy wood at fo great a price, as it is in *England, Spaine, France, Italy*, and *Holland*, and all other prouifions for the nourifhing of mans life ; liue well by their trade : when labour is all required to take thofe neceffaries without any other tax; what hazard will be here, but doe much better? And what commoditie in *Europe* doth more decay then wood? For the goodneffe of the ground, let vs take it fertill, or barren, or as it is : feeing it is certaine it beares fruites, to nourifh and feed man and beaft, as well as *England*, and the Sea thofe feuerall forts of fifh I haue related. Thus feeing all good prouifions for mans fuftenance, may with this facility be had, by a little extraordinarie labour, till that tranfported be increafed; and all neceffaries for fhipping, onely for labour : to which may bee added the afsiftance of the Saluages, which may eafily be had, if they be difcreetly handled in their
kindes,

kindes; towards fishing, planting, and destroying woods. What gaines might be raised if this were followed (when there is but once men to fill your store houses, dwelling there, you may serue all *Europe* better and farre cheaper, then can the *Iceland* fishers, or the *Hollanders*, *Cape blank*; or *New found Land*: who must be at as much more charge, then you) may easily be coniectured by this example.

2000. pound will fit out a ship of 200. & 1 of a 100 tuns: If the dry fish they both make, fraught that of 100. and goe for *Spaine*, sell it but at ten shillings a quintall; but commonly it giueth fifteen, or twentie: especially when it commeth first, which amounts to 3 or 4000 pound: but say but tenne, which is the lowest, allowing the rest for waste, it amounts at that rate, to 2000 pound, which is the whole charge of your two ships, and their equipage: Then the returne of the money, and the fraught of the ship for the vintage, or any other voyage, is cleere gaine, with your shippe of a 100 tuns of Train and oyle, besides the beuers, and other commodities; and that you may haue at home within six monethes, if God please but to send an ordinarie passage. Then saning halfe this charge by the not staying of your ships, your victual, ouerplus of men & wages; with her fraught thither of things necessarie for the planters, the salt being there made: as also may the nets & lines, within a short time: if nothing were to bee expected but this, it might in time equalize your *Hollanders* gaines, if not exceed them: they returning but wood.

wood, pitch, tarre, and such grosse commodities, you wines, oyles, fruits, silkes, and such *Straits* commodities, as you please to prouide by your Factors, against such times as your shippes arriue with them. This would so increase our shipping and sailers, and so employ and encourage a great part of our idlers and others that want imployments fitting their qualities at home, where they shame to doe that they would doe abroad; that could they but once taste the sweet fruites of their owne labours, doubtlesse many thousands would be aduised by good discipline, to take more pleasure in honest industrie, then in their humours of dissolute idlenesse.

Who can desire more content, that hath small meanes; or but only his merit to aduance his fortune, then to tread, and plant that ground hee hath purchased by the hazard of his life? If he haue but the taste of virtue, and magnanimitie, what to such a minde can bee more pleasant, then planting and building a foundation for his Posteritie, gotte from the rude earth, by Gods blessing & his owne industrie, without preiudice to any? If hee haue any graine of faith or zeale in Religion, what can hee doe lesse hurtfull to any; or more agreeable to God, then to seeke to conuert those poore Saluages to know Christ, and humanitie, whose labors with discretion will triple require thy charge and paines? What so truely sutes with honour and honestie,.

nestie, as the discouering things vnknowne ? cre-
cting Townes, peopling Countries, informing the
ignorant, reforming things vniust, teaching virtue;
& gaine to our Natiuemother-countrie a kingdom
to attend her, finde imployment for those that are
idle, because they know not what to doe : so farre
from wronging any, as to cause Posteritie to remember thee; and remembring thee, euer honour
that remembrance with praise ? Consider: What
were the beginnings and endings of the Monarkies
of the *Chaldeans*, the *Syrians*, the *Grecians*, and *Romanes*, but this one rule ; What was it they would
not doe, for the good of the commonwealth, or
their Mother-citie ? For example: *Rome*, What
made her such a Monarchesse, but onely the aduentures of her youth, not in riots at home; but in dan-
gers abroade ? and the iustice and iudgement out
of their experience, when they grewe aged. What
was their ruine and hurt, but this ; The excesse of
idlenesse, the fondnesse of Parents, the want of experience in Magistrates, the admiration of their
vndeserued honours, the contempt of true merit,
their vniust iealosies, their pollticke incredulities,
their hypocriticall seeming goodnesse, and their
deeds of secret lewdnesse ? finally, in fine, growing
onely formall temporists, all that their predecessors
got in many years, they lost in few daies. Those by
their pains & vertues became Lords of the world;
they by their case and vices became slaues to their
seruants. This is the difference betwixt the vse of
Armes in the field, & on the monuments of stones;
the

the golden age and the leaden age, profperity and
miferie, iuftice and corruption, fubftance and fha-
dowes, words and deeds, experience and imagi-
nation, making Commonwealths and marring
Commonwealths, the fruits of vertue and the
conclufions of vice.

Then, who would liue at home idly (or thinke
in himfelfe any worth to liue) onely to eate, drink,
and fleepe, and fo die? Or by confuming that care-
lefly, his friends got worthily? Or by vfing that
miferably, that maintained vertue honeftly? Or,
for being defcended nobly, pine with the vaine
vaunt of great kindred, in penurie? Or (to maintaine a filly fhewe of brauery) toyle out thy
heart, foule, and time, bafely, by fhifts, tricks,
cards, & dice? Or by relating newes of others actions, fharke here or there for a dinner, or fupper;
deceiue thy friends, by faire promifes, and diffimu-
lation, in borrowing where thou neuer intendeft
to pay; offend the lawes, furfeit with exceffe, burden thy Country, abufe thy felfe defpaire in want,
and then couzen thy kindred, yea euen thine owne
brother, and wifh thy parents death (I will not
fay damnation) to haue their eftates? though thou
feeft what honours, and rewards, the world yet
hath for them will feeke them and worthily de-
ferue them.

I would be fory to offend, or that any fhould
miftake my honeft meaning: for I wifh good to
all, hurt to none. But rich men for the moft part
are growne to that dotage, through their pride in
their

their wealth, as though there were no accident could end it, or their life. And what hellish care do such take to make it their owne miferie, and their Countries fpoile, efpecially when there is moft neede of their imployment? drawing by all manner of inuentions, from the Prince and his honeft fubiects, euen the vitall fpirits of their powers and eftates: as if their Bagges, or Bragges, were fo powerfull a defence, the malicious could-not affault them; when they are the onely baite, to caufe vs not to be onely affaulted; but betrayed and murdered in our owne fecurity, ere we well perceiue it.

May not the miferable ruine of *Conftantinople*, their impregnable walles, riches, and pleafures laft taken by the *Turke* (which are but a bit, in comparifon of their now mightines) remember vs, of the effects of priuate couetoufnefs? at which time the good *Emperour* held himfelfe rich enough, to haue fuch rich fubiects, fo formall in all exceffe of vanity, all kinde of delicacie, and prodigalitie. His pouertie when the *Turke* befieged, the citizens (whofe marchandizing thoughts were onely to get wealth, little conceiuing the defperate refolution of a valiant expert enemy) left the Emp. fo long to his conclufions, hauing fpent all he had to pay his young, raw, difcontented Souldiers; that fodainly he, they, and their citie were all a prey to the deuouring *Turke*. And what they would not fpare for the maintenance of them who aduentured their liues to defend them, did ferue onely their

enemies

enemies to torment them, their friends, and countrey, and all Chriſtendome to this preſent day.
Let this lamentable example remember you that
are rich (ſeeing there are ſuch great theeues in the
world to robbe you) not grudge to lend ſome proportion, to breed them that haue little, yet willing
to learne how to defend you : for, it is too late
when the deede is a-doing. The *Romanes* eſtate
hath beene worſe then this: for, the meere coue-
touſneſſe and extortion of a few of them, ſo moo-
ued the reſt, that not hauing any imployment, but
contemplation; their great iudgements grew to ſo
great malice, as themſelues were ſufficient to deſtroy themſelues by faction: Let this mooue you
to embrace imployment, for thoſe whoſe educati-
ons, ſpirits, and iudgements, want but your pur-
ſes; not onely to preuent ſuch accuſtomed dan-
gers, but alſo to gaine more thereby then you
haue. And you fathers that are either ſo fooliſhly
fond, or ſo miſerably couetous, or ſo willfully ignorant, or ſo negligently careleſſe, as that you will
rather maintaine your children in idle wantonneſs,
till they growe your maſters; or become ſo baſe-
ly vnkinde, as they wiſh nothing but your deaths;
ſo that both ſorts growe diſſolute : and although
you would wiſh them any where to eſcape the
gallowes, and eaſe your cares; though they ſpend
you here one, two, or three hundred pound a yeer;
you would grudge to giue halfe ſo much in ad-
uenture with them, to obtaine an eſtate, which in
a ſmall time but with a little aſſiſtance of your
proui-

prouidence, might bee better then your owne.
But if an Angell should tell you, that any place yet
vnknowne can afford such fortunes; you would
not beleeue him, no more then *Columbus* was be-
leeued there was any such Land as is now the well
knowne abounding *America*; much lesse such
large Regions as are yet vnknowne, as well in *A-
merica*, as in *Affrica*, and *Asia*, and *Terra incog-
nita*; where were courses for gentlemen (and them
that would be so reputed) more suiting their qualities, then begging from their Princes generous
disposition, the labours of his subiects, and the
very marrow of his maintenance.

I haue not beene so ill bred, but I haue tasted
of *Plenty* and *Pleasure*, as well as *Want* and *Mi-
serie*: nor doth necessity yet, or occasion of dis-
content, force me to these endeauors: nor am I ignorant what small thanke I shall haue for my
paines; or that many would haue the Worlde
imagine them to be of great iudgement, that can
but blemish these my designes, by their witty ob-
iections and detractions: yet (I hope) my reasons
with my deeds, will so preuaile with some, that I
shall not want imployment in these affaires, to
make the most blinde see his owne senselesnesse, &
incredulity; Hoping that gaine will make them affect that, which Religion, Charity, and the Common good cannot. It were but a poore deuice in
me, To deceiue my selfe; much more the King, &
State, my Friends, and Countrey; with these in-
ducements: which, seeing his Maiestie hath giuen
permi-

permiſsion, I wiſh all ſorts of worthie, honeſt, induſtrious ſpirits, would vnderſtand: and if they deſire any further ſatisfaction, I will doo my beſt to giue it: Not to perſwade them to goe onely; but goe with them: Not leaue them there; but hue with them there. I will not ſay, but by ill prouiding and vndue managing, ſuch courſes may be taken, may make vs miſerable enough: But if I may haue the execution of what I haue proiected; if they want to eate, let them eate or neuer digeſt Me. If I performe what I ſay, I deſire but that reward out of the gaines may ſute my paines, quality, and condition. And if I abuſe you with my tongue, take my head for ſatisfaction. If any diſlike at the yeares end, defraying their charge, by my conſent they ſhould freely returne. I ſcare not want of companie ſufficient, were it but knowne what I know of thoſe Countries; & by the proofe of that wealth I hope yearely to returne, if God pleaſe to bleſſe me from ſuch accidents, as are beyond my power in reaſon to preuent: For, I am not ſo ſimple, to thinke, that euer any other motiue then wealth, will euer erect there a Commonweale; or draw companie from their eaſe and humours at home, to ſtay in *New England* to effect my purpoſes. And leſt any ſhould thinke the toile might be inſupportable, though theſe things may be had by labour, and diligence: I aſſure my ſelfe there are who delight extreamly in vaine pleaſure, that take much more paines in *England*, to enioy it, then I ſhould doe heere to gaine wealth ſufficient:

ent: and yet I thinke they should not haue halfe such sweet content: for, our pleasure here is still gaines; in *England* charges and losse. Heer nature and liberty affords vs that freely, which in *England* we want, or it costeth vs dearely. What pleasure can be more, then (being tired with any occasion a-shore) in planting Vines, Fruits, or Hearbs, in contriuing their owne Grounds, to the pleasure of their owne mindes, their Fields, Gardens, Orchards, Buildings, Ships, and other works, &c. to recreate themselues before their owne doores, in their owne boates vpon the Sea, where man woman and childe, with a small hooke and line, by angling, may take diuerse sorts of excellent fish, at their pleasures? And is it not pretty sport, to pull vp two pence, six pence, and twelue pence, as fast as you can hale and veare a line? He is a very bad fisher, cannot kill in one day with his hooke and line, one, two, or three hundred Cods: which dressed and dryed, if they be sould there for ten shillings the hundred, though in *England* they will giue more then twentie; may not both the seruant, the master, and marchant, be well content with this gaine? If a man worke but three dayes in seauen, he may get more then hee can spend, vnlesse he will be excesiue. Now that Carpenter, Mason, Gardiner, Taylor, Smith, Sailer, Forgers, or what other, may they not make this a pretty recreation though they fish but an houre in a day, to take more then they eate in a weeke: or? if they will not eate it, because there is so much better

choice

choife; yet fell it, or change it, with the fifher men, or marchants, for any thing they want. And what fport doth yeeld a more pleafing content, and leffe hurt or charge then angling with a hooke, and crofsing the fweete ayre from Ile to Ile, ouer the filent ftreames of a calme Sea? wherein the moft curious may finde pleafure, profit, and content. Thus, though all men be not fifhers: yet all men, whatfoeuer, may in other matters doe as well. For necefsity doth in thefe cafes fo rule a Commonwealth, and each in their feuerall functions, as their labours in their qualities may be as profitable, becaufe there is a necefsary mutuall vfe of all.

For Gentlemen, what exercife fhould more delight them, then ranging dayly thofe vnknowne parts, vfing fowling and fifhing, for hunting and hauking? and yet you fhall fee the wilde haukes giue you fome pleafure, in feeing them ftoope (fix or feauen after one another) an houre or two together, at the skuls of fifh in the faire harbours, as thofe a-fhore at a foule; and neuer trouble nor torment your felues, with watching, mewing, feeding, and attending them: nor kill horfe and man with running & crying, *See you not a hauk?* For hunting alfo: the woods, lakes, and riuers, affoord not onely chafe fufficient, for any that delights in that kinde of toyle, or pleafure; but fuch beafts to hunt, that befides the delicacy of their bodies for food, their skins are fo rich, as may well recompence thy dayly labour, with a Captains pay.

For

For labourers, if thofe that fowe hemp, rape, turnups, parfnips, carrats, cabidge, and fuch like; giue 20, 30, 40, 50 fhillings yearely for an acre of ground, and meat drinke and wages to vfe it, and yet grow rich: when better, or at leaft as good ground, may be had and coft nothing but labour; It feemes ftrange to me any fuch fhould there grow poore.

My purpofe is not to perfwade children from their parents ; men from their wiues; nor feruants from their mafters: onely, fuch as with free confent may be fpared: But that each parifh, or village, in Citie, or Countrey, that will but apparell their fatherleffe children, of thirteene or fourteen years of age, or young maried people, that haue fmall wealth to liue on; heereby their labour may liue exceeding well: prouided alwaies that firft there bee a fufficient power to command them, hooffes to receiue them, meanes to defend them, and meet prouifions for them ; for, any place may bee ouerlain: and it is moft neceffarie to haue a fortreffe (ere this grow to practice) and fufficient mafters (as, Carpenters, Mafons, Fifhers, Fowlers, Gardiners, Husbandmen, Sawyers, Smiths, Spinfters, Taylors, Weauers, and fuch like) to take ten, twelue, or twentie, or as ther is occafion, for Apprentifes. The Mafters by this may quicklie growe rich; thefe may learne their trades themfelues, to doe the like; to a generall and an incredible benefit, for King, and Countrey, Mafter, and Seruant.

A MODELL OF CHRISTIAN CHARITY

John Winthrop, *A Modell of Christian Charity. Written on board the Arbella, on the Atlantic Ocean* (1630), in *Collections of the Massachusetts Historical Society*, 3rd series (Boston: Charles C. Little and James Brown, 1838), vol. vii, pp. 33–48.

John Winthrop (1605–76), in common with most of the early writers included in this volume, was simultaneously a religious and political leader. Born in England, he came from a family of considerable wealth and power, and had been educated at Cambridge. It was during his time at Cambridge that he first became familiar with the Puritan religion. Trained as a lawyer, Winthrop immigrated to Salem, Massachusetts, in 1630. He wrote voluminously on the topics of religion, politics and economics, and is perhaps best remembered for his journals recording life in the early Massachusetts Bay Colony. Winthrop served as governor of Massachusetts four times (1629–34, 1637–40, 1642–4, 1646–9). His journal provided information on the political structure and decision-making, not to mention the weather and everyday life, in Massachusetts during the middle of the seventeenth century.

His *Modell of Christian Charity* was written en route to Massachusetts and served as a basis for understanding his approach to Puritanism and a Puritan society. This piece has been reproduced from a hand written version found in the Winthrop family papers in the New York Historical Society. Although not in the handwriting of John Winthrop, the Massachusetts Historical Society was sufficiently convinced of its authenticity to include the writing in their *Collections of the Massachusetts Historical Society*, from which the piece below has been reproduced.

Winthrop's firmly-held belief was that every society was necessarily divided by God into the rich and powerful and the poor in need of leadership. He consistently emphasised collectivism in preference to individualism, and believed that the Puritans of Massachusetts Bay Colony had been divinely guided to establish and rule a religious colony in North America. Winthrop was a highly conservative individual and a great believer in theocracy, as opposed to democracy. He was, in fact, responsible for the banishment of Anne Hutchinson, America's first female religious leader, for her heretical teachings.

A Modell of Christian Charity not only spelled out Winthrop's religious views, but it was also a good example of religious discourse designed to achieve particular economic outcomes. Two features are important: the responsibility of the rich to provide charity to the poor, as defined by God, and the rules of lending, specifying that lending is only permitted when there is a reasonable probability of repayment. Individuals should be guided by justice and mercy in their decision-making. Thus, if there is no probability of the repayment of a loan, the money should be given as a gift. While the relationship defined was aimed at promoting charity, it also had practical results in terms of governorship and maintaining peace and order in society. Winthrop preached that only the most unworthy of the poor would rise up against their well-meaning and charitable rulers. Hence, this piece illustrates how religion served as the dominant instrument of social control in the early colonies. The use of religion in defining political roles is also evident in the writings of John Cotton (see Volumes I and II), who found his place within the Massachusetts Puritan tradition established by Winthrop.

MODEL OF CHRISTIAN CHARITY.

BY JOHN WINTHROP ESQ.

FIRST GOVERNOR OF THE COLONY OF THE MASSACHUSETTS BAY.

———————

[We introduce this interesting Paper by the following letter to the Corr. Sec. of Mass. Hist. Society.]

DEAR SIR,

Agreeably to your request, I forward to you a copy of the WIN-THROP MS. belonging to the New York Historical Society, as transcribed by the Assistant Librarian, under the direction of the Society, in accordance with a resolution I had the honor to submit at a late meeting. A member of your Publishing Committee, whom I had informed of the existence of this document, communicated to me the desire of the Committee to have it inserted in their forthcoming volume of Collections, and as it is the production of a man whose fame is inseparably connected with the history of Massachusetts, there seemed to be a manifest propriety in acceding to the request. The Society, therefore, readily consented that it should be communicated to the public, through that medium.

I am satisfied, by comparing it with the original, that the copy has been accurately made; occasionally, however, a word was illegible, rendering it necessary to leave blanks. The MS. is evidently in the obscure handwriting prevalent at the period to which it is referred, though probably not in that of the author. It is supposed to have been presented to the Society by the late Francis B. Winthrop, Esq., of this city, (the oldest brother of the Hon. Thomas L. Winthrop, late Lieutenant Governor of Massachusetts,) a lineal descendant of the author, into whose possession I am informed most of the old family papers came, nearly all of which have since perished. Among these was an original letter from Charles II. to Governor Winthrop of Connecticut, which was in existence a few years ago in this city.

Although aided in my inquiries by B. R. Winthrop, Esq., Recording Secretary of this Society, and of the same family, (who, by the way, is also, on his mother's side, a lineal descendant from Governor Stuyvesant, of the Rival Colony of New Netherlands, afterwards New York.) I regret to be unable to furnish any additional information relative to this interesting relic of the "brave leader and famous Governor" of the Colony of Massachusetts Bay.

Very Respectfully,

Your faithful

and obedient Servant,

GEORGE FOLSOM.

NEW YORK, *April* 19, 1838.

A

MODELL OF CHRISTIAN CHARITY.

WRITTEN

ON BOARD THE ARBELLA, ON THE ATLANTIC OCEAN.

By the Hon. John Winthrop Esqr. In his passage (with a great company of Religious people, of which Christian tribes he was the Brave Leader and famous Governor;) from the Island of Great Brittaine to New-England in the North America. Anno 1630.

CHRISTIAN CHARITIE.

A Modell hereof.

GOD ALMIGHTY in his most holy and wise providence, hath soe disposed of the condition of mankind, as in all times some must be rich, some poore, some high and eminent in power and dignitie ; others mean and in submission.

The Reason hereof.

1 *Reas.* First to hold conformity with the rest of his world, being delighted to show forth the glory of his wisdom in the variety and difference of the creatures, and the glory of his power in ordering all these differences for the preservation and good of the whole ; and the glory of his greatness, that as it is the glory of princes to have many officers, soe this great king will haue many stewards, counting himself more honoured in dispensing his gifts to man by man, than if he did it by his owne immediate hands.

2 *Reas.* Secondly that he might haue the more occasion to manifest the work of his Spirit : first upon the wicked in

moderating and restraining them : soe that the riche and mighty should not eate upp the poore nor the poore and dispised rise upp against and shake off theire yoake. 2ly In the regenerate, in exerciseing his graces in them, as in the grate ones, theire love, merċy, gentleness, temperance &c., in the poore and inferior sorte, theire faithe, patience, obedience &c.

3 *Reas.* Thirdly, that every man might have need of others, and from hence they might be all knitt more nearly together in the Bonds of brotherly affection. From hence it appears plainly that noe man is made more honourable than another or more wealthy &c., out of any particular and singular respect to himselfe, but for the glory of his creator and the common good of the creature, man. Therefore God still reserves the propperty of these gifts to himself as Ezek. 16. 17. he there calls wealthe, *his gold and his silver*, and Prov. 3. 9. he claims theire service as his due, *honor the Lord with thy riches* &c.—All men being thus (by divine providence) ranked into two sorts, riche and poore ; under the first are comprehended all such as are able to live comfortably by their own meanes duely improved ; and all others are poore according to the former distribution. There are two rules whereby we are to walk one towards another : Justice and Mercy. These are always distinguished in their act and in their object, yet may they both concurre in the same subject in eache respect ; as sometimes there may be an occasion of showing mercy to a rich man in some sudden danger or distresse, and alsoe doeing of meere justice to a poor man in regard of some perticular contract &c. There is likewise a double Lawe by which wee are regulated in our conversation towardes another ; in both the former respects, the lawe of nature and the lawe of grace, or the morrall lawe or the lawe of the gospell, to omitt the rule of justice as not propperly belonging to this purpose otherwise than it may fall into consideration in some perticular cases. By the first of these lawes man as he was enabled soe withall is commanded to love his neighbour as himself. Upon this ground stands all the precepts of the morrall lawe, which concernes our dealings with men. To apply this to the works of mercy ; this lawe requires two things. First that every man afford his help to another in every

want or distresse. Secondly, that hee performe this out
of the same affection which makes him carefull of his
owne goods, according to that of our Savior, (Math.) *Whatsoever ye would that men should do to you.*   This was
practised by Abraham and Lot in entertaining the angells
and the old man of Gibea.   The lawe of Grace or of the
Gospell hath some difference from the former ; as in these
respects, First the lawe of nature was given to man in the
estate of innocency ; this of the Gospell in the estate of
regeneracy. 2ly, the former propounds one man to another,
as the same flesh and image of God ; this as a brother in
Christ allsoe, and in the communion of the same Spirit,
and soe teacheth to put a difference between christians
and others.   *Doe good to all, especially to the household
of faith ;* upon this ground the Israelites were to putt a
difference betweene the brethren of such as were strangers
though not of the Canaanites.

3ly.   The Lawe of nature would give no rules for
dealing with enemies, for all are to be considered as
friends in the state of innocency, but the Gospell commands
loue to an enemy. Proofe. *If thine Enemy hunger, feed
him ; Loue your Enemies, doe good to them that hate you.*
Math. 5. 44.

This lawe of the Gospell propounds likewise a difference
of seasons and occasions.   There is a time when a christian must sell all and give to the poor, as they did in the
Apostles times.   There is a time allsoe when christians
(though they give not all yet) must give beyond their
abillity, as they of Macedonia, Cor. 2, 6.   Likewise community of perills calls for extraordinary liberality, and soe
doth community in some speciall service for the churche.
Lastly, when there is no other means whereby our christian
brother may be relieved in his distress, we must help him
beyond our ability rather than tempt God in putting him
upon help by miraculous or extraordinary meanes.

This duty of mercy is exercised in the kinds, Giueving,
lending and forgiving.—

Quest. What rule shall a man observe in giueving in
respect of the measure ?

Ans. If the time and occasion be ordinary he is to giue
out of his abundance. *Let him lay aside as God hath
blessed him.* If the time and occasion be extraordinary,

he must be ruled by them ; taking this withall, that then a man cannot likely doe too much, especially if he may leave himselfe and his family under probable means of comfortable subsistence.

Object. A man must lay upp for posterity, the fathers lay upp for posterity and children, and *he is worse than an infidell that pronideth not for his owne.*

Ans. For the first, it is plaine that it being spoken by way of comparison, it must be meant of the ordinary and usuall course of fathers, and cannot extend to times and occasions extraordinary. For the other place the Apostle speaks against such as walked inordinately, and it is without question, that he is worse than an infidell who through his owne sloathe and voluptuousness shall neglect to provide for his family.—

Object. *The wise man's Eies are in his head,* saith Solomon, *and foreseeth the plague ;* therefore he must forecast and lay upp against evill times when hee or his may stand in need of all he can gather.

Ans. This very Argument Solomon useth to persuade to liberallity, Eccle.: *Cast thy bread upon the waters,* and *for thou knowest not what evill may come upon the land.* Luke 26. *Make you friends of the riches of iniquity ;* you will ask how this shall be ? very well. For first he that giues to the poore, lends to the lord and he will repay him even in this life an hundredfold to him or his.—*The righteous is ever mercifull and lendeth and his seed enjoyeth the blessing ;* and besides wee know what advantage it will be to us in the day of account when many such witnesses shall stand forth for us to witnesse the improvement of our tallent. And I would know of those whoe pleade soe much for laying up for time to come, whether they holde that to be Gospell, Math. 16. 19. *Lay not upp for your-selves Treasures upon Earth &c.* If they acknowledge it, what extent will they allowe it ? if only to those primitive times, let them consider the reason whereopon our Saviour groundes it. The first is that they are subject to the moathe, the rust, the theife. Secondly, They will steale away the hearte ; *where the treasure is there will ye heart be allsoe.* The reasons are of like force at all times. Therefore the exhortation must be generall and perpetuall, withallwayes in respect of the love and affection to riches and in regard of the things themselves when any speciall seruice for the churche or perticular Distresse of our brother doe call for the use of them ; otherwise it is not only lawfull but necessary to lay upp as Joseph did to haue ready uppon such occasions, as the Lord (whose stewards wee are of them) shall call for them from us ; Christ giues us an Instance of the first, when hee sent his disciples for the Ass, and bidds them answer the owner thus, the Lord hath need of him : soe when the Tabernacle was to be built, he sends to his people to call for their silver and gold, &c ; and yeildes noe other reason but that it was for his worke. When Elisha comes to the widow of Sareptah and findes her preparing to make ready her pittance for herselfe and family, he bids her first provide for him, he challengeth first God's parte which she must first give before shee must serve her owne family. All these teach us that the Lord lookes that when hee is pleased to call for his right in any thing wee haue, our owne interest wee haue, must stand aside till his turne be served. For the other, wee need looke noe further then to that of John 1. *he whoe hath this world's goodes and seeth his brother to neede and shutts upp his compassion from him, how dwelleth the loue of God in him*, which comes punctually to this conclusion ; if thy brother be in want and thou canst help him, thou needst not make doubt, what thou shouldst doe ; if thou louest God thou must help him.

Quest. What rule must wee observe in lending ?

Ans. Thou must observe whether thy brother hath present or probable or possible means of repaying thee, if there be none of those, thou must give him according to his necessity, rather then lend him as he requires ; if he hath present means of repaying thee, thou art to look at him not as an act of mercy, but by way of Commerce, wherein thou arte to walk by the rule of justice ; but if his means of repaying thee be only probable or possible, then is hee an object of thy mercy, thou must lend him, though there be danger of losing it, Deut. 15. 7. *If any of thy brethren be poore &c., thou shalt lend him sufficient.* That men might not shift off this duty by the apparent hazzard, he tells them that though the yeare of Jubile were at hand (when he must remitt it, if hee were not able to repay it before) yet he must lend him and that chearefully. *It may not greive thee to giue him* (saith hee) and because some might object, why soe I should soone impoverishe myself and my family, he adds with all thy worke &c ; for our Saviour, Math. 5. 42. *From him that would borrow of thee turne not away.*

Quest. What rule must we observe in forgiuing ?

Ans. Whether thou didst lend by way of commerce or in mercy, if he hath nothing to pay thee, must forgive, (except in cause where thou hast a surety or a lawfull pleadge) Deut. 15. 2. Every seaventh yeare the Creditor was to quitt that which he lent to his brother if he were poore as appears ver. 8. *Save when there shall be no poore with thee.* In all these and like cases, Christ was a generall rule, Math. 7. 22. *Whatsoever ye would that men should doe to you, doe yee the same to them allsoe.*

Quest. What rule must wee observe and walke by in cause of community of perill ?

Ans. The same as before, but with more enlargement towards others and lesse respect towards ourselves and our owne right. Hence it was that in the primitive Churche they sold all, had all things in common, neither did any man say that which he possessed was his owne. Likewise in theire returne out of the captivity, because the worke was greate for the restoring of the church and the danger of enemies was common to all, Nehemiah directs the Jews to liberallity and readiness in remitting theire debts to theire brethren, and disposing liberally to such as wanted, and stand not upon their owne dues which they might have demanded of them. Thus did some of our Forefathers in times of persecution in England, and soe did many of the faithful of other churches, whereof wee keepe an honorable remembrance of them ; and it is to be observed that both in Scriptures and latter stories of the churches that such as have beene most bountifull to the poore saintes, especially in those extraordinary times and occasions, God hath left them highly commended to posterity, as Zacheus, Cornelius, Dorcas, Bishop Hooper, the Cuttler of Brussells and divers others. Observe againe that the Scripture gives noe caussion to restraine any from being over liberall this way ; but all men to the liberall and cherefull practise hereof by the sweeter promises ; as to instance one for many, Isaiah 58. 6. *Is not this the fast I have chosen to loose the bonds of wickedness, to take off the heavy burdens, to lett the oppressed go free and to breake every yoake, to deale thy bread to the hungry and to bring the poore that wander into thy house, when thou seest the naked to cover them ; and then shall thy light brake forth as the morning and thy healthe shall growe speedily, thy righteousness shall goe before God, and the glory of the Lord shall embrace thee ; then thou shalt call and the Lord shall answer thee* &c., Ch. 2. 10. *If thou power out thy soule to the hungry, then shall thy light spring out in darkness, and the Lord shall guide thee continually, and satisfie thy soule in draught, and make falt thy bones, thou shalt be like a watered garden, and they shalt be of thee that shall build the old wast places* &c. On the contrary most heavy cursses are layed upon such as are straightened towards the Lord and his people, Judg. 5. *Cursse the Meroshe because he came not to help the Lord. Hee whoe shutteth his cares from hearing the cry of the poore, he shall cry and shall not be heard ;* Math. 25. *Goe ye cursed into everlasting fire &c. I was hungry and ye fedd mee not,* Cor. 2. 9. 16. He that soweth sparingly shall reape sparingly. Haveing already sett forth the practice of mercy according to the rule of God's lawe, it will be useful to lay open the groundes of it allsoe, being the other parte of the Commandment and that is the affection from which this exercise of mercy must arise, the Apostle tells us that this *love is the fullfilling of the lawe,* not that it is enough to loue our brother and soe noe further ; but in regard of the excellency of his partes giueing any motion to the other as the soule to the body and the power it hath to sett all the faculties on worke in the outward exercise of this duty ; as when wee bid one make the clocke strike, he doth not lay hand on the hammer, which is the immediate instrument of the sound, but setts on worke the first mouer or maine wheele ; knoweing that will certainely produce the sound which he intends. Soe the way to drawe men to the workes of mercy, is not by force of Argument from the goodness or necessity of the worke ; for though this cause may enforce, a rationall minde to some present act of mercy, as is frequent in experience, yet it cannot worke such a habit in a soule, as shall make it prompt upon all occasions to produce the same effect, but by frameing these affections of loue in the hearte which will as naturally bring forthe the other, as any cause doth produce the effect.

The deffinition which the Scripture giues us of loue is this. *Love is the bond of perfection,* first it is a bond or ligament. 2ly it makes the worke perfect. There is noe body but consists of partes and that which knitts these partes together, giues the body its perfection, because it makes eache parte soe contiguous to others as thereby they doe mutually participate with each other, both in strengthe and infirmity, in pleasure and paine. To instance in the most perfect of all bodies ; Christ and his Church make one body ; the severall partes of this body considered a parte before they were united, were as disproportionate and as much disordering as soe many contrary quallities or elements, but when Christ comes, and by his spirit and loue knitts all these partes to himselfe and each to other, it is become the most perfect and best proportioned body in the world, Eph. 4. 16. *Christ, by whome all the body being knitt together by every joint for the furniture thereof, according to the effectuall power which is in the measure of every perfection of partes, a glorious body without spott or wrinkle;* the ligaments hereof being Christ, or his love, for Christ is love, 1 John 4. 8. Soe this definition is right. *Love is the bond of perfection.*

From hence we may frame these conclusions. 1. First of all, true Christians are of one body in Christ, 1 Cor. 12. 12. 13. 17. *Ye are the body of Christ and members of their parte.* All the partes of this body being thus vnited are made soe contiguous in a speciall relation as they must needes partake of each other's strength and infirmity; joy and sorrowe, weale and woe. 1 Cor. 12. 26. *If one member suffers, all suffer with it, if one be in honor, all rejoyce with it.* 2ly. The ligaments of this body which knitt together are loue. 3ly. Noe body can be perfect which wants its proper ligament. 5ly. This sensibleness and sympathy of each other's conditions will necessarily infuse into each parte a native desire and endeavour, to strengthen, defend, preserve and comfort the other. To insist a little on this conclusion being the product of all the former, the truthe hereof will appeare both by precept and patterne.   1 John 3. 10.   *Yee ought to lay doune your lives for the brethren.*   Gal. 6. 2. *beare ye one another's burthen's and soe fulfill the lawe of Christ.*   For patterns wee haue that first of our Saviour whoe out of his good will in obedience to his father, becomeing a parte of this body and being knitt with it in the bond of loue, found such a natiue sensibleness of our infirmities and sorrowes as he willingly yielded himselfe to deathe to ease the infirmities of the rest of his body, and soe healed theire sorrowes. From the like sympathy of partes did the Apostles and many thousands of the Saintes lay doune theire lives for Christ.   Againe the like wee may see in the members of this body among themselves.   1 Rom. 9.   Paule could have been contented to have been separated from Christ, that the Jewes might not be cutt off from the body.   It is very observable what hee professeth of his affectionate partaking with every member ; *whoe is weake* (saith hee) *and I am not weake ? whoe is offended and I burne not ;* and againe, 2 Cor. 7. 13. *therefore wee are comforted because yee were comforted.*   Of Epaphroditus he speaketh, Phil. 2. 30. *that he regarded not his owne life to do him service.*   Soe Phebe and others are called *the servants of the churche.* Now it is apparent that they served not for wages, or by constrainte, but out of loue.   The like we shall finde in the histories of the churche in all ages ; the sweete sympathie of affections which was in the members of this body one towards another ; theire chearfullness in serueing and suffering together ; how liberall they were without repineing, harbourers without grudgeing, and helpfull without reproaching ; and all from hence, because they had feruent loue amongst them ; which onely makes the practise of mercy constant and easie.

The next consideration is how this loue comes to be wrought.   Adam in his first estate was a perfect modell of mankinde in all their generations, and in him this loue was perfected in regard of the habit.   But Adam, rent himselfe from his Creator, rent all his posterity allsoe one from another ; whence it comes that every man is borne with this principle in him to loue and seeke himselfe onely, and thus a man continueth till Christ comes and takes possession of the soule and infuseth another principle, loue to God and our brother, and this latter haueing continuall supply from Christ, as the head and roote by which he is vnited, gets the predomining in the soule, soe by little and little expells the former. 1 John 4. 7. *loue cometh of God and every one that loueth is borne of God*, soe that this loue is the fruite of the new birthe, and none can have it but the new creature. Now when this quallity is thus formed in the soules of men, it workes like the Spirit upon the drie bones. Ezek. 39. *bone came to bone*. It gathers together the scattered bones, or perfect old man Adam, and knitts them into one body againe in Christ, whereby a man is become againe a living soule.

The third consideration is concerning the exercise of this loue, which is twofold, inward or outward. The outward hath beene handled in the former preface of this discourse. From unfolding the other wee must take in our way that maxime of philosophy. *Simile simili gaudet,* or like will to like ; for as of things which are turned with disaffection to eache other, the ground of it is from a dissimilitude or ariseing from the contrary or different nature of the things themselves ; for the ground of loue is an apprehension of some resemblance in the things loued to that which affects it. This is the cause why the Lord loues the creature, soe farre as it hathe any of his Image in it ; he loues his elect because they are like himselfe, he beholds them in his beloued sonne. So a mother loues her childe, because shee throughly conceives a resemblance of herselfe in it. Thus it is betweene the members of Christ; eache discernes, by the worke of the Spirit, his oune Image and resemblance in another, and therefore cannot but loue him as he loues himself. Now when the soule, which is of a sociable nature, findes anything like to itselfe, it is like Adam when Eve was brought to him. She must be one with himselfe. *This is flesh of my flesh* (saith he) *and bone of my bone.* Soe the soule conceives a greate delighte in it ; therefore shee desires nearness and familiarity with it. Shee hath a greate propensity to doe it good and receiues such content in it, as fearing the miscarriage of her beloved, shee bestowes it in the inmost closett of her heart. Shee will not endure that it shall want any good which shee can giue it. If by occasion shee be withdrawne from the company of it, shee is still looking towardes the place where shee left her beloved. If shee heard it groane, shee is with it presently. If shee finde it sadd and disconsolate, shee sighes and moanes with it. Shee hath noe such joy as to see her beloved merry and thriving. If shee see it wronged, shee cannot bear it without passion.   Shee setts noe boundes to her affections, nor hath any thought of reward. Shee findes recompense enough in the exercise of her loue towardes it. Wee may see this acted to life in Jonathan and David. Jonathan a valiant man endued with the spirit of love, soe soone as he discovered the same spirit in David had presently his hearte knitt to him by this ligament of loue ; soe that it is said he loued him as his owne soule, he takes soe great pleasure in him, that hee stripps himselfe to adorne his beloved.   His father's kingdome was not soe precious to him as his beloved David, David shall haue it with all his hearte.   Himself desires noe more but that hee may be neare to him to rejoyce in his good. Hee chooseth to converse with him in the wildernesse even to the hazzard of his oune life, rather than with the greate Courtiers in his father's Pallace. When hee sees danger towards him, hee spares neither rare paines nor perill to direct it. When injury was offered his beloued David, hee would not beare it, though from his oune father. And when they must parte for a season onely, they thought theire heartes would have broake for sorrowe, had not theire affections found vent by abundance of teares. Other instances might be brought to showe the nature of this affection ; as of Ruthe and Naomi, and many others ; but this truthe is cleared enough.   If any shall object that it is not possible that loue shall be bred or upheld without hope of requitall, it is graunted ; but that is not our cause; for this loue is alluayes vnder reward.   It never giues, but it alluayes receives with advantage ; First in regard that among the members of the same body, loue and affection are reciprocall in a most equall and sweete kinde of commerce.

2nly. In regard of the pleasure and content that the exercise of loue carries with it, as wee may see in the naturall body. The mouth is at all the paines to receive and mince the foode which serves for the nourishment of all the other partes of the body ; yet it hath noe cause to complaine ; for first the other partes send backe, by severall passages, a due proportion of the same nourishment, in a better forme for the strengthening and comforting the mouthe. 2ly the laboure of the mouthe is accompanied with such pleasure and content as farre exceedes the paines it takes. Soe is it in all the labour of love among Christians. The partie louing, reapes loue again, as was showed before, which the soule covetts more then all the wealthe in the world. 3ly. Nothing yeildes more pleasure and content to the soule then when it findes that which it may loue fervently; for to love and live beloved is the soule's paradise both here and in heaven. In the State of wedlock there be many comforts to learne out of the troubles of that Condition ; but let such as have tryed the most, say if there be any sweetness in that Condition comparable to the exercise of mutuall loue.

From the former Considerations arise these Conclusions.—1. First, This loue among Christians is a reall thing, not imaginarie. 2ly. This loue is as absolutely necessary to the being of the body of Christ, as the sinews and other ligaments of a naturall body are to the being of that body. 3ly. This loue is a divine, spirituall, nature ; free, active, strong, couragious, permanent ; undervaluing all things beneathe its propper object and of all the graces, this makes us nearer to resemble the virtues of our heavenly father. 4thly It rests in the loue and wellfare of its beloued. For the full certain knowledge of those truthes concerning the nature, use, and excellency of this grace, that which the holy ghost hath left recorded, 1 Cor. 13, may give full satisfaction, which is needful for every true member of this louely body of the Lord Jesus, to worke upon theire heartes by prayer, meditation continuall exercise at least of the speciall [influence] of this grace, till Christ be formed in them and they in him, all in eache other, knitt together by this bond of loue.

It rests now to make some application of this discourse, by the present designe, which gaue the occasion of writing of it. Herein are 4 things to be propounded ; *first* the persons, 2ly the worke, 3ly the end, 4thly the meanes. 1. For *the persons*. Wee are a company professing ourselves fellow members of Christ, in which respect onely though wee were absent from each other many miles, and had our imployments as farre distant, yet wee ought to account ourselves knitt together by this bond of loue, and,

live in the exercise of it, if wee would have comforte of
our being in Christ.   This was notorious in the practise
of the Christians in former times ; as is testified of the
Waldenses, from the mouth of one of the adversaries
Æneas Sylvius "mutuo ament pere antequam norunt,"
they use to loue any of theire owne religion even before
they were acquainted with them.   2nly for the *worke* wee
have in hand.   It is by a mutuall consent, through a
speciall overvaluing providence and a more than an ordinary approbation of the Churches of Christ, to seeke out
a place of cohabitation and Consorteshipp under a due
forme of Government both ciuill and ecclesiasticall.   In
such cases as this, the care of the publique must oversway
all private respects, by which, not only conscience, but
meare civill pollicy, dothe binde us.   For it is a true
rule that particular Estates cannot subsist in the ruin of
the publique.   3ly The *end* is to improve our lives to doe
more service to the Lord; the comforte and encrease of
the body of Christe, whereof we are members ; that ourselves and posterity may be the better preserved from the
common corruptions of this evill world, to serve the Lord
and worke out our Salvation under the power and purity
of his holy ordinances.   4thly for the *meanes* whereby this
must be effected.   They are twofold, a conformity with
the worke and end wee aime at.   These wee see are
extraordinary, therefore wee must not content ourselves
with usuall ordinary meanes.   Whatsoever wee did, or
ought to have done, when wee liued in England, the
same must wee doe, and more allsoe, where wee goe.
That which the most in theire churches mainetaine as
truthe in profession onely, wee must bring into familiar
and constant practise; as in this duty of loue, wee must
loue brotherly without dissimulation, wee must loue one
another with a pure hearte fervently.   Wee must beare
one anothers burthens.   We must not looke onely on our
owne things, but allsoe on the things of our brethren.
Neither must wee thinke that the Lord will beare with
such faileings at our hands as he dothe from those among
whome wee have lived; and that for these 3 Reasons ; 1.
In regard of the more neare bond of mariage between him
and us, wherein hee hath taken us to be his, after a most

strickt and peculiar manner,·which will make them the more jealous of our loue and obedience.   Soe he tells the people of Israell, *you onely have I knowne of all the families of the Earthe, therefore will I punishe you for your Transgressions.*   2ly, because *the Lord will be sanctified in them that come neare him.*   We know that there were many that corrupted the service of the Lord ; some setting upp altars before his owne ; others offering both strange fire and strange sacrifices allsoe ; yet there came noe fire from heaven, or other sudden judgement upon them, as did upon Nadab and Abihu, whoe yet wee may think did not sinne presumptuously.   3ly When God gives a speciall commission he lookes to have it strictly observed in every article,   When he gave Saule a commission to destroy Amaleck, Hee indented with him upon certain articles, and because hee failed in one of the least, and that upon a faire pretense, it lost him the kingdom, which should have beene his reward, if hee had observed his commission. Thus stands the cause betweene God and us.   We are entered into Covenant with Him for this worke.   Wee haue taken out a commission.   The Lord hath given us leave to drawe our own articles.   Wee haue professed to enterprise these and those accounts, upon these and those ends.   Wee have hereupon besought Him of favour and blessing.   Now if the Lord shall please to heare us, and bring us in peace to the place we desire, then hath hee ratified this covenant and sealed our Commission, and will expect a strict performance of the articles contained in it ; but if wee shall neglect the observation of these articles which are the ends wee have propounded, and, dissembling with our God, shall fall to embrace this present world and prosecute our carnall intentions, seeking greate things for ourselves and our posterity, the Lord will surely breake out in wrathe against us ; be revenged of such a [sinful] people and make us knowe the price of the breache of such a covenant.

Now the onely way to avoyde this shipwracke, and to provide for our posterity, is to followe the counsell of Micah, *to doe justly, to love mercy, to walk humbly with our God.* For this end, wee must be knitt together, in this worke, as one man.   Wee must entertaine each other in brotherly affection. Wee must be willing to abridge ourselves of our superfluities, for the supply of other's necessities. Wee must uphold a familiar commerce together in all meekeness, gentlenes, patience and liberality. Wee must delight in eache other ; make other's conditions our oune ; rejoice together, mourne together, labour and suffer together, allwayes haueving before our eyes our commission and community in the worke, as members of the same body. Soe shall wee *keepe the unitie of the spirit in the bond of peace.* The Lord will be our God, and delight to dwell among us, as his oune people, and will command a blessing upon us in all our wayes. Soe that wee shall see much more of his wisdome, power, goodness and truthe, than formerly wee haue been acquainted with. Wee shall finde that the God of Israell is among us, when ten of us shall be able to resist a thousand of our enemies ; when hee shall make us a prayse and glory that men shall say of succeeding plantations, "the Lord make it likely that of *New England*." For wee must consider that wee shall be as a citty upon a hill. The eies of all people are uppon us. Soe that if wee shall deale falsely with our God in this worke wee haue undertaken, and soe cause him to withdrawe his present help from us, wee shall be made a story and a by-word through the world. Wee shall open the mouthes of enemies to speake evill of the wayes of God, and all professors for God's sake. Wee shall shame the faces of many of God's worthy servants, and cause theire prayers to be turned into curses upon us till wee be consumed out of the good land whither wee are a goeing.

I shall shutt upp this discourse with that exhortation of Moses, that faithfull servant of the Lord, in his last farewell to Israell, Deut. 30. *Beloued there is now sett before us life and good, Death and evill, in that wee are commanded this day to loue the Lord our God, and to loue one another, to walke in his wayes and to keepe his Commandements and his Ordinance and his lawes,* and the articles of our Covenant with him, that *wee may liue and be multiplied, and that the Lord our God may blesse us in the land whither wee goe to possesse it. But if our heartes shall turne away, soe that wee will not obey, but shall be seduced, and worshipp and serue other Gods,* our pleasure and proffitts, *and serue them ;* it is propounded unto us this day, *wee shall surely perishe out of the good land whither wee passe over this vast sea to possesse it ;*

Therefore lett us choose life
that wee, and our seede
may liue, by obeyeing His
voyce and cleaveing to Him,
for Hee is our life and
our prosperity.

———————

GOD'S PROMISE TO HIS PLANTATIONS

John Cotton, *God's Promise to his Plantations 2 Sam 7. 10. Moreover I will appoint a place for my people Israell, and I will plant them, that they may dwell in a place of their owne, and move no more. As it was delivered in a Sermon* (London, 1634), pp. 1–20.

Born in Derby, England, and educated at Trinity College, Cambridge, John Cotton (1584–1652) took the position of vicar of St Botolph's Church in Boston, Lincolnshire, in 1612, where he remained for twenty-one years. During this time, his views tended increasingly towards Puritanism. By 1632, legal action was taken against him for nonperformance of church duties and he immigrated to the Massachusetts Bay Colony, becoming the head of the First Church of Boston. He held this position until his death, becoming a highly influential leader in both civil and religious affairs.

God's Promise to his Plantations is one of three writings by Cotton which are reproduced in this volume. They discuss the role of religion in society, particularly in regard to the establishment of civil government. Attention is paid in both political and religious terms to the problems of continuity versus change, freedom versus control, and hierarchy versus equality. In *God's Promise to his Plantations*, Cotton argues that if the colonists of Massachusetts Bay follow the will of God (including the organisation of society through religion) then God, in turn, will promise them safety and peace and, implicitly, wealth. In this piece, beyond his formulation of the Puritan work ethic, Cotton is concerned with economic organisation and motivations. For example, one reason Cotton offers for a man's right to immigrate is the better employment of god-given talents. Another reason is that a man may immigrate not to avoid the repayment of debts contracted, but for better opportunities to earn the sum necessary for repayment.

GODS
PROMISE
TO HIS
PLANTATIONS

2 Sam 7. 10.

Moreover J will appoint a place for my people Israell,
*and I will plant them, that they may dwell in a
place of their owne, and move no more.*

As it was delivered in a Sermon,

By IOHN COTTON, B. D.
and Preacher of Gods
word in *Boston.*

PSALME 22. 27. 30. 31.

*All the ends of the world shall remember and turne unto the
Lord, and all the kindreds of the Nations shall worship
before thee.
A seede shall serve him, it shall be accounted to the Lord for
a generation.
They shall come, and shall declare his righteousnesse unto a
people that shall be borne, that he hath done this.*

LONDON,
Printed by *William Jones* for *John Bellamy,* and
are to be sold at the three *Golden Lyons* by the
Royall Exchange. 1634.

2 Sam. 7. 10.

Moreover I will appoint a place for my people
Israell, and I will plant them, that they may
dwell in a place of their owne, and move no
more.

 N the begining of this chap-
ter we reade of *Davids* pur-
pose to build God an house,
who thereupon consulted
with *Nathan* about it, one
Prophet standing in neede of
anothers help in such waigh-
tie matters. *Nathan* incourageth the King unto
this worke, verse 3. God the same night meetes
Nathan and tells him a contrary purpose of his:
Wherein God refuseth *Davids* offer, with some
kind of earnest and vehement dislike, *verse* 4. 5.
Secondly, he refuseth the reason of *Davids* offer,
from his long silence. For foure hundred yeares
together he spake of no such thing, unto any of
the Tribes of *Israel* saying, *Why build you not me*
an house? in 6. 7. verses.
Now lest *David* should be discouraged with
                                            this

this anfwer, the Lord bids *Nathan* to fhut up his fpeech with words of encouragement, and fo he remoues his difcouragement two wayes.

Firft, by recounting his former fauours difpen-fed unto *David*.   Secondly , by promifing the continuance of the like or greater: and the ra-ther , becaufe of this purpofe of his. And five bleffings God promifeth unto *David,* and his, for his fake.

The firft is in the 10. verfe: *I will appoint a place for my people Ifraell.*

Secondly, feeing it was in his heart to build him an houfe, God would therefore, *build him an houfe renowned for ever.* verfe 11.

Thirdly, that he would accept of an houfe from *Salomon,* verfe 12.

Fourthly, hee will be a Father to his fonne, verf. 14. 15.

Fifthly, that he will *eftablifh the throne of his houfe for ever.*

In this 10 verfe is a double bleffing promifed:

Fiift,   the defignment of a place for his peo-ple.

Secondly, a plantation of them in that place, from whence is promifed a threefold bleffing.

Firft, they fhall dwell there like Free-holders in a place of their owne.

Secondly, hee promifeth them firme and du-rable poffeffion, they fhall move no more.

Thirdly, they fhall have peaceable and quiet refting there, The fonnes of wickedneffe fhall afflict them no more: which is amplified by their former troubles, as before time.   From

From the appointment of a place for them, which is the firſt bleſſing, you may obſerve this note,

The placeing of a people in this or that Countrey is from the appointment of the Lord.

This is evident in the Text, and the Apoſtle ſpeakes of it as grounded in nature, *Acts* 17.26. *God hath determined the times before appointed, and the bounds of our habitation. Dut.2 chap.5.9.* God would not have the *Iſraelites* meddle with the *Edomites,* or the *Moabites,* becauſe he had given them their land for a poſſeſſion. God aſſigned out ſuch a land for ſuch a poſterity, and for ſuch a time.

Wherein doth this worke of God ſtand in appointing a place for a people?

Firſt, when God eſpies or diſcovers a land for a people, as in *Ezek.* 20. 6. he brought them into a land that he had eſpied for them: And that is, when either he gives them to diſcover it themſelves, or heare of it diſcovered by others, and fitting them.

Secondly, after he hath eſpied it, when he carrieth them along to it, ſo that they plainly ſee a providence of God leading them from one Country to another: As in *Exod.* 19.4. *You have ſeene how I have borne you as on Eagles wings, and brought you unto my ſelfe.* So that though they met with many difficulties, yet hee carried them high above them all, like an eagle, flying over ſeas and rockes, and all hinderances.

Thirdly, when he makes roome for a people

to

to dwell there, as in *Pfal.* 80. 9. *Thou preparedst roome for them.* When *Ifaac* fojourned among the *Philiftines*, he digged one well, and the *Philiftines* ftrove for it, and he called it *Efek.* and he digged another well, and for that they ftrove alfo, therefore he called it *Sitnah* : and he removed thence, and digged another well, and for that they ftrove not, and he called it *Rohoboth*, and faid, *For now the Lord hath made roome for us, and we fhall be fruitfull in the Land.* Now no *Efek*, no *Sitnah*, no quarrel or contention, but now he fits downe in *Rohoboth* in a peaceable roome.

Now God makes room for a people 3 wayes:

Firft, when he cafts out the enemies of a people before them by lawfull warre with the inhabitants, which God cals them unto. as in *Pf.*44.2 *Thou didft driue out the heathē before them.* But this courfe of warring againft others, & driving them out without provocation, depends upon fpeciall Commiffion from God, or elfe it is not imitable.

Secondly, when he gives a forreigne people favour in the eyes of any native people to come and fit downe with them either by way of purchafe, as *Abraham* did obtaine the field of *Machpelah*; or elfe when they give it in courtefie, as *Pharaoh* did the land of *Gofhen* unto the fons of *Iacob.*

Thirdly, when hee makes a Countrey though not altogether void of inhabitants, yet voyd in that place where they refide. Where there is a vacant place, there is liberty for the fonne of *Adam* or *Noah* to come and inhabite, though they neither buy it, nor aske their leaves. *Abraham* and

and *Isaac*, when they　*　sojourned amongst the
Philistims, they did not buy that land to feede
their cattle, because they said There is roome e-
nough. And so did *Iacob* pitch his Tent by *Se-*
chem, Gen. 34. 21. There was *roome enough*, as *Ha-*
mor said, *Let them sit downe amongst us*. And in
this case if the people who were former inhabitants did disturbe them in their possessions, they
complained to the King, as of wrong done unto
them : As *Abraham* did because they tooke away
his well, in *Gen. 21. 25*. For his right whereto he
pleaded not his immediate calling from God,
(for that would have seemed frivolous amongst
the Heathen) but his owne industry and culture
in digging the well, verse 30. Nor doth the
King reject his plea, with what had he to doe to
digge wells in their soyle ? but admitteth it as a
Principle in Nature, That in a vacant soyle, hee
that taketh possession of it, and bestoweth culture
and husbandry upon it, his Right it is. And the
ground of this is from the grand Charter given
to *Adam* and his posterity in Paradise, *Gen.* 1.28.
Multiply, *and replenish the earth, and subdue it*. If
therefore any sonne of *Adam* come and finde a
place empty, he hath liberty to come, and fill,
and subdue the earth there. This Charter was
renewed to *Noah*, *Gen.* 9. 1. *Fulfill the earth and*
multiply So that it is free from that comon Grant
for any to take possession of vacant Countries.
Indeed no Nation is to drive out another without speciall Commission from heaven, such as
the *Israelites* had, unlesse the Natives do unjustly
wrong

*This sojour-
ning was a
constant resi-
dence there, as
in a possession
of their owne;
although it be
called sojour-
ning or dwel-
ling as man-
gers, because
they neither
had the sove-
raigne govern-
ment of the
whole Coun-
try in their
owne hand,
nor yet did in-
corporate them
selves into the
Common
wealth of the
Natives, to
submit them-
selves unto
their govern-
ment.

wrong them, and will not recompence the wrongs done in peaceable fort, & then they may right themfelves by lawfull war, and fubdue the Countrey unto themfelves.

This placeing of people in this or that Country, is from Gods foveraignty over all the earth, and the inhabitants thereof: as in *Pfal.* 24.1. *The earth is the Lords, and the fulneffe thereof.* And in *Ier.* 10. 7. God is there called, *The King of Nations:* and in *Deut.* 10. 14. Therefore it is meete he fhould provide a place for all Nations to inhabite, and haue all the earth replenifhed. Onely in the Text here is meant fome more fpeciall appointment, becaufe God tells them it by his owne mouth; he doth not fo with other people, he doth not tell the children of *Seer,* that hee hath appointed a place for them: that is, He gives them the land by promife; others take the land by his providence, but Gods people take the land by promife: And therefore the land of *Canaan* is called a land of promife. Which they difcerne, firft, by difcerning themfelves to be in Chrift, in whom all the promifes are yea, and amen.

Secondly, by finding his holy prefence with them, to wit, when he plants them in the holy Mountaine of his Inheritance: *Exodus.* 15. 17. And that is when he giveth them the liberty. and purity of his Ordinances. It is a land of promife, where they have provifion for foule as well as For body. *Ruth* dwelt well for outward refpects while fhee dwelt in *Moab,* but when fhee commeth to dwell in *Ifrael,* fhee is faid to come under
der

der the wings of God: *Ruth* 2. 12. When God wrappes us in with his Ordinances, and warmes us with the life and power of them as with wings, there is a land of promife.

This may teach us all where wee doe now dwell, or where after wee may dwell, be fure you looke at every place appointed to you, from the hand of God: wee may not rufh into any place, and never fay to God, By your leave; but wee muft difcerne how God appoints us this place. There is poore comfort in fitting downe in any place, that you cannot fay, This place is appointed me of God. Canft thou fay that God fpied out this place for thee, and there hath fetled thee above all hinderances? didft thou finde that God made roome for thee either by lawfull defcent, or purchafe, or gift, or other warrantable right? Why then this is the place God hath appointed thee; here hee hath made roome for thee, he hath placed thee in *Rehoboth*, in a peaceable place: This we muft difcerne, or els wee are but intruders upon God. And when wee doe withall difcerne, that God giveth us thefe outward bleffings from his love in Chrift, and maketh comfortable provifion as well for our foule as for our bodies, by the meanes of grace, then doe we enjoy our prefent poffeffion as well by gracious promife, as by the common, and juft, and bountifull providence of the Lord. Or if a man doe remove, he muft fee that God hath efpied out fuch a Countrey for him.

Secondly, though there be many difficulties
yet

yet he hath given us hearts to overlooke them all, as if we were carried upon eagles wings.

And thirdly, fee God making roome for us by fome lawfull meanes.

But how fhall I know whether God hath appointed me fuch a place, if I be well where I am, what may warrant my removeall?

There be foure or five good things, for procurement of any of which I may remove. Secondly, there be fome evill things, for avoiding of any of which wee may tranfplant our felves. Thirdly, if withall we finde fome fpeciall providence of God concurring in either of both concerning our felves, and applying general grounds of removall to our perfonall eftate.

Firft, wee may remove for the gaining of knowledge. Our Saviour commends it in the Queene of the fouth, that fhe came from the utmoft parts of the earth to heare the wifdome of *Salomon*: *Matth.* 12. 42. And furely with him fhe might haue continued for the fame end, if her perfonall calling had not recalled her home.

Secondly, fome remove and travaile for merchandize and gaine-fake; *Daily bread may be fought from farre, Prov.* 31. 14. Yea our Saviour approveth travaile for Merchants, *Matth,* 13. 45, 46. when hee compareth a Chriftian to a Merchantman feeking pearles: For he never fetcheth a comparifon from any unlawfull thing to illuftrate a thing lawfull. The comparifon from the unjuft Steward, and from the Theefe in the night, is not taken from the injuftice of the one, or the

theft

theft of the other; but from the wisedome of the one, and the sodainnesse of the other; which in themselves are not unlawfull.

Thirdly, to plant a Colony, that is, a company that agree together to remove out of their own Country, and settle a Citty or common wealth elsewhere. Of such a Colony wee reade in *Acts* 16. 12. which God blessed and prospered exceedingly, and made it a glorious Church. Nature teacheth Bees to doe so, when as the hive is too full, they seeke abroad for new dwellings: So when the hive of the Common wealth is so full, that Tradesmen cannot live one by another, but eate up one another, in this case it is lawfull to remove.

Fourthly, God alloweth a man to remove, when he may employ his Talents and gift better elsewhere, especially when where he is, he is not bound by any speciall engagement. Thus God sent *Ioseph* before to preserve the Church: *Iosephs* wisedome and spirit was not fit for a shepheard, but for a Counsellour of State, and therefore God sent him into *Egypt*. *To whom much is given of him God will require the more* : *Luk* 12. 48.

Fifthly, for the liberty of the Ordinances. 2 *Chron.* 11. 13, 14, 15. When *Ieroboam* made a desertion from *Iudah*, and set up golden Calves to worship, all that were well affected, both Priests and people, sold their possessions, and came to *Ierusalem* for the Ordinances sake. This case was of seasonable use to our fathers in the dayes

dayes of Queene *Mary*; who removed to *France* and *Germany* in the beginning of her Reign, upon Proclamation of alteration of religion, before any persecution began.

Secondly, there be evills to be avoyded that may warrant removeall. Firft, when fome grievous finnes overfpread a Country that threaten defolation. *Mic.* 2. 6. to 11 verfe: When the people fay to them that prophecie, *Prophecie not*; then verfe 10. *Arife then, this is not your reft.* Which words though they be a threatning, not a commandement; yet as in a threatning a wife man forefeeth the plague, fo in the threatning he feeth a commandement, to hide himfelfe from it. This cafe might have beene of feafonable ufe unto them of the *Palatinate*, when they faw their Orthodox Minifters banifhed, although themfelues might for a while enjoy libertie of confcience.

Secondly, if men be overburdened with debts and miferies, as *Davids* followers were; they may then retire out of the way (as they retired to *David* for fafety) not to defraud their Creditors (for *God is an avenger of fuch things*, 1 *Theff.* 4. 6.) but to gaine further opportunity to difcharge their debts, and to fatisfie their Creditors. 1 *Sam.* 22. 1, 2.

Thirdly, in cafe of perfecution, fo did the Apoftle in *Acts* 13. 46, 47.

Thirdly, as thefe generall cafes, where any of them doe fall out, doe warrant removeall in generall: fo there be fome fpeciall providences or
                                                      particular

particular cafes which may give warrant unto
fuch or fuch a perfon to tranfplant himfelfe, and
which apply the former generall grounds to particular perfons.

First, if foveraigne Authority command and
encourage fuch Plantations by giving way to
fubjects to tranfplant themfelves, and fet up a
new Commonwealth. This is a lawfull and expedient cafe for fuch particular perfons as be defigned and fent : *Matth.* 8. 9. and for fuch as
they who are fent, have power to command.

Secondly, when fome fpeciall providence of
God leades a man unto fuch a courfe. This may
alfo fingle out particulars. *Pfal.* 32. 8. *I will inftruct, and guide thee with mine eye*. As the childe
knowes the pleafure of his father in his eye, fo
doth the child of God fee Gods pleafure in the
eye of his heavenly Fathers providence. And
this is done three wayes.

First, if God give a man an inclination to this
or that courfe, for that is the fpirit of man ; and
God is the father of fpirits : Rom. 1. 11,12. 1 *Cor.*
16. 12. *Paul* difcerned his calling to goe to *Rom,*
by his τὸ πρόθυμον, his ready inclination to that
voyage ; and *Apollos* his loathing to goe to *Corinth, Paul* accepted as a juft reafon of his refufall
of a calling to goe thither. And this holdeth,
when in a mans inclination to travaile, his heart
is fet on no by-refpects, as to fee fafhions, to de-
ceive his Creditours, to fight Duels, or to live
idly, thofe are vaine inclinations ; but if his heart
be inclined upon right judgement to advance the
Gofpel,

Gofpell, to maintaine his family, to ufe his Talents fruitfully, or the like goood, this irclination is from God. As the beames of the Moone darting into the Sea leades it to and fro, fo doth a fecret inclination darted by God into our hearts leade and bowe (as a byas) our whole courfe.

Secondly, when God gives other men hearts to call us as the men of *Macedon* did *Paul*, *Come to us into Macedonia, and helpe us*. When wee are invited by others who have a good calling to refide there, we may goe with them, unlefle we be detained by waightier occafions. One member hath intereft in another, to call to it for helpe, when it is not diuerted by greater employment.

Thirdly, there is another providence of God concurring in both thefe, that is, when a mans calling and perfon is free, and not tyed by parents, or Magiftrates, or other people that have intereft in him. Or when abroad hee may doe himfelfe and others more good than he can doe at home. Here is then an eye of God that opens a doore there, and fets him loofe here, inclines his heart that way, and outlookes all difficulties. When God makes roome for us, no binding here, and an open way there, in fuch a cafe God tells them, he will appoint a place for them.

Secondly, this may teach us in every place where God appoints us to fit downe, to acknowledge him as our Landlord. The earth is the Lords and the fulnefle thereof, his are our Countries, our Townes, our houfes; and therefore let us acknowledge him in them all. The Apoftle

ftle makes this ufe of it amongft the *Athenians,*
Acts 17   26, 27. *He hath appointed the times, and*
places of our habitation, that we might feeke and grope
after the Lord. There is a threefold ufe that we are
to make of it, as it appeareth there; Let us feek after the Lord, why? Becaufe if thou commeft into
an houfe thou wilt aske for the owner of it: And
fo if thou commeft into a forreigne land, and
there findeft an houfe and land provided for
thee, wilt thou not enquire, where is the Landlord? where is that God that gave me this houfe
and land? He is miffing, and therefore feek after
him.

Secondly, thou muft feele after him, grope
after him by fuch fenfible things, ftrive to at-
taine the favour of your Landlord, and labour
to be obedient to him that hath given you fuch a
place.

Thirdly, you muft labour to finde him in his
Ordinances, in prayer and in Chriftian communion. Thefe things I owe him as my Landlord,
and by thefe I finde and enjoy him. This ufe the
very Pagans were to make of their feverall Plantations: And if you knew him before, feeke him
yet more, and feele after him till you finde him
in his Ordinances, and in your confciences.

Thirdly, when you have found God making
way and roome for you, and carrying you by
his providence unto any place, learne to walke
thankfully before him, defraud him not of his
rent, but offer your felves unto his fervice: Serve
that God, and teach your children to ferve him,
                                           that

that hath appointed you and them the place of your habitation.

    2. Obſervation. *A people of Gods plantation ſhall enjoy their owne place with ſafety and peace.*

This is manifeſt in the Text: I will plant them and what followes from thence? They ſhall dwell in their owne place. But how? Peaceably, they ſhall not be moved any more. Then they ſhall dwell ſafely, then they ſhall live in peace. The like promiſe you reade of in *Pſal.* 89.21, 22. *The enemie ſhall not exact upon them any more.* And in *Pſal.* 92. 13. *Theſe that be planted in the houſe of the Lord, ſhall flouriſh in the Courts of our God. Gods plantation is a flouriſhing plantation, Amos* 9.15.

Queſt.
    What is it for God to plant a people?

Anſw.
    It is a Metaphor taken from young Impes; I will plant them, that is, I will make them to take roote there; and that is, where they and their ſoyle agree well together, when they are well and ſufficiently provided for, as a plant ſuckes nouriſhment from the ſoyle that fitteth it.

    Secondly, When hee cauſeth them to grow as plants doe, in *Pſal.* 80.8,9,10,11. When a man growes like a tree in tallneſſe and ſtrength, to more firmeneſſe and eminency, then hee may be ſaid to be planted.

    Thirdly, When God cauſeth them to *fructifie Pſal.* 1. 5.

    Fourthly, When he eſtabliſheth them there, then he plants, and rootes not up.

    But here is ſomething more eſpeciall in this planting;

planting; for they were planted before in this land, and yet he promiseth here againe, that he will plant them in their owne land : which doth imply, first, That what ever former good estate they had already, he would prosper it, and increase it.

Secondly, God is said to plant a people more especially, when they become *Trees of righteousnesse, Isay* 61.3. That they may be called trees of righteousnesse, the planting of the Lord. So that there is implyed not onely a continuance of their former good estate, but that hee would make them a good people, a choice generation: which he did, first, by planting the Ordinances of God amongst them in a more glorious manner, as he did in *Salomons* time.

2. He would give his people *a naile,* and *a place in his Tabernacle, Isay* 56.5. And that is to give us part in Christ: for so the Temple typified. So then hee plants us when hee give us roote in Christ.

Thirdly, When he giveth us to *grow up in him as Calves in the stall: Mal.* 4.2, 3

Fourthly, & to *bring forth much fruit, Ioh.* 15.1.2

Fifthly, and to continue and abide in the state of grace. This is to plant us in his holy Sanctuary, he not rooting us up.

This is taken from the kinde acceptance of *Davids* purpose to build God an house, because *Reason.* he saw it was done in the honesty of his heart, therefore he promiseth to give his people a place wherein they should abide for ever as in a house of rest.   Secondly,

Secondly, it is taken from the office God takes upon him, when he is our planter, hee becomes our husbandman; and *if he plant us, who shall plucke us up?* *Isay* 27.1,2. *Iob* 34.29. When he giveth quiet, who can make trouble? If God be the Gardiner, who shall plucke up what he sets downe? Every plantation that he hath not planted shall be plucked up, and what he hath planted shall surely be established.

Thirdly, from the nature of the blessing hee conferres upon us: When he promiseth to plant a people, their dayes shall be as the dayes of a Tree, *Isay* 65.22. As the Oake is said to be an hundred yeares in growing, and an hundred yeares in full strength, and an hundred yeares in decaying.

Quest.

But it may be demanded, how was this promise fulfilled by the people, seeing after this time they met with many persecutions, at home, and abroad, many sonnes of wickednesse afflicted them; *Ieroboam* was a sonne of wickednesse, and so was *Ahab*, and *Ahaz*, and divers others.

Answ.

Because after *Davids* time they had more setlednesse than before.

Secondly, to the godly these promises were fulfilled in Christ.

Thirdly, though this promise was made that others should not wrong them, yet it followes not but that they might wrong themselves by trespassing against God, and so expose themselves to affliction. Whilst they continued Gods plantation, they were a noble Vine, a right seede;

feede, but if *Israel* will deftroy themfelves, the
fault is in themfelves. And yet even in their captivity the good amongft them God gracioufly
provided for : The *Basket of good figges* God fent
into the land of *Caldea* for their good: *Ier* 24. 5.
But if you rebell againft God, the fame God that
p'anted yo i will alfo roote you out againe, for all
the evill which you fhall doe againft your felyes:
Ier. 11. 17. When the Ifraelites liked not the
foile , grew weary of the Ordinances , and for-
fooke the worfhip of God, and faid, *What part
have we in David?* after this they never got fo
good a King, nor any fettled reft in the good
land wherein God had planted them. As they
waxed weary of God, fo hee waxed wearie of
them, and caft them out of his fight.

To exhort all that are planted at home, or in
tend to plant abroad, to looke well to your plantation; as you defire that the fonnes of wickedneffe may not afflict you at home, nor enemies a-
broad, looke that you be right planted, and then
you need not to feare, you are fafe enough: God
hath fpoken it, I will plant them, and they fhall
not be moved, neither fhall the fonnes of wickedneffe afflict them any more.

What courfe would you have us take ? *Queft.*

Have fpeciall care that you ever have the Or *Anfw.*
dinances planted amongft you , or elfe never
looke for fecurity. As foone as Gods Ordinances ceafe, your fecurity ceafeth likewife ; but if
God plant his Ordinances among you, feare not,
he will maintaine them. *Ifay* 4. 5. 6. *Vpon all their*
glory

glory there shall be a defence; that is, upon all **Gods**
Ordinances: for so was the Arke called *the Glory
of Israel,* 1 *Sam.* 4. 22.

Secondly, have a care to be implanted into
the Ordinances, that the word may be ingrafted
into you, and you into it: If you take rooting in
the ordinances, grow up thereby, bring forth
much fruite, continue and abide therein, then
you are a vineyard of red wine, and the Lord
will keepe you, *Isay* 27. 2. 3. that no sonnes of
violence shall destroy you. Looke into all the
stories whether divine or humane, and you shall
never finde that God ever rooted out a people
that had the Ordinances planted amongst them,
and themselves planted into the Ordinances: never did God suffer such plants to be plucked up;
on all their glory shall be a defence.

Thirdly, be not unmindfull of our *Ierusalem*
at home, whether you leave us, or stay at home
with us. *Oh pray for the peace of Ierusalem, they shall
prosper that love her, Psal.* 122. 6. *They shall all be
confounded and turned backe that hate Sion,* Psal.
129. 5. As God continueth his presence with
us (blessed be his name) so be ye present in spirit
with us, though absent in body: Forget not the
wombe that bare you, and the brest that gave
you sucke. Even ducklings hatched under an
henne, though they take the water, yet will still
have recourse to the wing that hatched them:
how much more should chickens of the same fea-
ther, and yolke? In the amity and unity of brethren, the Lord hath not onely promised, but
                                          commanded

commanded a bleffing, even life for evermore: *Pfal.* 133. 1, 2.

Fourthly, goe forth, every man that goeth, with a publick fpirit, looking not on your owne things onely, but alfo on the things of others: *Phil.* 2. 4. This care of univerfall helpfulneffe was the profperity of the firft Plantation of the Primitive Church: *Acts* 4. 32.

Fifthly, have a tender care that you looke well to the plants that fpring from you, that is, to your children, that they doe not degenerate as the Ifraelites did; after which they were vexed with afflictions on every hand. How came this to paffe: *Ier.* 2. 21. *I planted them a noble Vine, holy, a right feede, how then art thou degenerate into a ftrange Vine before mee?* Your Anceftours were of a noble divine fpirit, but if they fuffer their children to degenerate, to take loofe courfes, then God will furely plucke you up. Otherwife if men have a care to propagate the Ordinances and Religion to their children after them, God will plant them, and not roote them up. For want of this, the feede of the repenting *Ninivites* was rooted out.

Sixthly, and laftly, offend not the poore Natives, but as you partake in their land, fo make them partakers of your precious faith: as you reape their temporalls, fo feede them with your fpiritualls: winne them to the love of Chrift, for whom Chrift died. They never yet refufed the Gofpell, and therefore more hope they will now receive it. Who knoweth whether God have

reared

reared this whole Plantation for such an end ?

Secondly, for confolation to them that are planted by God in any place, that since rooting and eftablifhing from God, this is a caufe of much encouragement unto you, that what hee hath planted he will maintaine, every plantation his right hand hath not planted fhalbe rooted up, but his owne plantation fhall profper, & flourifh. When he promifeth peace and fafety, what enemie fhall be able to make the promife of God of none effect ? Neglect not walls, and bulwarkes, and fortifications for your owne defence; but ever let the name of the Lord be your ftrong Tower; and the word of his Promife tho Rocke of your refuge. His word that made heaven an earth will not faile, till heaven and earth be no more *Amen*

FINIS.

A DISCOURSE ABOUT CIVIL GOVERNMENT IN A NEW PLANTATION

John Cotton, *A Discourse about Civil Government in a New Plantation Whose Design is Religion* (Cambridge, 1663), pp. 3–24.

John Cotton's *Discourse About Civil Government* discusses the rights of the church to appoint and remove civil magistrates. Cotton argues that by having the elder burgesses – who were also leading members of the church – choose the civil magistrates, individuals would be able to pursue and enjoy their prosperity under the stability and order created by the 'Ordinances of God'. The authority of the elected magistrates was extensive, and while decisions or orders may be presented to all the members of the church, it was not necessary that this be the case. Further, while members of the church may retain the right to question their elders' decision-making, there was no provision for church members to seek the removal of all elected magistrates. By carefully placing most of the decision-making with elected magistrates chosen from leading families, Massachusetts maintained a highly ordered and hierarchical society.

However, Cotton's views on order and governance were not held universally in Massachusetts. Dissent against Cotton's strictly ordered and stratified society can be found in the writings of Roger Williams and Thomas Hooker, reproduced later in this volume. On finding Cotton's teachings inflexible, both men left Massachusetts to establish Rhode Island and Connecticut, whose governance was based on a more liberal interpretation of Puritanism.

A
DISCOURSE
ABOUT
CIVIL GOVERNMENT
IN A
NEW PLANTATION

Whofe *DESIGN* is

RELIGION.

Written many Years fince,

By that Reverend and Worthy Minifter of the GOSPEL,

JOHN COTTON B.D.

And now Publifhed by fome UNDERTAKERS of
a New Plantation, for General Direction
and Information.

CAMBRIDGE:

Printed by *Samuel Green* and *Marmaduke Johnfon.*

MDCLXIII.

A DISCOURSE
ABOUT
CIVIL GOVERNMENT IN A NEW
PLANTATION·

Where all, or the most considerable part of free Planters profess their de-
sire and purpose of enjoying, & securing to themselves and their Po-
sterity, the pure and peaceable enjoyment of the Ordinances of
Christ in Church-fellowship with his People, and have liberty to
cast themselves into that Mould or Form of a Common-wealth,
which shall appear to be best for them. Tending to prove the Ex-
pediency and Necessity in that case of intrusting free Burgesses.
wth are members of Churches gathered amongst them according to
Christ, with the power of Chusing from among themselves Ma-
gistrates, and men to whom the Managing of all Publick Civil
Affairs of Importance is to be committed. And to vindicate the
same from an Imputation of an Under-Power upon the Churches
of Chrst, which hath been cast upon it through a Mistake of the
true state of the Question.

Reverend Sir,

THe Sparrow being now gone, and one dayes respite from publick Labours on the Lords-day failing to me in course, I have sought out your Writing, and have reviewed it, and finde (as I formerly expressed to your self) that the Question is mis stated by you; and that the Arguments which you produce to prove that wch is not denied, are (in reference to this Question) spent in vain, as arrows are when they fall wide of the Marks they should hit, though they strike in a White which the Archer is not called to shoot at.

A 2   Th-

The terms wherein you ſtate the Queſtion, are theſe:

Whether the Right and Power of Chuſing Civil Magiſtrates belongs unto the Church of Chriſt?

To omit all critical Inquiries, in your thus ſtating the Queſtion, I utterly diſlike two things.

1. That you ſpeak of *Civil Magiſtrates indefinitely, and without limitation*; under which notion, all Magiſtrates in the world are included, *Turks*, and *Indians*, and *Idolaters*, as well as *Chriſtians*. Now no man, I think, holdeth or imagineth, that a Church of Chriſt hath power and right to Chuſe all Civil Magiſtrates throughout the World: For,

1. In ſome Countreys there is no Church of Chriſt, all the inhabitants being Heathen men and Idolaters; and amongſt thoſe who are called *Chriſtians*, the number of the Churches of Chriſt will be found to be ſo ſmall, and the Members of them ſo few and mean, that it is impoſſible that the Right and Power of Chooſing Civil Magiſtrates in all places, ſhould belong to the Churches of Chriſt

2. Nor have the Churches countenance of State in all Countreys, but are under Reſtraint and Perſecution in ſome; as the *Jews* in *Ægypt* under *Pharaoh*, and in the Captivity in *Babylon*, and the *Chriſtian Churches* 300 years after Chriſt perſecuted by *Roman Emperours*: and in theſe dayes thoſe Reformed Churches *ſub cruce* in *Antwerp*, and other Popiſh Countreys.

3. In ſome Countreys the Churches are indeed under the Protection of Magiſtrates, as Forreigners, permitted quietly to ſit down under their Wings: but neither are the Members capable of Magiſtracy there, nor have they power of Voting in the Choice of Magiſtrates: Such was that Church of Strangers gathered in *London* by *Johannes Alaſ̃*, with allowance of State under the Broad Seal of *England* in *Edw. 6.* Such are the *Dutch* and *French* Churches in *England*, and other Churches in the *Netherlands* at this day.

4. In ſome Countreys ſundry Nations are ſo mingled, that they have ſeverally an equal Right unto ſeveral parts of the Countrey, and therefore though they live in the ſame general Countrey, yet they are governed by different Laws, and have ſeveral Magiſtrates

Choſen

Chosen by themselves severally, neither of them being capable of Magistracy in the others parts, nor having Right and Power of Chusing Civil Magistrates there. Thus were the *Israelites* joyned with the *Canaanites*, that were left in *Canaan* unsubdued: and thus are the *English* planted in these parts of *America*, where sundry Nations of *Indians* dwell near them, and are Proprietaries of the places which they inhabit. Now he that should affirm, that the Churches of Christ, as such, have Right and Power of Chusing Civil Magistrates in such places, seemeth to me more to need Physick then Arguments, to recover him from his Errour.

2. The second thing that I dislike in your stating the Question, is, in that you make *the Churches of Christ to be the subject of this Right and Power of chusing Civil Magistrates.* For 1. The Church so considered is a Spiritual Political Body, consisting of divers Members Male and Female, Bond and Free; sundry of which are not capable of Magistracy, nor of Voting in the Choice of Magistrates, inasmuch as none have that Right and Power but free Burgesses, among whom Women and Servants are not reckoned, though they may be, and are Church-members. 2. The Members of the Churches of Christ are considerable under a twofold respect answerable to the twofold man, which is in all the Members of the Church whilst they are in this world, *the inward & the outward man.* 2 Cor. 4. 16. Whereinto the onely wise God hath fitted and appointed two sorts of Administrations, *Ecclesiastical* and *Civil.* Hence they are capable of a twofold Relation, and of Action and Power sutable to them both; *viz. Civil* and *Spiritual,* and accordingly must be exercised about both in their seasons, without confounding those two different states, or destroying either of them, whilest what they transact in civil Affairs, is done by virtue of their civil Relation, their Church-state onely fitting them to do it according to God.

Now that the state of the Question may appear, I think it seasonable and necessary to premise a few Distinctions, to prevent all mistakes, if it may be.

First then, let us distinguish between the two Administrations or *Distinct.* 1. Polities, *Ecclesiastical* and *Civil,* which men commonly call *the Church,* and *Common-wealth.* I incline rather to them who speaking of a *Christian Communion,* make the Communion to be the

G. nus,

Genus, and the State Ecclesiastical and Civil to be the *Species* of it. For in a Christian Communion there are two elected different Administrations or Polities or States, Ecclesiastical & Civil: Ecclesiastical Administrations, are a *Divine Order appointed to Believers for holy communion of holy things*: Civil Administrations, are *An Humane Order appointed by God to men for Civil Fellowship of humane things*. Thus *Junius* defineth them; and maketh 1. Order *the Genus of them both*. 2. God *the Efficient and Author of them both*. 3. Gods Glory *the last End of them both*. 4. Man *the common Subject of both* And so they agree very well in the *General Nature, Efficient , End and Subject* ; yet with difference in all. For,

1. Though both agree in this, that there is Order in their Administrations, yet with this difference, that the Guides in the Church have not a Despotical, but Oeconomical Power only, (a) being *not Lords over Christs heritage, but stewards and ministers of Christ and of the Church*; the Dominion and Law-giving Power being reserved to *Christ* alone, as *he only Head of the Church*. But in the other State he hath given Lordly Power, Authority and Dominion unto men ().

2. Though both agree in this, that *Man is the common Subject of them both*, yet with this difference, Man by Nature being a Reasonable and Sociable Creature, capable of Civil Order, is or may be the Subject of Civil Power and State: But Man by Grace called out of the world to fellowship with Jesus Christ, and with his People, is the only Subject of Church-power ; yet so, as the Outward man of Church members is subject to the Civil Power in common with other men, whilest their Inward man is the Subject of Spiritual Order and Administrations.

3. Though they both agree in this, that *God is the Efficient and Author of them both, and that by Christ*, yet not *eidem ratione*. For, God as the Creator and Governour of the world is the Author of Civil Order and Administrations: But God as in Covenant with his People in Christ, is the Author of Church-Administrations. So likewise Christ, as the Essential Word and Wisdome of God creating and governing the World is the Efficient and Fountain of Civil Order & Administrations (): But as Mediator of the New Covenant, & Head of the Church (), he establisheth Ecclesiastical Order.

4. Though

(a) John 23.
Matth 34.11.
1 Cor. 3. 5, 21
1 Cor. 1.1 24
& 4 5. & 5.20.
1 Pet 5.1.
Matth 28 18.
(b) Luke 22.25
John 13 10.
Pet. 2.13.

() Joh. 1.1.3.10
Col 1.17.
Heb 1.2,3.
Prov 8 15
() Eph. 1.22 &
23 & 4.4.11.

4. Though they both agree in this, that they have *the same last End*, viz. *The Glory of God*, yet they differ in their next Ends; for the next End of Civil Order and Administrations, is *The Preservation of Humane Societies in outward Honour, Justice and Peace*. But the next Ends of Church Order and Administrations, are *The Conversion, Edification, and Salvation of Souls, Pardon of Sin, Power against Sin, Peace with God, &c.*

5 Hence ariseth another Difference about the *Objects* of these different States: for though both agree in this, that they have the common *Welfare* for their aime and scope, yet the things about which the Civil Power is primarily conversant, are *Botica, τὰ Βιότικα*, 1 *Cor.* 6. 4. or *τὰ πρὸς τὸν βίον, the things of this life*, as Goods, Lands, Honour, the Liberties and Peace of the outward man. The things whereabout the Church Power is exercised, are *τὰ πρὸς τὸν θεὸν*, Heb 5. 1. *The things of God, as the Souls and Consciences of men, the Doctrine and Worship of God, the Communion of the Saints*. Hence also

3. They have different Laws: 2 Different Officers. 3. Different Power, whereby to reduce men to Order, according to their different Objects and Ends. Now that a just harmony may be kept between these two different Orders and Administrations, two Extremes must be avoided: 1. That they be not confounded, either by giving the Spiritual Power, which is proper to the Church, into the hand of the Civil Magistrate, as *Erastus* would have done in the matter of Excommunication. If any Magistrate should presume to thrust himself by his Authority or otherwise, into a Work which properly belongs to a Church-Officer, let him remember what befell *Saul* and *Uzzah* for so doing: or 2. By giving Civil Power to Church-Officers, who are called to attend onely to Spiritual matters and *the things of God*, and therefore may not be distracted from them by Secular intanglements. I say, Church-Officers, not Church-members; for they (not being limited as the Officers are by God) are capable of two different imployments, suting with two different *Use* in them, in different respects, as hath been said: and as they may lawfully be imployed about things of this life, so they are of all men fittest, being sanctified and dedicated to God to carry on all worldly and civil business to Gods ends, as we shall declare

in

in due time.   But concerning Church-Officers I am able with Gods help to prove, that the devolving of Civil Power upon Pasto s of Churches, (upon how specious pretences soever it began) gave that Rise to the *Man of Sin*, which at last set his feet on the necks of the Princes of the Earth, yea, of the Emperours of the World. It was your mistake, when you too confidently affirmed, That *the limiting of the Right and Power of choosing Civil Officers unto free Burgesses that are Members of Churches, brought that Tyranny into the Romish Church, which all the Churches of Christ complain of.*   It would well have become you to have better digested your own thoughts, before such words had passed through your lips; for you will never be able to produce any good Author that will confirm what you say.   The truth is quite contrary; for that I may instance in *Rome* it self: Had Churches been rightly managed, when the most considerable part in that City embraced the Christian Faith, in the ceasing of the *Ten Persecutions*, that onely such as had been fit for the State, had been admitted into Church-fellowship, that they alone had had power, out of themselves to have chosen Magistrates, such Magistrates would not have been chosen, as would have given their Power to the Pope; nor would those Churches have suffered their Pastors to become Worldly Princes and Rulers, as the Pope and his Cardinals are; nor would they have given up the Power of the Church from the Church into the Officers hands, but would have called upon them to *fulfill their Ministry which they had received of the Lord*; and if need were, would by the power of Christ have compelled them so to do: And then where had the Popes Supremacy been, which is made up of the Spoils of the Ecclesiastical and Civil State? but had by the course which now we plead for, been prevented.

2.   The second Extreme to be avoided, is, That these two different Orders and States, *Ecclesiastical* and *Civil*, be not set in opposition as contraries, that one should destroy the other, but as co-ordinate States, in the same place reaching forth help mutually each to other, for the welfare of both, according to God: So that both Officers and Members of Churches be subject, in respect of the outward man, to the Civil Power of those who bear Rule in the Civil State according to God, and teach others so to do: And that
the

the Civil Magiftrates and Officers, in regard of the inward man, fubject themfelves Spiritually to the power of Chrift in Church-Ordinances, and by their Givil Power preferve the fame in outward Peace and Purity; and this will beft be attained, when the Paftor may fay to the Magiftrate, as *Gregory Nazianzin* wrote to the Magiftrate of *Nazianzum, Scio te ovem meis gregis effe facri gregis facram ovem* I know thou art a fheep of my Flock, a holy fheep of a holy Flock. Again, *Cum Chrifto imperas, cum Chrifto etiam adminiftras, ab eo eft tibi gladius, hoc d narium arte puru n eis qui dedit confervetur*; that is, Thou ruleft with Chrift, and adminiftreft to Chrift; thou haft the Sword from him: let this gift which thou haft received from him, be kept pure for him. And when the Civil Magiftrate in his Church-ftate, anfwereth *Ambrofe* his defcription of a good Emperour: *Ipfe Imperator bonus intra Ecclefiam, non fupra Ecclefiam eft* A good Magiftrate is within the Church, not above it. Laftly, when according to *Junius* his defcription of the Power of the Chriftian Magiftrate in Church-matters, he accounts it his duty to embrace in Fellowfhip with the whole Church, *ut verum Chrifti & Ecclefie memi rum*, the Laws given by God in the Church, and the means fanctified by him to nourifh the inward man, and to protect and defend the fame: [*Tanquam Magiftratus à Deo Ordinatus*] for, faith he, *As he is a Chriftian*, he is *fancta ovis de fancto Chrifti grege*, (i. e. A holy fheep of Chrift's holy flock. But as a Magiftrate he is *Cuftos Ordinis vindexq; publici*,] that is, A preferver of publick order. Such were (befides the good Kings of *Judah*) *Conftantine, Theodofius*, &c. in fome meafure, though very defective. So much fhall ferve to have been fpoken concerning the firft Diftinction.

The fecond *Diftinction* to be premifed for clearing the true ftate of the Queftion, is, [*Inter Remp. conftitutam & conftituendam*] Between a Common-wealth already fetled, and a Common-wealth yet to be fetled, and wherein men are free to chufe what Form they fhall judge beft. For I conceive, when *Paul* exhorted the *Romans* to *be fubject to the higher Powers*, who at that time were Heathen men, and Perfecutors, he confidered that Civil State as fetled, and futed his Advice accordingly. But if he had been to Direct them about laying the Foundation of a Chriftian Common-wealth, he would

Diftinct. 2.

would not have advised them to chufe fuch Governours as were out of the Church; but would have ferioufly forewarned them of the danger whereunto the Church would have been expofed thereby, and that unavoidably   And that this may not be thought a flight and uncertain conjecture, let us confider what advice he gave in like cafes · Ye know, that writing to perfons already Married he exhorteth *the beleeving wife to live wth to the unbeleeving husband*; yet the fame Apoftle directeth the fame Church in cafe they were free to make their own choice, to avoid fuch matches : *Be not unequally yoked* (faith he) *with Infidels , for what fellowfhip hath righteoufnefs with unrighteoufnes : and what part hath the believer with the infidel ?*   In like manner, when *Peter* exhorted Chriftian *Servants to be fubject to their Maſters with all fear, not onely to the good and gentle, but alfo to the froward,* he did accommodate his inftruction to their prefent condition. But had he been to direct them in another ftate being free, to chufe what might be beft for themfelves, he would have expreffed himfelf otherwife, as may appear by this. The fame Spirit that infpired *Peter* thus to advife in this cafe, guided *Paul* further in a different cafe : *Art thou called being a fervant,* (faith he) *care not for it ; but if thou maiſt be free, ufe it rather.*   And that if he had written to a company of Bel'evers in a New Plantation, where the Foundations of the Church and Civil State, and the communion of both, was to be laid for many Generations to come, he would have advifed them to take the fame courfe which we plead for, may appear by his reproving the Church in *Co inth,* for carrying *their differences before Heathen Magiftrates to be judged by them,* though he prefs them to be *fubject to their power*   Had the unbelieving Magiftrates cited them to appear before their Judgement-feats, he taught them both by Precept and by his Example to fubmit.   But when they were at liberty to compofe civil Differences among themfelves, and yet they would voluntarily, and of their own accord, chufe to bring their cafes before thofe that were without the Church, this he blameth in them; and that fo farre as he demandeth why *they do not rather fuff r* then take fuch a courfe ? plainly intimating, that men that profefs the fear of God if they be free to make choice of their Civil Judges, (as in this New Plantation we are) they fhould rather chufe fuch as are Members of the Church for that purpofe,

then

1 Cor 7 13.

2 Cor 6 14,15

1 Pet.2.18.

1 Cor 7.21.

1 Cor. 5.1,

then others that are not in that estate. The same Rule holdeth by proportion in all things of like nature: for *Parium par est ratio.*

The third *Distinct* to be premised for clearing the truth in this *Distinct.* 3. Point, is *between free Burgesses and free Inhabitants in a Civil State.* Concerning whom, there must be had a different consideration. This difference of People living under the same Civil jurisdiction, is held and observed in all Countreys, as well Heathen as others, as may at large be proved, if it were needful, out of the Histories of all Nations and Times; and the Experience of our Times, as well in our own Native Countrey, as in other places, confirmeth it. In all which, many are Inhabitants that are not Citizens, that are never likely to be numbred among α"ρχοντες, or Rulers: Answerably it is in the case now in question. So that when we urge, that Magistrates be chosen out of free Burgesses, and by them, and that those free Burgesses be chosen out of such as are Members of these Churches, we do not thereby go about to exclude those that are not in Church-Order, from any Civil Right or Liberty that is due unto them as Inhabitants and Planters, as if none should have Lots in due proportion with other men, nor the benefit of Justice under the Government where they live, but onely Church-members; (for this were indeed to have the Common-wealth swallowed up of the Church) but seeing there ever will be difference between the World and the Church in the same place, and that both men of the world are allowed of God the use and enjoyment of the help of Civil Government, for their quiet and comfortable subsistence in the world: and Church-members (though called out of the world into fellowship with Christ, yet) living in the world, having many worldly necessities and businesses in common with men of the world that live among them, stand in need of the civil Power to right them against civil injuries, and to protect them in their right, and outward orderly use of their Spirituals, against those that are apt to be injurious to them in the one, or in the other respect; which being without, are not under the Churches Power; and yet living within the Verge of the same Civil Jurisdiction, are under the Civil Power of the Magistrates. Hence it is, that we plead for this Order to be set in Civil Affairs, that such a course may be taken as may best secure to our selves and our posterities the faithful managing of

Civil

* By *Church Members* in all this Diſcourſe, is meant ſuch as are in full Communion.

Civil Government for the *common welfare* ſo well in the Church as without; which will then moſt certainly be effected, when the publick Truſt and Power of theſe matters is committed to ſuch men as are moſt approved according to God; and theſe are Church-members *, as ſhall afterward, God aſſiſting, be proved.

Diſtinct. 4.

The fourth *Diſtinction* to be premiſed for clearing the truth, and to prevent miſtakes in this Queſtion, ſhall be *between the Actions of Church-members*. For ſome actions are done *by them all, joyntly as a Spiritual Body*, in reference to Spiritual ends; and ſome actions are done onely *by ſome of the Body*, in reference to Civil ends. Actions of the firſt ſort, are ſaid to be done *by the Church of Chriſt, as a Church of Chriſt*; ſuch are *Admiſſion of members, and Excommunication of them according to Chriſt's order*, and other actions of that kinde; but theſe fall not under our Queſtion, which is wholly about *the tranſaction of Civil Affairs*: ſo that, your whole Diſpute wanteth a good ground, and your labour about it might well have been ſpared. Actions of the ſecond ſort, are of a larger extent, and reach to buſineſſes of a *Civil Nature*, ſuch as that *Civil Judgement* whereof *Paul* ſpeaketh, 1 *Cor.* 6. ἐν τοῖς ἐξ...ξοῖς, in *matters that concern this life, as the Lives, Goods*, (and which is dearer to them then both) *the Reputations of men, and their outward Liberty and Peace*. Concerning which, Members fitly choſen out of the Church, and made free Burgeſſes, are fitter to judge and determine according to God, then other men, and that for weighty Reaſons; ſome whereof are rendred by *Paul* in that Chapter, whereunto others may be added, when we ſhall argue that Point, the Lord helping us.

Diſtinct. 5.

The fifth *Diſtinction* to be premiſed for the clearing of the truth in this Point, is *between Places, where all, or the moſt conſiderable part of firſt and free Planters, profeſs their deſire and purpoſe of entring into Church-fellowſhip according to Chriſt, and of enjoying in that State all the Ordinances in purity and peace, and of ſecuring the ſame unto their poſterity, ſo farre as men are able;* and *thoſe Places where all or the moſt conſiderable part of the firſt and free Planters are otherwiſe minded, and profeſs the contrary.* Our Queſtion is of the firſt ſort, not of the ſecond. As for thoſe of the ſecond ſort, if the *major*, or more conſiderable part among them, will be like Heathen men, without ſuch Church-fellowſhip, as is according to Chriſt in all things, a Heathen man,

man or meer civil worldly Politition, will be good enough to be their Magiftrate ; or if they defire to fet up *idolatry and Superftition*, an Idolatrous and fuperftitious Governor in the Civil State will beft fute their ends ; and fo they may be faid to their juft reproof and fhame, *Like Prieft, like People* ; and *Like King, like People*. Thus fometimes the Lord hath fpoken againft a licentius people concerning their prophets, *He that will prophecy of wine and ftrong drink, he fhall be the pro-* Micah 2.11 *phet to this people.* He that fometimes giveth fuch *Guides in the Church* to a people in his indignation, doth alfo fometimes give *Magiftrates & Rulers* to a people in the Civil State in his wrath, when men are forfaken of him, and given up more to affect outward fancy and vanity, then *Gods Order* as when the *people of Ifrael fought a King*, without refpect to the *right Tribe*, from whence by Gods order they ought to expect one, *He gave them a King in his anger, and took him away in* Hofea 13.11 *his wrath.* In fuch cafe, what fhall the people of God do that live in fuch a place ? furely if God give them liberty, and ability, they fhould attend to the voice of God, which hath faid in a like cafe to his people, *Arife and depart, this is not your reft* ; and follow *the fteps of Chrifts* Micah 2 10 *flock* to any place, where he caufeth his flock to feed, and lye down under Cantic.1.6,9. a comfortable fhadow *at noon* : As in *Jeroboam's* time, the *Levites left their fuburbs, and came to Judah and Jerufalem, and after them of all the Tribes of Ifrael, fuch as fet their hearts to feek the Lord God of Ifrael, and ftrengthned the Kingdome of Judah*, where Gods Ordinances both concerning Civil Government and Religious Worfhip were better obferved. But if Divine Providence doth neceffitate their ftay and abode in fuch places, they are to *pray for thofe in Authority*, 1 Tim.2.12 that they may become fuch, as *under whom they may live a quiet and peaceable life, in all godlinefs and honefty* ; and to be *fubject to their Power*, even in thofe things wherein they may not obey their Commands, nor feek their help, 1 Cor. 6. 1, 2 till God fhall give them liberty from that Yoke, either by removing them to thofe places where fitter Magiftrates bear Rule in Civil matters, or by giving them opportunity of Chufing more futable ones from among themfelves.

So much fhall ferve to have been fpoken to the *Diftinctions*, which having thus premifed, we now proceed to declare the true ftate of the Queftion : which is as followeth.

Q. Whether

The true state of the Question.

Q   *Whether a new Plantation, where all or the most considerable part of free Planters profess their purpose and desire of securing to themselves and to their posterity, the pure and peaceable enjoyment of Christ's Ordinances; Whether, I say, such Planters are bound in laying the Foundation of Church and Civil State, to take order, that all the free Burgesses be such as are in fellowship of the Church or Churches which are, or may be gathered according to Christ; and that those free Burgesses have the only power of chusing from among themselves Civil Magistrates, and men to be intrusted with transacting all publick Affairs of Importance, according to the rules and directions of Scripture?*

I hold the Affirmative part of this Question upon this ground, that this course will most conduce to the good of both States; and by consequence to the *common welfare of all,* whereunto all men are bound principally to attend in laying the *Foundation of a Common wealth;* lest Posterity rue the first Miscarriages, when it will be too late to redress them. They that are skilful in Architecture observe, *that the breaking or yielding of a stone in the groundwork of a Building but the breadth of the back of a knife, will make a cleft of more then half a foot in the Fabrick aloft.* So important (saith mine Author) *are fundamental Errours.* The Lord awaken us to look to it in time, and send us his Light and Truth to lead us into the safest wayes in these beginnings.

The Question being thus stated, I now proceed with Gods help to prove the Affirmative part: and thus I argue, to prove that *the Form of Government which is described in the true stating of the Question is the best, and by consequence, that men that are free to chuse (as in new Plantations they are) ought to establish it in a Christian Common-wealth.*

Argum. 1.
(a) Deut. 33.29.
1 Sa. 33.22.
Judg. 8.23.

Theocratie, *or to make the Lord God our Governour* (a), *is the best Form of Government in a Christian Common-wealth, and which men that are free to chuse (as in new Plantations they are) ought to establsh.* The Form of Government *described in the true stating of the Question is* Theocratie, *or that wherein we make the Lord God our Governour. Therefore that Form of Government which is described in the true stating of the Question, is the best Form of Government in a Christian Common-wealth, and which men that are free to chuse (as in new Plantations they are) ought to establish.* The Proposition is clear of it self. The Assumption I prove thus:

That Form of Government where 1. *The people that have the power of*
chusing

abusing their Governours are in Covenant with God (b) 2. Wherein the men chosen by them are godly men, and fitted with a spirit of Government (c): 3. In which the Laws they rule by are the Laws of God (d): 4. Wherein Laws are executed, Inheritances allotted, and civil differences are composed, according to Gods appointment (e): 5. In which men of God are consulted with in all hard cases, and in matters of Religion (f), is the Form which was received and established among the people of Israel whil'st the Lord God was their Governour, as the places of Scripture alledged shew; and is the very same with that which we plead for, as will appear to him that shall examine the true stating of the Question. The Conclusion follows neceſſarily.

That Form of Government which giveth unto Christ his due prehemi- Argum. 2. nence, is the best Form of Government in a Christian Common-wealth, and which men that are free to chuse (as in new Plantations they are) ought to establish. The Form of Government described in the true stating of the Question, is that which giveth unto Christ his due prehemmence. Therefore the Form of Government which is described in the true stating of the Question, is the best Form of Government in a Christian Commonwealth, and which men that are free to chuse (as in new Plantations they are) ought to establish.

The Propoſition is proved out of two places of Scripture, *Col.* 1. 15. to 19. with *Eph.*1.21,22. From which Texts it doth appear, that it is a preheminence due to Chriſt, that all things, and all Governments in the world, ſhould ſerve to Chriſts ends, for the welfare of the Church whereof he is the Head. For 1. In relation to God, he hath this by Right of Primogeniture, as he is *the firſt-born, and ſo Heir of all things, higher then the Kings of the earth.* 2. In relation to the World, it is ſaid, *All things were made by him, and for him, and do conſiſt in him,* and therefore it is a preheminence due to him, that they all ſerve him. 3. In relation to the Church, it is ſaid, *He hath made all things ſubject under his feet, and hath given him over all things to be Head of the Church, that in all things he might have the preheminence.* And indeed that he upholdeth the Creatures, and the Order that is in them, it is for his Churches ſake; when that is once compleat, the world ſhall ſoon be at an end. And if you reade the ſtories of the great Monarchies that have been, and judge of them by Scripture-light, you will finde they ſtood or fell, according as God purpoſed:

Marginal notes:
(b) Exod. 19.5.
Deut.1.13,14.
(c) Exod.18.21.
Deut.1 13.
(d) Numb.11.
24,25.
Iſa. 33. 22
(e) Num 35 29.
& 6 27 & 2.3.
1 Cor 6.1,2.
(f) Deut. 17 8.
10 11. & 19.16,
17
2 Cor.10.4. to 11

to make ufe of them about fome fervice to be done about his Church.
So that the onely confiderable part for which the world ftandeth at
this day, is the Church: and therefore it is a Preheminence due to
Chrift, that his Headfhip over the Church fhould be exalted and acknowledged, and ferved by all.   In which refpect alfo the Title of
The fir t-born is given to the Members of the Church, and they are
called *The firft-fruts of his Creatures*, to fhew both their preheminence above others, and that they are fitteft to ferve to Gods ends.

The Affumption (*That the Form of Government defcribed in the true
ftating of the Queftion, doth give unto Chrift his due preheminence*)
will eafily be granted by thofe that fhall confider what Civil Magiftrates and Rulers in the Common wealth thofe are, who are fitteft
to ferve to Chrift's ends for the good and welfare of his Church;
which will be evident from two places of Scripture : Firft, in *Pf.* 2.
10,11,12 you have a defcription of thofe that are fitted to order
Civil Affairs in their Magiftracy to Chrift's ends; they are fuch as
are not only wife and learned in matters of Religion but alfo do
reduce their knowledge into practife : they *Worfhip the Lord in fear*,
and not only fo, but *Kifs the Son*, which was a folemn & outward *Pro-*
feffion of love a), and of *Subj-ction* (b), and of *Religious Worfhip* (c),
and fo fitly ferveth to exprefs their joyning themfelves to the Church
of Chrift.   Secondly, in *Ifa.49.23.* it is promifed to the Church,
that *Kings and Queens fhall be their nurfing-fathers and nurfing-mothers*,
and therefore it is added, *They fhall worfhip with their faces to the earth,*
and lick up the duft of thy feet; which is a proverbial expreffion of
their voluntary humbling of themfelves to Chrift in his Ordinances,
(taken from the manner of the *Perfians*, in declaring their Subjection
to their Emperour (d), which the Apoftle calls *a voluntary fubmif-*
fion to the Gofpel (e), which is the fpirit of the Members of the Churches of Chrift.   And for this Reafon it is, that the Lord, when he
moulded a Communion among his own People, wherein all Civil
Adminiftrations fhould ferve to holy ends, he defcribed the men to
whom that Truft fhould be committed, by certain Properties, which
alfo qualified them for fellowfhip in Church-Ordinances, as *Men of*
ability and power over their own affections (f); fecondly, *fearing God,*
Truly Religious, Men of Courage, hating Covetoufnefs, men of Wifdom,
men of underftanding, and *men known or* approved of *among the people*
of

(a) 1 Pet.5.14.
(b) Gen 41.40.
I Sam 10.1.
(c) Hof 13 2.

(d) *Val. Max.*
lib 7 chap 3.
(e) 2 Cor 9.13.

(f) Exod 18.21
Deut 1 13.

of God; & chosen ly the Lord from among their Brethren, & not a stranger, which is no Brother: the most of which concurre to describe
Church-members in a Church rightly gathered and ordered, who
are also in respect of their un on with Christ and-fellowship together, called *brethren* frequently in the New Testament, wherein the
equity of that Rule is established to us.   *Object. Christ will* **Object.**
have his due Preheminence, though the Civil Rulers oppose him, and per-
secute the Churches, as in Rome: *Therefore it is not necessary that this*
course be taken in Civil affairs to establish Christs Preheminence.
Answ. The Question is of a Christian Commonwealth that should wil- **Answ.**
lingly subject themselves to Christ, not of a Heathen State that shall
perforce be subdued unto Christ. It is concerning what Gods people
being free should chuse, not what his enemies are compell'd unto.

That Form of Government wherein the best provision is made for the **Argum. 3.**
good both of the Church and of the Civil State, is the best- Form of Go-
vernment in a Christian Communion, and which men that are free to chuse
(as in new Plantations they are) ought to establish. The Form of Govern-
ment described in the true stating of the Question, is that wherein the best
provision is made for the good both of the Church and Civil State. There-
fore the Form of Government described in the true stating of the
Question, is the best Form of Government in a Christian Communion,
and which men that are free to chuse (as in new Plantations they are)
ought to establish.   The Proposition (if need be) may be confirmed from the end of all Civil Government & Administrations which
is *the publick and common Good*, whether Natural, as in *the preservation*
of Life and Safety; or Moral, as *Justice and Honesty in Humane Socie-*
ties; or Civil, as *Peace, Liberty of Commerce;* or Spiritual as *to pro-*
tect the Church in Spiritual, though outward, Order and Administra-
tions in peace & purity. And th s last is principally to be attended unto,
and therefore such as are intrusted with this care, are called *The Mi-*
nisters of God, to note the principal end whereunto they serve, *viz.*
The things wherein God is most directly and immediately honoured, which is in promoting man's Spiritual good, so farre as they
are enabled by their Civil Power.

The Assumption (*That the Form of Government in the Common-*
wealth which we plead for, is that wherein the best provision is made for
the good both of the Church and of the Civil State) may appear by the
blessing

bleffing of God which ufually is upon the Communion; where the
fcuring of the Spiritual good of men, in the peace and purity of
Gods Ordinances, is principally attended unto by all forts as may be
proved by the ftate of things in the Communion of *Ifrael*, whil'ft the
fervice of the Lord was with due care attended to *all the dayes of Io-*
fhua, and all the dayes of the Elders that over-lived Iefhua, which had
knowne all the workes of the Lord which he bid done, for ir. . Many
more places of Scripture might be alledged; but I will onely note
Pfal. 72. wherein all forts of good are affured to the Common-
wealth, wherein *the fear of God,* that is Matters of Religion are fo
regarded, as the prefervation thereof to after-ages is duely provided
for. which how can it be done, if the courfe defcribed in the true
ftating of the Queftion be neglected by thofe that are free to caft
the Common-wealth into what Mould they pleafe?

Iofh. 24. 31.

Junius Ecclef.
lib 3. chap. 5.

This *Junius,* a Learned and Godly man, and much exercifed in
State Affairs, as appears by the Story of his Life, faw clearly; and
therefore fpeaking of the Confent and Harmony of the Church and
Civil State. in the concurrence of their feveral Adminiftrations to the
welfare of a Chriftian Common-wealth, he expreffeth it by the
conjunction of the Soul and Body in a Man; and concludeth, that
Nothing will be of fo much avail to the welfare of civil Adminiftrations,
as will the beft Adminiftrations of the Church giving attendance to the
holy and juft Communion of Saints, (ut ad parentem officiorum omni-
um) *as to the Patent of all Duties.* and, that *Nothing will fo fecure*
and Strengthen Church-Adminiftrations, as that fecurity (quam præ-
bitura eft jufta pi. Magiftratus atque fidelis Πολιτεία) *which the*
juft Adminiftrations of a godly and faithful Magiftrate will afford.
Now *Pii & Fideles, Men that are godly and faithful,* are fuch as are
defcribed in our ftating of the Queftion. And having thus faid,
he breaks out into an affectionate Admiration of the Happinefs of a
Communion fo ordered: *Ecquid obfecro futurum eft, fi optima Eccle-*
fia, cum Republicâ optima coalefcat? O beatum populum, in quo uno ore,
& uno animo, utraq; adminiftratio, ad fanctam communionem cum ci-
vili Societate continendam, & augendam confpiraverit' Non minus il-
lam hæc adminiftratio, fed altera alteram firmem, confirmat, labantem,
ftatuminat, collapfam erigit Which I thus Englifh: *What I pray may be*
expected in future times, if the beft Church, and the beft Common-wealth

g *oiv*

grew up together ? Oh bleſſed people, among whom each Adminiſtration ſhall conſpire with one mouth, and one minde, to conjoyn and advance the Communion of Saints with the Civil Society ! Out of theſe Adminiſtrations will not detract from the other, but each will confirm the other if it ſtand, and ſtay it if it be falling, and raiſe it up if it be faln down. And a little after he thus concludeth, *Magiſtratum cui credita eſt civilis adminiſtratio non in Eccleſia ſolum, ſed etiam ex Eccleſia eſſe affirmamus ;* We affirm, that the Magiſtrate to whom the Civil Adminiſtration is committed, is or ought to be not onely in the Church, but alſo taken out of the Church. Thus *Junius* thought, and taught, and publiſhed to the world. And indeed what is more equal, then that he who by Office is to be a *Miniſter of God,* ſhould be choſen by and out of thoſe who are by open Profeſſion in the Church-eſtate, the Servants of the Lord and have more helps to know his Minde, and deep engagements to ſeek his Ends, and obſerve his Will, then other men ? But if any be otherwiſe minded, let them ſhew ſome other courſe, wherein the publick good may be promoted according to God, with aſſurance of a bleſſing by virtue of the Promiſes.

The fourth Argument ſhall be taken out of 1 *Cor* 6. ver. 1, to 8. *Argum.* 4. Whence I thus argue: *That Form of Government wherein the power of Civil Adminiſtrations is denied unto unbelievers, and committed to the Saints, is the uſt Form of Government in a Chriſtian Common-wealth, and which men that are free to chuſe (as in new Plantations they are) ought to eſtabliſh* The Form of Government deſcribed in the true ſtating of the Queſtion, is that wherein the power of Civil Adminiſtrations is denied to unbelievers, and committed to the Saints. Therefore the Form of Government deſcribed in the true ſtating of the Queſtion, is the beſt Form of Government in a Chriſtian Common, and which men that are free to chuſe (as in new Plantations they are) ught to eſtabliſh. The Propoſition is evident from the Scripture alledged. For, the thing which *Paul* blameth in them, is not, that living under unbelieving Magiſtrates, they ſubmitted to their Civil Judicature when they were cited to appear before their Judgement-ſeats but this reproveth, that when they were free to chuſe other Judge, (as in voluntary references they were) they would out of choice be judged under the unjuſt and not under Saints. His Arguments againſt this are many and weighty. 1. From the danger of thus exalting unbelievers, and

and abafing the Sa'nts, in thefe words, *Dare any of you having a mat-ter againft another, be judged under the unjuft, and not under the Saints?* 2. From the quality of unbelieving Judges whom he calleth *unjuft,* becaufe they are deftitute of the righteoufnefs that is by Faith, and which is the Fountain of all true Moral Juftice, and becaufe they were ill-affected to Chriftians, and to the Church of Chrift, and apt to vex them injurioufly, if they had any bufinefs before them; and becaufe though fome men out of Chrift may be found civilly honeft, and morally juft, as were alfo fome Heathen-men, yet you can have no affurance of their juftice, feeing this is the genius and nature of all men out of Chrift to be unrighteous. 3. From the property of Church-members, whom he calls *Saints,* that is, men confecrated to God and to his ends in all things; for fo they are in their Church-eftate, and by virtue of their Covenant are bound fo to be: when as others are (or at leaft are not manifefted to be otherwife according to Gods order) worldly-minded, or felf-feekers, *minding their own things, and not the things of Jefus Chrift.* The 4 h Argument is *a majo s,* for he faith. *The Saints fhall judge the world,* and blames their igno-rance that queftion it: *Know ye not that the Saints fhall judge the world* and thence inferreth, that they fhould much more have judge-ment ἐν τοῖς ξιωϊικοῖς *in matters that concern this life,* fuch are Humane Contracts, mens Goods, and Lives, and outward Liberties. The 5 t Argument is from the Wifdom wherewith the Church of God is furnifhed for all Civil bufineffes: *Is there not a wife man among you?* as if he fhould fay, It cannot be that more wifdome fhould be for tranfacting of bufineffes according to God, in men that are out of the Church, then in thofe that are in the Church? howfoever much worldly wifdome is fometimes given to men of the world, yet not fufficient to reach Gods ends that is the Priviledge of Saints, they onely are *wife as Serpents*, the other men may be as *fubtile as Foxes.* And feeing it is by Chrift that *Kings reign, and Princes decree juftice,* how can it be fuppofed that Chrift, who is the Head of the Church, will furnifh others with a Spirit of Wifdome and Govern-ment in Civil Matters, and deny it to the Church, Members of his own Body, whom he alone fanctifieth to his end?

   The Affumption (*That the Form of Government in the Common-wealth which we plead for, is that wherein the power of civil Admin-firations*

Prov. 8. 15.

stration is denied to unbelievers, and committed to the Saints) is **evident**
of it self. For whom doth the Apostle call *Saints* there, but Members of the Church? when he had said before, they *were justified in Christ Jesus, Saints by calling.* Hence it is that he speaks of men 1 Cor. 1 2. esteemed in the Church, *v. 4.* and of men that can judge between *Brethren, v. 5.* which is a Title given to Church-members ordinarily in the New Testament

If it be objected, *He speaketh there of Church-members, in oppo-* **Object.** *sition to Infidels which persecuted the truth, not in opposition to men that may fear God, and be accounted Believers, though they be not in Church-fellowship.*

I Answer, The fear of God, and Faith of those men, may be justly **Answ.** doubted, whose setled abode is in a place where Churches are gather'd and order'd according to Christ and yet are not after a convenient time joyned to them: For if in those times and places where the Name of Christ was a Reproach, men were no sooner converted, then they were *added to the Church*, and their being added to the Church, was made an evidence of their conversion; what may we think of those men who living in times and places where the Ordinances of the Gospel may be enjoyed in purity, with peace in Church-fellowship, do yet live without the Church? 2. Though there be sundry degrees of distance from the Church, to be found among men that are out of Church fellowship, as the Heathen are further off then moral Christians, yet the same Spirit of unrighteousness and enmity against Christ, worketh and bears rule in an unconverted Christian, as doth in an unbaptized Heathen: He is unsanctified as the other is, and so unsutable to Gods ends in civil Administrations; and therefore it will not be safe, nor according to the Rule, that where a Church is gathered according to Christ, the Members should be neglected, and such men intrusted with managing the Publick Affairs, as are not in fellowship with them.

The fifth Argument may be taken from the Nature and Power **Argum. 5.** of Church-Order, which when it is managed according to Christ's appointment, affordeth best security to a Christian State, for the faithful discharge of any Trust that shall be committed to those that are under it. Whence I thus argue: *That Form of Government wherein the power of chusing from among themselves, men to be intrusted with managing*

managing all publick Affairs of Importance, is committed to them who are furnished with the best helps for securing to a Christian State the faithfull discharge of such a Trust, is the best Form of Government in a Christian Common-wealth, and which men that are free to chuse (as in new Plantations they are) ought to establish. The Form of Government described in the true stating of the Question is such. *Therefore the Form of Government described in the true stating of the Question, is the best Form of Government in a Christian Common-wealth, and which men that are free to chuse (as in new Plantations they are) ought to establish.* The Proposition is undeniable.

The Assumption (*That the Form of Government which we plead for, is that wherein the power of chusing men to be intrusted with managing of all publick Affairs of Importance, is committed to them who are furnished with the best helps for securing to a Christian State the faithful discharge of such a Trust*) may be confirmed, by shewing what these Helps are; viz. 1. That the Members of the Church are *Saints by calling*, i.e. men *separated from the world, and the pollutions thereof, out of which they are called, and dedicated to God,* as the *first-born*, and the *first-fruits* were; and they are qualified, by *his spirit of wisdome and understanding, the spirit of counsel and strength, the spirit of knowledge and the fear of the Lord*, in some measure through Fellowship with Christ, to serve God and men *in holiness and righteousness all the dayes of their lives.* 2. That these *Saints by calling* being in Church-Order according to Christ's appointment, are in Covenant with God, and one with another; whereby they are most strictly bound to do faithfully, whatsoever they do to God or men. 3. That by virtue of this Order, they are bound to mutual helpfulness, in Watching over one another, Instructing, Admonishing, and Exhorting one another to prevent sin, or to recover such as are faln, or to encourage one another, and strengthen them in well-doing.

Thus are they bound in a threefold Cable unto all Faithfulness *in all things to God and Man.* The like assurance cannot be had in any other way, if this course be neglected.

Argum. 6.   The sixth Argument, with which I will conclude, that I may not weary you with Reading, as I have wearied my self with Writing) shall be taken from *The Danger of devolving this Power upon those that are not in Church-Order.* From whence the Apostle would have

*1 Cor 1.2.
John 15 19.
Heb 12.23.
James 1. 18.
Isai 11.1,2.
Luke 1.75.
Psal.5 4.5.
Deut.26.17,18.*

have men to be affrighted : *Dare any of you having businesse* ¹Cor.6.1. *against another, be judged under the unjust, and not under the Saints?* The Danger therefore that is to be feared in reference to the *Church,* is, The disturbance of the Churches Peace, when Power shall be put into their hands, who being of worldly spirits, hate the Saints and their Communion ; and being of the *seed of the Serpent, are at* John 15.18. *enmity against the seed of the Woman* ; and being Satans instruments, Gen 3.15. who is the *God of this World,* are resisting and fighting against Christ Revel.12.7. Zech.3.1. his Kingdome and Government in the Church. **2.** Adde hereunto, The Danger of corrupting Church Order, either by compelling them to receive into fellowship unsutable ones, or by imposing upon them Ordinances of men, and worldly Rudiments ; or by establish-Col.2.22,23. ing Idolatrous Worship ; or by strengthning Hereticks in subverting the common Faith, as those *Arrian Emperours,* and Idolatrous Kings and States have done, of which we reade so many instances.

Secondly, the Danger to be feared in reference to the Civil State, is, **1.** The raising of Factions to the disturbance of Publick Peace, whil'st some Magistrates out of the Church, watch their seasons to strengthen themselves against those that are in the Church, till they have wrought them out of Office and Power in the Civil State : and in the mean time, what other can be expected from such unequal mixture in State, but that they should be as *the toes of the feet* of *Ne-* Dan.2.42,43. *buchadnezzar's image,* which *were part of iron, and part of clay,* they should be partly broken, and partly strong, and not comfortably joyn one with another, as iron cannot be mixed with clay. The second Danger to the Civil State, will be, A perverting of *Justice* by Magistrates of worldly spirits, through Bribery, respect of persons, unacquaintance with the Law of God, and injuriousness to the servants of God. But I must break off, lest I grow too tedious. How easily might I adde the Consent of all Nations to this Truth in some proportion, who generally practise accordingly ? In our Native Countrey, none are intrusted with managing of Publick Affairs, but *Members of the Church of England,* (as they call them.) In *Holland,* when the *Arminian* Party had many Burgomasters on their side, *Grave Maurice* came into divers of their Cities with Troops of Souldiers, by Order from the *States Generall,* and put those *Arminian* Magistrates out of Office, and caused them to chuse onely such

such as were of the *Dutch Churches*. And in *Rotendam* (and I think it is so in other Towns) the *Vrentscap* (who are all of them of the *Dutch Church*, and free Burgers) do out of their own company chuse the Burgomaster, and other Magistrates and Officers. In all Popish Countreys and Plantations, they observe it strictly, to intruft none with the managing of Publick Civil Affairs, but such as are *Catholicos* (as they speak) and of the *Roman Church*. Yea, in *Turkey* it self, they are careful that none but a man devoted to *Mahomet* bear publick Office. Yea, these very *Indians* that Worship the Devil, will not be under the Government of any *Sagamores*, but such as joyn with them in Obfervance of their *Pawawes* and *Idolatries*: That it feems to be a Principle imprinted in the mindes and hearts of all men in the equity of it, *That such a Form of Government as best serveth to Establish their Religion, should by the consent of all be Established in the Civil State.*

Other things I might adde, but I hope enough hath been said for Defence and Confirmation of what I have affirmed touching this matter. If you remain unsatisfied, I shall defire that you will placidly, and lovingly, and impartially weigh the Grounds of my judgement, and communicate yours if any remain against it, in writing. For though much writing be wearisome unto me, yet I finde it the safer way for me   Now the God of Peace and Truth lead us into all wayes of Peace and Truth, to the Praise of his Grace through *the Lord Jesus Christ*, who is *the Way, the Truth, and the Life*. To whom be in all things the *Preheminence, and Glory, and Praise.* Amen.

F I N I S.

ERRATA.   Page 8 line 19. for the *state* read that eftate. *Ibid.* for that *read* and. p. 11 l. 27. *read* and having.

EXCERPTS FROM
THE BLOUDY TENET, OF PERSECUTION

Roger Williams, *The Bloudy Tenet, of Persecution, for cause of Conscience, discussed, in A Conference betweene Truth and Peace, who in all tender affection, present to the High Court of Parliament, (as the Result of their Discourse) these, (amongst other Passages) of highest consideration* (London, 1644), chapters 6, 9, 16 and 51, pp. 24–6, 29–30, 48–9 and 80–1.

Born in England and educated at Pembroke College, Cambridge, Roger Williams (c. 1603–83) immigrated to Massachusetts in 1630, and was called to serve in the Puritan Church in Boston. Upon arriving in Boston in 1631, Williams declined to serve in the church and engaged instead in severe criticism of the Massachusetts Puritans for enforcing religious precepts with the powers of civil government. Having become an opponent of the Puritan regime, the rulers of the church refused him a position as a teacher in the church at Salem. Williams was instead received in the Plymouth Colony (1631–3), where he assumed the role of pastor of the Congregation. However, his pastorship did not last, as he was tried by the General Court of Massachusetts Bay and found guilty of spreading 'dangerous opinions' in 1635. He was subsequently banished from the colony and forced to flee with his followers over the winter of 1635–6 to Rhode Island. Williams founded a settlement there, at Providence, which became known for its democratic institutions.

In *The Bloudy Tenet*, Williams discusses the role of civil disobedience in society. He calls for the separation of church and state, arguing that throughout English history the state had frequently suppressed religion, causing persecution and hence engendering civil disobedience. Such disruption has proved to be detrimental to society and, in turn, to the economy; it certainly hindered the individual's pursuit of his or her profession, as disruption and civil war decrease trade. Williams argues that the decisions made by civil government should lie with the people and not with civil magistrates, who were elected by a limited number of Puritan church members. Williams's call for greater individual freedom in religious and political affairs also translates into greater economic freedom, as Williams supported the 'free market' and the individuals' right to pursue economic gain.

THE
BLOUDY
TENET,
OF PERSECVTION,
for cause of *CONCIENCE,*
diſcuſſed, in

A Conference *betweene*

TRVTH and PEACE,

WHO,
In all tender affection, preſent to the
High Court of PARLIAMENT, (as the
Reſult of their *Diſcourſe*) theſe, (amongſt
other *Paſſages*) of *higheſt conſideration.*

Printed in the Yeere 1644.

CHAP. VI.

Peace. THe next *distinction* concerning the manner of *persons* holding forth the aforesaid *practices* (not only the *waighter duties* of the *Law*, but points of *doctrine* and *worship* lesse principall.)

" Some (saith he) hold them forth in a *meeke* and *peaceable* way: some
" with such *arrogance* and *impetuousnesse*, as of it selfe tendeth to the
" disturbance of *civill peace.*

Truth. In the examination of this *distinction* we shall discusse.

Firit, what is *civill Peace*, (wherein we shall vindicate thy name the
better.)

Secondly, what it is to hold forth a Doctrine or Practice in this *impetuousnesse* or *arrogancy.*

First, for *civill peace*, what is it but *pax civitatis*, the peace of the Citie, whether an *English* City, *Scotch*, or *Irish* Citie, or further abroad,
French, *Spanish*, *Turkish* Citie, *&c.*

Thus it pleased the Father of *Lights* to define it, *Ierem*, 29. 7. Pray
for the *peace* of the *City*; which peace of the *City*, or *Citizens*, so com-
pacted in a *civill* way of *union*, may be intire, unbroken, safe, &c. not-
with-

withstanding so many thousands of *Gods people* the *Iewes*, were there in *bondage*, and would neither be *constrained* to the *worship* of the City *Babell*, nor restrained from so much of the *worship* of the true *God*, as they then could practice, as is plaine in the practice of the 3 Worthis, *Shadrach*, *Misach*, and *Abednego*, as also of *Daniel*, Dan. 3. & Dan. 6. (the peace of the *City* or *Kingdome*, being a farre different Peace from the Peace of the *Religion* or *Spirituall worship*, maintained & professed of the Citizens. This *Peace* of their *worship* (which *worship* also in some Cities being various) being a false Peace, *Gods People* were and ought to be *Nonconformitants*, not daring either to be *restrained* from the *true*, or *constrained* to *false Worship*, and yet without breach of the Civill or *Citie-peace*, properly so called.

Peace. Hence it is that so many glorious and flourishing *Cities* of the World maintaine their *Civill* peace, yea the very *Americans* and wildest *Pagans* keep the peace of their *Townes* or *Cities*; though neither in one nor the other can any man prove a true *Church* of God in those places, and consequently no spirituall and heavenly peace: The Peace *spirituall* (whether true or false)being of a higher and farre different nature from the Peace of the place or people, being meerely and essentially *civill* and *humane*.

Truth. O how lost are the sonnes of men in this point ? To illustrate this :The *Church* or *company* of *Worshippers*(whether true or false) is like unto a Body or Colledge of *Physitians* in a *Citie*; like unto a *Corporation*, *Society*, or *Company* of *East-Indie* or *Turkie-Merchants*, or any other *Societie* or *Companie* in *London*: which Companies may hold their *Courts*, keepe their *Records*, hold *disputations* ; and in matters concerning their *Society*, may dissent, divide, breake into *Scismes* and *Factions*, sue and implead each other at *Law*, yea wholy breake up and dissolve into pieces and nothing, and yet the peace of the *City* not be in the least measure impaired or disturbed ; becaufe the *essence* or being of the *Citie*, and so the *well-beeing* and *peace* thereof is essentially distinct from those particular *Societies* : the *City-Courts*, *Citie-Lawes*, *Citie-punishments* distinct from theirs. The *City* was before them, and stands absolute and intire, when such a *Corporation* or *Society* is taken downe. For instance further, the *City* or *Civill state* of *Ephesus* was essentially distinct from the *Worship* of *Diana* in the City, or of the *whole citie*. Againe, the *Church* of *Christ* in *Ephesus* (which were Gods people, converted and call'd out from the *worship* of that City unto *Christianity* or *worship* of *God* in *Christ*) was distinct from both.

Now

Now suppose that *God* remove the *Candlestick* from *Ephesus*, yea though the *whole worship* of the *Citie of Ephesus* should be altered : yet (if men be true and honestly ingenuous to *City-covenants, Combinations* and *Principles*) all this might be without the least impeachment or infringement of the *City of Ephesus.*

Thus in the City of *Smirna* was the City it selfe or Civill estate one thing, The Spirituall or Religious state of *Smirna,* another ; The Church of Christ in *Smirna,* distinct from them both ; and the *Synagogue* of the *Jewes,* whether literally *Jewes* (as some thinke) or mystically, false *Christians,* (as others) called the *Synagogue* of *Sathan,* Revel. 2. distinct from all these. And not withstanding these spirituall oppositions in point of *Worship* and *Religion,* yet heare we not the least noyse (nor neede wee, if Men keepe but the Bond of *Civility*) of any *Civill breach,* or *breach* of *Civill peace* amongst them : and to persecute Gods people there for Religion, that only was a breach of Civilitie it selfe.

CHAP. IX.

2. *Ob.* **I**T will here be faid, Whence then arifeth civill diffentions and
Peace. uproares about matters of Religion?

Truth. I anfwer: When a Kingdome or State, Towne or Family,
lyes and lives in the guilt of a falfe God, falfe Chrift, falfe worfhip: no
wonder if fore eyes be troubled at the appearance of the light, be it never fo fweet: No wonder if a body full of corrupt humours bee troubled at ftrong (though wholfome) Phyfick? If perfons fleepy and loving to fleepe be troubled at the noife of fhrill (though filver) alarums:
No wonder if *Adonijah* and all his company be amazed and troubled at
the found of the right Heyre King *Salomon*, **1** *King.* **1.** If the Husbandmen were troubled when the Lord of the Vineyard fent fervant after
fervant, and at laft his onely Sonne, and they beat, and wounded, and
kill'd even the Sonne himfelfe, becaufe they meant themfelves to feize
upon the inheritance, unto which they had no right, *Matth.* **21.** **38.**

Hence

Hence all thofe tumults about the Apoftles in the *Acts*, &c. whereas good eyes are not fo troubled at light ; vigilant and watchfull perfons loyall and faithfull, are not fo troubled at the true, no nor at a falfe Religion of Jew or Gentile.

Secondly, breach of civill peace may arife, when falfe and idolatrous practices are held forth, and yet no breach of civill peace from the doctrine or Practice, or the manner of holding forth, but from that wrong and prepofterous way of fuppreffing, preventing, and extinguifhing fuch doctrines or practices by weapons of wrath & blood, whips, ftockes, imprifonment, banifhment, death, &c. by which men commonly are perfwaded to convert Heretickes, and to caft out uncleane fpirits, which only the finger of God can doe, that is the mighty power of the Spirit in the Word.

Hence the Towne is in an uproare, and the Country takes the Alarum to expell that fog or mift of Errour, Herefie. Blafphemy, (as is fuppofed) with Swords and Guns ; whereas tis Light alone, even Light from the bright fhining Sunne of Righteoufneffe, which is able, in the foules and confciences of men to difpell and fcatter fuch foggs and darkeneffe.

Hence the Sons of men, (as *David* fpeakes in another cafe, *Pfal.* 39.) difquiet themfelves in vaine, and unmercifully difquiet others, as (by the helpe of the Lord) in the fequell of this difcourfe fhall more appeare.

CHAP. XXVI.

NOw if any imagine that the time or date is long, that in the meane-feafon they may doe a *world of mifchife* before the *Worlds end*, as by infection.&c.

Truth. Firft, I anfwer, that as the *civill* State keepes it felfe with a *civill Guard*, in cafe thefe *Tares* fhall attempt ought againft the *peace* and *Welfare* of it, let fuch *civill offence* be punifhed, and yet as *Tares* oppofite to *Chrifts Kingdome*, let their *Worfhip* and *Confciences* be tolerated.

Secondly, the *Church* or *fpirituall ftate*, *City*, or *Kingdome* hath *lawes*, and *orders*, and *armories*, (whereon there hang a thoufand *Bucklers, Cant.*4.) *Weapons* and *Ammunition*, able to breake down the ftrongeft *Holds*, 1 *Cor.* 10. and fo to defend it felfe againft the very *Gates* of *Earth* or *Hell*.

Thirdly, the *Lord* himfelfe knows who are his, and his *foundation* remaineth fure, his *Elect* or chofen cannot perifh nor be finally deceived.

Laftly, the *Lord Iefus* here in this Parable layes down 2 *Reafons*, able to content and fatisfie our *hearts*, to beare patiently this their *contradiction* and *Antichriftianity*, and to permit or let them alone.

Firft, leaft the good Wheat be pluckt up and rooted up alfo out of this *field* of the *world*, if fuch *combuftions* & *fightings* were, as to pluck up all the falfe profeffours of the name of *Chrift*, the *good wheat* alfo would

would enjoy little peace, but be in danger to be pluckt up and torne out of this world by such bloody *ſtormes and tempeſts.*

And therefore as *Gods people* are commanded, *Jer.* 29. to pray for the peace of *materiall Babell,* wherein they were captivated, and 1 *Tim.* 2. to pray for all men, and ſpecially *Kings and Governors,* that in the peace of the *civill State* they may have peace. So contrary to the opinion and practice of moſt (drunke with the Cup of the *Whores fornication*) yea, and of *Gods* owne people faſt aſleep in *Antichriſtian Dalilahs* laps, *obedience* to the command of *Chriſt* to let the *tares* alone, will prove the onely meanes to preſerve their Civill Peace, and that without obedience to this command of Chriſt, it is impoſſibe (without great tranſgreſſion againſt the *Lord* in carnall policy, which will not long hold out) to preſerve the *civill* peace.

Beſide, Gods people the good Wheat are generally pluckt up and perſecuted, as well as the vileſt idolaters, whether Jewes or Antichriſtians, which the Lord Jeſus ſeemes in this *Parable* to foretell.

The ſecond *Reaſon* noted in the *Parable* which may ſatisfie any man from wondring at the *patience* of *God,* is this : when the *world* is ripe in ſinne, in the ſinnes of *Antichriſtianiſme* (as the Lord ſpake of the ſinnes of the *Amorites, Gen.* 12.) then thoſe holy and mighty *Officers* and *Executioners,* the *Angels,* with their ſharpe and cutting *ſickles* of eternall vengeance, ſhall downe with them, and bundle them up for the *everlaſting barnings.*

Then ſhall that Man of Sin, 2 *Theſſ.* 2. be conſumed by the breath of the mouth of the *Lord Jeſus,* and all that *worſhip* the *Beaſt* and his picture, and receive his *mark* into their *forehead* or their *hands,* ſhall drinke of the Wine of the *wrath of God* which is poured out without mixture into the Cup of his *indignation,* and he ſhall be tormented with *fire and brimſtone* in the preſence of the holy *Angels,* and in the preſence of the *Lambe:* and the ſmoake of their *torment* ſhall aſcend up for ever and ever, *Rev.* 14. 10. 11.

CHAP. LII.

Truth. A Fourth Argument from this Scripture I take in the 6. verſe, from *Tribute, Cuſtome, &c.* which is a meerly civill *Reward* or *Recompence* for the *Magiſtrates* worke. Now as the *wages* are, ſuch is the *Worke*: But the *Wages* are meerely *civill, Cuſtome, Tribute, &c.* not the *contributions* of the Saints or *Churches* of *Chriſt* (proper to the *Spirituall* and *Chriſtian ſtate*) and ſuch *worke* only muſt the *Magiſtrate* attend upon, as may properly deſerve ſuch *civill wages*, reward or recompence.

Laſtly, that the *Spirit of God* never intended to direct or warrant the *Magiſtrate* to uſe this Power in *ſpirituall* affaires and *Religions* worſhip: I argue, from the *terme* or *title* it pleaſeth the wiſedome of God to give ſuch *Civill Officers*, to wit, (verſ. 6.) *Gods Miniſters.*

Now at the very firſt bluſh, no man denies a double *Miniſterie.*

The one appointed by *Chriſt* Ieſus in his *Church*, to *gather*, to *governe, receive in, caſt out*, and order all the affaires of the *Church*, the *Houſe, Citie,* or *Kingdome* of *God*, Epheſ.4. 1 Cor. 12.

Secondly, a Civill *Miniſtry* or *office*, meerely *humane* and *civill*, which Men agree to conſtitute (called therefore an humane *creation*, (1 Pet. 2.) and is as true and lawfull in thoſe Nations, Cities, Kingdomes, &c. which never heard of the true *God*, nor his holy Sonne Ieſus, as in any part of the World beſide, where the Name of Ieſus is moſt taken up.

From all which *premiſes*, viz. that the ſcope of the *Spirit of God* in this Chapter is to handle the matters of the *ſecond Table* (having handled the matters of the *firſt*, in the 12. ſince the Magiſtrats of whom *Paul* wrote, were naturall, ungodly, perſecuting, and yet lawfull Magiſtrates, and to be obeyed in all lawfull Civill things.

Since all *Magiſtrates* are *Gods Miniſters*, eſſentiall *civill*, bounded

dead to a *civill* worke, with *civill* weapons or inftuments, and paid or rewarded with *civill* rewards. From all which, I fay, I undeniably collect, that this *Scripture* is generally miftaken, and wrefted from the fcope of Gods Spirit, and the nature of the place, and cannot truely be alledged by any for the Power of the *Civill Magiftrate* to be exercifed in *fpirituall* and *Soule-matters*.

EXCERPTS FROM
THE BLOUDY TENENT, WASHED, AND MADE WHITE IN THE BLOUD OF THE LAMBE

John Cotton, *The Bloudy Tenent, Washed, and Made White in the Bloud of the Lambe: being discussed and discharged of bloud-guiltinesse by just Defence. Wherein The great Questions of this present time are handled…whereunto is added a Reply to Mr. Williams Answer, to Mr. Cottons Letter* (London, 1647), chapters 6, 9, 26 and 51, pp. 10–13, 17–21, 49–51 and 105–9.

John Cotton wrote this piece in response to Roger Williams's *Bloudy Tenet* (1644). These two texts demonstrate the growing dialogue in the American colonies regarding individual rights and religious choice. Implicitly these arguments contain some discussion of the economic rights that were also accorded to the colonists. Whereas Williams calls for the protection and promotion of individual liberty for economic prosperity, Cotton argues that it is religious order that is necessary.

THE

BLOUDY TENENT,

WASHED,

And made white in the bloud of the
Lamb : being difcuffed and difcharged of
bloud-guiltineffe by juft Defence.

WHEREIN

The great Queftions of this prefent time are
handled , *viz.* How farre Liberty of Confcience
ought to be given to thofe that truly feare God? And how farre
reftrained to turbulent and peftilent perfons, that not onely raze the foundation of Godlineffe, but difturb the Civill
Peace where they live? Alfo how farre the Magiftrate may proceed in the duties of the firft Table? And that all Magiftrates
ought to ftudy the word and will of God , that they may frame
their Government according to it

DISCUSSED.

As they are alledged from divers Scriptures, out of
the Old and New Teftament. Wherein alfo the practife of
Princes is debated, together with the Judgement of Ancient and late Writers of moft precious efteeme.

Whereunto is added a Reply to Mr. WILLIAMS
Anfwer, to Mr. COTTONS Letter.

BY JOHN COTTON Batchelor in Divinity, and
Teacher of the Church of Chrift at *Bofton* in *New-England.*

LONDON,
Printed by *Matthew Symmons* for *Hannah Allen,* at the *Crowne* in
Popes Head-Alley. 1 6 4 7.

Chap. 6.

A Reply to his sixth Chapter Discussing Civill peace, and the Disturbance of it.

IN this Chapter, the Discusser undertaketh to declare what Civill peace is, and to shew, that the Toleration of different Religions, is no Disturbance of Civill Peace.

First, for Civill peace, what is it, saith he, but Pax Civitatis, whether English , *or* Irish , Spanish *or* Turkish *City.*

Reply.

Be it so , and if the Civill State , or Common-wealth containe many Citties , or Townes, and so become a whole Countrey or Common-wealth, let Civill Peace be the peace of the Countrey, or of the Common-wealth. But what is then the peace of the Citty,or Countrey? Is it not *Tranquillitas Ordinis* the tranquility of order in every Society,wherein the Publicke Weale of the Citty, or Countrey is concerned ? And is it not the proper worke of the Civill Magistrate to preserve the Civill Peace, and to prevent or reforme the disturbance of the Tranquility or Peace of any such Societyes, in whose Peace, the Peace or Weale of the Citty or Society is concerned ? Suppose a Society of Merchants or Cloath-

yers,

yers, or Fishmongers, or Drapers, or the like : If the Weale of the
Citty or Countrey be concerned in these (as it is much concerned
in them all) It is not for the safety of the Civill Sate to suffer any
of these so to be disturbed, as wholely to breake up , and to be dis-
solved.

*No matter (saith the Discusser) though they doe wholly breake up into
peices and dissolve into nothing. For neverthelesse the Peace of the Citty
is not thereby in the least measure impaired or disturbed : because the
Essence or being of the Citty is Essentially distinct from those particular
Societyes &c. The Citty was before them, and standeth absolute and
Entire, when they are taken downe &c.*

Reply.

If by Peace be meant (as in Scripture Language it is)all welfare,
It would argue a man that liveth in the world, to be too much Ignorant of the state of the world, *to say that in the breaking up and
dissolving of such perticular Societyes, the Peace of the Citty or Countrey
is not in the least measure impaired, or disturbed.*

For 1. Though such Societyes of Merchants and other Trades,
be not of the Essence of the Citty ; yet they be of the integrety of
the Citty. And if the defect of one Tribe In *Israel* was a great trouble
to all the Common-wealth of *Israel* (*Judges,* 21.2, 3.) then sure
the breaking up and dissolving of so many particular usefull Societyes cannot but much impaire and disturbe the Peace and wellfare of the Citty and Countrie.

2. Though these Societyes of Trades be not of the Essence of
the Citty, yet they are amongst the conservant causes of the Citty:
as without which the Citty cannot long flourish, no nor well subsist, Common sense will acknowledge so much.

Now then if all these particular Societyes and severall Com-
panyes of Trades, they and their peace and wellfare doe much
concerne the wellfare and peace of the Citty and Countrey , and
therefore it behooveth the Civill Government to provide for their
peace and wellfare : I demand, whether the Church also, (which
is a particular Society of Christians) whether, I say, the Peace and
wellfare of it, doe not concerne the Peace and wellfare of the Citty
or Countrey where they live ?

If it be denyed it is Easily proved .

First,

First, *David* saith they shall prosper that love the Peace of *Jeru-salem*, and seeke the good of it ; *Psalm.* 122. 6 *&c.* And *Solomon* saith, *where the Righteous rejoyce there is great Glory*, Pro. 28. 12. And what is the Church, but a Congregation of Righteous men ? If the Rejoycing of the Church be the glory of a Nation, surely the disturbing, and distracting, and dissolving of the Church, is the shame and Confusion of a Nation.

2. Consider the Excellency and Preheminence of the Church above all other Societyes. *She is the fairest amongst women*, Cant. 1. 8. and 6. 1. *She is the Citty and House of God*, Revel. 21. 2. Psal. 48. 1. 1. Tim. 3. 15. The world and all the Societyes of it, are for the Church, 1 *Cor.* 3. 21, 22. The world would not subsist, but for the Church : nor any Countrey in the world, but for the service of the Church. *And can the Church then breake up, into peices, and dissolve into nothing, and yet the Peace and wellfare of the Citty, not in the least measure impaired or disturbed ?*

3. It is a matter of just displeasure to God, and sad greife of heart to the Church, when Civill States looke at the estate of the Church, as of little, or no concernment to themselves. *Zach.* 1. 15. *Lament.* 1. 12.

Object 1. *Many glorious and flourishing Cittyes of the world main-taine their Civill Peace : yea the very Americans, and wildest Pagans, keep the Peace of their Townes, and Cittyes, though neither in the one, nor in the other can any man prove a true Church of God in these places.*

Ans. It is true, where the Church is not, Cittyes and Townes may enjoy some measure of Civill Peace, yea and flourish in outward prosperity for a time, through the Patience and Bounty and Long-sufferance of God. *The times of Ignorance God winketh at* Act. 17. 30. But when the Church cometh to be Planted amongst them, If then Civill States doe neglect them, & suffer the Churches to corrupt, and annoy themselves by pollutions in Religion, the the staffe of the Peace of the Common-wealth will soone be broken, as the Purity of Religion is broken in the Churches. The Common-wealth of *Rome* flourished five hundred yeares before the Kingdome of God in his Church came amongst them : and the decayes of the Common-wealth occasioned by the persecutions of the Church, were Repaired by the Publick establishment of

the

the Churches peace in Chriſtian Emperors. But when the Churches begun to pollute themſelves by the Idolatrous worſhip of Images, and the Chriſtian Emperors tooke no care to reforme this abuſe in Churches, the Lord ſent in (amongſt other barberous nations) the *Turkes* to puniſh, not onely degenerate Churches, but alſo the Civill State for this wickedneſſe. And therefore the Holy Ghoſt upbraideth them for their continuance in Image worſhip, though the *Turke* were let looſe from the River *Euphrates*, to ſcourge them for it, *Rev.* 9. 14. 20. Goe now, and ſay, the eſtate of the Church whether true, or falſe, (pure or corrupt) doth not concerne the Civill Peace of the Sate.

Object. 2. *The Peace of the Church (whether true or falſe) is ſpirituall, and ſo of an higher and farre different nature from the peace of the Cou____, or People, which is meerely and Eſſentially Civill and humane.*

Anf. 1. Though the inward peace of the Church be ſpirituall and heavenly : yet there is an outward peace of the Church due to them (even from Princes and Magiſtrates) in a way of godlineſſe and honeſty, 1. *Tim.* 2. 1. 2. But in a way of ungodlineſſe, and Idolatry, it is an wholeſome faithfulneſſe to the Church if Princes trouble the outward peace of the Church, that ſo the Church finding themſelves wounded and pricked in the houſe of their friends, they may repent, and ret____ to their firſt Husband, *Zach.* 13. 6. *Hoſea.* 2. 6. 7.

Anf. 2. Though the peace of the Countrey or Common-wealth be Civill and humane, yet it is diſtracted and cutt off, by diſturbing the ſpirituall purity, and peace of the Church. *Jehu* cutting ſhort his Reformation, God cutt ſhort the coaſts of the Civill State. 2 *King.* 10. 31. 32.

Anf. 3. Civill Peace (to ſpeake properly) is not onely a peace in ____ things, for the Object; but a peace of all the perſons of the Citty, for the Subject. The Church is one Society in the Citty, as well as is the Society, of Merchants, or Drapers, Fiſhmongers, and Hiberdaſhers, and if it be a part of Civill Juſtice, out of regard to Civill Peace, to protect all other Societyes in peace according to the wholeſome Ordinances of their Company, is it not ſo, much more to protect the Church-Society in peace, according to the wholeſome Ordinances of the Word of Chriſt ?

CHAP. 9.

A Reply to his ninth Chapter, Touching the Causes of Civill Dissensions, and uprores about Matters of Religion.

Discusser.

Whence then arise Civill Dissensions and uprores in matters of Religion? I Answer, 1. When a State liveth and lieth in the guilt of a false God, false Christ, false Worship: then no wonder, if soare eyes be troubled at the appearance of light,——whereas good eyes are not troubled at the Light. Vigilant and watchfull Persons, Loyall and Faithfull are not so troubled at the true, no nor at a false Religion of Jew or Gentile.

Discharge,

Difcharge.

This is as little to the purpofe, as that which went before. The diftinction fpake of holding forth Erroneous and unlawful things, in a way tending of it felfe, to the difturbance of Civill Peace. This Difcuffion holdeth forth another way tending to the difturbance of Civill Peace, not of it felfe, but by occafion or by Accident, to wit, when the holding forth of Light and Truth difturbeth the fore Eyes of a corrupt State. If *per fe*, and *per Accidens* (of it felfe, and by occafion) be all one: If the holding forth of Truth, and Error be all one, then this Difcuffion hath fhaken the diftinction of holding forth Error, not in an humble and meeke way, but in a way of Arrogance and Impetuoufneffe. But when he faith, *vigilant and faithfull Perfons are not fo troubled, no not at the falfe Religion of Jew or Gentile*: If he meane not fo much troubled at the falfe Religion, as corrupt Sates be at the true Religion: there may be truth in the fpeech, but it onely argueth, That corrupt nature is more zealous in the defence of its owne will-worfhip, then the faithfull be in the defence of the Truth. But furely the faithful are called to contend Earneftly for the Faith, (*Jude* 3.) and have as much caufe to be troubled at the holding forth of the Worfhip of *Baal*, as corrupt States be at the holding forth of the Worfhip of *Jehovah*. If his meaning be, that vigilant and faithfull Perfons, are not fo troubled at the falfe Religion of *Jew* or *Gentile*, but that they can Tolerate them to live amongft them in a Civill Body, we fay fo too: And therefore the *Indians*, who have fubmitted to the Government of this jurifdiction, are not compelled to the Profeffion or acknowledgement of our Religion, either by Force of Armes, or Pœnall Lawes. But yet if Chriftians fhould feduce Chriftians to turne Apoftates from the Faith, and to imbrace *Judaifme*, or *Paganifme*: Or if *Jewes* or *Pagans* living amongft us fhould openly blafpheme the God of heaven, & draw away Chriftians to *Atheifme*, or *Judaifme*, I fhould not account them either vigilant, or faithfull Chriftians, that were not troubled at fuch a deftroying of the true Religion, and propagating of the falfe. *Paul* blamed the falfe Teachers to be the Troublers of the Churches of *Galatia*, Gal. 5. 10, 12. *Acts* 15. 24.

Difcuffer.

2, *Breach of Civill Peace may arife when falfe and Idolatrous practifes*
are

are held forth, and yet no Breach of Civill Peace from the Doctrine, or Practise, or the manner of holding them forth, but from the wrong and preposterous way of Suppressing, and preventing and extinguishing such Errors by weapons of wrath and Bloud, Whips, Stocks, Imprisonment, Banishment, Death, by which men are commonly perswaded to convert Heretickes, and to cast out uncleane spirits, which onely the finger of God can doe, that is, the mighty Power of the Spirit of the Word. It is light alone that is able to dispell and scatter such mists and foggs of darknesse in the soules and Consciences of

Hence the Sonnes of men disquiet themselves in vaine, and unmercifully disquiet others.

Defender.

Then it seemeth, that if the *Mariners* of the *Ship* wherein *Jonah* sayled when he fled from the Presence of God, if they I say did cast *Jonah* over board into the Sea, this preposterous way of theirs in suppressing the Error of his way, was it which raised the storme and Tempest, whereby the *Ship* was tossed to and fro, & disturbed, yea & in jeopardy to be sunk and destroyed. But the Text speakes to the contrary, when they had cast *Jonah* forth into the Sea, the Sea ceased from his raging, *Jonah* 1. 15.

But what was the sinne of *Jonah* ? was it not some sinne against the second Table, some act of unrighteousnesse against his Neighbour ? It was a direct and immediate breach of a rule of his Propheticall Office, a sin against the second Commandement of the First Table. But was not the Sea, in which this tempest arose against *Jonah*, and against the whole *Ship* for his sake, was it not the Sea of *Tiberias*, which being within the Confines of the Holy Land, the Sea also was Holy, and would not suffer such a sin unpunished ? No, the Sea of *Tiberias* is within the Confines of *Galilee*, and other parts of the Land of *Israel* ; But this was the *Mediterranean* Sea, between *Joppa* and *Tarshish*. *Jonah* 1. 3. But were not these *Mariners*, *Israelites*, who might have some speciall charge from God, to roote out all Idolatry and false Worship from amongst them, which bindeth not us *Gentiles ?* No, they were *Pagans* and *Gentiles*, as appeareth in that every one of them cryed out, unto his own God.

But why did not God send out the tempest to punish those *Pagan*

gan *Mariners* rather, for their Idolatry then *Jonah* for his Erroneous Practise in running away from the true God ?

God in times paft fuffered all Nations to walke in their owne wayes *Acts*, 14. 16. And fo did his Vicegerents the good Kings of *Ifrael* doe the like : *David* did not compell the tributary Nations to worfhip the God of *Ifrael*. No more doth our Colony here compell the tributary *Indians* to worfhip our God. But if an *Ifraelite* forfake God, he difturbeth not onely the Common-wealth of *Ifrael*, but the Barks of *Pagans*, and *Heathen* ftates as *Jonah* did this *Ship*, by his departure from God. Therefore a Chriftian by departing from God, may difturbe a *Gentile* civill State. And it is no prepofterous way for the Governours of the State, according to the quality of the difturbance raifed by the ftarting afide of fuch a Chriftian, to punifh both it and him by civill cenfure.

Nor doth the Civill State in fuch punifhments attend fo much, how to procure the converfion of Heretickes, or Apoftates, or fuch like fcandalous turbulent offenders : as how to prevent the perverfion of their founder peopie (*Gangraenam amoveas, ne pars fincera trahatur :*) or elfe to worke the fubverfion of fuch , as doe fubvert both truth and peace.

And yet as legall terrours are ordinary meanes bleffed of God to prepare hard and ftout hearts to converfion: fo fuch legall punifhments God is in like fort pleafed to bleffe to the confufion, and reformation of falfe Prophets, as was foretold by *Zacharie*, it fhould come to paffe in the dayes of the new Teftament, *Zach*. 13. 4,5,6.

Object. Yea, but it is light alone that is able to difpell and fcatter fuch mifts and foggs of darkneffe in the foules and Confciences of men.

Anf. True: But yet the judgements of God are as the Light that goeth forth, *Hofea* 6. 5. And the judgements of men executed according to the Word, are fanctified of God to prevent the fpreading of Idolatry and feducement to it ; All *Ifrael* fhall heare and feare, and doe no more prefumptuoufly, *Deut*. 13. 11. Nor is the righteous proceeding in Civill States a difquieting of themfelves, *or any unmercifull difquieting of others*. For it is no difquieting to a juft man to doe Juftice : and the difquieting of men in finne, it is no unmercifull dealing, but a compaffionate healing either of themfelves or others. The falfe Prophet reclaimed by ftigmatizing with
wounds

wounds in his hands, will freely accknowledge, thus was I wounded in the House of my friends (*Zach.* 13. 6.) Friends are not unmercifull difquieters.

Object. The Judgements of God which goe forth as the light are
not of the Judgements of his hand, but of his mouth, for fo he ex-
pleineth himfelfe in that place of *Hofea*, I have hewen them by the
Prophets, I have flaine them by the words of my mouth: And thy
Judgements were as the light that goeth forth.

Anf. The Judgements of God, whether of his mouth or of his
hand, doe both of them goe forth as light. For when the Judgements of God are upon the earth, (and he fpeaketh of the judgments
of his hands,) *the Inhabitants of the world fhall learne righteoufneffe,*
Ifai. 26. 9. And that whereby we learne righteoufneffe, is light.
Befides when the Lord is faid to have hewen, and flaine his Apo-
ftate people by his Prophets, and by the words of his mouth ; He
doth not onely meane the fpirituall hewing, and flaying of their
foules, but alfo the temporall judgements, Famine, Warre, and
Peftilence, which the Prophets threatned, and the Hand of God,
and *Hazael* executed in the hewing and flaying of them.

C H A p. 26. *A Reply to his* Chap. 26.

Touching the danger of letting alone AntiChriftians.

Difcuffer.

If any imagine, that the Antichriftians being let alone may doe a worla of mifchiefe before the worlds end, by the infeltion of others.

I Anfwer, 1. The Civill State keepeth it felfe with a Civill fword: let Civill offences be punifhed : and yet let their worfhip and Confciences be tolerated.

2. The Church hath a thoufand bucklers and weapons, able to break downe the ftrongeft bauld (2 Cor. 10.) and fo to defend it felfe againft the gates of earth or hell.

3. The Lord knoweth who are his : his chofen cannot finally be deceived

Laftly the Lord Jefus himfelfe in this Parable giveth 2. Reafons able to content and fatisfie our hearts.

Firft, leaft the good wheat be pluckt up out of the feild of the world. Gods People, the good wheat are generally pluckt, and perfecuted, as well as the vileft Idolaters, whether Jewes or Antichriftians, which the Lord Jefus feemeth here to foretell.

Second reafon is, when the world is ripe in finne, in the finnes of Antichriftianifme, thofe mighty Angells of God will come with their fharpe
ficlkes

*fickles , and downe with them, and bundle them up for everlasting bur-
nings, then shall the man of sin be confumed by the breath of the mouth of
the Lord Jesus &c.*

Defender.

Reply, 1. To his first *Answer :* It is true, the Civill State keepeth it felfe with a Civill fword, if Civill offences be punished. But
when he would have their worship & Confciences tolerated, what
if their worship and Confciences incite them to Civill offences?
How shall then the Civill State keepe it felfe fafe with a Civill
Sword.

As fuppofe a man that worshippeth the Beaft, and maketh Confcience of obeying his commandements , shall thinke himfelfe
bound to fubvert the Civill Prince, or State, who is excommunicated by the Beaft? If fuch a man muft be tolerated in his worship,
and Confcience, what fword can provide for the fafety of fuch a
Prince or State?

Reply.

2. To his fecond *Answer* , It is true, the Church wanteth no
Armories to defend it felf, and amongft others, excommunication.
But if their members be leavened with Antichriftian Idolatry and
fuperftition, and yet muft be tolerated in their Idolatrous and fu-
perftious worship, will not a little leaven (fo tolerated) leaven the
whole lumpe? And how then is the fafety of the Church
guarded?

Reply.

3. To his 3. *Anfw.* It is true the Lord knoweth who are his :
and none of his Elect shall perish. But neverthelefe, Is it not a
tempting of God, to prefume upon Gods Election for our falva-
tion, and to neglect the meanes of our prefervation ? In like cafe,
Paul knew by revelation , that all his fellow paffengers in the ship
should be faved : but yet he profeffed that if the Marriners went
out of the ship, they could not be faved Acts, 27. 24, with 3 1. So is
it here, The Elect of God shall be faved : but yet if Idolaters , and
Seducers be tolerated (as *Jezabell* was in *Thyatira*) to feduce the
fervants of Chrift to pollution and Apoftacy , the Church will
ftand guilty before God of the feduction and corruption of the
people of God..

Reply.

Reply.

4. To his 4 *Answer* (the 2. Reasons alledged by him out of the Text:) To the first: There is no feare of plucking up the wheat, by rooting out Idolaters, and Seducers. If any of Gods People should fall into Idolatry, and Apostacy, yea and should prove an instrument to seduce others also into the like wickednesse: yet the censures inflicted on them, would be blessed of God to their recovery,& healing: yea and if they were cut off by the Civill sword, yet the example and terrour of their punishment, would be blessed of God to preserve their brethren: who would all of them heare and feare, and doe no m· · such wickednesse. Neither is the just punishment of such, any just pretence to punish the innocent lambs of Christ.

Reply.

To the Second Reason out of the Parable, It may justly be Replyed, that the charge given to the Angells to execute vengeance at the last day upon such Idola· , if that were sufficient to plead for the toleration of Idolaters, It would as well plead for the toleration of Murtherers, Robbers, Adulterers, Extortioners &c. for all these will the holy and mighty Angells of God gather into bundles at the last day, and cast them into everlasting burnings.

The place in 2 *Theff.* 2. doth not say, that the man of sin shall then be consumed with the breath of the mouth of the Lord Jesus: for he shall begin to be consumed long before , by all the seven vials of the wrath of God , *Revel.* 16. which have bin, and will be in powring out, many ages, before the great Harvest, of the end of the world. Yea I beleive also, He shall be destroyed many ages before then : as the Apostle *John* foretelleth in *Chap.* 20. 21. 22. of the *Revelation.* And though it be translated, (in 2 *Theff.* 2. 8.) The Lord shall destroy him with the brightnesse of his coming : yet the word is , ἐν τῇ ἐπιφανείᾳ τῆς Παρουσίας αὐτοῦ ; and Παρουσία doth as well, and more fistly signifie Presence, then comming. The Lord will destroy Antichrist with the brightnesse of his Presence in his sacred and Civill Ordinances, sundry ages before the brightnesse of his comming to Judgement. Otherwise we should set *John* & *Paul* at variance, who spake by one and the same Spirit of Truth.

Chap. 51. *A Reply to his* Chap. 51.

Discusser.

A Fourth *Argument from this* Scripture (Rom. 13.) *I take (in* ver. 6.) *which is a meerely civill reward for the Magistrates worke. Now as the wages be, such is the worke, but the wages are meerely Civill , Custome, Tribute , not the contributions of the Saints or Churches of Christ,* &c.

Defender.

Defender.

The Contributions of the Saints and Churches, are truly called by the Apostle carnall things, *Romans* 15. 27. and againe, 2 *Cor.* 9. 11. But shall a man therefore thus reason, as the wages be, such is the worke: But the wages are carnall things: therefore such is the worke of the Ministers of the Gospel, to whom such wages are paid? It is true the contributions of the Saints, may be called Holy, because they are given to God, and (by his appointment) to the maintenance of such as minister in his house about his holy things: But these are mentall relations, no reall differances in the things given to Magistrates, and Ministers: The wages given to them both, are carnall things. And consider them both in their proper ends: as the rewards given to Ministers, are given for their service about holy things: so the rewards given to Magistrates are given for their service about righteous things. Now if the Purity of Doctrine, worship, and Government be righteous priviledges of all the Churches in the Common-wealth, surely Magistrates doe not well deserve all their wages, that suffer the Churches to be bereaved, and dispoyled of their spirituall priviledges, which is the greatest and best part of their Birthright.

Besides, the Apostle commandeth the Churches, and Saints not onely to pay to Magistrates, Tribute, and Custome, (which are civill things:) but also to poure out all manner of Prayers, and Supplications, Intercessions, and given of thanks for them, 1 *Tim.* 1. 1, 2. And surely these are spirituall dues, and not Earthly. And therefore Magistrates owe to the Churches, and Saints some Spirituall recompences, which the Apostle also there nameth, that we may live a quiet and peaceable Life in all godlinesse and honesty, *ver.* 2. If therefore the Churches and Saints be not suffered to live a quiet and peaceable Life in Godlinesse and honesty : or if they be suffered to live a quiet and peaceable life in ungodlinesse and dishonesty, the Magistrates fall short of returning spirituall recompence for the spirituall Duties and services performed for them.

Discusser.

Lastly, that the Spirit of God never intended to direct or warrant the Magistrate, to use his power in spirituall affaires and Religions, I

argue

argue from the Terme, or Title given by God, to such civill Officers, to wit, Gods Ministers, ver. 6.

Defender.

One would thinke the Argument would rather evince the contrary. For what is a Minister, but a Servant? and what is a servant, but he that is at his Masters command (for his efficient cause:) and for his Masters ends, as his finall cause? How shall then a Magistrate carrie himselfe, as a Minister of God, and yet fall short (and intended so to doe) both of Gods Commandements in his Lawes? and of Gods worship, and glory in the execution of them?

Discusser.

But at the very first blush, any man will acknowledge a double Ministery: the one appointed by Christ in his Church, to order the affaires thereof, Ephes. 4. 1 Cor. 12. The other a Civill Ministery or office, meerely humane and Civill, which men agree to constitute, (therefore called an humane Creation, 1 Pet.) and is as true and lawfull in those Countries, that never heard of the true God, and his holy Sonne Jesus, as in any part of the world, where the Name of Christ is not taken up.

Defender.

If Magistrates be the Ministers of God (as *Paul* calleth them:) then their Ministery or office is not meerely humane, but as the Apostle saith, it is of God, and ordained of God, *Rom.* 13. 1. And if it be of God, it must also be for God: or else he is a Minister and servant not of God, but of the world. It is true, men agree to constitute it, to wit, this or that forme of it (in respect of which influence of men, it is called an humane Creation:) but the Truth is, Government it selfe is of God, and ordained by God, and every lawfull forme of Government (whether Monarchy, Aristarchy, or Democracy, or some mixt of these, according to the State of the People) they are all of God, and so acknowledged, and authorized by God in his word, and though they be as true and lawfull in those Nations that never heard of the true God, or of his holy Sonne Jesus: yet it was from the guidance and appointment of God in the very light of Nature, that such Nations did erect such and such Governments, and Governments for the good of humane society, and that not onely in worldly matters, But in matters also of Religion.

Whence

Whence it is, that in all civill Nations, whofe *Acts* are recorded, either in facred or prophane Authors, their Magiftrates have had not onely a due care of Juftice and honefty, but a reverend care of Religion alfo : *Jofeph* in *Egypt* provided for the prefervation of the Lands of the Priefts without Impeachment, and that not out of refpect to their fuperftition (which he could not but diflike :) but out of regard to the *Ægyptian* Lawes, & Cuftomes, to preferve their Religion, and the maintenance thereof, inviolate, *Gen.* 47. 22. In *Babell*, *Nebuchadnezzar* being convinced of the foveraigne Divinity of the God of *Ifrael*, made a capitall Law againft the blafphemers of his Name, *Dan.* 3. 29. *Darius* of the *Medes* and *Perfians* enacted a Royall Law to like purpofe, *Dan.* 6. 26. The like did *Artaxerxes*, *Ezra.* 7 26. and *Darius* before him, *Ezra.* 6. 11. In *Athens* they had a Law againft Ἀσέβεια, Irreligion, upon which fuffered three famous Philofophers, *Socrates*, *Theodorus*, and *Protagoras*. *Socrates*, as *Laertius* reporteth in his Life, was accufed by *Melitus* τῆς Ἀσεβείας, who commenced his Action againft him in thefe words Ἀδικεῖ Σωκράτης, ὅς ἡ Πόλις νομίζει Θεὺς, ὐ νομίζων, ἕτερα δὲ Δαιμόνια καινὰ εἰσηγύμενΘ.

Theodorus was firnamed ἌθεΘ, and as *Socrates* was condemned to death by poyfon, fo was this man alfo, as *Laertius* reporteth out of *Amphicrates* in the life of *Ariftippus*. *Protagoras*, (as *Tully* reporteth of him, *de Natura Deorum Lib.* 1.) having thus expreffed himfelfe in the beginning of his Booke, concerning the Gods (I have not to fay, whether they be, or whether they be not) his Bookes were publickly burnt, and himfelfe banifhed out of City and Country. How the *Ephefians* ftood affected to the deftroyers of their Religion, appeareth by the excufe which the Towne-Clarke made for *Paul* and his Companions, you have brought thefe men hither faith he, which are neither robbers of Churches, nor yet blafphemers of your Goddeffe, *Acts* 19. 37. The *Romans* how zealous they were in defence of their Religion, the flaughter of many thoufand Chriftians will be a perpetuall Monument to all Ages. All which things I recite not to juftifie the mifapplying of their zeale to the maintenance of falfe Gods, but to make it appeare, that as the Pagan Nations who never heard of the true God, and of his Sonne Jefus, did erect by inftinct of Nature, Governments, and Magiftrates : fo by the fame inftinct,

their

their Lawes and Magiftrates tooke care of the maintenance of that Religion, which they tooke to be of God. What a fhame were it, that Pagan Magiftrates fhould be more carefull and zealous of the honour of their Idols, then Chriftians of the Honour of the knowne true God, the Lord our Creator, Redeemer, and Sanctifier?

EXCERPTS FROM
A SURVEY OF THE SUMME OF CHURCH-DISCIPLINE

Thomas Hooker, *A Survey of the Summe of Church-Discipline. Wherein, the Way of the Churches of New-England is warranted out of the Word, and all Exceptions of weight, which are made against it, answered: Whereby also it will appear to the Judicious Reader, that something more must be said, then yet hath been, before their Principles can be shaken, or they should be unsetled in their practice* (London, 1648), chapters 1 and 2, pp. 1–34.

Born in England, and a graduate of Queen's College, Cambridge, the Puritan Thomas Hooker (1586–1647) held several religious positions in England before being forced to flee to Holland in 1630 to escape religious persecution. In 1633 he immigrated to Massachusetts Bay Colony and became the pastor of a church in New Towne, Cambridge. After experiencing difficulties with the Massachusetts religious authorities in 1636, Hooker lead a group of Puritans to establish the city of Hartford, Connecticut. He served there as pastor until his death.

Hooker was best known for advocating the extension of voting rights beyond church members and for arguing that all people had a god-given right to choose their own magistrate. For this, he is sometimes known as the 'father of American democracy'. His *Fundamental Orders* (1639) served as Connecticut's first constitution and embodied many of his own political ideas. He defends these views in *A Survey of the Summe of Church-Discipline*.

Yet, despite Hooker's radical views on political participation, the necessity of maintaining order is the primary theme of *A Survey*. Hooker argues that logic is a divine instrument that helps to guide interpretations of the Bible and can be used to apply the rules therein to society. Through the use of logic, a fundamental system of order can be found that – among other things – promotes political rule by the community's religious elders, who understand the logic. Such power was not just political, but also economic, and included the enforcement of property rights and the granting of privileges and monopolies. The rules of lending and usury were all controlled by the religious elders, who thus had broad control over the economic organisation of society.

A
SURVEY
of the Summe of
Church-Difcipline.

WHEREIN,

The Way of the CHURCHES of

NEW--ENGLAND

is warranted out of the Word,
and all Exceptions of weight, which
are made againſt it, anſwered : Whereby
alfo it will appear to the Judicious Reader,
that ſomething more muſt be ſaid, then
yet hath been, before their Principles can be ſhaken, or they
ſhould be unſetled in
their practice.

By THO. HOOKER, late Paſtor of the Church at
Hertford upon *Connecticott* in *N. E.*

ISA. 62. 1.

*For Sions ſake I will not hold my tongue · and for Jeruſalems ſake, I will not
reſt : untill the righteouſneſſe thereof break forth as the light, and the ſalva-
tion thereof be as a burning lamp*

2 COR. 13. 8. *For we can due nothing againſt the truth, but for the truth.*

LONDON,

Printed by *A. M.* for *John Bellamy* at the three Golden Lions
in *Cornhill*, near the Royall Exchange. M.DC.XLVIII.

A
SURVEY
of the Summe of
Church-Difcipline.

CHAP. I.
Ecclefiafticall Policy Defined.

Ecclefiafticall Policy is a skill of ordering the affairs
of Chrifts houfe, according to the pattern of his word.

 *Kill.*] When we fpeak of fpirituall things, we
defire to fpeak in the words which the wife-
dome of the holy Ghoft teacheth, and fo we
fhall compare fpirituall words and fpirituall
things together. And therefore it is, though
the Government, whereof we are now to
intreat, fhareth, with other of the like
rank, in the generall nature common to
them and it, and thence may (as it is) truely be called, an Art or
Policy, as civil governments are ftiled : and there be a like parity and proportion of reafon, in regard of the nature of the
work : yet we attend the language of the Apoftle, who, when
he would inftruct *Timothy,* touching the fubject now to be in-

B   t iated

treated of, and furnish him with directions fitting and sufficient thereunto, he terms it, *by knowledge or skill, how to demean himself in the house of God,* 1 Tim.3 15.

Its the knowledge of the duty of some rule that lieth upon him. Thus knowledge how to converse and carry our selves in Church-work, as the effect, leads us by the hand to look to the cause, whence it comes, namely the rule by the staple-precepts whereof, as by the Kings standard, this knowledge hath its being, and is bounded in its operations, the effect thus is expressed, but the cause is implied.

Ordering.] Its the art of ordering the affairs of the Church, For so the Apostle speaks, *Colos.2.5. When I behold your faith and order,* as if he would referre the whole work of the Gospel to these two heads, *Doctrine* and *Discipline.* So much of Religion, as concernes the nature and work of Faith inwardly in the soul towards God and man, that is contained in the first branch, *Faith.* *Order,* which is the second and opposite member, includes the exercise of *Discipline* and censures of the Church, so far, as by rule they are expressed, and concern the rectifying of the carriage of such, who are in confœderation each with other.

This word taken in its native and narrow signification, implies *the right posture of things in their proper places and ranks,* when they are marshalled by the rule of *Method,* according to their especiall precedencies and dependencies they have, each upon other. And here by a Metonimy of the Adjunct, The managing of all Church-Ordinances, according to all the *formes thereof,* as *Ezekiel* speaks, the outgoings thereof, and incomings thereof, with that piety and spirituall prudence, as is most sutable to all, that time, place, and persons, and practises, can require, as dispensed by some, received by others, is understood.

Ch 43.11.

So that, when all offices and ordinances are managed in this manner, in a comely demeanour, the Church is then truely visibly Militant, becomes *terrible like a well ordered army with banners.* But when you loose the ranks, and rout the company, by disorderly administrations, it is the overthrow of the Army, and so of the Church.

House of Christ.] It is the expression of the Apostle in the place formerly quoted, 1 Tim.3.15. *That thou maiest know how to behave thy self in the house of God, which is the Church*

of

of the living God. God is the father of all the family in heaven and earth. Chrift the Head and Redeemer, the holy Ghoft the Comforter.

As the Head, fo the Church which is his Body, admits a double confideration.

Chrift is a Head, { Myfticall, by Spirituall influence.
{ Politicall, by his efpeciall guidance in the means, and difpenfation of his Ordinances.

The Church alfo is a Body. { Myfticall,
{ Politicall.

The myfticall Body is the Church of true Beleevers, who being effectually called by his word and fpirit, by faith yeelding to the call, are fpiritually united unto Chrift, from whom, as from a head, all fpirituall life and motion is communicated on his part, and received on theirs. And this takes up the *Invifible Church*, becaufe the union, and fo the relation, is the truth of it, is inward, and not to be feen by fenfe. *Of ... we do not now inquire.* It is that we doe beleeve. *The Politicall body or Church vifible* refults out of that relation, which is betwixt the profeffours of the faith, when by voluntary confent they yeeld outward fubjection to that government of Chrift, which in his word he hath prefcribed, and as an externall head exercifeth by his word, fpirit, and difcipline, by his ordinances and officers over them, who have yeelded themfelves fubjects to his Headfhip and fupream Authority. For Chrift having humbled himfelf to the death, the curfed death upon the croffe, God the Father hath given him a name, above every thing that is named. Hath given him all things: Hath committed all power into his hand: and hath delegated unto him, the immediate difpenfation of this power. *For the Father judgeth no man*, and by a parity of reafon, in a right fenfe, he calls quickens, rules no man, but hath committed the immediate difpenfation of all to the Sonne : which power he exercifeth invifibly in their hearts by the operations of his fpirit : but exercifeth it vifibly by his ordinances and officers in his Church, as upon his fubjects, who profeffe allegiance and homage to him. So the Apoftle, *Ephef.* 4. *When he afcended up on high, and led captivity captive, he gave gifts to men, fome to be Paftors, fome to be Teachers*, all fet in his Church, and all for the good of his Church.

Phil. 2.9.
Joh. 13.3.
Mat.28.18
Joh.5,22.

And

And as he hath a golden Scepter for the guidance of his ſervants, ſo, as a Judge, he hath an iron rod to break his enemies in pieces like a potters veſſell. *Bring hither mine enemies*, that will not have me *to rule over them, and ſlay them before my face.*

Hence obſerve *obiter* and by the way, that the root of this power lieth firſt in Chriſt, as a Head, and is communicated by vertue of that commiſſion received from the Father. *All power in heaven and earth is given to me*, therefore *Preach and Baptiſe*, *Matth.* 28. 18, 19.

We now ſee the proper and adequate ſubject about which ecclefiaſticall policy is exerciſed, to wit,

The affaires of his houſe,] The things that appertain to the viſible Church, his viſible Kingdome on earth. And to this place appertain the diſputes, touching the difference betwixt Eccleſiaſticall and civil Policy, what kinde of influence they have each into other, together with the tyrannicall uſurpation of that man of ſinne, and the falſe claim that Antichriſt makes to both the ſwords, with all the pretences he deviſeth to ſerve his own turn, and the falſe colours he puts upon his proceedings, when he would allay his cruelty, with a far-fetcht device, as though he did all *in ordine ad ſpiritualia,* and by the colour of that order, he might diſorder and overturn the whole frame of all Kingdomes and commonwealths, if they will not ſtoop to his tyranny and uſurpation.

All thoſe controverſies take here their proper conſideration, as in their proper place. But our intendment being to comprehend things in ſhort, we ſhall wholly leave ſuch tedious diſputes, which would trouble our work, and weary the Reader.

Certain it is, Eccleſiaſticall policy confines it ſelf within the affairs of the Church, as within its proper compaſſe. *My Kingdome,* ſaith our Saviour, *is not of this World;* and ſo the weapons of his Kingdome are ſpirituall weapons, as in the inference our Saviour fully concludes. *If my Kingdom were of this world, then would my ſervants fight,* that I ſhould not be delivered to the Jews. But his Kingdome is not of this world, therefore his ſervants will not fight.

Men ſuſtain a double relation.

As members of the commonwealth they have civil weapons, and in a civil way of righteouſneſſe, they may, and ſhould uſe them.   But

But as members of a Church, their weapons are fpirituall, and the work is fpirituall, the cenfures of the Church are fpirituall, and reach the fouls and confciences of men.

According to the pattern of the Word.] This claufe points where the laws of this Kingdom are to be found, and whence to be fetched. As *Mofes* faw his pattern in the Mount, according to which he was to mold, all things in the Tabernacle : So we have ours left upon record in the Holy Scriptures, unto which we muft not adde, and from which we muft not take any thing. Chrift the King of his Church, and Mafter of his Houfe, he only in reafon, can make laws that are Authenticke for the government thereof.

And here we fhall take leave to ftay a little, and make this ground good before we paffe, becaufe we fhall have fpeciall ufe of it, as a main pillar to bear up the building, of the following difcourfe, againft the cavils of Papifts and Formalifts.

We fhall firft explicate, and then argue.

Church-government then is attended in a double refpect,

Either in regard of the {*Effentialls,* or *Circumftantialls,* of it.

Effentialls required to the compleating of Church-government are, {Partly in the perfons that difpenfe. Partly in the ordinances that are difpenfed.

In the perfons that difpenfe, the kindes of officers that are appointed to that work : the nature, bounds, and limits of their offices, all thefe are effentialls.

The ordinances which thefe are to difpenfe, as preaching, prayer, feals, Church-cenfures, &c. all thefe are to be found in the word, and fhould be fetched from the word: and now under the Gofpel, they are and ought to be the fame ; in all places, amongft all people, at all times, in all fucceeding generations, untill the coming of Chrift.

Media cultus funt immutabilia.

It is not left in the power of perfons, Officers, Churches, nor all ftates in the world, to add, or diminifh, or alter any thing in the leaft meafure. But as God did appoint all in the Old Teftament, and thofe his inftitutions, did endure their Ever (as the Scripture fpeaks) i. untill the coming of Chrift, when the fame power which appointed them, changed them, So in the New Teftament where we are to expect no alteration,

Gen. 17 fui in lo- rum.

Chrift

Chrift the Law-giver he only appoints, none but he can, and he hath made known his will, that he will not change them.

The *Circumftantialls* of Difcipline, as time, place, the carrying on of thefe difpenfations in civill decencies, fuitable to the quality of the things, and conditions of the time, as peace and perfecution: the generall rules of thefe are in the word delivered: but the particular application admits varieties, mutabilities and alterations, according as neceffities or conveniences fhall appear by emergent occafions.

That there is an immutable rule, touching the *effentialls* of difcipline, left in the word, and thence to be fetched, we are now to prove.

1. Argument.

All parts of Gods worfhip are by God alone appointed, in the word revealed, and thence to be fetched.

This is evident from the nature of worfhip, which only proceeds from Gods will, and the appointment of it is his peculiar prerogative. For came it from the will of man, it would be will-worfhip. *Deut.* 12. and laft. Its here true, what God doth not command God doth not accept: It is the charge he laies againft all fuperftitious and falfe devices of men; *They never came into his minde or heart*, and therefore never have his approbation. Who required thefe things? He only knows what will beft pleafe himfelf, and his own will can make beft choice.

But all Offices and Ordinances of Difcipline are parts of Gods Worfhip: being duties required in the fecond command, and thither are to be referred, by the grant of all.

2.

The effentialls ftand, either by the neceffity of precept, and fo immutably required, or elfe they are left arbitrary to the will of man to appoint.

But they are not left arbitrary.

The firft part is evident by the fulneffe of the divifion.

All things fpirituall are either Chriftian duties, or elfe are left to Chriftian liberty.

The fecond part is thus proved.

If it be not in man to inable an Officer to his work, or offices or Ordinances to attain their end: Then it is not in his power

to

to appoint Officer or Ordinance in the Church. For such appointment should be crosse to wisdome in attempting it, and so frustrate in regard of the end, in not attaining it.

But it is not in man to inable to the work, or to make the Ordinance attain its end: because the work is spirituall, and the end supernaturall: And herein lies especially the difference betwixt civill and Ecclesiasticall power, *Dominium* and royall Soveraignty may be seated in the one, *i.e.* in the Commonwealth; because they can communicate power from themselves to others, and inable others to attain civill ends, and to accomplish civill work, and in that respect they are called, κτίσις ανθρωπίνη, A humane Creation. But in the Church there is only *ministerium* received from Christ alone, and therefore they cannot delegate from themselves, and by their own institution any Officer, but only attend the institution of Christ.

There is no man can have his Curate or Vicar, his *Vicarius*, because he is bound, in his own particular, to his place of Ministery: he can appoint none because he can give power to none.

3.

That which is a fundamentall point of Religion, that hath divine Institution, and so becomes immutable, unlesse Christ himself repeal it. For principles of that nature must have divine authority to appoint and to remove.

But Church Discipline is a fundamentall point of Religion. Heb.6. *Laying on of hands, being by a Metonymy of the adjunct* put for Ordination, Ordination one particular, put for the whole of Church Discipline.

4.

If God received this as his peculiar to himself under the Law, To appoint Offices Ordinances in his word according to his will, Then it is unlawfull now for any man to arrogate it: because his soveraignty is as much now as then, his word as perfect, there is no reason which can cast the balance another way.

But this he did take as his peculiar in the Old Testament. *2 Chro.29.25.*

Hence by the way we may lay in a caveat against significant Ceremonies instituted by man in Gods worship, as superstitious,

such

such I mean which are appointed to stir up the dull and dead minde of man to the remembrance of his duty towards God, by some speciall signification, whereby he might be edified.

1.

Becaufe these under this Inftitution are *media cultus*, and are so more efficacious to carry the minde and heart to God, as the Papifts require, and such as all Orthodoxe Divines condemn. Nay if it be by teaching and ftirring towards thefe supernaturall works, as Gods fpirituall worfhip.

Its that which the Lord condemns in Images, *which tell lies.* Its that which the Lord threatens to punifh. *Isa,29.19. That his fear is taught by the preseps of men.*

2.

Becaufe such ceremonies are of the fame kinde and homogeneall with the fignificative part of the actions of the Sacrament, and upon the groud may be faid to have a reall and true efficacy of teaching, which properly is a part of worfhip: fince that part of the Sacrament, which is placed in fignification is fo. Doth Baptifme confecrate the child to God? fo doth the croffe. Doth Baptifme fignify the Covenant betwixt Chrift and the childe? fo doth the Croffe. For its openly faid by the Patrons thereof, *to betoken the ingagement* betwixt Chrift and the child, that he fhall be Chrifts fervant, and fouldier to follow his colours and fight under his banner unto his dying day. And this Image though it hath no tongue to fpeak of its own, yet it fpeaks by this inftituted fignification put upon it and preffed by the power of the Prelates.

3.

Thofe Ceremonies which are fet in the fame rank with Gods own Ceremonies, in regard of their end and ufe, As thofe are truly religious becaufe God is the appointer of them: So thefe muft be fuperftitious, becaufe mans will is the Inftitutour of them: the parity and proportion of reafon holds on both fides.

But fignificant Ceremonies thus inftituted, are of the like nature with fome of Gods own rites. Inftance the Phylacteries. *Numb.15.39,* they were appointed for this end by the Lord, to be remembrancers and admonifhers of the Law to thofe that ufed them, and the fame place thefe Ceremonies fupply, and are ordained for the fame purpofe,

The

The Circumstantials of *Discipline*, as Time, Place, outward Decency and Comelinesse in the managing of Gods Ordinances : these admit of varieties and mutabilities, according to emergent occasions, which alter with the conditions of the Church.

There is a comelines and conveniency of Time and Places of meeting, and manner in their meeting, when the Churches are under persecution, which will be much altered, when the Churches enjoy peace and prosperity, and have Christian Kings and Queens for their nursing Fathers, and nursing Mothers. Yet in the carrying on of these *Circumstantials* according to the minde of Christ, among many other, these Rules lend a common influence, and are of speciall consequence and consideration.

I.

Though there be not, nor in truth can be particular precepts expressed in the Word, that may meet with all the speciall varieties of occurrences in this kinde ; yet there be generall Rules, under the reach whereof, all the particulars will come, and by which they may be regulated, and that without fail. *All must be done comelily and in order*, without rudenes or confusion, *For God is not the God of confusion, as in all the Churches*, 1 Cor. 14. 33. *All must be done to edification*, 1 Cor. 14. 26. *All to Gods glory*, 1 Cor. 10. 31.

2.

All these *Circumstantials* of Time, Place and Decency, they are *common* to things *Civil*, as well as *Sacred*, and serve indifferently and equally to further the usefull administration of both, and therefore cannot be conceived to be any part of religious worship, nor can be ranked within the compasse thereof, by any shew of reason, only the ancient maxime here takes place, *The later Arts useth the work of the former, Ars posterior utitur prioris opere* ; both civil and sacred administrations use these Circumstantials, as issuing from precedent Arts, and so put forth their own actions to the best advantage, for the attaining of their own ends. As each man may meet with instances many, by easie attendance.

There must be a right understanding of the meaning of the words, and so a *Grammaticall Analysis* of the phrase, where the promises or commands are expressed, before either our faith can believe the one, or a gracious, humble heart make choice aright of the other, and obey it. Both *beleeving* and *obeying* are religious

ous actions, and both suppose the use and work of *Grammar*, and so of *Logick*, about the promises and commands, and yet no man, that hath the exercise of reason about him, will say, that either *Grammar* or *Logick Analysis* are *religious* actions, much leffe religious worship.

3.

The *Will of no man*, neither Magistrate in the Common-wealth, nor Officer or Officers in the Churches, is the *rule* either of commanding or forbidding *things indifferent*. For if their wils were the rule, they could not erre in commanding or forbidding : for the rule cannot erre. They were not to give an account for those their commands, nor could be punished for any miscarriage in them. Then also, the will of the Inferiour were absolutely bound to yeeld obedience thereunto, and that without either queftioning or examining the nature of it. Yea blinde obedience would by this means be not only allowed, but of neceffity enjoyned. Nor could the Inferiour fin, in what ever he did in subjecting himfelf to the directions of the Superiour in fuch indifferent things. All which are contrary to common fenfe.

4.

The determination of indifferent things, either absolutely to be attended, or abfolutely to be laid afide, when there is no preponderations or neceffity to caft the balance either way, is *beyond* Warrant ; becaufe it thwarts the nature of the things, and that meerly out of the pleafure of the Impofer, which is not a rule to go by, fince God by rule hath left thefe either to be done, or not done, as occafions are prefented.

5.

Appointment and injunctions of things indifferent, which are either unprofitable, and have no good in their ufe, or be but fo far prejudiciall, as that they occafion a ftop in a Chriftian courfe upon any juft ground : Such appointments are to be repealed as unlawfull 1. For if Gods own *Ceremonies* were to be removed, *becaufe unprofitable*, then much more ours, *Heb. 7.18*. 2. If we muft anfwer for *idle words*, then for *idle Ceremonies*. 3. Things indifferent, when they are ufed, not in fubordination to help forward morall duties, their ufe is unlawfull. For herein lieth their ufe and good, that they may be in way to lend a lift to a higher end. But when they are unprofitable or prejudiciall in the fenfe before expreffed, then they are not in fubordination

nation to help forward the morall. *Ergo.* 4. That which crosseth the Place and Office of the Governour, that he must not doe or maintain : But to injoyn any thing that is unprofitable, is against his place, for his Office is to *rule for their good*, Rom. 13. 4. But unprofitable things are not such.

CHAP. II.

The Constitution of a visible Church *in the Causes thereof*: *The Efficient and Matter.*

THis *visible Church*, the subject adequate of our Enquiry, is to be attended in a double regard,

either in respect of the $\begin{cases} \text{Constitution, or} \\ \text{Gubernation of it.} \end{cases}$

The Church in her Constitution is considered two waies,

as *Totum* $\begin{cases} \textit{Essentiale,} \\ \text{Or} \\ \textit{Integrale.} \end{cases}$

As *totum Essentiale* or *Homogeneum,* look at it as in the first causes, out of which she exists, and comes to be gathered, and this is called, *Ecclesia prima.*

This Church hath the right of electing and choosing Officers, and when these are set in it, it becomes *totum Organicum.* Ames. *med.l.*1.*c.*33.18. The Corporation is a true body, when it hath no *Major,* nor other Officers, which happily she yearly chooseth.

We now come to enquire of the *visible Church in her first constitution and gathering.*

And in the handling of this, we shall take into consideration such speciall Questions, wherein there appears any difference betwixt us, and our Reverend and very learned Brethren, desirous to propound things, wherein difficulties yet appear unto us, hoping some further evidence may be given for the manifestation of the truth, which we only seek, if we know what we seek : and therefore would live and learn ; only while we thus beleeve, we thus speak.

The

The causes of a visible Church, which will make most for the clearing of the subject we have in hand,

are the { *Efficient*, As also the { *Materiall*, and *Formall*.

Of the Efficient.

Concerning the *Principall cause* and Institutour of a visible Church, there is a common concurrence of all sides, so far as I can reade, and therefore I shall ease the Reader of all large discourse in this behalf.

It shall be enough to point out the truth, as it is expressed in Scripture : namely, The institution of the Church issues from the speciall appointment of *God the Father, thorow the Lord Jesus Christ*, as the head thereof, *by the holy Ghost*, sent and set on work for that end. So the Apostle speaks most pregnantly and plainly, *Heb.3.31. For this man* (meaning *Christ*) *was counted Worthy of more honour then Moses, inasmuch as he that hath builded the house, hath more honour then the house. Christ is set over the Church*, which is, *the house of God, as the Sonne, Moses as a servant.* He the master-builder, *Moses* as an Inferiour and under-workman. And *verf.4. For every house is builded by some man, but he that buildeth all things is God.* This *ALL* is to be referred to the things that went before, to wit, the *things of the house.*

What ever belongs to the Church hath God in Christ the Authour of it. And hence in the old Testament it was given in charge to *Moses*, that as *he saw* all presented before him *in the Mount*, in a lively manner, so he must be cautelous and conscientious to hold himself to that patern, not to swerve an hairs breadth there-from, or to adde any thing of his own devising. And hence our Saviour claims this as his prerogative royall, *Mat. 16. Upon this rock I will build my Church.* It is his house, and he knows his own minde, and therefore he only will fashion it thereunto. And from hence it is,that in the time wherein *Ezekiel* would limme out, and that unto the life, the *Temple* to be erected in the *new Testament*, he there laies out all the particulars by Gods speciall appointment ; The *Outgoings* and *Incomings, Forms, Fashions, Laws* thereof, and the *Ordinances* thereof.

Touching *the Inferiour helping cause*, viz, *The Civil Magistrate*, how

As M R. acknow. ledgeth l, 1 p.10, Ezek.43. 11.

how farre he may be said to have a hand in the erecting of Chur-ches, It is that which hath exercised the heads and pens of the most judicious, and is too large for this place, and our purpose, we willingly passe it by, being not yet perswaded that the chief Magistrate should stand a Neuter, and tolerate all Religions.

Of the Matter.

Proceed we to make enquiry of the *Matter*, and there (though it hath not so much Art in it, yet because it hath more, and indeed more evidence, in regard of all, to whom we addresse this our enquiry; sith it concerns all, who seek the good of Church-fellowship, as all need it, if they were worthy to share therein. Our first Conclusion is negative.

Conclusion I.

Parish precincts, or the abode and dwelling within the bounds and liberties of such a place, doth not give a man right, or make him matter fit for a visible Congregation.

Reason 1. *No civil rule can properly convey over an Ecclesiasticall right.* The rules are *in specie* distinct, and their works and ends also, and therefore cannot be confounded.

Civil power hath a *nourishing* and *preserving* faculty of Ecclesiasticall Orders, Officers, and their severall operations. *Kings shall be nursing Fathers,* &c. But in their *proper constitutions,* they cannot meet. *Imperare* and *praedicare* are not compatible, hath been a ruled case, admitting no contradiction in an ordinary way: one is compleat, and hath all the causes without the other, and therefore one doth not receive his constitution in whole or in part from the other. Civil power may compell Ecclesiasticall persons to do, what they ought in their offices, but doth not confer their Offices upon them. The Kingdom of Christ is spirituall, and not of this world. That Proposition then is beyond controul. The second is open to experience.

But the taking up an abode or dwelling in such a place or precincts is by the rule of policy and civility. A man hath it by inheritance from his parents, or purchaseth it by his money, or receives it by gift or exchange. *Ergo,* This can give him no Ecclesiasticall right to Church-fellowship.

Reas. 2. That right which any man hath in Church-fellowship, Excommunication out of a Church can, nay doth take away. For Excommunication is, according to the intent of the Word, The

cutting

cutting off from all Church-communion : and what ever right before he had in his admiffion, is now difanulled by his Excommunication. *Let him be as an Heathen*, Mat.18.

But Excommunication doth not, nor can *take away a mans civil right* to the houfe and land, the civil priviledges he doth poffeffe, or remove him from the right of his habitation, civil office or authority, he is invefted in.

Ergo, *That is no Ecclefiaftical right.*

Reaf.3. If Parifh Precincts fhould have right to Church-fellowfhip, then Atheifts, Papifts, Turks and profane ones, who are enemies to the truth and Church, yea men of ftrange Nations and languages, who neither know, nor be able to do the duties of Church members, fhould be fit matter for a Church, becaufe they have abode in fuch places . yea thofe fhould have right to whom Chrift hath denied right, *Revel.*21.27.

Much more might here be added, but that the tenet is fo groffe, that I fuppofe any, ferioufly judicious, will fee the errour of it.

We fhall come nearer home then, and our

2^d Conclufion is,

Vifible Saints only are fit Matter appointed by God to make up a vifible Church of Chrift.

The terms fhall be, 1. *Opened.* 2. *The Queftion ftated.* 3.*The Conclufion proved.*

Saints as they are taken in this controverfie, and in the currant expreffions of Scripture, which look this way, and fpeak to this fubject (*Saints at Corinth, Saints at Philippi, at Rome, in Cafars houfe*) were members of the Churches, comprehending the Infants of confœderate believers under their Parents Covenant, according to 1 *Cor.*7.14. and fuch conftant expreffions of Saintfhip do intimate, that either *they were fuch*, or at leaft conceived to be *fuch in view* and *in appearance*. I fay in *appearance*: for when the Scripture fo terms and ftiles men, we muft know that *Saints* come under a double apprehenfion. *Some are fuch* according to *Charity. Some* according *to truth. Saints* according to *charity* are fuch, who in their practice and profeffion (if we look at them in their courfe, according to what we fee by experience, or receive by report and teftimony from others, or laftly, look we at their expreffions) *they favour fo much, as though they had been with Jefus. From all which*, as farre as *rationall charity* directed *by rule* from the *Word*, a man cannot but conclude, That *there*

may

may be some seeds of some Spirituall work of God in the soul. These we call *visible Saints* (leaving *secret things to God*) in our view, and according to the reach of rationall charity, which can go no further, then to hopefull fruits. We say and *hope*, and so are *bound* to *conceive they are Saints*: though such be the secret conveyances, and hidden passages of hypocrisie, that they may be gilt, not gold, seemingly such only, not savingly, known to God and their own hearts, not known to others. So *Judas*, *Demas*, *Simon Magus*, *Ananias*, &c. And therefore our Saviour proceeds with such, not *as God* who knows the heart, but in a *Church-way*, as those who judge the tree by the fruit. *De occultu non judicat Ecclesia*, That which the Church doth not see, it cannot censure. *Some mens sins go before, & some come after*, 1 *Tim*. 5. 24.

The STATE then of the *QUESTION* is this, Persons, though they be hypocrites inwardly, yet if their conversations and expressions, be such, so blamelesse and inoffensive, that according to *reason* directed by the *Word*, we cannot conclude, but in *charity* there *may be, and is some speciall spirituall good* in them; *These are fit matter of a visible Church* appointed and allowed by Christ : and that for these Reasons.

Reason 1.

From *the nature of a visible Church* rightly constituted,

It is truly stiled, and truly judged by Scripture light to be the *visible body of Christ*, over whom he is a *Head*, by *Politicall Government* and guidance, which he lends thereunto, 1 *Cor*, 12. 12. And that it is a visible politick body, appears quite thorow the whole Chapter, but especially, *v.* 27, 28. Because in *that Church God sets Orders and Officers, Some Apostles, Teachers, Helpers, Governments*. The like to this, *Ephes*. 4. 12, 13. Where these *Officers* are, it is supposed there be *visible* concurrences of many *Saints* consenting, both to *choose* such, and to *subject* unto such being chosen. Whence the Argument proceeds,

> *The members of Christs body are fit alone to be members of a true Church*, because that is the body of Christ, *ex concessis*.
> *But only visible Saints, who according to the rules of reasonable charity may be conceived to have some speciall good in them, are only members of Christs body.*

For to have a member, which nor doth, nor ever did receive any power or vertuall impression of any operation in the kinde of
it

it from the head, is not onely againſt reaſon, but againſt that *reference and correſpondence, which the members have to the head.* Now viſible Saints onely, according to former explicati-on, can be ſaid by the rules of reaſonable charity, to have ſome vertuall influence of ſome ſpirituall operation from Chriſt as a Head.

Therefore *Such onely are members of a Church.*

Reaſon. 2.

Thoſe are fit to be members of Chriſts Church, that are ſub-jects in Chriſts Kingdome.

The *Church is the viſible kingdome* in which *Chriſt* reigns, by the ſcepter of his word and ordinances, and the execution of diſcipline. *To whomſoever he is a Head,* over them he *will be King.* He is our *King*; He is our *Lawgiver.* The *Church* is his *Houſe,* and he is *Maſter* and *Ruler* of it. They who carry themſelves, in *profeſſed rebellion,* they are *Traitors,* not ſubjects. The members of the *Body* are under the *motion* and gaidance of the *Head. Wolves* and *Cancers* are contrary to it. Members are in *ſubordination,* Wolves and Cancers are in *oppoſition* to the Head.

Iſa.33.23.

But viſible Saints (as formerly deſcribed) *are onely ſub-jects in this kingdome.*

Chriſt is the *King of Saints* (not of drunkards and whore-mongers, Athieſts, *&c.*) they alone proclaim ſubjection in their practiſe : They onely attend to know and doe the will and com-mand of God, or in caſe they ſwerve aſide, and be carried un-awares and unwittingly into conſpiracie, yet are they willing to ſee, ready to yeeld, and come in again. But ſuch, who cry, *hail Maſter, kiſſe Chriſt* and *betray him :* that in words pro-feſſe the truth, but in *deeds deny* it, and are to *every good work* *reprobate, Sonnes of Belial,* who can bear no yoke, but *break all cords, and caſt all commands behinde their backs,* theſe are *convicted rebells,* but are not *ſubjects* of Chriſts kingdome.

As a *Generall* of the field, he will overpower theſe, and *deſtroy* them *as* his *enemies,* but not *govern* them as *leige people,* and therefore he profeſſeth to ſuch as ſent after him, that they would not have him to rule over them, that they were his enemies. *Bring hither mine enemies, and ſlay them before mine eyes.*

Reaſon. 3.

If theſe who be viſible Saints, be not thoſe that are only fit to be members,

members, then those who are not visible Saints, that is such who in the judgement of rationall charity, are gracelesse persons for the present, and give up themselves to the swinge of their distempers, they may be members.

The consequence is beyond dispure, for contradicents divide the breadth of being.

> *If visible Saints onely be not ;*
> *Then non-visible may be.*

But this draws many absurdities with it : For then such who to the judgement of charity are *members of the devil*, may be conceived *members of Christ*. *Those*, who to the eye of reason, are *servants to sin*, may be *servants of righteousnesse* and of Christ : and those, who are under the *kingdom of darknesse* by the rule of reasonable charity, by *the same rule*, at *the same time*, they may be judged under the *kingdome of light*. Those may be counted fit to *share in the covenant* and the priviledges thereof, as Sacraments and Church society, who *are strangers from the covenant, and without God in the world*. All which are absurdities, that common sense will not admit.

If it be replied, that all these may be verified of cunning hypocrites not yet discovered.

I answer : The Argument leaves no place for the appearance of such an objection: for the terms in open expression are pointed directly against such, that in the judgement of charity were not Saints : and then the difference is exceeding wide. *Those that are darknesse*, and the *servants of sin inwardly*, may to the *view of charity* seem to *be light*, and servants of Christ *outwardly*, and yet in *charity* be led by light. But that he who in his outward practice should appear to be a slave to sin, and subject to the kingdome of darknesse, should yet be conceived to be a servant to God and subject to his kingdome : Surely *charity* must not onely pluck out her eies to see by anothers spectacles, but loose eies and spectacles and all, and cease to be *charity* ; yea be turned into *fury* and madnes.

Reason. 4.

Those who by God are *excluded* from *his covenant* and medling with *that, as unfit, they* are *not fit* to have *communion* with the *Church*: For to *that* all the *holy things of God* do in an especiall manner *appertain*.

Its *Gods house,* and there all Gods treasury lies : The *keyes of*
the

the kingdome are given to them: To them all *the oracles,* ordinances and priviledges do belong, *&c.*

But *those* who *hate to be reformed,* and *caft away his commands,*
God profeffeth, *they have nothing to do to take his cove-*
nant into their mouth, Pfal. 50 16,17.

To this Mr *R.* l.t.p.116. *anfw.* 2. things.

1. "*That the wicked are forbidden in cafe, fo lang as they hate*
"*to be reformed, but not fimply : but this hinders not, but that*
"*they may be ordinary hearers, and fo members of a vifible*
"*Church.*

To which I fhall crave leave to *reply* feverall things.

1. The anfwer, in the 1. branch of it yeelds the caufe, and
grants all that was defired or intended, namely ; *while they hate*
to be reformed they have no title, which is all that is ftriven for :
for if they come to fee their fin, and to reform their evil waies,
and give in evidence of their *godly forrow* and *repentance,* then
they are no longer haters of reformation, but true reformers and
repentants in the judgement of charity, and then *vifible Saints,*
and fit to be made materialls in the temple, when the rubbifh
and unhewnneffe of their diftempers are taken away. But
while they remain haters, they have no title, *ex conceffis.* Therefore *that while,* they are not vifible Saints ; which is all the
argument required, and is now yeelded.

Whereas its added, "*that it hence follows not, that they*
"*fhould not be ordinary hearers of the word.*

Anfwer : It is true, it was never intended nor inferred ;
therefore the argument is untouched. For we fay, as you, it doth
not follow, nor need be required, for help either of the reafon
or the queftion. For let it be fuppofed, they may fo doe, nay
for ought we know, they fhould fo doe, and we yet have what
we would.

It is yet further added, "*That being ordinary hearers and fo*
"*members of a Church :* Such an expreffion I will not now inquire how neer the caufe it comes, I cannot but yet conceive, it is
far from the truth.

1. If ordinary *hearing* make a man a member, then *excommu-*
nicate perfons, who are cut off from memberfhip, are members,
for they may ordinarily hear ; *ex conceffit.*

2. Then *Turks, Papifts,* all forts of contemners of the
truth, *Indians, Infidells,* fhall be members, for they may
be,

be, and in many places are ordinary hearers.

3. Then in publique cities, where severall congregations meet, at severall houres, *one* and the *same* man may be an ordinary hearer in them a'l, and so a man may be a member of three or four congregations.

The second thing Mr R. answers, is, "*That this argument nothing concludes against them, because such adulterers, and slanderers, which are forbid to take Gods law into their mouthes, are to be cast out: but the question is, if they be not cast out, Whether the Church for that be no true Church.*

To which I say, The first part yeelds the cause again, for if they should be cast out, there is no reason they should be received or taken in, nor have they right thereunto, nor be they fit matter for that work.

The second clause doth wholly misse the mark again. For the question is, touching the *constitution* of a Church, of what matter it should be made, It is not touching *separation* from a Church: for the errour is in taking in such as be not fit. So that the argument is yet unanswered, yea by these answers, further confirmed.

So much may serve for the confirmation of the conclusion for the present, more shall be added in an opportune place.

But before we leave the conclusion, we shall make some *inferences* from it, which may further help us in our proceedings and purpose in hand. Something hence may be collected for the discovery of sundry *mistakes* in the *Separatists*, wherein they go *aside* from the truth. Something observed, for *to clear their* way, wherein they go along with it.

Inference. I.

If *visible Saints* be *fit matter* for to make a Church, *Then* Church *fellowship* presupposeth them to be *such*, but properly doth not *make* them *such*.

Inference. 2.

And hence, such *mistakes* in *judgement* or *practice* that do *not hinder* men from *being visible Saints*, doe not *unfit men* from *being members* of a Church.

Inference. 3.

Hence, the *holding* of the *visible Churches in England* to be *true Churches* (suppose it were an *errour*, which *it is not*) doth not *hinder* men from being *fit matter* for a visible Church.

Infe-

Inference. 4.

Hence laftly, the *not being* in a *Church*, doth *not hinder private* Chriftian *communion.*

The two laft inferences, are the *Tenets* of thofe of the *Separation*, not onely extreamly *rigid*, but very *unreafonable.* For if they be fit matter for publique communion, they are much more fit for private: But men are or fhould be vifible Chriftians before they come into Church fellowfhip, and are thereby fitted for it, and therefore much more fitted for private communion.

Something alfo may be obferved *to clear the way* where *they go along with the truth.* Namely,

Hence, They who hold *vifible Saints* in the judgement *of charity* to be fit Matter, though they be not inwardly fanctified, cannot in reafon be thought to maintain *onely fuch, that be effectually called, juftified, and fanctified,* to be the *onely matter* of a rightly-conftituted Church.

And therefore I could have heartily wifhed, that Mr *Rcut.* would not have difputed againft that which they freely and profefledly grant, to wit, " That *hypocrites, becaufe their falfenes* " *is coloured and covered over with appearances of piety, and fo* " *cannot be cenfured (as not difcovered) may be received into* " *Church communion, without the breach of any rule, becaufe* " *the Church therein goeth according to the rule of charity, being* " *bound to hope all to be good* (upon grounds which fhall be af-" terwards laid) *which reafon inlightned by rule cannot prove to* " *be bad.* This is yeelded and therefore need not to have been proved.

But the pinch *of the difference* lieth in this,

Whether fuch as walk in a way of profannelfe, or remain pertinacioufly obftinate in fome wickednelfe, though otherwife profefling and practifing the things of the Gofpel, have any allow-arce from Chrift, or may be counted *fit matter,* according to the terms of the Gofpel, to *conftitute a Church.*

This is that which *is controverted,* and fhould have been e-victed by argument. There is no colour for fuch a confequence : If *hypocrites* be received into the Church, according to the rule of rationall charity and allowance from God, Then may *profane* perfons alfo.

It is true, The expreffions of *fome* of our *brethren,* as thofe alfo of the *Separation,* are fomewhat narrow at the firft fighe,

and

and feem to require exactnes in the higheſt ſtrain : yet were they but candidely interpreted by the received principles, according to which they are known to proceed, they would carry a fair conſtruction, to any brotherly conceiving : of this I ſpeak, be-cauſe I doe obſerve, and I cannot but profeſſe I doe obſerve it with trouble and grief, that Mr *R.* a man of ſuch learning and ſharpneſſe of judgement, and in other things, and at other times of pious moderation, ſhould yet ſo commonly, and frequently, and if I miſtake not, without occaſion offered many times, load the expreſſions of thoſe, againſt whom he writes, with ſuch a ſenſe, that their own grounds, to his own knowledge, do directly oppoſe, and their own words, by an eaſie interpretation, may ad-mit a contrary meaning.

I ſhall conſtrain my ſelf therefore upon ſo juſt an occaſion, to indeavour to clear this coaſt, that if it be the will of God, I may for ever ſilence *miſconceivings*, or *miſinterpretations* in this caſe : and therefore I ſhall labour,

1. To *lay out the meaning* of thoſe of the *Separation*, out of their *own Words.*

2. Punctually to expreſſe, *how farre rationall charity*, rectified by the word, will *goe*, in giving *allowance* to the *viſibility of Saints.*

3. I hope I ſhall make it appear, that We require no *more Saint-ſhip* to make men *fit matter for a viſible Church*, then Mr *R.* his *own grounds* will give us leave.

1.

1. The *minde* and *meaning* of thoſe *our brethren of the Sepa-ration* is written in ſo great characters, that he who runs may reade it, if he will, nor can he readily miſtake, unleſſe he will. Mr *Ainſworth* againſt Mr *Bernard.* p.174. *Saints by calling are the onely matter of a viſible Church* : yet, with all We hold, *that many are called but few choſen.* Hence he cannot hold, that they are true beleevers, nor truely converted, or truely ſancti-fied, for then they ſhould have been all choſen and elected, which in open words he doth peremptorily deny. The *ſenſe* then can *be no other* but this, That *Saints by externall and outward cal-ling* are fit matter of a Church, for had they been *inwardly called* they had alſo been *elected.*

This being the meaning of their Tenet, if Mr *R.* be pleaſed to look into his firſt book, *ch.9.p.100.* he will finde that he there gives his reader to underſtand, that he and Mr *Ainſworth* are of the

the fame minde. For he laies it as a firm corner-ftone, the firft conclufion that he propounds, for the true underftanding of the true conftitution of a Church. "*Saints by externall call-*"*ing are the true members of a visible Church.* Thefe are *his* words, and Mr *Ainfworths* are the *very fame*, onely *he* faies the *true* matter, Mr *Ainfw.* faies the *onely matter;* wherein there can be no odds in regard of the fubftance of the thing intended ; for *true matter* is that which now is in-quired after, and if all other matter befide them is falfe, then they are the *onely matter,* in truth, of the Church.

Hear we Mr *Robinfon,* A man pious and prudent, expreffe his own opinion, in his own words, who thus, *Juftific. of Separ.* pag. 112. propounds the queftion, and the ftate of it betwixt him and Mr *Bernard.* "*Before I come to the point in contro-*"*verfie, I will lay down two cautions* (faith he) *for the preven-*"*ting of errour in the fimple, and of cavelling, in fuch as defire to*"*contend. 1. It muft be confidered, that here the queftion is,*"*about the visible or externall Church, which is by men difcern-*"*able, and not of that Church, which is internall and invisible,*"*which onely the Lord knoweth, we speak here of visible and ex-*"*ternall holines onely, whereof men may judge, and not of that*"*which is within and hid from mens eyes. For we doubt not, but*"*the pureft Church upon earth may confift of good and bad in*"*Gods eye, of fuch that are truely fanctified and faithfull, and*"*of fuch, who have onely for a time, put on the outfide and vi-*"*zard of fanctity, which the Lord will in due time pluck off,*"*though in the mean time, mans dim fight cannot pierce*"*through it.*

So that we have expreffions full. The Church confifts of fome who are faithfull and fincere hearted : Some counterfet and falfe hearted. Some really good, fome really bad, onely thofe who appear fo bad and vile fhould not be accepted. And doth not Mr R. fay the fame ?

In the fame place Mr *Robinf.* addes. "*I defire it may be re-*"*membred, that the queftion between Mr Bern. and me, is, a-*"*bout the true and naturall members, whereof the Church is*"*orderly gathered and planted, and not about the decaied and*"*degenerate eftate of the Church and members. For we know*"*that naturall children may become rebellious, the faithfull*"*city a harlot, the filver droffe, and the wine corrupt with water,*
"*the*

" *the whole vine so planted, whose plants were all naturall, may*
" *degenerate into the plants of a strange vine.*

The expreſſions are ſo plain that there needs no explication, nor can a man, that will deal candidly, miſtake, unleſſe one ſhould ſet himſelf on purpoſe to pervert a writers meaning.

He that holds ſuch may be received into the Church, who may degenerate from ſubjection and obedience, to rebellion, from faithfulneſſe to falſeneſſe, from a profeſſion pure and ſincere in appearance and approbation of men, to a rotten, profane and unſavoury carriage : He muſt needs hold, that falſe, counterfeit, and hollow hearted hypocrites may be members of a Congregation.

When therefore we meet with ſuch phraſes printed and recorded, *Onely the Saints, faithfull, called, and sanctified are to be members of a Congregation*, He muſt needs be exceeding weak, or exceeding wilfull, that will not eaſily and readily give ſuch a conſtruction as this, *Namely, Persons visibly, externally ſuch to the judgement of Charity, not alwaies really and internally ſuch by the powerfull impreſſion of Gods grace.* Let therefore ſuch miſtakes be for ever ſilenced in the mindes and mouths of ſuch as are wiſe hearted and moderate. We have *thus cleared the expreſſions* of our *Brethren of the Separation.*

WE ſhall *now punctually expreſſe our own apprehenſions,* and with as much openneſſe and ſimplicity as our ſhallowneſſe can attain unto, *puntiulus ergo agamus.*

1. It is *not the eminency of holineſſe*, that we look at in the entertainment of members, but *the uprightnes of heart :* Its not the *ſtrength* and growth of grace, but the *trueth* that we attend. *Rom.*14.1. *Heb.*5.13.

2. *This truth* we know is, and may be accompanied with many *failings and infirmities*, which more or leſſe may break out and appear to the apprehenſion of the judicious.

3. *The judgement* of this truth of *grace*, (as clouded and covered with failings,) is *not certain and infallible*, either to *Church* or *Christian. Philip* was deceived by *Simon Magus, Paul miſjudged of Demas*, all the Diſciples conceived as well of *Judas*, as of themſelves, though he was a *Thief* (and bare the bag) nay though a *Devill* in Gods righteous ſentence which he paſſed upon him. *Joh.*6. & laſt. The Sum is, *The heart of man is*
deceitfull

deceitfull above all things, and *desperately* wicked, *who can know it?* The Lord himfelf takes that as his place, *I the Lord try the heart, and fearch the reins*. Ier. 17. 9

4. This *judgement*, ther, of others *fincerity*, *eft tantum opinio, non fcientia*, and therefore the moft difcerning may be deceived therein, they may proceed according to the *rules of Charity*, and yet not paffe a fentence according to the *reality of truth*.

5. *Charity* is not *cenforius* yet *judicious* (fhe wants neither eyes nor watchfullneffe) *hopes all*, and *beleeves all things*, that are *hopefull* or *beleeveable*, 1 Cor 13 6. ever yeelds and inclines to *the better part*, unleffe *evidence* come to the *contrary*, when fhe hath not ground fufficient to prove an evill. She conceives her felf bound to caft the ballance the other way, and to believe there is *fome good* (*take it in fubjecto capaci whereof now we fpeak*) As in the eye, there muft be either fight or blindeneffe : So in the foul there muft be either *fome* meafure of *grace*, or elfe *habituall wickedneffe*, or that we call *a graceleffe* condition.

If *Love* directed by the *rules of reafon and religion* hath not *fufficient evidence* of the one, fhe *believes the other*. and in probabilities, where the weight of the arguments fal's, love falls that way, and fhe hath warrant fo to do, and by that means her perfwafion comes to be poifed.

6. The *grounds* of *probabilities* by which *charity* is poifed according to rule, are either taken from the *practice* or from *the knowledge* of the party.

The way and ground of our proceeding according to both may be expreffed in this *propofition*.

He that profeffing the faith, lives not in the neglect of any known duty, or in the commiffion of any known evill, and hath fuch a meafure of knowledge as may in reafon let in Chrift into the foul, and carry the foul to him Thefe be grounds of probabilities, by which charity poifed according to rule may and ought to conceive, there be fome beginnings of fpirituall good. I fhall explicate both in a word.

1. *He muft not live in a fin*] Its *not having* but *living in fin* : not to be furprifed and taken afide with a diftemper, but to trade in it, is that we here attend. And it muft be *known fin*] alfo, Such, to wit, whereof a man is *informed* and convinced

by

by the power of the word, and the evidence of reason, otherwise sincerity may stand with a continued course in an unknown
corruption, as the fathers did continue in poligamy. But he
that commits some grosse evill, and expresseth no repentance
for it, or after conviction persists in the practise of known wickednesse: rationall charity accounts such *workers of iniquity,*
evill doers, *such as be of the world,* and he *in wickednesse,* and
by *this the children of the Devil, are known from the children*
of God, He that hates his Brother, and doth unrighteousnesse.
In a word, such, if they were under the discipline of Christ, would
be counted pertinacious and should be cast out of a Congregation, therefore should not be received into it.

1 Joh. 3, 8.
& 5 19.
& 3. 10.
2 Tim. 3.
5.

2. *There must be so much knowledge as may let in Christ into*
the soul, and lead the soul to him] for there is a breadth of ignorance in some, like a dungeon so dark and loathsome, that reasonable charity will readily conclude there *can be no grace:*
Isa. 27. 11. *It is a people that have no understanding: there-*
fore he that made them will not save them: Without understan-
ding the minde is not good.

And in this sense and according to this explication, we
do directly deny that proposition of M^r. *Rutt. lib. 2. pag.*
259.

"*This Proposition is false* (saith he) *Those only we are to*
"*admit to the visible Church, whom we conceive to be Saints,*
"*and are in the judgement of charity perswaded they are*
"*such.*

This proposition, in the meaning formerly mentioned, we
say, is true; and we require no more Saintship to make persons
members of a visible Church, then M^r. R. *his own grounds* will
give us leave and allowance to do.

It is one principle maintained by M^r. R. *that profession* and
baptisme doe *constitute a member of a visible Church.*
lib. 2, p. 25.

Whence I *Reason.*

What is required of a man of years to fit him in the judgement
of the Chuch for Baptisme, that and so much is required
to make him a member.

But visible holinesse (ut supra) *is required to fit a man of*
years to be baptized.

The consequence admits no deniall, because to be baptized
and

and to be admitted a member, infer each other.

The *assumption* is proved by the constant and received practice of *John the Baptist*, Mat.3.5.6.

When *Jerusalem* and *Judea*, Scribes, people and Souldiers came to be baptised, *they confessed their sinnes*, ver. 6. It was *such a confession*, as amounted to *repentance*, for the Baptist so interprets it : *Bring forth fruits worthy repentance and amendment of life*, verse.7.8. and their own words evidence as much, *Luke.*3.56. *What shall we do?* The advice of the Apostle requires as much. *Repent and be baptized*, Acts.2.38. and the works of this Repentance, and the aim of Baptisme imports as much. For the remission of sinne doth call for such competent knowledge of Christ, and of remission of sins in him, that they may make way for the sight of the need of a Saviour, and also of going to him.

Again 2. when M*r*.*R*.thus writes,*lib2.p.99*, "*The ignorants and simple ones among the Papists,have not rejected the Gospel obstinately in respect it was never revealed to them,yet the simple ignorance of points principally fundamentall makes them a non-Church.*

Whence I *Reason* thus.

That *Ignorance which maketh persons to be no Church, that will hinder a person from being a true member* of a Church.

But there is a *simple ignorance of points fundamentall that makes people a non-Church*, by his own confession.

Therefore, by his grant, there is an Ignorance, that will keep a man from being a member of a true Church. and there is no point more fundamentall, then Christ to be the foundation stone, laid by God, whereon our faith and we must be built.

A Third ground we take from M*r*.*R*. is p.196.*l*.2. where he hath these words. *Faith to speak properly doth give us right to the seals,and to speak accurately,a visible profession of the Faith doth not give a man right to the seals, but only it doth notifie and declare to the Church that the man hath right to the seals, because he beleeves, and that the Church may lawfully give them to him.*

Whence I *Reason*.

That

That profeffion which muft notifie to the Church, that a perfon is a true beleever, that muft notifie THAT HE HATH TRUE GRACE.

But the profeffion that M.R. *requires, muft notifie to the Church that a perfon is a true beleever.*

And if it notifie thus true faith, it muft prefent fuch grounds of probability to charity rectified by the rules of reafon and religion, that they will caft and carry the fcales of a mans judgement that way, and the evidences of grace to a charitable and reafonable confideration will overweigh all the evidences that come in competition or comparifon with them, otherwife they cannot notifie a party to be a beleever, but fway judicious charity to the contrary fide.

3. Conclufion,

Churches conftituted of fit matter may be corrupted by the breaking forth of fcandals, and peftered with fcandalous, perfons which may fo far be tolerated, untill in a judiciall way, the cenfures of the Church be exercifed upon them, according to the rule of Chrift, and they thereby reformed or elfe removed and cut off from the body.

There be *three branches* in the conclufion, which hold forth evidence of truth at the firft fight, and therefore we fhall not ftay long upon proof.

That *Churches rightly conftituted may foon be corrupted,*] the Scriptures are pregnant which teftifie it, and experience is fo plain, it is paft gainfaying, at *Corinth, Galatia, Sardis, Laodicea,* &c. And above all, this is to be feen in the *Church of the Jews,* the canker of falfeneffe in doctrine, and corruption in manners, had fo far eaten into the very *effence* of the Church, *Hof.* 2. 2 9. that the Lord threatned her to give her *a bill of divorce,* and to caft her out of his fight as not his wife.

2. Yet in fuch declining times, when difeafes grow deadly, there is allowed, and *a toleration of neceffity muft be fo far granted, untill* Juridice *by a judiciall proceeding the evil be examined, the parties convinced, cenfures applied for Reformation*]For the Ordinances of Chrift and rules of the Gofpel ferve, not only for the *conftitution* of a Church, but for the *prefervation* of it. That is the main fcope of our Saviour his government: firft, to gain a finner if it may be, *for he came not to condemn*
                                                                    t'e

the World (men can condemn themfelves faft enough) *but to fave it,* and the cenfures of the Church are fufficient to recover the fick and defeafed, as well as to nourifh the found.

And hence our Saviour requires time of triall, if they may be healed, and untill that be over, they muft be tolerated. Cutting off is only ufed when things come to extremity. *If he will not hear, let him be as an Heathen,* &c. Therefore had he heard and fubmitted to the cenfure of the Church, and been gained thereby to repentance and reformation, there had needed no further proceeding.

But in cafe they prove incorrigeable and irrecoverable by the phyfick ufed, they are then to be abandoned. *Purge out the old leaven,* 1 Cor. 5. caft out fuch an one.

And hence it is evident, the corrupting of a Church conftituted gives no allowance to bring in corrupt members to the conftitution of a Church, but the contrary, if a pertinacious member fhould be removed by the rule of the Gofpel, then fuch a one fhould not be admitted.

Thefe Conclufions premifed : the arguments of Mr. *Rutt, againft the vifibility of Saints to be right matter of a Church, Will admit an eafie anfwer.*

"1. *Argument,* is taken *from the manner of receiving mem-* "*bers in the Apoftles Church, where there was nothing but a pro-* "*feffed willingneffe to receive the Gofpel, howbeit they received* "*it not from the heart.*

Anfw. There is *not only a profeffed willingneffe to receive the Gofpel, but a practicall reformation,* that in the judgement of charity gives *ground of hope there is fomething reall, before the contrary appear.* And therefore *Peter* who received *Simon Magus,* upon his approbation of the truth and outward conformity thereunto in the courfe of his life, when his practife proclaimed the contrary, the Apoftle rejected him, as one in *the gall of bitterneffe and bond of iniquity,* who had no fhare in Chrift, and therefore certainly would not fuffer him to fhare in the priviledges of communion, fo perfifting without repentance.

2. Argument. "*If the vifible Church be a draw-net, where* "*are fifh and filth: an houfe, where are veffels of filver* "*and gold, and bafer veffels of braffe and wood: Then in*

"B

" *a Church rightly constituted, there may be beleevers*
" *and hypocrites.*

Answ. The argument is wholly yeelded, and the cause not touched, much lesse concluded, as may appear by the state of the question taken in a right meaning.

The like may be said to the third argument, touching the man that came to the wedding, not having on a wedding garment, for it seems by the text, he carried it so cunningly in appearance, that onely the *Master of the feast* perceived it, others did not discover it, before his coming in.

The *three last arguments* having one and the same bottom to bear them up, admit one and the same answer.

" If the *Churches of Israel, Judah, Galatia, Sardis, Laodicea,*
" *were Churches truely constituted, and yet in them were many*
" *wicked, prophane, unclean ; then visible Saints are not onely*
" *fit matter allowed by Christ to make up a visible Church.*

But they were Churches truely constituted, and yet had clean and unclean mixed among them. Therefore,

Answ. *The consequence is denied,* and the cause is given in the *third conclusion,* because such are onely by rule to be tolerated for a time, untill the censures be tried upon them. But if then they prove incorrigible they are to be removed and excommunicated. So that the edge of the argument may be turned most truely against the cause it would prove.

If in all these Churches the unclean and profane were to be excommunicated : Then such as they, were not to be admitted. But by Gods command they were to be excommunicated.

Therefore such as they were *not to be admitted.* Its certain *Christ* allows the Toleration of some in the Church for a time, whom he doth not allow to be taken in as fit matter to make up a Church.

The *rest of his Arguments* propounded in his second book. *p.*251. labour of the *same mistake,* and the *like answer* releeves the reader without the least trouble. For let him carry the conclusions formerly propounded along with him in his consideration, and refresh his memory with the *caveat* and *caution* that was put in by Mr *Robinson,* when I cleared the opinion of those our *Brethren* of the *Separation*; That our Question is not, whether members now received, and visible Christians in the eye of charity may so degenerate and break out into scandalous cour-

ses

ſes and apoſtaſies, that they may be ſcandalous, and that groſſely : But the Queſtion is, whether in the orderly gathering of the Church, ſuch according to the way and warrant of Chriſt can, and ought to be received.

And therefore to diſpute, The Church now gathered hath wicked and ungodly in it, and ſuch as be not viſible Saints : Therefore it may be gathered of ſuch, is ſo broad unconſequence, and makes the Church door ſo wide, that Mr *R.* his own princi- ples will proclaim it to be the broad way that leads croſſe to the tenure of the Goſpel. For I would make a collection, that ſhall carry a parity of reaſon with Mr *R.* his Inference, which cannot ſtand with his own grounds.

1. Such as were in the Church of *Iſrael,* in *Deut.* 29.
2. Such as the *falſe Apoſtles, Nicolaitans, followers of Ba- laam* and *Jezebels doctrine,* who were members of the Churches of *Aſia.* 3. Such who were *Schiſmaticks, Rai- lers, Partakers of the tables of devils,* 1 Cor. 6. 10. with *chap.* 10. 20.

Rev. 2. & 3. 1.

Such may be received members, according to the order of Chriſt.

But ſuch as theſe are openly ſcandalous.

Therefore ſuch as be openly ſcandalous may be received into the viſible Church.

And this doth not only ſet open the Church door, but pulls down the Church-ſide, and its that which M. *R.* himſelf gain- ſaies, and that profeſſedly and *in terminis.* lib. 2. p. 251. Let him therefore but defend his own opinion, and the like defence will maintain our cauſe from the force of theſe arguments.

His fourth argument taken from the 3000. in *Act.* 2. is an- ſwered before.

His fifth. is p. 253. Thus :

" *If we are to bear one anothers burthen, and ſo fulfill the law*
" *of Chriſt, and if grace may be beſide many ſins, yea if* Simon
" Magus *his profeſſion was eſteemed ſufficient for to give him bap-*
" *tiſme : Then it is not required, that all the members of the*
" *viſible Church, be viſible Saints, as before explicated.*

Anſw. The conſequence fails, for all this may be, namely, there may be many weakneſſes, and yet viſible expreſſions of re- pentance to reaſonable charity, and it is certain there were ſuch in *Simon Magus.* For what *Peter* exacted at the hands of thoſe, *Act.* 2. 38. *Repent and be baptized* ; he would and did follow
the

the rule of Chriſt which he had received and delivered to others, and therefore required as much at his hands.

The examples of *Aſa* and *Solomon*, the one breaking out into open perſecution, the other into toleration of groſſe Idolatry, are here very impertinent, and prejudiciall to M.R. his own defence and confeſſion: For if ſuch as theſe may be received; then openly ſcandalous may be entertained, which he denies, *ubi ſupra*.

His *ſixth argument* is,

" *If onely viſible Saints ſhould be received, then we are not* " *onely to try our ſelves, but to examine and judge carefully one* " *another, and that every one muſt labour to be ſatiſfied in con-* " *ſcience anent the regeneration one of another.*

Anſw. M.R. maintains we ſhould be ſatisfied in the judgement of charity that perſons are ſuch: for he holds, " *1. that we muſt* " *beware they be not ſcandalous.* 2. They muſt be *ſuch as may* " *be baptized by the order of Chriſt* ; and theſe muſt repent and " profeſſe their faith in the Lord Jeſus. 3. They muſt be *ſuch as* " *by their profeſſion muſt notifie they be true beleevers*, ut ſupra. *lib.2.pag.196.* Therefore, They muſt try and examine them that they be ſuch, and theſe grounds give warrant thereunto.

Argument *ſeventh.*

" *If many be brought and called to the viſible Church on pur-* " *poſe both in Gods revealed intention in his word to convert* " *them; and in the Churches, that they may be converted: Then* " *the Church doth not conſiſt of thoſe who are profeſſed* *converts.*

Anſw. The *propoſition* fails. Thoſe who are *converts in the judgement of charity*, may yet in Gods intention be brought into the Church, that they may be truely converted.

But if he mean, that the Church doth of purpoſe receive them into the Church to be converted, then it is croſſe to his own Tenet, and a perſon may be received to the ſeals of the Covenant, who doth not notifie that he hath faith, nay the Church may receive them to the ſeals, whom ſhe knows have no right to the ſeals; for ſhe knows they are not inviſible members, which in M. R. his judgement onely gives them right.

Having thus cleared our way, We ſhall take leave in few words, to take into further conſideration and examination ſome *expreſſions* of M. R. in *chap.9.p 99.l.1.* where neer the end he hath theſe words.   1. *Aſſer-*

1. *Aſſertion.* of M.R.

1. "*We ſay that there is nothing more required, as touching* "*the eſſentiall property and nature of being members of a* "*Church as viſible, but that they profeſſe before men the faith;* "*deſire the Seals of the Covenant, and crave fellowſhip with the* "*viſible Church.*

2. *Aſſertion.* of M.R.

2. "*Preaching the Goſpel is called a note of a true Church.*

We ſhall take theſe into *conſideration*, in the order that they are propounded; and

To the 1. *Aſſertion.*

Thoſe that have a ſhew of godlines and deny the power thereof

The Apoſtles charge is, that, *we ſhould turn away from ſuch*. *i.e.* Renounce all voluntary, and unneceſſary familiarity with ſuch: For the condition, unto which we are called by God, may happily neceſſitate a man or woman to hold conſtant and intimate familiarity with ſuch, in point of conſcience, by vertue of their calling. A godly and pious *wife* muſt doe the *duties* of a *wife* in the moſt inward and intimate manner of familiarity with her *huſband*, though *profane* and *wicked*: *The bond of relation neceſſitates thereunto.* But were it that ſhe was free, ſhe were bound in conſcience neither to match, nor to maintain any ſpeciall familiarity: becauſe ſhe is now at her choice, and her *ſociety* is *voluntary*, and thence to be avoided. Whence the argument groweth on.

Argument. 1.

If I muſt not enter into a voluntary or unneceſſary familiari- ty with ſuch, who have a ſhew of godlineſſe and deny the power thereof: Then am I bound much more, not to enter into a ſpeciall and ſpirituall ſociety and fellowſhip of the faith.

Becauſe this is much more, then ordinary and civil familiarity, and there is much more danger.

But this firſt part is the charge of the Apoſtle, therefore the *ſecond is undeniable.*

Argument. 2.

Again the Apoſtles advice is plain and peremptory. *If a Brother be an Idolater, or covetous,* &c *with ſuch a one eat not,* I *Cor.5.11.*

If

If he be unfit for civil, much more for spirituall society and communion, and therefore both are to be avoided, as far as in my power, and according to my part, I shall be able. For it sometimes so falls out, that I cannot remove a wicked person from my spirituall communion, because it is not in my power to cast him out, whom a congregation will keep in, yet I must by vertue of the Apostles charge, ever oppose, and protest against the admission of such, and the other of the brethren should according to God, keep him out of communion, as unfit wholly for spirituall fellowship, who is not fit for civill familiarity.

Argument. 3.

They who should be cast out of a congregation by the rule of Christ, those are unfit to be received in.

But men may have all those three properties (suppose a common and ordinary drunkard) i.e. *Professe the faith,* is *eager after the seals, most desirous of society with the Church;* as counting it a disparagement not to be born, if not admitted to the Sacrament ; *and yet such a one should be cast out ; therefore also kept out.*

To the 2. *Assertion* of Mr *R.* Which is,

"*That it is vain to say the preaching of the Word is no essentiall* "*mark of the true Church, is made good by distinguishing three* "*things.* 1. *Single and occasionall preaching.* 2. *Setled* "*preaching or the setling of the candlestick,* 3. *The preached* "*word with the seals.* Whence the answer in the summe issues "thus. *It is not the single, but the setled preaching of the word,* "*established and remaining in the Church, which is a mark of it.*

Answ. However the tenet seems to be vain, yet it will not vanish so easily.

By setled preaching of the word] Is meant a constant opening and applying the Scriptures in one place to one people.

By mark] Is meant, not any *common accident* or *adjunct* which doth indifferently agree to other things, as well as the Church, for then it could never be said to *notifie the Church,* in that it may notifie many things besides. But it must be a *differencing* and *distinguishing note,* and therefore it must be *proprium quarto modo,* as they call it, and *inseparable.*

These things confessed, which received rules of reason evince; I thence dispute.

That

That which is separable from the Church, and common to something beside that, cannot be a note of the Church.

This is evident from the right explication of the terms.

But setled preaching of the word, and constant opening and applying the Scripture to one people, in one place, is separable from the Church.

As suppose a Minister should preach many years, to a company of Infidels in one place. Nay suppose a lecturer speak constantly to a company of people, which resort from severall Churches, unto the same Auditory.

Here is *setled preaching,* and yet here is *no Church* ; and therefore *this is a seperable adjunct, and no note.*

If it be *replied,* that you must consider setled preaching, *as* established and remaining *in the Church.*

To that the *answer* is ; This plea is yet too narrow, to cover the nakednesse and weaknesse of this assertion. For upon this grant, the dispute must follow one of these two waies. The *setled* preaching of the word taken *with the Church,* is a mark of the *Church :* and this is irrationall, to make the *Church* a *mark of it self.* Or the meaning must be this ; Setled preaching, *whilst it remains in the Church,* is a *note* of the *Church :* but this nothing helps, for the inference remains as feeble as before. For if such a setled preaching be but a common adjunct or separable accident, in the nature of it, let it be where it will be, it will never, nay it can never be *a proper* note to that thing, as *Sensitiva facultas in homine,* is *not* a *mark* of a *man,* though *in a man.*

A BRIEF ACCOUNT OF THE PROVINCE OF PENNSYLVANIA

William Penn, *A Brief Account of the Province of Pennsylvania Lately Granted by the King, under the Great Seal of England, to William Penn and his Heirs and Assigns.* (London, 1681), pp. 1–8.

William Penn (1644–1718) was the son of Admiral Sir William Penn who rose to prominence during the English Civil War and the Restoration of the Stuarts. Penn attended Christ Church College in Oxford, England, for two years, but was expelled for his refusal to participate in Anglican Church observances. During this time, Penn was first attracted to the Puritan faith and then the Quaker faith. Becoming an active Quaker, Penn was imprisoned in 1669 for writing *The Sandy Foundation Shaken*, an attack on the Anglican Church. While in prison, he wrote his most famous piece, *No Cross, No Crown*, in which he spelled out his interpretation of Quakerism. However, Penn's situation improved as King Charles II granted him ownership of Pennsylvania for debts owed to his father in 1681; this was in addition to his extensive holdings in Ireland which had been granted to his father. Penn framed the first government for the Providence of Pennsylvania in 1682 and served as the proprietary governor from 1682 to 1692 and from 1694 to 1718. He also superintended Philadelphia's town planning, despite infrequent visits to North America.

Though Penn was perhaps America's leading intellectual figure in the seventeenth century, conflicts were evident in his writings between his views on the organisation of government, society and economy and Quaker religious beliefs. True to the Quaker philosophy, Penn's writings encouraged hard work and frugality and deplored consumption of luxuries and vice. Penn's Quakerism was firmly in favour of order and the submission of man's own will to his religious elders.

In another piece, *Information and direction to such persons as are inclined to America* (1686), Penn calculates the costs of immigrating to America, presenting the advantages to be gained from labour in the tradition of John Smith. This is an interesting piece in the use of numerical calculation to demonstrate the weighing of costs and benefits. This is not seen again until Hugh Vans's *Inquiry into the nature and uses of Money* (1740) which is reproduced in Volume III of this collection.

A brief Account of the

Province of Pennsylvania,

Lately Granted by the

K I N G,

Under the GREAT

Seal of England,

TO

WILLIAM PENN

AND HIS

Heirs and Assigns.

Since (by the good Providence of *God*, and the Favour of the *King*) a Country in *America* is fallen to my Lot, I thought it not lefs my Duty, then my Honeft Intereft, to give fome publick notice of it to the World, that thofe of our own or other Nations, that are inclin'd to Tranfport Themfelves or Families beyond the Seas, may find another Country added to their Choice; that if they fhall happen to like the Place, Conditions, and Government, (fo far as the prefent Infancy of things will allow us any profpect) they may, if they pleafe, fix with me in the Province, hereafter defcribed.

I. *The* KING'S *Title to this Country before he granted it.*
It is the *Jus Gentium*, or Law of Nations, that what ever Wafte, or unculted Country, is the Difcovery of any Prince, it is the right of that Prince that was at the Charge of the Difcovery: Now this *Province* is a Member of that part of *America*, which the King of *Englands* Anceftors have been at the Charge of Difcovering, and which they and he have taken great care to preferve and Improve.

II. William

II. *William Penn's* Title from the *KING.*

An Abſtract of the Patent

GRANTED BY THE

K I N G,

To William Penn, &c.

The Fourth of *March,* 1681.

I. WE do Give and Grant (upon divers conſiderations) to William Penn his Heirs and Aſſigns for ever all that Tract of Land in America with all Iſlands thereunto belonging That is to ſay from the beginning of the fortieth degree of North Latitude unto the forty third Degree of North Latitude whoſe Eaſtern bounds from Twelve Engliſh Miles above New-Caſtle (alias Delaware Town) runs all along upon the ſide of Delaware River.

II. Free and undiſturb'd uſe and paſſage into and out of all Harbours Bays Waters Rivers Iſles and Inlets belonging to or leading to the ſame Together with the Soyl Fields Woods Underwoods Mountains Hills Fenns Iſles Lakes Rivers Waters Rivulets Bays and Inlets Scituate in or belonging unto the Limits and Bounds aforeſaid Together with all ſorts of Fiſh Mines Mettles, &c. To have and to hold to the only behoof of the ſaid William Penn his Heirs and Aſſigns for ever To be holden of us as of our Caſtle of Windſor in free and common ſoccage paying only two Beaver ſkins yearly.

III. And of our further Grace we have thought it fit to erect and we do hereby erect the aforeſaid Countrey and Iſlands into a Province and Seigniory and Do call it Pennſilvania and ſo from henceforth we will have it call'd.

IV That repoſing ſpecial confidence in the wiſdom and juſtice of the ſaid William Penn we Do grant to him and his Heirs and their Deputies for the good and happy Government thereof to ordain and e-nact and under his and their ſeals to publiſh any Laws whatever for the publick uſes of the ſaid Province by and with the Advice and Appro-bation of the Free-holders or the ſaid Countrey or their delegates ſo as they be not repugnant to the Law of this Realm and to the Faith and Allegiance due unto us by the legal Government thereof.

.V. Full power to the ſaid William Penn, &c. to appoint Judges Lieutenants Juſtices Magiſtrates and Officers for what cauſes ſoever and with what Power and in ſuch Form as to him ſeems convenient alſo to be able to Pardon and Aboliſh Crimes and Offences and to do all and every other thing that to the compleat Eſtabliſhment of Juſtice un-to Courts and Tribunals forms of Judicature and manner of proceed-

ings

ings do belong and our pleasure is and so we enjoyn and require that such Laws and Proceedings shall be most absolute and available in Law and that all the Leige People of us our Heirs and Successors inviolably keep the same in those parts saving to us final appeals.

VI. That the Laws for regulating Property as well for the discent of Lands as enjoyment of Goods and Chattels and likewise as to Felonies shall be the same there as here in England until they shall be altered by the said William Penn his Heirs or Assigns and by the Freemen of the said Province or their Delegates or Deputies or the greater part of them.

VII. Furthermore that this new Colony may the more happily encrease by the multitude of People resorting thither therefore we for us our Heirs and Successors do hereby grant License to all the Leige People present and future of us, &c. (excepting such as shall be specially forbidden) to Transport themselves and Families unto the said Country there to Inhabit and Plant for the publick and their private Good.

VIII. Liberty to Transport what Goods or Commodities are not forbidden paying here the Legal Customs due to us, &c.

IX. Power to divide the Countrey into Counties Hundreds and Towns to Incorporate Towns into Burroughs and Burroughs into Cities to make Fairs and Markets with convenient Priviledges according to the merit of the Inhabitants or the fitness of the place And to do all other thing or things touching the premises which to the said William Penn his Heirs or Assigns shall seem meet and requisite albeit they be such as of their own nature might otherwise require a more special commandment and warrant then in these presents is express'd.

X. Liberty to Import the Growth or Manufactures of that Province into England paying here the Legal duty.

XI. Power to erect Ports Harbours Creeks Havens Keys and other places for Merchandizes with such Jurisdiction and Priviledges as to the said William Penn, &c. shall seem expedient.

XII. Not to break the Acts of Navigation neither Governour nor Inhabitants upon the penaltys contained in the said Acts.

XIII. Not to be in League with any Prince or Country that is in War against us our Heirs and Successors.

XIV. Power of safety and defence in such way and manner as to the said William Penn, &c. seems meet.

XV. Full power to Assign Alien Grant Demise or Enfeoff of the premises so many and such parts and parcels to those that are willing to purchase the same as the said William Penn thinks fit to have and to hold to them the said Persons their Heirs or Successors in fee Simple or fee Tail or for term of Life or Lives or years to be held of the said William Penn, &c. as of the said Seigniory of Windsor by such Services Customs and Rents as shall seem fit to the said William Penn his Heirs and Assigns and not immediately of us our Heirs or Successors and that the said Persons may take the premises or any Parcel thereof of the said William Penn, &c. and the same hold to themselves their Heirs and Assigns the Statute Quia emptores Terrarum in any wise notwithstanding.   XVI.

XVI. We give and grant License to any of those Persons to whom the said William Penn, &c. has granted any Estate of Inheritance as aforesaid with the consent of the said William Penn to erect any parcel of Lands within the said Province into Mannors to hold Courts Baron and view of Francke-pledge, &c by Themselves or Stewards.

XVII. Power to those Persons to Grant to others the same Tenures in fee simple or otherwise to be held of the said Mannors respectively and upon all further Alienations the Land to be held of the Mannor that it held of before the Alienation.

XVIII. We do Covenant and Grant to and with the said William Penn his Heirs and Assigns that we will not set or make any Custom or other Taxation upon the Inhabitants of the said Province upon Lands Houses Goods Chattels or Merchandizes except with the consent of the Inhabitants and Governour.

XIX. A charge that no Officers nor Ministers of us our Heirs and Successors do presume at any time to attempt any thing to the contrary of the premises or in any sort withstand the same but that they be at all times aiding to the said William Penn and his Heirs and to the Inhabitants and Merchants their Factors and Assigns in the full use and benefit of this our Charter.

XX. And if any Doubts or questions shall hereafter arise about the true sense or meaning of any Word Clause or Sentence contained in this our Charter We will Ordain and Command that at all times and in all things such Interpretation be made thereof and allowed in any of our Courts whatsoever as shall be adjudged most advantageous and favourable unto the said William Penn his Heirs and Assigns so as it be not against the Faith and Allegiance due to us our Heirs and Successors.

In Witness whereof we have caused our Letters to be made Patents. Witness our self at *Westminster*, &c.

The KING's Declaration

TO

The Inhabitants and Planters of the Province of

PENNSYLVANIA.

CHARLES R.

Whereas His Majesty in consideration of the great merit and faithful services of Sir William Penn deceased, and for divers other good Causes him thereunto moving, hath been Graciously pleased by Letters Patents bearing Date the Fourth Day of March last past, to Give and Grant unto William Penn Esquire, Son and Heir of the said Sir William Penn, all that Tract of Land in America,

America, called by the Name of Pennsylvania, as the same is Bounded on the East by Delaware River, from Twelve miles distance Northwards of New Castle Town, unto the three and fourtieth Degree of Northern Latitude, if the said River doth extend so far Northwards, and if the said River shall not extend so far North-ward, then by the said River so far as it doth extend: And from the Head of the said River, the Eastern Bounds to be determined by a Meridian Line to be drawn from the Head of the said River, unto the said Three and fourtieth Degree, the said Province to extend Westward five Degrees in Longitude, to be Computed from the said Eastern Bounds, and to be Bounded on the North, by the Beginning of the Three and fourtieth Degree of Northern Latitude, and on the South, by a Circle Drawn at Twelve Miles distance from New-Castle Northwards, and Westwards unto the Beginning of the Fourtieth Degree of Northern Latitude, and then by a straight Line Westwards to the limit of Longitude above mentioned, together with all Powers, Preheminencies, and Jurisdictions necessary for the Government of the said Province, as by the said Letters Patents, Reference being thereunto had, doth more at large appear.

His Majesty doth therefore hereby Publish and Declare his Royal Will and Pleasure, That all persons Setled or Inhabiting within the Limits of the said Province, do yield all Due Obedience to the said William Penn, His Heirs and Assigns, as absolute Proprietaries and Governours thereof, as also to the Deputy or Deputies, Agents or Lieutenants, Lawfully Commissionated by him or them, according to the Powers and Authorities Granted by the said Letters Patents ; Wherewith His Majesty Expects and Requires a ready Complyance from all Persons whom it may concern, as they tender His Majesties Displeasure.

Given at the Court at *Whitehall* the Second day of *April*, 1681. In the Three and thirtieth year of Our Reign.

By His Majesties Command,

C O N W A Y.

III. *The Reason of the Grant.*

The reason and ground of this Grant from the *King*, to Him and his Heirs, &c, Was his Petition to the *King*, in which he set forth, *His Fathers Services, his own Sufferings and Losses, in relation to his Fathers Estate*; And lastly, *His long and costly Attendance without success*. In right, and consideration of which, the *King* was graciously pleased to make the aforesaid Grant; to which Title, the said *William Penn* adds that of the *Natives* by purchase from them.

IV. *Of the Country, and its Produce.*

It lies 600. Miles *South* of the *Latitude* of *England* ; and as it is of the same side of the *Line*, so it is about the same degree with *Mompellier* in *France*, or *Naples* in *Italy*: The Air is generally clear and sweet, the *Summer* is longer and Hotter, and *Winter* shorter, and sometimes Colder than in *England*: The Soil is said to be as good as any in those parts. It commonly produceth *Oak, Cedar, Mulbery, Chesnut, Walnut, Firr, Cyprus, Ash, Beech, Popaler, Saxafras, Medaler, Plumbs, Grapes, Peaches, Strawberries, Huckleberries, Cranberries, Hopps,*

Hopps, &c. *English* Fruit takes kindly, and produceth fuddainly and plentifully: The Woods are furnifhed with Store of Wild Fowl, as *Turkeys*, *Pheafants*, *Heath-Cocks*, *Patridges*, *Pidgeons*, &c. The Earth well Watered with *Springs* and *Rivers*, and the Rivers ftored with Fifh, as *Sturgion*, *Sheepfheads*, *Drums*, *Cat-fifh*, *Shads*, *Eeles*, and abundance more: With Fowl, as *Swans*, *Gray* and *White Geefe*, *Duck*, *Mallard*, &c. The Corn of the Country ufed by the *Indians*, produceth four hundred fold, is Good and Hearty, both in Milk, and made into Bread; the price two Shillings fix pence the Bufhel: There is alfo good *English* Corn, as *Wheat*, *Barly*, *Rye*, and *Oates*, *Wheat* under four Shillings the Bufhel, *Barly and Rye*, under three Shillings the Bufhel, *Oates* about two Shillings the Bufhel: There are alfo very good *Peafe*, and *Beans* of feveral forts. The *Beef* is good, but *Pork* is very Sweet: The *Beef* at three pence, the *Pork* at two pence half-penny the pound; *Butter* at fix pence a pound, *Peaches* to Eat, or make Drink of, at eight pence the Bufhel, a *Cow* and *Calf* about the Spring of the Year, at five pounds, a pair of *Oxen* at ten pounds, a good *Breeding Sow* at thirty Shillings, a *Young good breeding Mare*, at eight pounds. But it is to be Noted, that thefe foregoing prifes and fums, are to be paid *with one half of the Value in* Englifh *Goods*, at the Rates they are bought at in *England*, for example, four pounds *English* paies for the *Breeding Mare*, that is Rated at eight pounds, the like with the reft

The Country alfo abounds with feveral forts of Wild Creatures, as *Elkes*, *Deer*, *Beavers*, *Racoons*, *Minks*, *Martins*, *Wild Catts*, *Otters*, &c. fome of which are good Food, and Cheap, as a Fat *Buck* at two Shillings, *English* Goods, others of them confiderable for their Furs: The way of Traffique, is to fend to the *Southren* Plantations, *Corn*, *Beef*, *Pork*, *Fifh*, *Sider*, and *Pipe-ftaves*; the *Skins* and *Furs* for *England*. The Conveniency that belongs to the *Province* in point of *Navigation*, is two fold; the one through *Chefapeak Bay*, and the other *Delaware Bay*, by which Ships of great Burthen may come and Trade to the faid *Province*.

V. *Of the prefent Inhabitants.*

That part of the Country which is at all Inhabited, is at the head of *Chefapeak Bay*, and on the *Weft* fide of *Delaware* River, they are by Nation, *Sweeds*, *Dutch*, *English*, who are capable of giving Entertainment to New Commers, till they can provide for themfelves.

VI *What the Country is believed capable of*

It is thought by feveral knowing Perfons, that have Travelled thofe parts of *America*, and have been well acquainted with places in *Europe* of the fame degree, that there may be *Silke*, and *Wine*, if not *Oyle*; and for *Flax*, *Hemp*, *Woad*, *Madder*, *Liquorifh*, *Pot-afhes*, and *Iron*, there needs to be no queftion.

VII. *Of the Government.*

1ft. The *Governour* and *Free-holders*, have the power of *making Laws*, fo that no Law can be made; nor Money raifed, *But by the Peoples confent*.

2ly. That the *Rights* of the People of *England* are in force there

3ly. That making no Law againft *Allegiance*, they may make all Laws requifite for the Profperity, and Security of the faid *Province*.

VIII. *Of the Conditions.*

The *Province* is caft at a penny an Acre; But he fets apart feveral parcels, which he calls *Shares*; thefe he fells; faving a *Quit-rent*, neceffary for to fecure the Title and Tenure: That is, whereas 5000. Acres (which makes a *Share*) comes (at a penny an Acre) to 20. *l.* 16. *s.* 8. *d.* yearly, for 100 *l.* down, he fells off the yearly Rent of 18. *l.* 6. *s.* 8 *d.* and referves but 50 *s,* which may be reduc'd as the purchafer pleafes, but fomething muft be referved for the Security of the *Title*: To which, the *Royalties* proper to Mannors in *England*, as *Hunting*, *Fowling*, *Fifhing*, with all common *Mines*, *Minerals*, and a Proportion of *Royal Mines* alfo (if found within any ones propriety) is affixed by the general Conceffions.

And that fuch as are not able to purchafe, yet willing to go, and capable to to pay their Paffage, and their Servants, may not be excluded. It is hereby Declared, that every fuch Perfon, for himfelf, and Wife, and every Child, *Male* or *Female*, if fixteen Years of Age, fhall have right to take up at *3. d.* per Acre, Fifty Acres by the Head, to him and his Heirs for ever, in lieu of Purchafing, which fhall be by the *Surveyor* of the Country fet out fo foon as the faid perfon comes to take it up : And to encourage fuch Children and Servants to ferve their *Parents*, *Mafters*, or *Miftreffes*, the full time for which they are Engaged, Diligently and Faithfully ; Every fuch Child or Servant, fhall have Right to take up 50. Acres at but two Shillings *Quit-Rent* for ever, which makes him a *Free-holder* of the Country.

IX *Perfons fitteft for Plantations.*

Thofe perfons that Providence feems to have fitted for Plantations, are *Induftrious Hufbandmen, Laborious Handicrafts*. As *Carpenters, Ship-wrights, Ropemakers, Smiths, Brick-makers, Weavers, Taylors, Tanners, Coopers, Mill-wrights, Joyners, Shooe-makers, Turners, Potters, fuch as drefs Flax, Hemp, and Wool*; With many others.

It feems alfo a fit place for *Younger Brothers, and Men of fmall Eftates*, who with the Induftry of a few Servants, may in two or three years time, be plentifully accommodated, Alfo all Ingenious Men, that are lovers of *Planting, Gardening*, and the like quiet, and ufeful Imployments.

A *Plantation* feems a fit place for thofe Ingenious Spirits, that being Low in the World, are much clog'd and oppreffed about a Lively-hood; for the means of Subfifting being eafy there, they may have time, and opportunity to Gratify their Inclinations; and thereby improve Science, and help Nurferies of People.

There are an other fort of Perfons, not only fit for, but neceffary in *Plantations*; and that is, Men of Univerfal Spirits, that have an Eye to the good of Pofterity; and that both underftand, and delight to promote good *Difcipline*, and *Juft Government* among a Plain and Well intending People : Such Perfons may find room in *Colonies*, for their good *Counfil and Contrivance*, who are fhut out from being of much ufe or fervice to great *Nations*, under fettled Cuftoms.

But they that go, muft wifely count the Coft, *For they muft either work themfelves, or be able to imploy others*. A *Winter* goes before a *Summer*, and the firft work will be Countrey Labour, to *clear Ground*, and *raife Provifion*; other things by degrees.

X. *What is fit for the Journey, and firft to be done there.*

1ft. The Paffage for Men and Women is *Five Pounds* a head, for Children under Ten Years, *Fifty Shillings*; Sucking Children *Nothing*, for Freight of Goods, *Forty Shilling per* Tun; but one Cheft to every Paffenger Free.

2ly. The Goods fit to take with them for ufe or fale; are all Utenfils for *Hufbandry and Building*, and *Houfe-hold-ftuff*, Alfo all forts of things for *Apparel*, as *Cloath, Stuffes, Linnen*, &c. Wherein all that defire, may be more particularly Informed, by *Philip Ford*, at the *Hood and Scarf* in *Bow-lane* in *London*

Laftly, Being by the Mercy of God fafely *Arrived*; be it in *October*, Two Men may clear as much Ground for Corn, as ufually brings by the following Harveft about *Twenty-Quarters*; In the mean time they muft buy Corn, which they may have as aforefaid; and if they buy them two *Cows*, and two *Breeding Sows*; with what the *Indians* for a fmall matter will bring in, of *Fowl, Fifh, and Venifon* (which is incredibly Cheap, as a *Fat Buck* for *Two Shillings*) that, and their induftry will fupply them. It is Apprehended, that *Fifteen Pounds* ftock for each Man (who is firft well in Cloaths, and provided with fit working Tools for himfelf) will (by the Bleffing of God) carry him thither, and keep him, till his own *Plantation* will Accommodate him. But all are moft ferioufly cautioned, how they proceed in the difpofal of themfelves; 'Tis true, *The Earth is the Lords, and the Fullnefs thereof*; and it feems to many, to be the time wherein thofe defolate *Weftern* parts of the World are to be Planted, and

and have their Day, as *Asia*, *Africa*, and *Europe* have had (of which there are divers Prophesies extant) yet let all have a Reverend regard to *God*'s Providence in their Removal, and be serious in it, rather seeking the Comforts of retirement, and a sufficiency for Life (like the Blessed *Patriarks* of Old) then Ease, Fulness, and Wealth.

And it is further Advised, that all such as go, would at least get the Permission, if not the good Likeing of their near Relations.; for that is both Natural, and a Duty incumbent upon all: And by this means will natural Affection be Preserved, and a Friendly and Profitable Correspondence maintained between them. In all which, *God Almighty* (who is the Salvation of the Ends of the Earth) Direct us, that His Blessings may attend our Honest Indeavours; and then the Consequence of all our Undertakings, will be to the Glory of His Great Name, and the true Happiness of Us, and our Posterity. *Amen*.

𝔚𝔦𝔩𝔩𝔦𝔞𝔪 𝔓𝔢𝔫𝔫.

POSTSCRIPT.

W Hoever are desirous to be concern'd in this Province, they may be treated with, and further Satisfied, at Philip Fords in Bow-lane in Cheap-side, and at Thomas Rudyards, or Benjamin Clarks in George-yard in Lombard-street, *London*.

There is likewise Printed a *Map of Pennsylvania*, together with a Description at the End of it; and some Proposals.

THE END.

LONDON,

Printed for *Benjamin Clark* in *George-yard* in *Lom-bard-street*. 1681.

A FURTHER ACCOUNT OF THE PROVINCE OF PENNSYLVANIA

William Penn, *A Further Account of the Province of Pennsylvania and its Improvements. For the Satisfaction of those that are Adventurers, and enclined to be so* (London, 1685), pp. 1–20.

In both *A Brief Account* and *A Further Account of the Province of Pennsylvania*, William Penn spells out the rights of individuals who live in or are immigrating to Pennsylvania. In *A Brief Account* particular attention is paid to property rights, rights of trade, and rights to granted land, as every person upon reaching sixteen years of age legally had the right to purchase land at a very low price. Additionally, *A Brief Account* provides recommendations on economic activities including what crops to farm and what occupations would be most rewarded, not to mention what immigrants should pack. *A Further Account* takes up many of these themes in detail, as Penn describes the economic system, history and geography of Pennsylvania, as well as the improvements being undertaken to develop the colony, such as improvements to roads and cities. Both pieces wonderfully describe how America was being 'sold' to peasants and labourers in Europe as a place of economic opportunity.

A
Further Account
Of the Province of
PENNSYLVANIA
AND ITS
IMPROVEMENTS.

For the Satisfaction of thofe that are Adventurers, and enclined to be fo.

IT has, I know, been much expected from me, that I fhould give fome farther Narrative of thofe parts of *America*, where I am chiefly interefted, and have lately been ; having continued there above a Year after my *former Relation*, and receiving fince my return, the frefheft and fulleft Advices of its *Progrefs* and *Improvement*. But as the reafon of my coming back, was a *Difference* between the *Lord Baltamore* and my felf, about the *Lands of Delaware*, in confequence, reputed of mighty moment to us, fo I wav'd publifhing any thing that might look in favour of the Country or inviting to it, whilft it lay under the Difcouragement and Difreputation of that Lord's claim and pretences.

But fince they are, after many fair and full hearings before the *Lords* of the *Committee* for *Plantations* juftly and happily *Difmift*, and the things agreed ; and that the *Letters* which daily prefs me from all Parts, on the fubject of *America,*

rica, are fo many and voluminous, that to anfwer them fe-
verally, were a Task too heavy, and repeated to perform, I
have thought it moft eafie to the Enquirer, as well as my felf,
to make this Account *Publick,* left my filence, or a more private intimation of things, fhould difoblige the juft inclinations
of any to *America,* and at a time too, when an extraordinary Providence feems to favour its Plantation, and open a
Door to *Europeans* to pafs thither.   That then which is my
part to do in this Advertifement is,

Firft, *To Relate our Progrefs, efpecially fince my laft of the
Month called* Auguft 83.

Secondly, *The Capacity of the Place for farther Improvement,
in order to Trade and Commerce.*

Laftly, *Which Way thofe that are Adventurers; or incline to be
fo, may imploy their Money to a fair and fecure Profit ;* fuch as
fhall equally encourage Poor and Rich, which cannot fail of
Advancing the Country in confequence.

I. We have had about N I N E T Y   S A Y L *of Ships with*
P A S S E N G E R S fince the beginning of 82. and not one
Veffel, defigned to the *Province,* through Gods mercy, hi-
therto mifcarried.

The Eftimate of the People may be thus made ; *Eighty*
to each Ship, which comes to S E V E N T H O U S A N D
T W O- H U N D R E D P E R S O N S : At leaft a *Thoufand*
there before, with fuch as from other Places in our neighbourhood are fince come to refide among us : And I prefume
the *Births* at leaft equal to the *Burials* : For having made
our firft Settlement high in the *Frefhes* of the Rivers, we do
not finde our felves fubject to thofe Seafonings that affect
fome other Countries upon the fame Coaft.

The People are a *Collection* of divers Nations in *Europe* : As,
French, Dutch, Germans, Sweeds, Danes, Finns, Scotch' Irifh, and
Englifh ;

Englifh ; and of the laft equal to all the reft : And which is admirable, not a Reflection on that Account : But as they are of one kind, and in one Place, and under One Allegiance, fo they live like People of *One County*; which Civil Union has had a confiderable influence towards the profperity of that Place.

II. Philadelphia, and our intended Metropolis, as I formerly Writ, is two Miles long, and a Mile broad, and at each end it lies *thot* mile, *upon a Navigable River*. The fcituation *high* and *dry*, yet replenifhed with *running ftreams*. Befides the High-Street, that runs in the midle from River to River, and is an *hundred foot* broad, it has Eight Streets more that run the fame courfe, the leaft of which is *fifty foot* in breath. And befides Broad-Street, which croffeth the Town in the middle, and is alfo an hundred foot wide, there are twenty ftreets more, that run the fame courfe, and are alfo fifty foot broad. The names of thofe Streets are moftly taken from the things that Spontaneoufly grow in the Country, *As Vine-Street, Mulbery-Street, Chefnut-Srteet, Wallnut-Street, Strawbery-Street, Cranbery-Street, Plumb-Street, Hickery-Street, Pine-Street, Oake-Street, Beach-Street, Afh-Street, Popler-Street, Saffafrax-Street, and the like.*

III. I mentioned in my laft Account, that from my Arival in *Eighty two*, to the Date thereof, being ten Moneths, we had got up *Four-fcore* Houfes at our Town, and that fome Villages were fetled about it. From that time to my coming away, which was a Year within a few Weeks, the Town advanced to *Three hundred and fifty feven Houfes*; divers of them, large, well built, with good Cellars, three ftories, and fome with *Belconies*.

IV. There is alfo a fair *Key* of about three hundred foot fquare, Built by *Samuel Carpenter*, to which a Ship of *five hundred Tuns* may lay her broade fide : and others intend to
follow

follow his example. We have alfo a Rope-walk made by *B. Wilcox*, and cordage for fhipping already fpun at it.

V. There inhabits moft forts of ufeful Trades-men, As *Carpenters, Joymers, Bricklayers, Mafons, Plafterers, Plumers, Smiths, Glafiers, Taylers, Shoemakers, Butchers, Bakers, Brewers, Glovers, Tanners, Felmongers, Wheelrights, Millrights, Shiprights, Boatrights, Ropemakers, Saylmakers Blockmakers, Turners* &c.

VI. There are *Two Markets* every Week and *Two Fairs* every Year. In other places Markets alfo, as at *Chefter* and *Nev-Caftle*.

VII. Seven *Ordinaries* for the Intertainment of *Strangers* and *Work-Men*, that are not Houfe-keepers, and a good Meal to be had for fixpence, fterl.

VI.I. The hours for Work and Meals to *Labourers*, are fixt, and known by Ring of *Bell*.

IX. After mine at Night, the *Officers* go the Rounds and no Perfon, without very good caufe, fuffered to be at any Publick-Houfe that is not a Lodger.

X. Tho this *Town* feemed at firft, contrived for the Purchafers of the *firft hundred fhares*, each fhare confifting of 5000 *Acres*, yet few going, and that their abfence might not Check the Improvement of the Place, and *Strangers*, that flockt to us, be thereby Excluded, I added that half of the Town, which lies on the *Skulkill*, that we might have Room for prefent and after Commers, that were not of that number, and it hath already had great fuccefs to the Improvement of the Place.

XI. Some *Veffels* have been here Built, and many *Boats*; and by that means, a ready Conveniency for Paffage of People and Goods.

XII. Divers *Brickerys* going on, many Cellars already Ston'd or Brick'd, and fome Brick Houfes going up.

XIII. The *Town* is well furnifh'd with convenient *Mills*;
and

and what with their *Garden Plats*, (the leaft half an Acre) the *Fifh* of the River, and their labour, to the *Country-man*, who begins to pay with the provifions of his own growth, they live Comfortably.

XIV. The Improvement of the place is beft meafur'd, by the *advance* of Value upon every mans Lot. I will venture to fay, that the worft Lot in the Town, without any Improvement upon it, is worth *four times* more then it was when it was lay'd out, and the beft *forty*. And though it feems unequal that the Abfent fhould be thus benefited by the Improvments of thofe that are upon the place, efpecially, when they have ferv'd no Office, run no hazard, nor as yet defray'd any Publick charge, yet this advantage does certainly redound to them, and whoever they are, they are great Debtors to the Country ; of which I fhall now fpeak more at large.

Of Country Settlements.

1. WE do fettle in the way of *Townfhips* or *Villages*, each of which contains 5000 Acres in fquare and at leaft *Ten Families*: The regulation of the Country, being a Family to each five hundred Acres : Some Townfhips have more, where the Intereft of the People is lefs then that quantity; which often falls out.

2. Many that had right to more Land, were at firft covetous to have their *whole* quantity, without regard to this way of fettlement, tho by fuch *Wildernefs* vacancies they had ruin'd the Country, and their own intereft of courfe. I had in my view, *Society, Affiftance, Eafy Commerce, Inftruction of Youth, Goverment of Peoples manners, Conveniency of Religious Affembling, Encouragement of Mechanicks, diftinct and beaten Roads*, and it has anfwer'd in all thofe refpects, I think, to an Univerfall Content.

3. Our

3. Our *Townships* lie square: generally the Village in the Center; the Houses either opposit, or else opposit to the middle, betwixt two houses over the way, for nearer neighborhood. We have another Method, that tho the Village be in the Center, yet after a different manner: Five hundred Acres are allotted for the Village, which among ten families comes to fifty Acres each: This lies square, and on the outside of the square stand the Houses, with their fifty Acres running back, whose ends meeting, make the Center of the 500 Acres, as they are to the whole. Before the Doors of those Houses, lies the high way, and cross it, every mans 450 Acres of Land, that makes up his Complement of 500 so that the Conveniency of Neighbourhood is made agreeable with that of the Land.

4. I said nothing in my last of any number of Townships, but there were at least *FIFTY* settled before my leaving those parts, which was in the moneth call'd *August* 1684.

5. I visitted many of them, and found them much advanc'd in their Improvements. *Houses* over their heads, and *Garden-Plots, Coverts* for their Cattle, an *encrease* of stock, and several Enclosures in Corn, especially, the first Commers; and I may say of some Poor men, even to the beginings of an Estate: The difference of labouring for themselves and for others; of an Inheritance and a Rack Lease, *being never better understood.*

Of The Produce of the Earth.

1. THE *EARTH*, by Gods-blessing, has more then answer'd our expectation; the poorest places in our Judgment, producing large Crops of Garden Stuff, and Grain. And though our Ground has not generally the symptoms of the fat Necks, that lie upon salt Waters in Provinces southern of us, our Grain is thought to *excell* and our Crops to be as large. We have had the mark of the good Ground amongst

amongſt us; from *Thirty to Sixty fold* of Engliſh Corn.

2. The Land requires leſs feed : *Three Pecks* of Wheat ſow an Acre; a Buſhel at moſt, and ſome have had the in-creaſe I have mention'd.

3. Upon Tryal, we find that the Corn and Roots that grow in *England*, thrive very well there, as *Wheat, Barly, Rye, Oats, Buck-Wheat, Peaſe, Beans, Cabbages, Turnips, Carrets, Parſnups, Colleflowers, Aſparagus, Onions, Charlots, Garlick, and Iriſh Potatos*; we have alſo the *Spaniſh*, and very good R I C E which do not grow here.

4. Our *Low* Lands are excellent for *Rape* and *Hemp* and *Flax*. A Tryal has been made, and of the two laſt, there is a Conſiderable quantity Dreſs'd Yearly.

5. The *Weeds* of our Woods feed our Cattle to the Mar-ket as well as Dary: I have ſeen fat Bullocks brought thence to Market before *Mid-Summer*. Our Swamps or Marſhes yeeld us courſe Hay for the Winter,

6. Engliſh *GRASS-SEED takes well*; which will give us fatting Hay in time. Of this *I* made an Experiment in my own Court Yard, upon ſand, that was dug out of my Cellar, with feed that had layn in a *Cask*, open to the weather two Winters and a Summer: I caus'd it to be ſown in the beginning of the month called *April*, and a fortnight before *Midſummer* it was fit to *Mow :* It grew very thick : But I ordered it to be fed, being in the nature of a Graſs Plott, on purpoſe to ſee if the Roots lay firm : And though it had been meer ſand, caſt out of the Cellar, but a Year before, the feed took ſuch Root, and held the earth ſo faſt, and faſtened it ſelf ſo well in the Earth, that it held and fed like old Engliſh Ground. I mention this, to confute the Objections that lie againſt thoſe Parts, as if that, firſt, Engliſh Graſs would not grow ; next, not enough to mow; and laſtly, not firm enough to feed, from the Levity of the Mould.

7. All

7. All forts of Englifh fruits that have been tryed, *take mighty well* for the time : The *Peach* Excellent, on ftanders, and in great quantities : They fun-dry them, and lay them up in lofts, as we do roots here, and ftew them with Meat in Winter time. *Mufmellons* and *Water Mellons* are raifed there, with as little care as Pumpkins in *England.* The *VINE* efpecially, prevails, which grows every where ; and upon experience, of fome *French People from Rochel, and the Ifle of Rhee,* *GOOD WINE* may be made there, efpecially, when the Earth and Stem are fin'd and civiliz'd by culture. We hope that good skill in our moft Southern Parts will yeild us feveral of the *Straights* Commodities, efpecially, *Oyle, Dates,* *Figgs, Almonds, Raifins* and *Currans.*

Of the Produce of our Waters.

1. **M**Ighty. WHALES roll upon the Coaft, near the Mouth of the Bay of *Delaware.* Eleven caught, and workt into Oyl one Seafon : We juftly hope a confiderable profit by a Whalery. They being fo numerous and the Shore fo fuitable.

2. STURGEON play continually in our Rivers in Summer : And though the way of cureing them be not generally known, yet by a Receipt I had of one *Collins,* that related to the Company of the Royal Fifhery, I did fo well preferve fome, that I had of them good there three months of the Summer, and brought fome of the fame fo for *England.*

3. ALLOES, as they call them in *France,* the Jews *Allice,* and our Ignorants, *Shads,* are excellent Fifh, and of the Bignefs of our largeft *Carp* : They are fo Plentiful, that Captain *Smyth's* Overfeer, at the *Skulki!,* drew 600 and odd at one Draught, 300 is no wonder, 100 familierly. They are excellent Pickled or Smokt'd, as well as boyld frefh : They are caught by nets only. 4. ROCKS

4. R O C K S are fomewhat rounder and larger, alfo a whiter fifh, little inferior in rellifh to our *Mullet :* We have them almoft in the like plenty. Thefe are often *Barrell'd like Cod,* and not much inferior for their fpending. Of both thefe the Inhabitants increafe their Winter ftore: Thefe are caught by Nets, Hooks and Speers.

5. The S H E E P S H E A D, fo called, from the refem-blance of its Mouth and Nofe to a Sheep, is a fifh much pre-ferr'd by fome, but they keep in falt Water; they are like a *Roach* in fafhion, but as thick as a *Salmon,* not fo long. We have alfo the *Drum,* a large and noble fifh, commended equal to the *Sheepfhead,* not unlike to a *Newfoundland Cod,* but larger of the two : Tis fo call'd from a noife it makes in its Belly, when it is taken, refembling a *Drum.* There are three forts of them, the *Black, Red* and *Gold colour;* the Black is fat in the Spring, the Red in the Fall, and the Gold colour believed to be the Black, grown old, becaufe it is obferv'd that young ones of that colour have not been taken. They generally ketch them by *Hook* and *Line,* as *Cod* are, and they fave like it, where the People are fkilful. There are abundance of leffer fifh to be caught of pleafure, but they quit not coft, as thofe I have mentioned, neither in Magnitude nor Number, except the *Herring,* which fwarm in fuch fhoales, that it is hardly Cre-dible; in little Creeks, they almoft fhovel them up in their tubs. There is the *Catfifh,* or *Flathead, Lampry, Eale, Trout, Perch black* and *white, Smelt, Sunfifh,* &c. Alfo *Oyfters, Cockles, Cunks, Crabs, Mufsles, Mannanofes.*

Of Provifion in General

1. I T has been often faid, we were ftarv'd for want of food; fome were apt to fuggeft their fears, others to infinuate their prejudices, and when this was contradicted, and they
affur'd

affur'd we had plenty, both of *Bread*, *Fiſh* and *Fleſh*; then 'twas objected, we were forc't to fetch it from other places at great Charges: but neither is all this true, tho all the World will think we muſt either carry Proviſion with us, or get it of the Neighbourhood till we had gotten Houſes over our heads, and a little Land in tillage. We fetcht none, nor were we wholly helpt by Neighbours; the *Old Inhabitants* ſupplied us with moſt of the *Corn* we wanted, and a good ſhare of *Pork* and *Beef*: tis true, *New-York*, *New-England* and *Road-Iſland*, did with their proviſions fetch our Goods and Money, but at ſuch Rates, that ſome ſold for almoſt what they gave, and others carried their proviſions back, expecting a *better* Market neerer, which ſhowed no ſcarcity, and that we were not totally deſtitute in our own River. But if my advice be of any Value, I would have them buy ſtill, and not weaken their Herds, by killing up their Young Stock *too ſoon*.

2. But the right meaſure of information muſt be the proportion of Value of Proviſions there; to what they are in more planted and mature Colonies. *Beef* is commonly ſold at the rate of *two pence per Pound*; and *Pork* for *two pence half-penny*; *Veal* and *Mutton* at *three pence*, or *three pence half penny*, that Country mony; an Engliſh Shilling going for *fifteen pence*. Grain ſells by the *Buſhel*; *Wheat* at *four ſhillings*; *Rye*, and excellent good, at *three ſhillings*; *Barly two ſhillings ſix pence*; *Indian Corn two ſhillings ſix pence*, *Oats two ſhillings*, in that money ſtill, which in a new Country, where Grain is ſo much wanted for ſeed, as well as food, cannot be called dear, and eſpecially if we conſider the Conſumption of the many new Commers.

3. There is ſo great an encreaſe of Grain, by the dilligent application of People to Husbandry, that within three Years, ſome Plantations have got *Twenty* Acres in Corn, ſome *Forty*, ſome *Fifty*.

4. They

4. They are very careful to encreafe their ftock, and get into *Dairies*, as faft as they can. They already make good *Butter* and *Cheefe*. A good *Cow* and *Calf* by her fide may be worth *three pounds* fterling, in goods at firft Coft. A pare of Working *Oxen*, *eight pounds*: A pare of fat ones, *Little* more, and a plain Breeding *Mare* about *five pounds* fterl.

5. For *Fifh*, it is brought to the Door, both frefh and falt. Six *Alloes* or *Rocks* for *twelve pence*, and falt fifh, at *three fardings* per *pound*, *Oyfters* at 2 s. per *bufhel*.

6. Our D R I N K has been *Beer* and *Punch*, made of *Rum* and *Water*: Our Beer was moftly made of *Moloffes*, which well boyld, with *Saffafras* or *Pine* infufed into it, makes very tollerable drink; but now they make *Mault*, and Mault Drink begins to be common, efpecially at *Ordinaries*, and the Houfes of the more fubftantial People. In our great Town there is an *able Man*, that has fet up a large *Brew. Houfe*, in order to furnifh the People with good Drink, both there, and up and down the River. Having faid this of the Country, for the time I was there, I fhall add one of the many Letters that have come to my hand, becaufe brief and full, and that he is known to be a Perfon of an extraordinary Caution as well as Truth, in what he is wont to Write or Speak.

Philadelphia *the 3 d. of the 6th. month (Auguft)* 1685.

Governour.

Aving an opportunity by a Ship from this River, (out of which feveral have gone this Year) I thought fit to give a fhort account of proceedings, as to fettlements here, and the Improvements both in Town and Country. As to the Country the Improvements are large, and fettlements very throng, by way of *T O W N S H I P S and V I L-L A G E S* Great inclinations to Planting Orchards, which are eafily raifed, and foon brought to perfection. Much Hay-Seed fown, and much

Planting

Planting of Corn *this Year, and great produce said to be, both if* Wheat, Rye *and* Rise ; Baily *and* Oates *prove very well, besides* Indian Corn *and* Pease *of several sorts; also* Kidny Beans, *and* English Pease *of several kinds, I have had in my own Ground, with English Roots,* Turnaps, Parsnaps, Carrets, Onions, Leeks, Radishes *and* Cabbidges, *with abundance of sorts of* Herbs *and* Flowers : *I know but of few seeds that have mist, except* Rosemary *seed, and being English might be old.* Also, *I have such plenty of* Pumpkins, Musmellons, Watermellons, Squashes, Coshaws, Bucks-hens, Cowcumbers *and* Simnells *of Divers kinds; admired at by new Commers, that the Earth should so plentifully cast forth, especially the first Years breaking up; and on that which is counted the* WORST SORT OF SANDY LAND. *I am satisfied, and many more, that the Earth is very fertil, and the Lord hath done his part, if Man use but a moderate Diligence.* Grapes, Mulberies, and many wilde Fruits, and natural Plums, *in abundance, this Year have I seen and eat of. A brave* Orchard *and* Nursery *have I planted, and thrive mightily, and Fruit the first Year. I endeavor choice of Fruits, and Seeds from many parts ; also* Hay-Seed ; *and have sowed a field this spring for tryal. First, I burn'd the leaves, then had it Grub'd, not the field, but the small Roots up, then sowed great and small* Clover, *with a little old Grass-seed, and had it only raked over, not Plowed nor Harrowed, and it grows exceedingly : also for experience I sowed some patches of the same sort in my Garden and Dunged some, and that grows worst. I have planted the Irish* Potatoes, *and hope to have a brave increase to Transplant next Year.* Captain Rapel *(the French man) saith, he made good.* WINE *of the* Grapes *(of the Country) last Year, and Transported some, but intends to make more this Year. Also a French man in this* Town *intends the same, for* Grapes *are very Plentiful.*

Now as to the Town of PHILADELPHIA *it goeth on in Planting and Building to* admiration, *both in the front & backward, and there are about* 600 Houses *in 3 years time. And since I built my* Brick House, *the foundation of which was laid at thy going, which I did design after a good manner, to incourage others, and that from building with Wood; it being the first, many take example, and some that built Wooden Houses, are sorry for it :* Brick *building is said to be* as cheap : *Bricks are exceeding good, and better then when I built : More Makers fallen in, and* Bricks *cheaper, they were before at* 16 s. *English per* 1000, *and now many brave* Brick Houses *are going up, with good Cellars.* Arthur Cook *is building him*

a

a brave Brick House near William Frampton's, on the frontier For William Frampton *hath since built* a good Brick house, by his Brew-house and Bake-house, *and let the other for an Ordinary.* John Wheeler, *from* New-England, *is building* a good Brick house, *by the* Blew Anchor; *and the two Brickmakers* a Double Brick *House and Cellars; besides several others going on.* Samuel Carpenter *has built* another *house by his. I am Building* another Brick *house by mine, which is three large Stories high, besides a good large Brick Cellar under it,* of *two Bricks and a half thickness in the wall, and the next story half under Ground, the Cellar hath an Arched Door for a* Vault *to go (under the Street) to the River, and so to bring in goods, or deliver out.* Humphery Murry, *from* New-York, *has built a large Timber house, with Brick Chimnies.* John Test *has almost finished* a good Brick *House, and a Bake-house of Timber;* and N. Allen *a good house, next to* Thomas Wynns *front Lot.* John Day *a good house, after the* London *fashion, most Brick, with a large frame of Wood, in the front, for Shop Windows; all these have* Belconies. Thomas Smith and Daniel Pege *are Partners, and set to making of* Brick *this Year, and they are very good;* also, Pastorus, *the German Friend, Agent for the* Company at Frankford, *with his* Dutch *People, are preparing to make* Brick *next year.* Samuel Carpenter, *is our* Lime burner *on his Wharf.* Brave L I M E S T O N E *found here, as the Workmen say, being proved. We build most Houses with* Belconies. Lots are much desir'd in the Town, great buying one of an other. *We are now laying the foundation of* a large plain Brick house, *for a Meeting House, in the Center, (sixty foot long, and about forty foot broad) and hope to have it soon up, many hearts and hands at Work that will do it. A large Meeting House,* 50 *foot long, and* 38 *foot broad, also going up, on the front of the River, for an evening Meeting, the work going on apace. Many Towns People setling their liberty Lands. I hope the* Society *will rub off the Reproaches some have cast upon them. We now begin to gather in some thing of our many great Debts.*

I do understand three COMPANIES FOR WHALE CATCHING *are designed to fish in the Rivers Mouth this season, and find through the great* Plenty *of fish, they may begin early. A Fisherman this Year found the way to catch* Whiteins *in this River, and it's expected many sorts of fish more then hath been yet caught, may be taken by the skilful. Fish are in such plenty, that many sorts on tryal, have been taken with Nets, in the Winter time:* The Sweeds *laughing at the* English *for going to try, have since tried themselves. The River so big, and full of several sorts of*

brave

brave fiſh, *that its believed, except frozen over, we may catch any time in the Winter. It's great pity, but two or three experienced* Fiſhermen *were here to Ply this River, to* ſalt *and* ſerve freſh to the Town. *A good way to* Pickle Sturgion *is wanting*; ſuch *abundance in this River,* even before the Town : *many are* Catcht, Boyld *and* Eaten. Laſt Winter *great* plenty of Dear *brought in by the* Indians *and* Engliſh *from the Country. We are generally very Well and Healthy here, but abundance Dead in* Maryland *this Summer* .

The Manufacture of Linnen *by the* Germans *goes on finely, and they make* fine Linnen : Samuel Carpenter *having been lately there, declares, they had gathered one* Crop of Flax, *and had* ſowed *for the* Second, *and* ſaw *it come up well: And they* ſay, *might have had forwarder and better, had they had* old ſeed, *and not* ſtayd ſo *long for the Growth of the* new ſeed to ſow again. *I may believe it, for large hath my experience been this Years, though in a* ſmall *peece of Ground, to the admiration of many.*

I thought fit to ſignify *thus much, knowing thou wouldſt be glad to hear of the People and Provinces welfare*; *the Lord preſerve us all, and make way for thy return, which is much deſired, not only by our Friends, but all* ſorts. *I am, &c. thy truly Loving Friend*

ROBERT TURNER.

Of Further Improvements for Trade and Commerce.

THoſe things that we have in proſpect for Staples of Trade, are *Wine, Linnen, Hemp, Potaſhes,* and *Whale Oyle* ; to ſay nothing of our *Proviſions* for the Iſlands, our *Saw-Mills, Sturgeon,* ſome *Tobacco,* and our *Furs* and *Skins,* which of themſelves are not contemptible ; I might add *Iron* (perhaps *Copper* too) for there is much *Mine* ; and it will be granted us, that we want no Wood, though I muſt confeſs, I cannot tell how to help preferring a domeſtick or ſelf ſubſiſtance, to a life of much profit, by the extream Toyl of forraign Traffick,

Advise

Advice to Adventurers how to imploy their Eſtates, with fair profit.

IT is fit now, that I give ſome Advertiſement to *Adven-turers*, which way they may lay out their Money to beſt advantage, ſo as it may yeild them fair returns, and with content to all concerned, which is the laſt part of my preſent task ; and I muſt needs ſay ſo much wanting, that it has perhaps given ſome occaſion to ignorance and prejudice to run without mercy, meaſure or diſtinction againſt *America*, of which *Pennſylvania* to be ſure has had its ſhare.

1. It is agreed on all hands, that the *Poor* are the *Hands* and *Feet* of the Rich. It is their labour that improves Countries; and to encourage them, is to promote the real benefit of the publick. Now as there are abundance of theſe people in many parts of *Europe*, extreamly deſirous of going to *America* ; ſo the way of helping them thither, or when there, and the return thereof to the Disburſers, will prove what I ſay to be true.

2. There are two ſorts, ſuch as are able to tranſport them-ſelves and Families, but have nothing to begin with there; and thoſe that want ſo much as to tranſport themſelves and Families thither.

3. The firſt of theſe may be entertained in this manner. Say I have 5000 Acres, I will ſettle *Ten Families* upon them, in way of Village, and build each an houſe, an out-houſe for Cattle, furniſh every Family with Stock ; as four *Cows*, two *Sows*, a couple of *Mares*, and a yoke of *Oxen*, with a Town *Horſe*, *Bull* and *Boar* ; I find them with Tools, and give each their firſt Ground-ſeed. They ſhall continue *Seven* Year, or more, as we agree, at *half encreaſe*, being bound to leave the Houſes in repair, and a *Garden* and *Orchard*, I pay-ing for the Trees & at leaſt *twenty Acres* of Land within *Fence*,

and

and *improved* to corn and grafs; the charge will come to about *fixty* pounds Englifh for each Family : At the feven years end, the Improvement will be worth, as things go now, 120 l. befides the value of the *encreafe* of the Stock, which may be neer as much more, allowing for cafualties ; efpecially, if the People are honeft and careful, or a man be upon the fpot himfelf, or have an Overfeer fometimes to infpect them. The charge in the whole is 832 l. And the value of ftock and improvements 2400 l. I think I have been modeft in my computation. Thefe *Farms* are afterwards fit foi *Leafes* at *full* rent, or how elfe the Owner fhall pleafe to difpofe of them.   Alfo the People will by this time be skilled in the Country, and well provided to fettle themfelves with ftock upon their own Land.

4. The other fort of *poor people* may be very beneficially tranfported upon thefe terms : Say I have 5000 *Acres* I fhould fettle as before, I will give to each Family 100 *Acres*, which in the whole makes 1000 ; and to each Family *thirty pounds* Englifh, half in hand, and half there, which in the whole comes to 300 l. After four years are expired, in which time they may be eafie, and in a good condition, they fhall each of them pay *five pounds, and fo yearly for ever, as a Fee-farm rent* ; which in the whole comes to 50 l. a Year. Thus a man that buys 5000. *Acres* may fecure and fettle his 4000 by the gift of one, and in a way that hazard and intereft allowed for, amounts to at leaft ten *per cent.* upon Land fecurity, befides the value it puts upon the reft of the 5000 *Acres.* I propofe that there be at leaft *two working hands* befides the *wife*, whether fon or fervant; and that they oblige what they carry ; and for further fecurity bind themfelves as fervants for fome time, that they will fettle the faid land accordingly, and when they are once feated, their inprovements are *fecurity* enough for the Rent.

5. There is yet another expedient, and that is, give to *ten Families* 1000 *Acres* forever, at a *fmall acknowledgement*, and
fettle

settle them in way of Village, as afore; by their feating thus, the Land taken up is fecured from others, becaufe the *method* of the Country is anfwered, and the value fuch a fettlement gives to the reft referved, is not inconfiderable ; I mean, the 4000 Acres; efpecially that which is *Contiguous* : For their *Children* when grown up, and Handicratts will foon covet to fix next them, and fuch after fettlements to begin at an *Improved Rent in Fee, or for long Leafes, or fmall Acknowledgements, and good Improvements*, muft advance the whole confiderably. I conceive any of thefe methods to iffue in a fufficient advantage to Adventurers, and they all give good encouragement to feeble and poor Families.

6. That which is moft advifeable for People, intended thither, to carry with them, is in fhort, all things relating to *Apparel, Building, Housholdftuf, Husbandry, Fowling,* and *Fishing.* Some *Spice, Spirits* and *double Bear*, at firft, were not amifs : But I advife all to proportion their Eftates thus ; one third in *Money*, and two thirds in *Goods.* Upon *peices of eight*, there will be almoft a third gotten, for they go at 6 s. and by goods well bought, at leaft *fifty* pounds fterl. for every hundred pounds ; fo that a man worth 400 l. here, is worth 600 l. there, without fweating.

Of the Natives.

1. BEcaufe many Stories have been prejudicially propagated, as if we were upon ill terms with the *Natives*, and fometimes, like *Jobs Kindred*, all cut off but the Meffenger that brought the Tidings; I think it requifit to fay thus much, that as there never was any fuch Meffenger, fo the dead People were *alive*, at our laft advices; fo far are we from *ill* terms with the *Natives*, that we have liv'd in great friendfhip. I have made feven Purchaffes, and in Pay and Prefents they have received

received at leaft *twelve hundred pounds* of me.   Our humanity.
has obliged them fo far, that they generally leave their guns
at home, when they come to our fettlements; they offer us no
affront, not fo much as to one of our *Dogs*; and if an of them
break our Laws, they fubmit to be punifht by them : and
to this they have tyed themfelves by an obligation *under their
hands*. We leave not the leaft indignity to them unrebukt, nor
wrong unfatisfied.   Juftice gains and aws them.   They have
fome Great Men amongft them, I mean, for Wifdom, Truth
and Juftice.   I refer, to my former Account about their
Laws, Manners and *Religious Rites*.

Of the Goverment.

THE *Goverment* is according to the words of the *Grant*,
as near to the Englifh as conveniently may be : In the
whole, we aim at *Duty* to the King, the Prefervation of *Right*
to all, the fuppreffion of *Vice*, and encouragement of *Vertue*, and
Arts ; with *Libert* to all People to worfhip Almighty God,
according to their *Faith* and *Perfwafion*.

Of the Seafons of Going, and ufual time of Paffage.

1. THO) Ships go hence at all times of the Year, it muft
be acknowledged, that to go fo as to arrive at *Spring*
or *Fall*, is beft.   For the Summer may be of the hotteft, for
frefh Commers; and in the Winter, the wind that prevails, is
the North Weft, and that blows off the Coaft, fo that fometimes
it is difficult to enter the *Capes*.

2. I propofe therefore, that Ships go hence about the middle
of the moneths call'd *February* and *Auguft*, which, allowing
two moneths for paffage, reaches time enough to plant in
the *Spring* fuch things as are carried hence to plant, and in the
Fall

Fall to get a small Cottage, and clear some Land against the next *Spring*. I have made a discovery of about a hundred Miles West, and find those back Lands richer in Soyl, Woods and Fountains, then that by *Delaware*; especially upon the *SASQUEHANAH River*.

3. I must confess I prefer the *Fall* to come thither, as believing it is more healthy to be followed with Winter then Summer; tho, through the *great goodness and mercy of God*, we have had an extrordinary portion of health, for so new and numerous a Colony, notwithstanding we have not been so regular in time.

4. The *Passage* is not to be set by any man; for Ships will be quicker and flower. Some have been *four* moneths, and some but *one* and as often. Generally between *six and nine weeks*. One year, of four and twenty Sayl, I think, there was not three above nine, and there was one or two under six weeks in passage.

5. To render it more healthy, it is good to keep as much upon *Deck* as may be; for the *Air* helps against the offensive smells of a *Crowd*, and a *close place*. Also to *scrape* often the Cabbins, under the Beds; and either carry store of *Rue* and *Wormwood*, and some *Rosemary*, or often sprinkle *Vineger* about the Cabbin. *Pitch* burnt, is not amiss sometimes against faintness and infectious scents. I speak my experience for their benefit and direction that may need it.

And because some has urged my coming back, as an argument against the place, and the probability of its improvement; Adding, that I would for that reason never return: I think fit to say, That *Next Summer*, God willing, I intend to go back, and carry my Family, and the best part of my Personal Estate with me. And this I do, not only of Duty, but Inclination and Choice. God will Bless and Prosper poor *America*.

I

I fhall conclude with this further *Notice*, that to the end fuch as are willing to embrace any of the foregoing propofitions for the *Improvement of Adventurers Eftates*, may not be difcouraged, from an inability to find fuch *Land Lords, Tennants, Mafters* and *Servants*, if they intimate their defires to my Friend and Agent *Philip Ford*, living in *Bow-Lane* in *London*, they may in all probability be well accommodated; few of any quality or capacity, defigned to the *Province*, that do not inform him of their inclinations and condition.

Now for you that think of going thither, I have this to fay, by way of caution; if an *hair* of our heads falls not to the ground, without the providence of God, Remember, *your removal* is of greater moment. Wherefore have a due reverence and regard to his good Providence, as becomes a People that profefs a belief in *Providence*. Go clear in your felves, and of all others. Be moderate in Expectation, count on Labour before a Crop and Coft before Gain, for fuch perfons will beft endure difficulties, if they come, and bear the Succefs, as well as find the Comfort that ufually follow fuch confiderate undertakings.

Worminghurft-Place, 12fth}
of the 10th Month 85.}   **William Penn.**

PAge 1. line 2. Read *thing*. p. 3. l 9 r. *that*. p. 11. l. laft r. *foon brought*. p. 12 l. 9. r. *buckfhorns*. p. 14. l. 21. r *Thofe things*. p. 17. l. 2. for *Bond*, read *Land*. l. 8. r. *on fmall* l. 17. l. *there* r. *their*. p. 20. l. 3. r. *Improvement*.

THE END.

EXCERPTS FROM
A PERSWASIVE TO MODERATION

William Penn, *A Perswasive to Moderation to Church Dissenters, in Prudence and Conscience: Humbly Submitted to the King and his Great Councel* (London, 1686), pp. 1–26 and 47–9.

William Penn's *Perswasive to Moderation* presents another two common themes in this collection: the benefits of religious freedom and the use of the church as an instrument of social (and economic) control. Penn argues that tolerance is the key to economic prosperity; a country that is intolerant loses its dissenters, labour and capital to another country, thereby impoverishing itself in the process. On the other hand, if tolerance is granted, dissenters from around the world will flock to the country, bringing wealth with them. In this text, we also see some of Penn's thoughts on the economic issue of money. He argues that overvaluation of coins (or currency) should be prohibited, and that the church should take a leading role in the supervision of this law. Penn's interest shows the growing clamour in America for monetary reform, which it was hoped would alleviate the chronic shortage of currency in the colonies. Penn also argues against the accumulation of vast quantities of wealth, indicating that avarice is one of the most evil of sins. Through hard work, saving, investment and supporting charities, individuals and countries can become wealthy. Thus, in many ways, Penn's Quakerism and Massachusetts Puritanism share a number of common economic themes.

A
PERSWASIVE
TO
Moderation
TO
Church Dissenters,
In Prudence and Conscience:
Humbly Submitted to the
KING
AND HIS
Great Councel.

By one of the Humblest and most Dutiful
of his Dissenting Subjects.

Let your Moderation *be known unto all men, for the Lord is at Hand,*
Phil. 4. 5.

A Christian Toleration *often dissipates their Strength, whom Rougher*
Opposition fortifies, K. Charls 1. to the late King.

A
PERSWASIVE
TO
Moderation &c.

ODERATION, the Subject of this Difcourfe, is in plainer Englifh, **Liberty of Confcience to Church Diffenters**: A Caufe I have, with all Humility undertaken to plead againft the Prejudices of the Times.

That there is fuch a thing as **Confcience**, and the **Liberty** of it, in reference to *Faith* and *Worfhip* towards God, muft not be denied, even by thofe, that are moft fcandal'd at the *Ill* ufe fome feem to have made of fuch Pretences. But to fettle the Terms. By **Confcience**, I underftand *the Apprehenfion and Perfwafion a man has of his Duty to God*: By **Liberty of Confcience**, I mean *A Free and open Profeffion and Exercife of that Duty; efpecially in Worfhip*: But I always premife this *Confcience* to keep within the bounds of *Morality*, and that it be neither *Frantick* nor *Mifchievous*, but a *Good Subject*, a *Good Child*, a *Good Servant in all the affairs of Life*: As exact to yield to *Cæfar* the things that are *Cæfar's*, as jealous of with-holding from *God* the thing that is *God's*: In brief, he
that

that acknowledges the civil *Government* under which he lives, and that maintains no Principle hurtful to his Neighbour in his civil Property : For he that in any thing violates his Duty to thefe Relations, cannot be faid to obferve it to God, who ought to have his *Tribute* out of it. Such do not reject their *Prince, Parent, Mafter* or *Neighbour*, but God who enjoyns that Duty to him. Thofe Pathetick words of Chrift will naturally enough reach the Caufe, *In that ye did it not to them, ye did it not to me*; for Duty to fuch Relations have a divine Stamp : And divine Right runs through more things of the World, and Acts of our Lives then we are aware of : And Sacriledge may be committed againft more then the Church. Nor will a Dedication to God, of the Robbery from Man, expiate the Guilt of Difobedience : For though Zeal could turn *Goffip* to Theft, his Altars would renounce the Sacrifice.

The *Confcience* then that I ftate, and the *Liberty* I pray, carrying fo great a *Salvo* and Deference to publick and private Relations, no ill defign, can with any Juftice, be fixt upon the Author, or Reflection upon the Subject, which by this time, I think, I may venture to call a **Toleration**

But to this fo much craved, as well as needed *Toleration*, I meet with two Objections of weight, the falving of which will make way for it in this Kingdom. And the firft is a Difbelief of the Poffibility of the thing. *Toleration of Diffenting Worfhips from that eftablifh't, is not practicable*(fay fome) *without danger to the State, with which it is interwoven.* This is Political. The other Objections is, *That admitting Diffenters to be in the Wrong (which is always premifed by the National Church) fuch Latitude were the way to keep up the Dif-union, & inftead of compelling them into a better Way, leave them in the poffeffion poſſeſſion and perſuit of their old Errors.* This is *Religious.* I think I have given the Objections fairly, 'twill be my next buſineſs to anſwer them as fully.

The ſtrength of the firſt Objection againſt this Liberty, is the *Danger* ſuggeſted to the *State*; the Reaſon is, the National Form being *interwoven* with the Frame of the Government. But this ſeems to me only ſaid, and not only (with ſubmiſſion) not prov'd, but not true: For the eſtabliſht Religion and Worſhip are no other ways interwoven with the Government, than that the Government makes profeſſion of them, and by divers Laws has made them the *Currant Religion*, and required all the Members of the State to conform to it.

This is nothing but what may as well be done by the Government, for any other Perſwaſion, as that. 'Tis true, 'tis not eaſie to change an eſtabliſh't Religion, nor is that the Queſtion we are upon; but *State Religions* have been chang'd without the change of the *States* We ſee this in the Governments of *Germany* and *Denmark* upon the *Reformation*: But more clearly and near our ſelves, in the caſe of *Henry* the *eighth*, *Edward* the *ſixth*, *Queen Mary* and *Elizabeth*; for the Monarchy *ſtood*, the Family *remained* and *ſucceeded* under all the Revolutions of State-Religion, which could not have been, had the Propoſition been generally true.

The change of Religion then, does not *neceſſarily* change the Government, or alter the State; and if ſo, *a fortiori*, Indulgence of Church-Diſſenters, does not *neceſſarily* hazard a change of the State, where the preſent State-Religion or Church remains the ſame, for That I premiſe.

Some may ſay, *That it were more facile to change from one National Religion to another, than to maintain the Monarchy and Church, againſt the Ambition and Faction of divers diſſenting Parties.* But this is improbable at leaſt. For it

we-

were to fay, That it is an eafier thing to change a whole
Kingdom, than with the Soveraign Power, followed with
Armies, Navies, Judges, Clergy, and all the *Conformiſts* of
the Kingdom, to fecure the Government from the Ambition
and Faction of *Diſſenters,* as differing in their Intereſts
within themfelves, as in their Perfwafions; and were they
united, have neither Power to awe, nor Rewards to allure
to their Party. They can only be formidable, when *headed*
by the Soveraign. They may ſtop a *Gap,* or make, by his
Acceſſion, a Ballance: Otherwife, till 'tis harder to fight
broken and divided Troops, than an entire Body of an Army,
it will be always *eaſier* to maintain the Government under
a Toleration of Diſſenters, than in a total change of Religion, and even then it felf, it has not fail'd to have been preferved. But whether it be more or lefs eafie, is not our point;
if they are many, the danger is of exafperating, not of
making them eafie; for the force of our Queftion is, Whether fuch Indulgence be fafe to the State? And here we
have the firft and laft, the beft and greateft Evidence for
us, which is **Fact** and **Experience,** the Journal and Refolves of Time, and Treafure of the Sage.

For, *Firſt,* the **Jews,** that had moft to fay for their Religion, and whofe Religion was **Twin** to their State (both
being joyn'd, and fent with Wonders from Heaven) *Indulg'd*
Strangers in their Religious Diffents. They requir'd but the
belief of the *Noachical* Principles, which were common to the
World: No *Idolator,* and but a *Moral Man,* and he had his
Liberty, ay, and fome *Priviledges* too, for he had an apartment in the Temple, and this without danger to the Government. Thus *Maimonides,* and others of their own Rabbics,
and *Grotius* out of them.

The *Wiſdom* of the **Gentiles** was very admireable in this,
that

that tho' they had many Sects of Philosophers among them, each diffenting from the other in their Principles, as well as Difcipline, and that not only in Phyfical things, but points Me-Metaphyfical, in which fome of the Fathers were not *free*, the School-men *deeply engaged*, and our prefent Accademies but too much *perplext*; yet they *indulg'd* them and the beft Livers with fingular Kindnefs: The greateft States-men and Captains often beccming *Patrons* of the Sects they beft affected, honouring their *Readings* with their Prefence and Applaufe. So far were thofe Ages, which we have made as the original of Wifdom and Politenefs, from thinking *Toleration* an Error of State, or dangerous to the Government. Thus *Plutrach*, *Strabo*, *Laertius*, and others.

To thefe Inftances I may add the Latitude of old *Rome*, that had almoft as many *Deities* as Houfes: For *Varro* tells us of no lefs than **thirty Thoufand** feveral **Sacra**, or Religious Rites among her People, and yet without a Quarrel: Unhappy fate of *Chriftianity!* the beft of Religions, and yet her Porteffors maintain lefs Charity than Idolaters, while it fhou'd be peculiar to them. I fear, it fhews us to have but little of it at Heart.

But nearer home, and in our own time, we fee the effects of a difcreet *Indulgence*, even too Emulation. **Holland**, that **Bogg** of the World, neither Sea nor dry Land, now the *Rival* of talleft Monarchs; not by *Conquefts*, *Marriages*, or acceffion of *Royal Blood*, the ufual wayes to Empire, but by her own fuperlative *Clemency* and *Induftry*; for the one was the effect of the other: She cherifht her People, whatfoever were their *Opinions*, as the reafonable ftock of the Country, the Heads and Hands of her Trade and Wealth; and making them eafie in the main point, their *Confcience*, fhe became great by them: This made her fill with People, and they fill'd her with *Riches* and *Strength*.

And

And if it should be said, *She is upon her Declenfion for all that.*
I Anfwer, All States muft know it, nothing is here *Immortal.*
Where are the **Babylonian, Perſian** and **Grecian** Empires?
And are not **Lacedemon, Athens, Rome** and **Carthage**
gone before her ?   Kingdoms and Common-Wealths have
their *Births* and *Growths,* their *Declenfions* and *Deaths,* as
well as private Families and Perfons: But 'tis owing, neither
to the *Armies* of *France,* nor *Navies* of *England,* but her own
Domeftick Troubles.

Seventy Two ſticks in her Bones yet : The growing
Power of the Prince of *Orange,* muft in fome degree, be an
Ebb to that States Strength ; for they are not fo unanimous
and vigrous in their Intereft as formerly : But were they fecure againft the danger of their own Ambition and Jealoufie,
any body might enfure their Glory at *five per Cent.*   But
fome of their greateft men apprehending they are in their
Climacterical Juncture, give up the Ghoft, and care not, if
they muft fall, by what hand it is.

Others chufe a *Stranger,* and think one afar off will give
the beft Terms, and leaft annoy them : whileft a confiderable Party have chofen a *Domeftick* Prince, *a Kin* to their
early Succeſſes by the *fore-Father's fide* (the Gallantry of his
Anceftors)   And that his own greatnefs and fecurity are
wrapt up in theirs, and therefore modeftly hope to find
their Account in his Profperity.   But this is a kind of Digref-
greflion, only before I leave it, I dare venture to add, that if
the Prince of *Orange* changes not the Policies of that State,
he will not change her Fortune, and he will mightily add to
his own.

But perhaps I fhall be told   *That no body doubts that* **Toler-**
ation *is an* agreeable *thing to a Common-Wealth, where every*
one thinks he has a fhare in the Government ; ay, that the one is the
confequence of the other, and therefore moft carefully to be avoided
by

by all Monarchical States. This indeed were fhrowdly to the purpofe, in *England*, if it were but true. But I don't fee how there can be one true Reafon advanc'd in favour of this Objection: *Monarchies*, as well as *Common-Wealths*, fubfifting by the Prefervation of the People under them.

But, *Firſt*, if this were true, it would follow by the *Rule* of *Contraries*, that a *Republick* could not fubfift with *Unity* and *Hierarchy*, which is *Monarchy* in the Church ; but it muft, from fuch *Monarchy* in *Church*, come to *Monarchy* in *State* too. But *Venice, Genova, Lucca*, feven of the *Cantons* of *Switzerland*, (and *Rome* her felf, for fhe is an *Ariſtocracy*) all under the loftieft *Hierarchy* in Church, and where is no *Toleration*, fhow in fact, that the contrary is true.

But, *Secondly*, this Objection makes a Common-Wealth the better Government of the two, and fo overthrows the thing it would eftablifh. This is effectually done, if I know any thing, fince a Common-Wealth is *hereby* rendred a more copious, powerful and beneficial Government to Mankind, and is made better to anfwer Contingencies and Emergencies of State, becaufe this fubfifts *either* way, but *Monarchy* not, if the Objection be true. The one profpers by *Union* in Worfhip and Difcipline, and by *Toleration* of diffenting Churches from the National. The other only by an *univerſal Conformity* to a National Church. I fay, this makes *Monarchy* (in it felf, doubtlefs, an admirable Government) *leſs Powerful, leſs Extended, leſs Propitious*, and finally *leſs Safe* to the People under it, than a *Common-Wealth* ; In that *no Security* is left to *Monarchy* under diverfity of Worfhips, which yet no man can defend or forbid, but may often arrive, as it hath in *England*, more than five times in the two laft Ages. And truly 'tis natural for men to chufe to fettle where they may be fafeft from the *Power* and *Miſchief* of fuch Accidents of State.

Upon

Upon the whole matter, it is to reflect the *laſt Miſchief* upon *Monarchy*, the worſt Enemies it has could hope to diſgrace, or endanger it by ; ſince it is to tell the People under it, that they muſt either *conform*, or be *deſtroyed*, or to ſave themſelves, turn *Hypocrites*, or *change* the Frame of the Government they under. A perplexity both to *Monarch* and *People*, that nothing can be greater but the comfort of knowing the Objection is *Falſe*. And that which ought to make every reaſonable man of this Opinion, is the cloud of Witneſſes that almſt every Age of *Monarchy* affords us.

I will begin with that of **Iſrael**, the moſt exact and ſacred Pattern of *Monarchy*, begun by a valiant Man, tranſlated to the beſt, and improv'd by the wiſeſt of Kings, whoſe Miniſters were neither *Fools*, nor *Fanaticks* : Here we ſhall Proviſion for Diſſenters. Their *Proſoliti Domicilii* were ſo far from being compelled to their National Rites, that they were expreſly forbid to *obſerve* them. Snch were the *Egyptians* that came with them out of *Egypt*, the *Gibeonites* and *Canaanites*, a great People, that after their ſeveral Forms, worſhipt in an *apartment* of the ſame Temple. The *Jews* with a Liturgy, they without one : The *Jews* had *Prieſts*, but theſe none : The *Jews* had variety of Oblations, theſe People burnt Offerings only. All that was required of them was the natural Religion of *Noah*, in which the Acknowledgement and and Worſhip of the true God, was, as it ſtill ought to be, the main point ; nay, ſo far they from Coercive Conformity, that they did not ſo much as oblige them to obſeve their *Sabbath*, though one of the ten Commandments : *Grotius* and *Selden* ſay more. Certainly this was great Indulgence, ſince ſo unſuitable an Uſage lookt like *prophaning* their Devotion, and a common *nuſance* to their National Religion. One would think by this, that their Care lay on the ſide of

preſerving

preferving their Cult from the *touch* or *acceſſion* of Diſſenters,&c not of *forcing* them, by *undoing* Penalties to conform. This muſt needs be evident: For if Gods *Religion* and *Monarchy* (for ſo we are taught to believe it) did not, & would not at a time, when Religion lay *leſs* in the Mind, and *more* in Ceremony, compel Conformity from Diſſenters, we hope we have got the beſt Preſidents on our ſide.

But if this Inſtance be of moſt Authority, we have another very exemplary, and to our point pertinent; for it ſhews what *Monarchy* may do : It is yielded us from the famous Story of **Mordecai**. He, with his *Jews*, were in a bad pleight with the King **Ahaſuerus**, by the ill Offices **Haman** did them : The Arguments he uſed were drawn from the common Topicks of **Faction** and **Sedition**, *That they were an odd and dangerous People under differing Laws of their own, and refuſed Obedience to his*; So denying his *Supremacy*. Diſſenters with a witneſs : Things moſt tender to any Government.

The King thus incenſed, commands the Laws to be put in Execution, and decrees the Ruin of *Mordecai* with all the *Jews*. But the King is timely intreated, his heart ſoftens, the Decree is revok'd, and *Mordecai* and his Friends ſaved. The Conſequence was, as extream Joy to the *Jews*, ſo Peace and Bleſſings to the King. And that which heightens the Example, is the *Greatneſs* and *Infidelity* of the Prince : Had the Inſtance been in a *Jew*, it might have been placed to his *greater Light* or *Piety* : In a petty Prince, to the *Paucity* or *Intireneſs* of his Territory : But that an *Heathen*, and King of One hundred and ſeven and twenty Provinces, ſhould *throughout* his vaſt Dominions not fear, but **practiſe Toleration** with good ſucceſs, has ſomething admirable in it.

If we pleaſe to remember the *Tranquility*, and ſucceſs of thoſe Heathen *Roman* Emperors, that allowed *Indulgence*; that *Auguſtus* ſent *Hecatombs* to *Jeruſalem*, and the wiſeſt honoured the

the *Jews*, and at leaſt ſpared the divers Sects of *Chriſtians*, it will certainly oblige us to think, that Princes, whoſe Religions are *nearer of Kin*, to thoſe of the Diſſenters of our times, may not unreaſonably hope for quiet from a diſcreet Toleration, eſpecially when there is nothing peculiar in *Chriſtianity* to render Princes unſafe in ſuch an *Indulgence*. The admirable *Prudence* of the Emperor **Jobianus**, in a quite contrary me-thod to thoſe of the Reigns of his Predeceſſors, ſettled the moſt **Imbroiled** time of the Chriſtian World, *almoſt to a Mi-racle*; for though he found the hearts of the *Arrian* and *Ortho-dox* carried to a barbarous height, (to ſay nothing of the *No-vations*, and other diſſenting Intereſts, the Emperor eſteem-ing thoſe Calamities the effect of Coercing Conformity to the Prince's or States Religion, and that this Courſe did not only waſte *Chriſtians*, but expoſe *Chriſtians* to the ſcorn of *Heathens*, and ſo ſcandal, thoſe whom they ſhould convert, he reſolutely declared, *That he would have none* **moleſted** *for the different ex-erciſe of their Religious Worſhip*; which (and that in a trice (for he reigned but ſeven Moneths) calm'd the impetuous Storms of Diſſention, and reduced the Empire, before agitated with the moſt uncharitable Conteſts) to a wonderful *Serenity* and *Peace*; Thus a *kindly Amity* brought a *civil Unity* to the *State*; which endeavours for a forc'd Unity never did to the Church, but had formerly filled the Government with incomparable *Miſeries*, as well as the Church with incharity: And which is ſad, I muſt needs ſay, that thoſe *Leaders* of the *Church* that ſhould have been the *Teachers* and *Examples* of Peace, in ſo ſingular a juncture of the *Churches* ferment, did, more then any *blow the Trumpet, and kindle the Fire of Diviſion*. So dange-rous is it to *Super-fine* upon the Text, and then *Impoſe*, it upon Penalty, for Faith.

Valantinian the Emperor (we are told by *Socrates Scho-laſticus) was a great Honourer of thoſe that favoured his own Faith*;

Faith; *but so, as he molested not the* Arrians *at all.* And *Mar-cellinus* further adds in his Honour, *That he was much Renown'd for his Moderate Carriage during his Reign*; *insomuch, that amongst sundry Sects of Religion, he troubled no man for his Conscience, imposing neither This nor That to be observed*; *much less with menacing Edicts and Injunctions*, did he compel *others, his Subjects, to bow the Neck, or* conform *to that which himself Worshipped, but left such Points as clear and untouch't as he found them.*

Gratianus & Theodsius the *great*, *Indulged* divers sorts of *Christians*; but the *Novations* of all the Dissenters were prefer'd: which was so far from *Insecuring*, that it preserv'd the *Tranquility* of the *Empire*. Nor till the time of *Celestine* Bishop of *Rome*, were the *Novations* disturbed; And the *Persecution* of them and the Assumption of the *secular Power* began much at the same time. But the *Novations* at *Constantinople* were not so dealt withal; for the *Greek* Bishops continued to permit them the quiet enjoyment of their dissenting Assemblies; as *Socrates* tells us in his fifth and seventh Book of Ecclesiastical Story.

I shall descend nearer our own times; for notwithstanding no Age has been more furiously moved, then that which *Jovianus* found, and therefore the Experiment of Indulgence *was never better made*, yet to speak more in view of this time of day, we find our Contemporaries, of remoter Judgments in Religion, under no manner of difficulty in this point. The Grand Signior, Great Mogul, Czars of Muscovia, King of Persia; the Great Monarchs of the East have *long allow'd and prosper'd with a Toleration*: And who does not know that this gave Great Tamerlan his mighty Victories? In these Western Countries we see the same thing.

Cardinal D' Ossat in his 92d Letter to *Villroy*, Secretary
to

to *Henry* the fourth of *France,* gives us Doctrine and Ex-
ample for the Subject in hand; "Besides (says he) that
"Necessity has no Law, be it in what case it will; our *Lord*
"*Jesus Christ* instructs us by his Gospel, *To let the Tares*
' *alone, left removing them, may endanger the Wheat.* That
"other *Catholick* Princes have allow'd it without *Rebuke.*
"That particularly the Duke of *Savoy,* who (as great a
"Zealot as he would be thought for the Catholick Religion)
"Tolerates the Hereticks in three of his Provinces, namely,
"*Angroyne, Lucerne* and *Perofe.* That the King of *Poland*
"does as much, not only in *Sweedland,* but in *Poland* it self.
"That all the Princes of the *Auftrian* Family, that are cele-
"brated as Pillars of the *Catholick Church,* do the like, not
"only in the Towns of the Empire, but in their *proper* Ter-
"ritories, as in *Auftria* it self, from whence they take the
"Name of their Honour. In *Hungary, Bohemia, Moravia,*
"*Lufatia, Stirria, Carniolia* and *Croatia* the like. That *Charles*
"the fifth, Father of the King of *Spain,* was the Perfon that
"taught the King of *France,* and other *Princes,* how to
"yield to fuch Emergencies. That his Son, the prefent
"King of *Spain,* who is efteemed *Arch-Catholick,* and that is,
"as the *Atlas* of the *Catholick Church, Tolerates* notwithftan-
"ding, at this day, in his Kingdoms of *Valentia* and *Gra-*
"*nada,* the *Moors* themfelves in their *Mahumatifme,* and has
"offer'd to thofe of *Zealand, Holland,* and other *Hereticks*
"of the Low-Countries, the *free Exercife* of their pretended
"Religion, fo that they will but acknowledge and Obey
"him in Civil Matters. It was of thofe Letters of this
extraordinary Man, for fo he was (whether we regard him
in his Ecclefiaftical Dignity, or his greater Chriftian and Civil
Prudence) that the great Lord *Falkland* faid, *A Minifter of*
State fhould no more be without Cardinal d' Offat's *Letters, than*
a Parfon without his Bible. And indeed, if we look into
France,

France, we fhall find the Indulgence of thofe Proteftants, hath been a flourifhing to that Kingdom, as their *Arms* a Succour to their King. 'Tis true, that fince they helpt the Minifters of his Greatnefs to Succefs, that haughty Monarch has chang'd his Meafures, and refolves their Conformity to his own Religion, or their Ruin; but no man can give another Reafon for it, than that he thinks it for his turn to pleafe that part of his own Church, which are the prefent necef- fary and unwearied Inftruments of his abfolute Glory. But let us fee the end of this Conduct, it will require more time to approve the Experiment.

As it was the Royal Saying of 𝔖𝔱𝔢𝔭𝔥𝔢𝔫, 𝔎𝔦𝔫𝔤 of 𝔓𝔬𝔩𝔞𝔫𝔡, That he was a *King of* 𝔐𝔢𝔫, *and not of* 𝔠𝔬𝔫𝔣𝔠𝔦𝔢𝔫𝔠𝔢 ; *a Com- mander of* 𝔅𝔬𝔡𝔦𝔢𝔰, *and not of* 𝔖𝔬𝔲𝔩𝔰. So we fee a *Toleration* has been practifed in that Country of a long time, with no ill *Succefs* to the *State* ; the Cities of *Cracovia*, *Racovia*, and many other Towns of *Note*, almoft wholly diffenting from the com- mon *Religion* of the *Kingdom*, which is *Roman Catholick*, as the others are *Socinian* and *Calvinift*, mighty oppofite to that, as well as to themfelves.

The King of 𝔇𝔢𝔫𝔪𝔞𝔯𝔨, in his large Town of *Altona*, but about a Mile from *Hambrough*, and therefore called fo, that is, *All-to-near*, is a pregnant proof to our point For though his Seat be fo remote from that place, and another ftrong and in- finuating State, fo near, yet under his *Indulgence* of divers Per- fwafions, they enjoy their *Peace*, and he that *Security*, that he is not upon better terms in any of his more *immediate* and *Uni- form* Dominions. I leave it to the thinking Reader, if it be not much owing to this *Freedom*, and that a contrary courfe were not the way for him to furnifh his Neighbours with means to Depopulate that place, or make it uneafie and chargeable to him to keep?

If we look into other Parts of 𝔊𝔢𝔯𝔪𝔞𝔫𝔶, where we find a
Stout

Stout and Warlike People, fierce for the thing they opine, or beleve, we shall find the Prince Palatine of the *Rhine*, has been safe, and more potent by his *Indulgence*, witness his *Improvements* at *Manhine*: And as (believe me) he acted the Prince to his People in other things, so in this to the Empire; for he made bold with the Constitution of it in the Latitude he gave his Subjects in this Affair.

The *Elector* of Bradenburg is himself a *Calvinist*, his people mostly *Lutheran*, yet in part of his *Dominions*, the *Roman Catholicks* enjoy their Churches quietly.

The Duke of Newburg, & a *strict* *Roman Catholick*, Brother-in Law to the present Emperor, in his Province of *Juliers*, has, not only at *Dewsburg*, *Mulheim*, and other places, but in *Duseldorp* it self, where the Court resides, *Lutheran*, and *Calvinist*, as well as *Roman Catholick* Assemblies.

The *Elector* of Saxony, by Religion a *Lutheran*, in his City of *Budissin*, has both *Lutherans* and *Roman Catholick* in the same Church, parted only by a Grate.

In Ausburg, they have two chief Magistrates, as their *Duumvirat*, one must always be a *Roman Catholick*, and the other a *Lutheran*.

The Bishop of Osnabrug is himself a *Lutheran*, and in the Town of his Title, the *Roman Catholicks*, as well as *Lutherans*, have their Churches: And which is more, the next Bishop must be a *Catholick* too: For like the Buckets in the Well, they take turns: One way to be sure, so that one be but in the Right.

From hence we will go to Sultzbach, a small Territory, but has a great Prince, I mean, in his own *extraordinary* Qualities; for, among other things, we shall find him act the Moderator among his People. By Profession he is a *Roman Catholick*, but has *Simultaneum Religionis Exercitium*, not only *Lutherans* and *Roman Catholicks* enjoy their different Worships, but
alternatively

alternatively in one and the same place, the same day ; so ballancing his Affection by his wisdom, that there appears neither Partiality in him, nor Envy in them, though of such opposite Perswasions

I will end these Forreign Instances with a Prince and Bishop, all in one, and he a *Roman Catholick* too, and that is the Bishop of *Mentz* ; who admits, with a very peaceable success such *Lutherans* with his *Catholicks*, to enjoy their Churches, as live in his Town of 𝕰𝖗𝖋𝖔𝖗𝖉. Thus doth Practice tell us, that neither *Monarchy* nor *Hierarchy* are in danger from a Toleration.   On the contrary, the Laws of the *Empire*, which are the Acts of the *Emperor*, and the *Soveraign Princes* of it, have Tolerated these three Religious Perswasions, *viz*. The *Roman Catholick, Lutheran* and *Calvinist*, and they may as well tolerate three more, for the same Reasons, and with the same Success.   For it is not their *greater nearerness* or consistency in Doctrine, or in Worship ; on the contrary, they differ much, and by that, and other Circumstances, are sometimes engaged in great Controversies, yet is a Toleration practicable, and the way of Peace with them

And which is closest to our Point, at home it self, we see that a *Toleration* of the 𝕵𝖊𝖜𝖘, 𝖋𝖗𝖊𝖓𝖈𝖍 and 𝕯𝖚𝖙𝖈𝖍 in *England*, all *Dissenters* from the *National Way* : And the connivance that has been in 𝕴𝖗𝖊𝖑𝖆𝖓𝖉 ; and the down-right *Toleration* in most of the *Kings* 𝕻𝖑𝖆𝖓𝖙𝖆𝖙𝖎𝖔𝖓𝖘 abroad, prove the Assertion, *That Toleration is not dangerous to Monarchy*. For Experience tells us, where it is in any degree admitted, the *Kings* Affairs *prosper* most ; *People, Wealth* and *Strength* being sure to follow such *Indulgence*.

But after all that I have said in Reason and Fact, why *Toleration* is safe to *Monarchy*, Story tells us that worse things have befallen *Princes* in Countries under *Ecclesiastical Union*, than in Places under divided Forms of Worship ; and so Tolerating raring. Countries ftand to the Prince, more then upon equal terms with *Conforming ones.* And where Princes have been expofed to hardfhip in tolerating Countries, they have as often come from the Conforming, as Non-conforming party; and fo the *Diffenter* is upon equal terms, to the Prince or State, with the *Conformift*.

The firft is evident in the **Jews**, under the conduct of *Mofes*; their Diffention came from the men of their own Tribes, fuch as **Corah, Dathan** and **Abiram**, with their pertakers. To fay nothing of the *Gentiles.*

The Miferies and Slaughters of *Mauritius* the Emperor, prove my Point, who by the greateft **Church-men** of his time was withftood, and his Servant that perpetrated the *Wickednefs, by them,* fubftituted in his room, becaufe more officious to their Grandure. What power but that of the *Church,* dethroned *Childrek,* King of *France,* and fet *Pippin* in his place? The Miferies of the Emperors, *Henry* the fourth and fifth, Father and Son, from their rebellious Subjects, raifed and animated by the power of *Conformifts;* dethroning both, as much as they could, are notorious. 'Tis alledg'd, that *Sigifmond* King of *Sweedland,* was rejected by that *Lutheran* Country, becaufe he was a *Roman-Catholick.*

If we come nearer home, which is moft futable to the reafons of the *difcourfe,* we find the **Church-men** take part with *William Rufus,* and *Henry* the firft againft *Robert* their elder Brother; and after that, we fee fome of the greateft of them *make Head* againft their King, namely *Anfelm* Arch-Bifhop of *Canterbury,* and his Party, as did his Succeffor *Thomas* of *Becket* to the fecond *Henry.* *Stephen* ufurp'd the Crown when there was a *Church Union:* And King *John* lived *miferable* for all that, and at laft dyed *by one of his own Religion too.* The Diffentions that agitated the Reign of his Son *Henry* the third, and the *Barrons* War, with *Bifhop Grofteeds* Bleffing

Blessing to *Mumford* their General : The *Deposition* and *Murther* of the second 𝕰𝖉𝖜𝖆𝖗𝖉, and 𝕽𝖎𝖈𝖍𝖆𝖗𝖉, and sixth 𝕳𝖊𝖓𝖗𝖞, and his Son the *Prince*. The *Usurption* of 𝕽𝖎𝖈𝖍𝖆𝖗𝖉 the third, and the *Murther* of the Sons of 𝕰𝖉𝖜𝖆𝖗𝖉 the fourth, in the Tower of *London*. The *civil War* that followed between him and the *Earl of Richmond*, afterwards our *wise* 𝕳𝖊𝖓𝖗𝖞 the *seventh*, were all perpetrated in a Country of *one Religion*, and by the hands of *Conformists*. In short, if we will but look upon the civil War that so long raged in this Kingdom, between the Houses of *York* and *Lancaer*, and consider that they professed but one and the same Religion, and both back't with numbers of Church-men too (to say nothing of the Miserable end of many of our Kings princely Ancestors in *Scotland*, especially the first and third *James*) will find cause to say, *That Church - Uniformity is not a Security for Princes to depend upon.*

If we will look next into Countries where *Dissenters* from the National Church are *Tolerated*, we shall find the ↄonformist not less Culpable than the *Dissenter*.

The *Disorders* among the 𝕵𝖊𝖜𝖘, after they were settled in the Land that God had given them, came not from those they tolerated, but themselves. They *cast off Samuel*, and the government of the *Judges*. 'Twas the Children of the *National* Church, that fell in with the Ambition of *Absolom*, and animated the Rebellion against their Father *David*. They were the same that revolted from *Solomon's* Son, and cryed in behalf of *Jeroboam, To your Tents, O Israel !*

Not two Ages ago, the Church of 𝕱𝖗𝖆𝖓𝖈𝖊, too generally fell in with the Family of 𝕲𝖚𝖎𝖘𝖊, against their lawful Soveraign, 𝕳𝖊𝖓𝖗𝖞 the fourth: Nor were they without Countenance of the greatest of their Belief, who stiled it an *holy War* : At that time, fearing (not without cause) the *Defection* of the Kingdom from the *Roman* See. In this conjuncture, th

Dissente

Diſſenters made up the beſt part of that King's Armies, and by their *Loyalty* and *Blood*, preſerv'd the *Blood Royal* of *France*, and ſet the Crown on the Head of that Prince.   That King was twice Aſſeſſinated, and the laſt time Murdered, as was *Henry* the third, his Predeceſſor; but they fell, one by the hand of a *Church-man*, the other, at leaſt by a *Conformiſt*.

'Tis true, that the next *civil War* was between the *Catho-licks* and the *Hugenots*, under the Conduct of **Cardinal Richliue**, and the **Duke of Rohan :**   But as I will not juſtifie the Action, ſo their *Liberties* and *Cautions* ſo ſolemnly ſettled by *Henry* the *fourth*, as the Reward of their ſingular Merit, being by the Miniſtry of that *Cardinal* invaded, they ſay, they did but defend their *Security*, and that rather againſt the *Cardinal*, than the *King*, whoſe ſoftneſs ſuffered him to become a Property to the great *Wit* and *Ambition* of that Perſon : And there is this Reaſon to believe them, that if it had been otherwiſe, we are ſuch that *King Charles* the *firſt* would not in the leaſt have countenanced their Quarrel.

However, the **Cardinal**, like himſelf, wiſely knew when to ſtop : For though he thought it the Intereſt of the Crown, to moderate their Greatneſs and check their Growth, yet having freſh in Memory the *Story* of the fore-going Age, he ſaw, *'twas wiſe to have a Ballance* upon occaſion.   But this was more than recompenc'd in their fixt Adheſion to the *Crown* of **France,** under the Miniſtry and Direction of the ſucceeding *Cardinal,* when their Perſwaſion had not only Number, and many good Officers to value it ſelf upon, but yielded their *King* the ableſt Captain of the Age, namely, **Turene :**   It was an *Hugenot* then, at the Head of almoſt an *Hugenot* Army, that fell in with a *Cardinal* himſelf (ſee the Union, Intereſt makes) to maintain the Imperial Crown of *France*, and that on a *Roman-Catholicks Head* : And together *with their own In-*
dulgence,

dulgence, that Religion, *as* National too, againſt the pretences of a *Roman-Catholick Army,* headed by a *Prince,* brave and learned of the ſame Religion.

I mention not this, to prefer one Party to another; for contrary Inſtances may be given elſe-where, as Intereſts have varied. In 𝕾𝔀𝔢𝔞𝔡𝔩𝔞𝔫𝔡 a Prince was rejected by 𝔓𝔯𝔬𝔱𝔢-𝔣𝔱𝔞𝔫𝔱𝔰: And in *England* and *Holland,* and many of the *Principalities* of *Germany,* 𝕽𝔬𝔪𝔞𝔫-𝕮𝔞𝔱𝔥𝔬𝔩𝔦𝔠𝔨𝔰 have approv'd themſelves Loyal to their *Kings, Princes* and *States:* But this ſuffices to us, that we gain the Point; for it is evident in Countries where *Diſſenters* are tolerated, the *Inſecurity* of the Prince and Government, *may as well come from the Conforming, as Diſſenting Party,* and that it comes not from Diſſenters, *be-cauſe ſuch.*

But how happy and admirable was this civil Union be-tween the 𝕮𝔞𝔯𝔡𝔦𝔫𝔞𝔩 and 𝕿𝔲𝔯𝔢𝔫𝔢? Two moſt oppoſite Re-ligions, both follow'd by People of their own Perſwaſion: One ſays his *Maſs,* t'other his *Directory:* Both invoke *One* Deity, by ſeveral ways, for *one Succeſs,* and it followed with *Glory,* and a *Peace* to this Day. O why ſhould it be other-wiſe now! What has been, may be: Methinks *Wiſdom* and *Charity* are on that ſide ſtill.

It will doubtleſs be objected, That the *Diſſenting Party of* 𝕰𝔫𝔤𝔩𝔞𝔫𝔡, fell in with the *State-Diſſenter* in our late *Civil, but Unnatural War:* And this ſeems to be againſt us, yet *Three* things muſt be confeſſed: *Firſt,* That the War rather *made the Diſſenters,* than the *Diſſenters made the War. Secondly,* That thoſe that were then in being, were not tolerated, as in *France,* but *proſecuted.* And *Laſtly,* That they did not lead, but *follow* great Numbers of *Church-goers,* of all *Qualities* in that unhappy *Controverſie;* & which began upon other *Topicks* than Liberty for *Church-Diſſenters.* And though they were herein blameable, Reaſon is Reaſon, in all *Climates* and

Latitudes.

Latitudes. This does not affect the Queſtion : Such Cala‑
mities are no *neceſſary Conſequences* of *Church-Diſſent,* becauſe
they would then follow in all places where *Diſſenters* are
tolerated, which we ſee they do not : But theſe may ſome‑
times indeed be the effects of a violent Endeavour of *Unifor‑
mity,* and that *under all Forms of Government,* as I fear they
were partly here under our *Monarch* . But then, this teaches
us to conclude, that a *Toleration* of thoſe, that a contrary
courſe makes *uneaſie* and *deſperate,* may prevent or cure *Inte‑
ſtine Troubles*; as *Anno* Forty Eight, it ended the Strife, and
ſettled the Peace of *Germany.* For 'tis not now the Queſtion,
how far men may be provoked, or ought to reſent it ; but
Whether Government is ſafe in a Toleration, eſpecially 𝔐𝔬𝔫𝔞𝔯‑
𝔠𝔥𝔶 ? And to this Iſſue we come in Fact, *That tis ſafe,* and
that *Conformiſts* (generally ſpeaking) have for their In‑
tereſts, as rarely known their Duty to their *Prince,* as *Diſ‑
ſenters* for their Conſciences. So that the danger ſeems to lie
on the ſide of *forcing Uniformity* againſt Faith, upon ſevere
Penalties, rather than of a diſcreet *Toleration.*

In the next place, I ſhall endeavour to ſhew the *Prudence*
and *Reaſonableneſs* of a *Toleration,* by the great Benefits that
follow it.

𝔗𝔬𝔩𝔢𝔯𝔞𝔱𝔦𝔬𝔫, which is an admiſſion of Diſſenting Worſhips,
with Impunity to the *Diſſenters,* ſecures *Property,* which is
civil Right, and That *Eminenty the* 𝔏𝔦𝔫𝔢 *and* 𝔭𝔬𝔴𝔢𝔯 *of the*
𝔐𝔬𝔫𝔞𝔯𝔠𝔥𝔶 : For if no man-ſuffer in his *civil Right* for the
ſake of ſuch *Diſſent,* the point of *Succeſſion* is ſettled without
a *civil War, or a Recantation*; ſince it were an abſurd thing
to imagin, that a man born to *five Pounds a year,* ſhould not be
liable to forfeit his Inheritance for *Non-conformity,* and yet a
*Prince of the Blood, and an Heir to the Imperial Crown, ſhould be
made incapable of Inheritance for his Church-Diſſent.*

The

The Security then of 𝔓𝔯𝔬𝔭𝔢𝔯𝔱𝔶 or 𝔠𝔦𝔟𝔦𝔩 𝔕𝔦𝔤𝔥𝔱, from being forfeitable for Religious Diſſent, becomes a ſecurity to
the *Royal Family*, againſt the Difficulties lately labour'd under
in the buſineſs of the *Succeſſion*.   And though I have no
Commiſſion for it, beſides the great Reaſon and Equity of
the thing it ſelf, I dare ſay, there can hardly be a *Diſſenter*
at this time of day ſo *void* of Senſe and Juſtice, as well as
Duty and Loyalty, as not to be of the ſame Mind.   Elſe it
were to deny that to the *Prince*, which he needs, and prays
from him.   Let us not forget the Story of 𝔖𝔦𝔤𝔦𝔰𝔪𝔲𝔫𝔡. of
Sweedland, of 𝔥𝔢𝔫𝔯𝔶 the fourth of *France*, and eſpecially of
our own 𝔔𝔲𝔢𝔢𝔫 𝔐𝔞𝔯𝔶.   Had *Property* been fix't, the *Line*
of thoſe Royal Families could not have met with any Let or
Interruption.   'Twas this Conſideration that prevail'd with
Judge *Hailes*, though a ſtrong *Proteſtant*, after King *Edward's*
Death, to give his Opinion for *Queen Mary's* Succeſſion,
againſt that of all the reſt of the Judges to the contrary :
Which noble Preſident, was recompene'd in the Loyalty of
Arch-Biſhop 𝔥𝔢𝔞𝔱𝔥, a *Roman-Catholick*, in favour of the Succeſſion of *Queen Elizabeth* :   And the ſame thing would be done
again, in the like caſe, by men of the ſame Integrity.

I know it may be ſaid, *That there is little Reaſon now for*
the Prince to regard this Argument in favour of Diſſenters, when
it was ſo little heeded in the caſe of the 𝔓𝔯𝔢𝔰𝔲𝔪𝔭𝔱𝔦𝔟𝔢 𝔥𝔢𝔦𝔯 *to*
the Crown.   But as this was the Act and Heat of Conforming men within Doors, ſo if it were in Counſel or Deſire,
the Folly and Injuſtice of any Diſſenters without Doors, ſhall
many entire Parties pay the Reckoning of the few buſie
Offendors ?   They would humbly hope, that the ſingular
Mildneſs and Clemency, which make up ſo great a part of
the King's publick Aſſurances, will not leave him in his Reflection here.

'Tis

'Tis the Mercies of Princes, that above all their Works, give them the nearest Resemblance to Divinity in their Administration. Besides, it is their Glory to measure their Actions by the Reason and Consequence of things, and not by the Passions that possess and animate private Breasts: For it were fatal to the Interest of a Prince, that the *Folly* or *Undutifulness* of any of his Subjects, should put him out of the way, or tempt him to be *unsteady* to his Principle and Interest: And yet, with submission, I must say, it would be the Consequence of Coercion: For by exposing *Property* for Opinion, the Prince exposes the Consciences and Property of his own Family, and plainly *Disarms* them of all Defence, upon any alteration of Judgment. Let us remember, that several of the same Gentlemen, who at first sacrificed civil Rights for Non-conformity in *common Dissenters*, fell at last to make the Succession of the *Crown*, the *Price of Dissent in the next Heir of the Royal Blood*. So dangerous a thing it is to hazard Property to serve a turn for any Party, or suffer such Examples in the case of the meanest Person in a Kingdom.

Nor is this all the benefit that attends the *Crown* by the preservation of civil Rights; for the *Power of the Monarchy* is kept more *Entire* by it. The King has the benefit of his Whole People, and the Reason of their *Safety* is owing to their *Civil*, and not Ecclesiastical Obedience: Their *Loyalty* to *Cæsar*, and not Conformity to the Church. Whereas the other Opinion would have it, that no Conformity to the Church, *No Property* in the State: Which is to clog and narrow the civil Power; for at this rate, *No Church-man*, No Englishman, and *No Conformist*, No Subject. A way to *alien* the King's People, and practise an Exclusion upon him, from, it may be, a fourth part of his Dominions. Thus it may happen, that the ablest States man, the bravest
Captain,

Captain, and the beft Citizen may be difabled, and the Prince forbid their Imployment to his Service.

Some Inftances of this we have had fince the late King's Reftoration: For upon the firft *Dutch-War*, Sir 𝔚illiam 𝔓enn being commanded to give in a Lift of the ableft Sea-Officers in the Kingdom, to ferve in that Expedition. I do very well remember he prefented our prefent King with a Catalogue of the knowingeft and braveft Officers the Age had bred, with this fubfcrib'd, *Thefe men, if his Majefty will pleafe to admit of their Perfwafions, I will anfwer for their Skill, Courage and Integrity.* He pickt them by their Ability, not their Opinions; and he was in the Right; for that was the beft way of doing the King's bufinefs. And of my own knowledge, *Conformity* robb'd the King at that time of Ten men, whofe greater Knowledge and Valour, than fome one ten of that Fleet, had in their room, been able to have faved a Battel, or perfected a Victory. I will name three of them. The firft was Old Vice-Admiral 𝔊oodfon; than whom, no body was more Stout, or a Sea-man. The fecond, Captain 𝔥ull, that in the *Saphire* beat *Admiral* 𝔈verfon, hand to hand, that came to the Relief of old *Trump.* The third was Captain 𝔓otter, that in the conftant *Warwick*, took Captain *Beach*, after eight hours fmart Difpute. And as evident it is, that if a War had proceeded between this Kingdom and *France*, feven years ago, the bufinefs of Conformity had deprived the King of many Land-Officers, whofe fhare in the late Wars of *Europe* had made knowing and able.

But which is worft of all, fuch are not fafe, with their diffent, under their own extraordinary Prince. For though a man were a great *Honourer* of his King, a *Lover* of his Country, an *Admirer* of the Government: In the courfe of his Life, fober, wife, induftrous and ufeful; if a Diffenter from

from the eftablifh't Form of Worfhip, in that condition there is no *Liberty* for his Perfon, nor *Security* to his Eftate: As *Ufelefs* to the Publick, fo *Ruin'd* in himfelf. For this *Net* catches the beft. Men true to their Confcience, and who indulged, are moft like to be fo to their Prince; whilft the reft are left to *coufen* him by their change; for that is the unhappy end of *forc'd Conformity* in the poor fpirited Compliers. And this muft always be the confequence of *neceffitating* the *Prince* to put *more* and *other Tefts* upon his People, than are requifit to fecure him of their Loyalty.

And when we fhall be fo happy in our meafures as to confider this Mifchief to the *Monarchy*, it is to be hop'd, it will be thought expedient to dif-intangle *Property* from *Opinion*, and cut the untoward Knot, fome men have tyed, that hath fo long hamper'd and gaul'd the Prince as well as People. It will be then, when civil Punifhments fhall no more follow Church faults, that the Civil Tenure will be recover'd to the Government, and the *Natures* of Acts, Rewards and Punifhments, fo diftinguifh't, as *Loyalty* fhall be the Safety of Diffent, and the whole People made ufeful to the *Government*.

It will, perhaps, be objected, *That Diffenters can hardly be obliged to be true to the Crown, and fo the Crown unfafe in their very Services; for they may eafily turn the Power given them to ferve it, againft it, to greaten themfelves.* I am willing to obviate every thing, that may with any pretence be offer'd againft our entreated Indulgence. I fay, No, and appeal to the *King* himfelf (againft whom the Prejudices of our late times ran higheft, and therefore has moft reafon to Refent) If he was ever better lov'd or ferv'd, than by the Old *Roundheaded* Sea-men, the *Earl of Sandwich*, Sir *William Penn*, Sir *J. Levfon*, Sir *G. Afcue*, Sir *R. Stainer*, Sir *J. Smith*, Sir *J. Jordan*, Sir *J. Harmon*, Sir *Chrif. Minns*,

Captain

Captain *Sanfum,Cuttins, Clark, Robinfom,Molton,Wager,Tern,
Parker, Haward, Hubbard, Fen, Langhorn, Daws, Earl, White*;
to fay nothing of many yet living, of real Merit, and many
inferior Officers, expert and brave. And to do our *Prince*
Juftice, he *deferv'd* it from them, by his Humility, Plain-
nefs and Courage, and the care and affection that he always
fhew'd to them.

If any fay, *That moſt of thefe men were* **Confozmiſts** : I
prefume to tell them, I know as well as any man, they
ferv'd the King never the better for that : On the contrary,
'twas all the ſtrife that fome of them had in themfelves, in
the doing that Service, that they muſt not ferve the King
without it ; and if in that they could have been Indulged,
they had perform'd it with the greateſt Alacrity. *Intereſt*
with not lye. Where People find their Reckoning, they
are fure to be *True*. For 'tis want of Wit that makes any
man *falfe* to himfelf. 'Twas he that knew all mens Hearts,
that faid, *Where the Treafure is, there the Heart will be alfo.*
Let men be eafie, fafe, and upon their Preferment with the
Prince, and they will be Dutiful, Loyal and moſt affectionate.

Mankind by nature *fears* Power, and *melts* at Goodnefs.
Pardon my Zeal, I would not be thought to plead for *Diffenters* Preferment ; 'tis enough they keep what they have,
and may live at their own Charges. Only I am for having
the Prince have Room for his Choice, and not be crampt and
ſtinted by Opinion ; but imploy thofe who are beſt able to
ferve him : And I think out of *Six* Parties 'tis better picking, than out of *One*, and therefore the Prince's Intereſt is
to be Head of all of them, which a *Toleration* effects in a
moment, fince thofe *Six* (divided Interefts, within themfelves) having but on *civil Head*, become one intire *civil
Body* to the Prince : And I am fure, I have *Monarchy* on my
fide.

fide, if *Solomon* and his *Wifdom* may ftand for it, who tells us, *That the Glory of a King is in the Multitude of his People.*

Nor is this all, for the Confequences of fuch an Univerfal Content would be of infinite moment to the *fecurity* of the *Monarchy*, both at *Home* and *Abroad.* At *Home*, for it would *Behead the Factions without Blood*, and *Banifh the Ringleaders without going abroad.* When the great Bodies of *Diffenters* fee the care of the Government for their *fafety*, they have no need of their Captains, nor thefe any ground for their pretences : For as they us'd the People to value themfelves, and raife their Fortunes with the *Prince*, fo the People follow'd their Leaders to get that eafe, they fee their Heads promifed, but could not, and the *Government* can, and does give them.

★   ★   ★   ★   ★

To make this more eafie in Grant and Practice, with our Superiors, I humbly propofe , *Firft*, That every Party do Subfcribe an Engagement of their Fidelity to the King and *Government*, in Terms the moft full and plain that may be : In which, as the King will have an Account of their *Number*, fo of their principles of *Duty* to the Government, and Abhorrance of all Faction and Rebellion. Without which I would not fpeak a word,

Secondly, That the Names and Abode of all Diffenters above the age of fixteen be Regeftred. As alfo the Number of their Meetings, their place and time.

Thirdly, That the Doors of their Meeting-Houfes be ever open during their time of Worfhip, and that it fhall be a *Præmunire* for

any

any Diſſenter to come Armed to any ſuch Meeting of Woiſhip.

Fourthly, That once in every Year, the Names of *Proſelites* be delivered in to the *Clark of the Peace* for every County, and that all of that Party, as well as thoſe new Adherents, do *renew* their Obligation of Obedience by Annual Subſcriptions, if required.

Fifthly, Becauſe it is not impoſſible that ſome or other may miſ-behave themſelves, and abuſe this Liberty, or be abuſed in the uſe of it. That in every County three Perſons of moſt Emi-nency, among *Diſſenters,* be *Yearly* Named to the Magiſtrates by each *Diſſenting Intereſt,* to ſtand a kind of Repreſentatives, both to inform them what they can, upon inquiry, of Perſons or Things among the *People* of that *Party,* which may in the leaſt be thought to affect the Government, and to have redreſs of Injuries done to Perſons in the ſober uſe of their-allowed Liberty.

And *Laſtly,* Becauſe this *Freedom* will be beſt kept and impro-ved to the publick Benefit, by maintaining a good and charitable Underſtanding between the divers Orders of *Chriſtians* within themſelves : 'Twere farther requiſit, That, No *Nick-Names* were continued, and all Terms of *Reproach,* on all hands, pu-niſhable : And That Controverſial Points were carefully avoided, and *Vice* decry'd, and *Holineſs* preſt, *Without which* (St *Paul* aſ-ſures us) *no man ſhall ſee the Lord.*

Theſe are the *Methods* that have had moſt weight with me, and the beſt I know to create a Reciprocal Confidence and Intereſt between the 𝔓rince and his *Conforming* and *Diſſenting People :* To be ſure, this Courſe hath ſucceeded well elſe-where, even in *Monarchical States;* And therefore in it ſelf not incon-ſiſtent with 𝔐onarchy, and very agreeable to 𝕮hriſtianity.

God Almighty inſpire the KING's *Heart, and the Hearts of his* Great Council, *to be the Glorious Inſtruments of this Bleſſing to the Kingdom.*

I ſhall conclude this 𝔓erſwaſive with the Judgment of ſome *Pious Fathers* and *Renowned Princes.*

AN ACCOUNT OF THE PROVINCE OF CAROLINA IN AMERICA

Samuel Wilson, *An Account of the Province of Carolina in America. Together with an Abstract of the Patent, and several other Necessary and Useful Particulars, to such as have thoughts of Transporting themselves thither* (London, 1682), pp. 5–27.

Little is known about Samuel Wilson. Joseph Dorfman indicates in his *Economic Mind in American Civilization* (1946) that Wilson was a doctor and served as the secretary to the Lords Proprietors of the Carolina Colony. Thus far, this collection has included writings by northern authors; this piece by Wilson offers an example of life in the southern colonies, which was significantly different. The most notable variant, beyond the type of agricultural activity, was that the southern colonies tended to be governed directly by the Crown and were not either Puritan or Quaker. Hence, both the social structure and the governing system in the northern colonies were significantly different from those in the south.

Wilson's *Account of Carolina* puts economic decision-making in a rational light, by taking the view that individuals will pursue their own advantages. This piece also lays the groundwork for the development of a slave-based economy as he argues that individuals expressly demand slave labour: 'What commodities shall I be able to produce, that will yield me money in other countries, that I may be enabled to buy Negro slaves (without which a planter can never do any great matter)'. Similar themes on individual rights are taken up in the second volume of this collection.

AN
ACCOUNT

OF THE

Province

OF

CAROLINA

IN

AMERICA.

TOGETHER WITH

An Abſtract of the PATENT,

and ſeveral other Neceſſary and Uſeful Particulars, to ſuch as have thoughts of Tran-
ſporting themſelves thither.

Publiſhed for their Information.

L O N D O N:

Printed by *G. Larkin* for *Francis Smith*, at the Elephant
and Caſtle in *Cornhil.*   1682.

AN

ACCOUNT

OF THE

Province

OF

CAROLINA

IN

AMERICA

CAROLINA, is that part of *Florida*, which lies between *twenty nine* and *thirty six* Degrees, and *thirty Minutes* of *Northern Latitude*: On the *East* it is washed with the *Atlantick Ocean*, and is bounded on the *West* by *Mare Pacificum* (or the South Sea) and within these bounds is contained the most healthy Fertile and pleasant part of *Florida*, which is so much commended by the Spanish Authors.

This *Province* of *Carolina*, was in the Year 1663. Granted by *Letters Pattents* in Propriety of his most Gracious *Majesty*, unto the Right Honourable *Edward*

ward Earl of *Clarendon*, George Duke of *Albemarle*, *William* Earl of *Craven*, *John* Lord *Berkely*, *Anthony* Lord *Afhly*, now Earl of *Shaftsbury*, Sir *George Carteret*, and Sir *John Colleton*, Knights and Barronets, Sir *William Berkeley* Knight, by which Letters Pattents the Laws of *England* are to be of force in *Carolina*: but the *Lords Proprietors* have power with the confent of the Inhabitants to make By-Laws for the better Government of the faid *Province*: So that no Money can be raifed or Law made, without the confent of the Inhabitants or their Reprefentatives. They have alfo power to appoint and impower Governours, and other Magiftrates to Grant Liberty of Confcience, make Conftitutions, &c. With many other great Priviledges, as by the faid Letters Pattents will more largely appear. And the faid Lords Proprietors have there fetled a Conftitution of Government, whereby is granted Liberty of Confcience, and wherein all poffible care is taken for the equal Adminiftration of Juftice, and for the lafting Security of the Inhabitants both in their Perfons and Eftates.

By the care and endeavours of the faid Lords Proprietors, and at their very great charge, two Colonys have been fetled in this *Province*, the one at *Albemarle* in the moft Northerly part, the other at *Afhly* River, which is in the Latitude of thirty two Degrees odd Minutes.

Albemarle bordering upon *Virginia*, and only exceeding it in Health, Fertility, and Mildnefs of the Winter, is in the Growths, Productions, and other things much of the fame nature with it: Wherefore I fhall not trouble the Reader with a perticular Defcription of that part; but apply my felf principally
to

to difcourfe of the Collony at *Afbly-River*, which being many Degrees more Southward than *Virginia*, differs much from it in the Nature of its Clymate and Productions.

Afbly-River was firft fetled in *April* 1670, the Lords Proprietors having at their fole charge, fet out three Veffels, with a confiderable number of able Men; eighteen Moneths Victuals, with Cloths, Tools, Ammunition, and what elfe was thought neceffary for a new Settlement, and continued at this charge to fupply the Collony for divers years after, until the Inhabitants were able by their own Induftry to live of themfelves; in which condition they have been for divers years paft, and are arrived to a very great Degree of Plenty of all forts of Provifions. Infomuch, that moft forts are already cheaper there, than in any other of the Englifh Collonys, and they are plentifully enough fupplied with all things from *England* or other Parts.

Afbly-River, about feven Miles in from the Sea, divides it felf into two Branches; the Southermoft retaining the name of *Afbly-River*, the North Branch is called *Cooper-River*. In *May*, 1680, the Lords Proprietors fent their Orders to the Government there, appointing the Port-Town for thefe two Rivers to be Built on the Poynt of Land that divides them, and to be called *Charles* Town, fince which time about an hundred Houfes are there Built, and more are Building daily by the Perfons of all forts that come there to Inhabit, from the more Northern Englifh Collonys, and the Sugar Iflands, *England* and *Ireland*; and many Perfons who went to *Carolina* Servants, being Induftrious fince they came out of their times with their Mafters, at whofe charge they were

Tranfper-

Tranfported, have gotten good Stocks of Cattle, and Servants of their own ; have here alfo Built Houfes, and exercife their Trades : And many that went thither in that condition, are now worth feveral Hundreds of Pounds, and live in a very plentiful condition, and their Eftates ftill encreafing. And Land is become of that value near the Town, that it is fold for twenty Shillings *per* Acre, though pillaged of all its valuable Timber, and not cleared of the reft, and Land that is clear'd and fitted for Planting, and Fenced, is let for ten Shillings *per annum* the Acre, though twenty miles diftant from the Town, and fix men will in fix weeks time, Fall, Clear, Fence in, and fit for Planting, fix Acres of Land.

At this Town, in *November*, 1680. There Rode at one time fixteen Sail of Veffels (fome of which were upwards of 200 Tuns) that came from divers parts of the Kings Dominions to trade there, which great concourfe of fhipping, will undoubtebly in a fhort time make it a confiderable Town.

The *Eaftern Shore of America*, whether it be by reafon of its having the great Body of the Continent to the Weftward of it, and by confequence the Northweft-Wind (which Flows contrary to the Sun) the Freezing-Wind, as the North-Eaft is in *Europe*, or that the Frozen Lakes which Lye-in, beyond *Canada*, and lye *North* and *Weft* from the Shore, Impregnate the Freezing Wind with more chill and congealing qnalities, or that the uncultivated Earth, covered for the moft part with large fhading Trees, breathes forth more nitrous Vapours,than that which is cultivated; or all thefe Reafons together, it is certainly much more cold than any part of *Europe*, in the fame Degree of Latitude of thirty nine and forty;

and

and more *North* , though above fix hundred Miles nearer the Sun than *England* ; is notwithftanding, many Degrees colder in the Winter.

The Author having been informed by thofe that fay they have feen it, that in thofe Parts it Freezeth above fix Inches thick in a Night, and great Navigable Rivers are Frozen over in the fame fpace of time ; and the Country about *Afhl, -River*, though within nine Degrees of the *Tropick*, hath feldom any Winter that doth not produce fome Ice, though I cannot yet learn that any hath been feen on Rivers or Ponds, above a quarter of an Inch thick, which vanifheth as foon as the Sun is an hour or two high, and when the Wind is not at *North-weft*, the weather is very mild. So that the *December* and *January* of *Afhly-River*, I fuppofe to be of the fame Temperature with the latter end of *March*, and beginning of *April* in *England*, this fmall Winter caufeth a fall of the Leaf, and adapts the Country to the production of all the Grains and Fruits of *England*, as well as thofe that require more Sun ; infomuch, that at *Afhly-River*, the Apple, the Pear, the Plum, the Quince, Apricock, Peach, Medlar, Walnut, Mulberry, and Chefnut, thrive very well in the fame Garden, together with the Orange, the Lemon, the Olive, the Pomgranate, the Fig and Almond ; nor is the Winter here Cloudy, Overcaft, or Foggy, but it hath been obferved that from the twentieth of *Auguft* to the tenth of *March*, including all the Winter Months, there have been but eight overcaft days, and though Rains fall pretty often in the Winter, it is moft commonly in quick Showers, which when paft, the Sun fhines out clear again.

The

The Summer is not near fo hot as in *Virginia*, or the other Northern American Englifh Collonys, which may hardly gain belief with thofe that have not confidered the reafon; which is its neernefs to the *Tropicks*, which makes it in a greater meafure than thofe parts more Northward partake of thofe Breezes, which almoft conftantly rife about eight or nine of the Clock, within the *Tropicks*, and blow frefh from the *Eaft* till about four in the Afternoon; and a little after the Sea-breeze dys away, there rifes a North-wind, which blowing all night, keeps it frefh and cool. In fhort, I take *Carolina* to be much of the fame nature with thofe delicious Countries about *Aleppo*, *Antioch*, and *Smyrna*: but hath the advantage of being under an equal Englifh Government.

Such, who in this Country have feated themfelves near great Marfhes, are fubject to Agues, as thofe are who are fo feated in *England*: but fuch who are planted more remote from Marfhes or ftanding Waters, are exceeding healthy; infomuch, that out of a Family confifting of never lefs than twelve Perfons, not one hath died fince their firft Arrival there, which is nine years: but what is more, not one hath been fick in all that time; nor is there one of the Mafters of Families that went over in the firft Veffels, dead of ficknefs in *Carolina*, except one, who was feventy and five years of Age before he came there; though the number of thofe Mafters of Families be pretty confiderable: divers perfons that went out of *England* Ptifical, and Confumptive, have recover'd, and others fubject in *England* to frequent fits of the Stone, have been abfolutely freed from them after they have been there a fhort time; nor is the

the Gout there yet known. The Ayr gives a ſtrony Appetite and quick Digeſtion, nor is it witetlh ſuitable effects, men finding themſelves apparntlẞ more lightſome, more prone, and more able to al Youthful Exerciſes, than in *England*, the Wom ẘ are very Fruitful, and the Children have freſh Sanguine Complexions.

The Soyle is generally very fertile, but hath ſome ſandy tracts ſo as to make an agreable variety, but even this Land produceth good Corne and is excellent paſture; Wheat, *Rye*, *Barly*, *Oates*, and Peas, thrive exceedingly, and the ground yeilds in greater abundance than in *England*, *Turnips*, *Parſnips*, *Carrots*, *Potatoes*, and *Edoes*, a ſubſtantial wholeſome nouriſhing Root growes well, and all excellent in their kindes they have near twenty ſorts of Pulſe that we have not in *England*, all of them very good food, inſomuch that the *Engliſh* Garden Bean is not regarded.

Near the Sea the Trees are not very large, they grow pritty neare together; farther up they are larger, and grow farther aſunder, and are in moſt parts free from Underwood, ſo that you may ſee near half a mile amongſt the bodyes of large tall timber trees, whoſe tops meeting make a very pleaſing ſhade, yet hinders not graſs, myrtle and other ſweet ſcenting ſhrubs here and there from growing under them: Amongſt theſe Groves of Timber Trees are here and there Savana's, (or graſsy plains) of ſeverall magnitudes clear of Trees, which hath occaſion'd ſome that have ſeene them to compare *Carolina* to thoſe pleaſant Parks in *England*, that have abundance of tall Timber Trees unlop'd, here you may hunt the Hare, Fox, and Deere all day long in the ſhade, and freely
ſpur

fpur your horfe through the*Woods*to follow the chafe.

This Country hath the Oak, Afh, Elm, Poplar, Beech,and all the other forts of ufefull Timber that *England* hath, and divers forts of lafting Timber that *England* hath not, as Cedar white and red, Cyprefs, Locuft, Bay and Laurell Trees, equal to the biggeft Oaks, large Mirtles,Hickery,black Wallnut,and Pyries big enough toMaft the greateft Ships, and divers other forts, which I cannot enumerate.

The woods abound with *Hares, Squirrels, Ratoons Fofsums, Conyes* and *Deere*,which laft are fo plenty that an Indian hunter hath kill'd nine fatt Deere in a day all fhott by himfelf, and all the confiderable Planters have an Indian hunter which they hire for lefs than twenty fhillings a year, and one hunter will very well find a Family of thirty people with as much Venifon andFoul,as they can well eat. Here are alfo in the woods great plenty of wilde *Turkeys, Partridges,* fomething fmaller than thofe of *England*, but more delicate, *Turtle Doves, Paraquetos,* and *Pidgeons* : On the grafsy plaines the whiftling *Plover* and *Cranes* and divers forts of Birds unknowne in *England*.

Carolina doth fo abound in Rivers,that within fifty miles of the Sea you can hardly place your felf feven miles from a Navigable River, and divers are navigable for good big Veffels above three hundred miles : The Rivers abound with variety of excellent Fifh, and near the Sea with very good Oyfters, in many of which are Pearl : the Author having feen Pearl that have been taken out of fome of them bigger than Rouncival Peafe, and perfectly round. On the Rivers and brooks are all the winter moneths vaft quantitys of *Swan, wild Geefe, Dack, Widgeon, Teale, Curlew, Snype, Shell Drake,* and a certaine fort of *black Duck*

Duck that is excellent meat, and ſtayes there all the year.

Neat Cattle thrive and increaſe here exceedingly, there being perticular Planters that have already ſeven or eight hundred head, and will in a few years in all probability, have as many thouſands, unleſs they ſell ſome part ; the Cattle are not ſubject to any Diſeaſe as yet perceiv'd, and are fat all the Year long without any Fother., the little Winter they have, not pinching them ſo as to be perceiv'd, which is a great advantage the Planters here have of the more Northern Plantations who are all forc'd to give their Cattle Fother, and muſt ſpend a great part of their Summers Labour in providing three or four Months Fother for their Cattle in the Winter, or elſe would have few of them alive in the Spring, which will keep them from ever having very great Heards, or be able to do much in Planting any Comodity for Forreign Markets; the providing Winter Food for their Cattle, taking up ſo much of their Summers Labour; So that many Judicious Perſons think that *Carolina* will be able by Sea, to ſupply thoſe Northern Collonys, with ſalted Beef for their Shipping, cheaper than they themſelves with what is bred amongſt them; for, conſidering that all the Woods in *Carolina* afford good Paſturage, and the ſmall *Rent* that is paid to the *Lords Proprietors* ſo Land, an Ox is raiſed at almoſt as little expence in *Carolina*, as a Hen is in *England.* And it hath by experience been found that Beef will take ſalt at *Aſhly-River* any Month in the Year, and ſave very well.

Ewes have moſt commonly two or three Lambs at a time ; their Wool is a good Staple, and they thrive very

very well, but require a Shepherd to drive them to Feed, and to bring them home at night to preferve them from the Wolves.

Hogs increafe in *Carolina* abundantly, and in a manner without any charge or trouble to the Planter, only to make them Sheds, wherein they may be protected from the Sun and Rain, and Morning and Evening to give them a little Indian Corn, or the pickings and parings of *Potatoes, Turnips,* or other Roots, and at the fame time blowing a Horn, or making any other conftant noyfe, to which being us'd, they will afterwards upon hearing it, repair home, the reft of their Food they get in the Woods, of Mafts, and Nuts of feveral forts; and when thofe fail, they have Grafs and Roots enough, the ground being never frozen fo hard as to keep them from Rooting, thefe conveniencies breeds them large, and in the Maft time they are very fat, all which makes the rearing them fo eafy, that there are many Planters that are fingle and have never a Servant, that have two or three hundred Hogs, of which they make great profit; *Barbados, Jamaica,* and *New-England,* affording a conftant good price for their Pork; by which means they get wherewithal to build them more convenient Houfes, and to purchafe Servants, and *Negro-flaves.*

There have been imported into *Carolina*, about an hundred and fifty Mares, and fome Horfes from *New-York,* and *Road-Ifland,* which breeds well, and the Coalts they have are finer Lim'd and Headed than their Dams or Sires, which gives great hopes of an excellent breed of Horfes, as foon as they have gotten good Stalions amongft them.

Negros

Negros, By reafon of the mildnefs of the Winter thrive and ftand much better, than in any of the more Northern Collonys,& require lefs clothes,which is a great charge fav'd.

With the Indians the *Englifh* have a perfect freind-fhip, they being both ufefull to one another . And care is taken by the *Lords Proprietors,*that no Injuftice fhall be done them ; In order to which they have eftablifhed a particular Court of Judicature, (compos'd of the fobereft and moft difinterefsed Inhabitants) to determine all differnces that fhall happen between the *Englifh* and any of the *Indians,* this they do upon a Chriftian and Moral Confideration, and not out of any apprehenfion of danger from them,for the *Indians* have been always fo ingaged in Wars one Town or Village againft another (their Government being ufually of no greater extent) that they have not fuffered any increafe of People, there having been feveral Nations in a manner quite extirpated by Wars amongft themfelves fince the *Englifh* fetled at *Afhly* River : This keeps them fo thin of people, and fo divided,that the *Englifh* have not the leaft apprehenfions of danger from them ; the *Englifh* being already too ftrong for all the *Indians* within five hundred Miles of them,if they were united, and this the *Indians* as well know,that they will never dare to break with the *Englifh,* or do an Injury to any particular perfon, for fear of having it reveng'd upon their whole Nation.

The *Lords Proprietors* do at prefent grant to all perfons that come there to Inhabit as follows, *viz.* To each Mafter or Miftrifs of a Family fifty acres, and for every able fon or man fervant they fhall carry or caufe to be tranfported into*Carolina* fifty acres more, and the like for each Daughter or woman fervant that

is

is marrigeable, and for ea chchild, man or woman 'fer-vant under fixteen years of age, forty acres, and fifty acres of Land to each fervant when out of their time, this Land to be injoy'd by them and their Heirs for ever, they paying a Penny an Acre Quit-rent to the Lords Proprietors, the Rent to commence in two years after their taking up their Land. But forafmuch as divers perfons who are already Inhabitants of *Carolina*, and others that have Intentions to tranfport them-felves into that *Province*, defire not to be cumber'd with paying of a Rent, and alfo to fecure to them-felves good large convenient tracts of Land, without being forc'd to bring thither a great number of fer-vants at one time ; The *Lords Proprietors* have been Prevail'd upon, and have agreed to fell to thofe who have a mind to buy Land, after the rate of fifty pound for a Thoufand Acres, referving a Pepper-Corn *per annum* Rent when demanded.

The way of any ones taking up his Land, due to him either by carrying himfelf or fervants into the Country, or by purchafing it of the *Lords Proprietors,* is after this manner : He firft feeks out a place to his mind that is not already poffeffed by any other, then applyes himfelf to the Governour and Proprietors Deputys, and fhew what rights he hath to Land, either by Purchafe or otherwife ; who thereupon iffue out their Warrant to the Surveyor-General to meafure him out a Plantation containing the number of acres due to him ; who making Certificate that he hath meafur'd out fo much Land and the Bounds, a Deed is prepar'd of courfe, which is figned by the Gover-nour and the Lords Proprietors Deputys, and the *Proprietors* Seal affixed to it and Regifter'd, which is is a good Conveyance in Law of the Land therein mention'd to the party and his Heirs for ever.

I

I have here, as I take it, defcribed a pleafant & fertile Country, abounding in health and pleafure, and with all things necefsary for the fuftenance of mankind, and wherein I think I have written nothing but truth, fure I am I have inferted no wilful falfhood. I have alfo told you how men are to have Land that go there to Inhabit. But a rational man will certainly inquire, When I have Land, what fhall I doe with it? what Comoditys fhall I be able to produce that will yeild me mony in other Countrys, that I may be inabled to buy *Negro* flaves (without which a Planter can never do any great matter) and purchafe other things for my pleafure and convenience, that *Carolina* doth not produce? To this I anfwer, That befides the great profit that will be made by the vaft heards of Cattle and Swine, the Country appears to be proper for the Commoditys following. *viz.*

Wine. *There are growing* naturally in the Country five forts of Grapes, three of which the French Vignaroons who are there, judge will make very good Wine, and fome of the *Lords Proprietors* have taken care to fend plants of the *Rhenifh, Canary, Clarret, Mnfcatt, Madera,* and Spanifh *Grapes,* of all which divers Vinyards are planted; fome wine was made this year that proved very good both in colour and tafte, and an indifferent good quantity may be expected the next year: The Country hath gentle rifing hills of fertile fand proper for Vines, and farther from the Sea, rock and gravel, on which very good grapes grow naturally, ripen well, and together, and very lufhious in tafte, infomuch as the French Proteftants who are there, and skill'd in wine, do no way doubt of producing great quantitys and very good.

Oyl. *There are* feverall *Olive* trees growing, which were carryed thither, fome from *Portugal,* and fome
from *Bermeudas*

mudas and flourish excedingly, and the Inhabitants take great care to propagate more, so that in all probability it will be an excellent Oyl-Country.

Silk. There is in *Carolina* great plenty of *Mulberry* Trees, such as are by experience found to feed the Silk-worm very well, yea as well as the white Mulberry, but there is of that sort also, which are propagated with a great deal of ease, a stick new cut and thrust into the ground, seldom failing to grow, and so like-wise if the Seed if them be sown.

Tobacco. *Tobacco* doth here grow very well, and is nearer to the nature of the *Spanish Tobacco* than that of *Virginia.*

Indigo. *Indigo* thrives well here, and very. good hath been made.

Cotton. *Cotton* of the *Cyprus* and *Smyrna* sort will grow well, and good plenty of the Seed is sent thither.

Flax & Hemp Thrives exceedingly.

Good plenty of Pitch and Tar is there made, there being particular persons that have made above a thousand barrels.

Here is great plenty of Oake for Pipe staves, which are a good Commodity in the *Maderas, Canaryes, Barbados*, & the *Leeward Islands.*

Sumack. *Sumack* growes in great abundance naturally, so undoubtedly would *Woad, Madder* & *Sa-Flower*, if planted.

Drugs. *Jallop, Sassaparilla, Turmerick, Sassafras, Snake-root,* & divers others.

In short. This Country being of the same Clymate and Temperature of *Aleppo, Smyrna, Antioch, Judea,* and the Province of *Nanking,* the richest in *China,* will (I conceive) produce any thing which those Countrys do, were the Seeds brought into it.

The

The Tools that men who goe thither ought to take with them are thefe, *viz.* An Ax, a Bill, and a broad Hoe, & grabbing Hoe, for every man, and a crofs cut Saw to every four men, a Whip-faw, a fet of Wedges and Fraus and Betle-Rings to every family, and fome Reaping Hooks and Sythes, as likewife Nails of all forts, Hooks, Hinges, Bolts & Locks for their Houfes.

The Merchandizes which fell beft in *Carolina*, are Linnen and Woollen, and all other Stufs to make clothes of, with Thread Sowing Silk, Buttons, Ribbons, Hats, Stockings, Shoes, &c. which they fell at very good rates, and for thefe goods any man may purchafe the Provifion he hath need of.

The Pafsage of a man or woman to *Carolina* is five Pound, Ships are going thither all times of the year. Some of the *Lords Proprietors*, or my felf, will be every Tuefday at 11 of the clock at the *Carolina*-Coffee-houfe in *Burching*-Lane near the Royal Exchange, to inform all people what Ships are going, or any other thing whatfoever.

An

An Abſtract of the Pattent gran-
ted by the King, the 30th of
June, in the 17th Year of his
Reign, under the Broad Seal of
England, unto *Edward* Earl of *Cla-
rendon, George* Duke of *Albermarle,
William* Earl of *Craven, John* Lord
Berkley, Anthony Lord *Aſhly*, Sir
George Carteret, and Sir *John Colle-
ton*, Knights and Barronets, and
Sir *William Berkeley* Knight, their
Heirs and Aſſigns.

Impri. 𝔄S a mark of our particular Favour,
we do give and Grant all that Pro=
vince, Territory, or Tract of Land, lying within
our Dominions of America; extending North, and
Eaſtward as far as the North-end of Caraliuck-
River, or inlet upon a ſtreight Weſterly Line to
Wyanoake-Creek, which lies within or about the
Degrees of 36 and 30 Minutes Nothern Lati-
tude, and ſo Weſt in a Direct line as far as the
South-Seas, and South and Weſtward as far as the
Degrees of 29 incluſive, Nothern Latitude: And
ſo Weſt in a Direct line as far as the South-Seas.

2. Alſo

2. Also all Ports, Harbours, Bays, Rivers, and Inlets belonging to the Province and Territory aforesaid.

3. All the Soyl, Land, Feild, Woods, Mountains, Ferns, Lakes, Rivers, Bays, and Inlets, within the limits before mentioned: with the Fishing of all sorts of Fish, together with the Royalty of the Sea upon that Coast: And all Veins, Mines, and Quarries of Gold, Silver, Gems, and Precious Stones, or any other thing whatsoever.

4. The Patronage and Advowsons of all Churches and Chappels, with Licence to build and found Churches, to exercise and enjoy as ample priviledges, &c. as any Bishop of Durham, in our Kingdom of England.

5. We do by these presents constitute the aforenamed Persons, their Heirs and Assigns, the true and absolute Lords and Proprietors of the said Province, to be holden of Us, our Heirs and Successours, as of our Mannor of East-Greenwich, in our County of Kent, in free and common Soccage, and not in capite, nor by Knights service, paying yearly for the same the fourth part of all Gold and Silver-Oar which shall from time to time be found, besides the yearly Rent of twenty Mark.

6. We do grant full power to the aforesaid Proprietors, to make several Counties, Baronies, and Collonies, within the said Province, with several and distinct Liberties, Priviledges, &c.

7. Also to make, ordain, and erect, and under their Seals to publish any Laws and Constitutions; by and with the advice, assent, and approbation of the Freemen of the said Province, or of

of the Freemen of the County, Barony, or Collony, for which such Law or Constitution shall be made, or of the greater part of them, or their Deligates: And likewise to erect any Courts of Judicature, and establish any Judges, Justices, Magistrates, or Officers, as well within the said Province, as at Sea. Also to pardon, whether before Judgment or after, all Crimes and Offences against the said Laws, and to do all and every other thing which to the compleat establishment of Justice unto Courts, Sessions, and Forms of Judicature, and manners of proceeding therein do belong, and we do enjoyn it shall be absolute firm and avayleable in Law, and all the Leige People of Us, our Heirs and Successors, within the said Province, do observe and keep the same. Provided the said Laws be consonant to Reason, and as near as may be conbeniently agreeable to the Laws and Customs of this our Kingdom of England.

8. And because such Assemblies of Freeholders cannot be so suddainly called as occasion may require, we do grant to the Proprietors, their Heirs and Assigns, by themselves or their Magistrates, full power to ordain wholsome Orders and Ordinances, within the Territory aforesaid; so as they be reasonable and not repugnant or contrary, but as near as may be agreeable to the Laws of England.

9. And to the end the said Province may be the more happily encreased by the multitude of people resorting thither; We for Us, our Heirs and Successors, do give and grant License to all the Leige people of Us, our Heirs and Successors (excepting those who shall be specially forbidden) to
Tran-

Transport themselves and Families into the said Province, and there to settle themselves and Inhabit.

10. That the Subjects and Leige people of Us, our Heirs and Successors, Transported, or to be Transported into the said Province, or such as shall descend from them, be Denizens and Leiges of Us, &c.

11. Full liberty and license to lade and fraight in any Ports whatsoever, of Us, &c and Goods not prohibited by the Laws of our kingdoms: saving to Us &c. the Customs and other Duties due for the said Goods.

12. Full liberty and license at any time from the Feast of Saint Michael the Arch-Angel, Anno. 1667. As well to import into any of our Dominions from the said Province of Carolina, these several Comodities, viz. Silk, Wines, Currants, Raysins, Capers, Wax, Almonds, Oyl and Olives, without paying any Custom, or other Duty for the same; and this to continue during the space of seven Years, to comence from and after the first Importation of four Tuns of any the said Goods, in any one Bottom or Vessel. As also to export and carry out of our Dominions into the said Province Custom-free, all sorts of Tools which shall be useful and necessary for the Planters there in the Improvements of the Premises.

I 3.

13. Full Power to Erect and Constitute Sea-Ports, &c. for Lading and Unlading of Goods, and likewise the Proprietors to have and enjoy the Customs and Subsidies in the Ports, &c. aforesaid for Goods, &c. there Laded or Unladed: The said Customs to be reasonably assessed by themselves, with the Consent of the Free People there, or the greatest part of them.

14. Full and absolute License, Power, and Authority, from time to time, for ever, to Assign Alien, Grant, Demise, or Enfeoff, the Premises or any part thereof, to be held by the said Person or Persons, their Heirs, &c. In Fee-simple, or Fee-tayl, or for term of Life, or Lives, or Years of the said Proprietors, by such Rents, Services, and Customs, as shall seem fit unto them.

15. Full Power and Authority to confer Honours, so as they be not such as are conferred upon any of the Subjects of England.

16. Further, we do give and grant full Power to erect as many Forts, Fortresses, Castles, Cities, Borroughs, Towns, Villages, &c. and furnish with Ordnance and all other Weapons, Ammunition, &c. as shall be thought fit, with all the Liberty, &c. within any Corporations in England. Also to erect as many Markets and Fairs, as shall be thought necessary. And likewise to erect so many Mannors with such Seigniories as to them shall seem meet. And in each Mannor to hold a Court-Baron with all things whatsoever thereunto belonging. And to

to hold biews of Frankpledge and Court-Leets, to be holden by Stewards deputed by the Proprietors, or by the Lords of other Mannors and Leetes.

17. To Levy, Muster, and Train, all sorts of Men.   To pursue an Enemy as well by Sea as Land, even without the limits of the said Province, and them to put to death by the Law of War, and to do all other things which to the Captain General of an Army belongs.

18. We do grant unto the Proprietors and Inhabitants of the said Province, that the said Province and Inhabitants thereof shall not be held or reputed any part of any Collony in America, or elsewhere, nor be depending on their Government: but that they be subject immediatly to our Crown of England. And that the Inhabitants of the said Province shall not be any ways lyable to appear or answer to any matter whatsoever out of the Province aforesaid, except in our Realm of England, &c.

19. Our will and pleasure is, and we do give and grant unto the Proprietors, free License, Liberty, and Authority, to give and grant to such Persons as cannot in their private Opinions conform to the publick exercise of Religion, such Indulgences or Dispensations as they shall think fit.

20. And if it shall happen that any doubts or questions shall arise concerning the true sense and understanding of any Word, Clause, or Sentence, contained in this our present Charter.   We will ordain and command, that at all times

times, and in all things such Interpretation be made thereof, and allowed in all and every of our Courts whatsoever, as Lawfully may be adjudged most advantagious and favourable to the aforesaid Proprietors, their Heirs and Assigns.

> In Witness whereof we have caused these our Letters to be made Pattents, Witness our Self at *Westminster*, the thirtieth day of *June*, In the seventeenth Year of our Reign.

F I N I S.

GOOD ORDER ESTABLISHED IN PENNSYLVANIA AND NEW-JERSEY IN AMERICA

Thomas Budd, *Good Order Established in Pennsylvania and New-Jersey in America, Being a true Account of the Country; With its Produce and Commodities there made* (Philadelphia, 1685), pp. 1–40.

Thomas Budd (1646–c. 1698) was a leading Pennsylvania Quaker merchant and the son of a Quaker martyr. Although this piece is meant to be a promotional pamphlet, Budd's *Good Order Established* provides an insight into the protection of property in Pennsylvania and New Jersey at the end of the seventeenth century. Budd argues that property and liberty should be protected in Pennsylvania and New Jersey regardless of religious belief. This piece shows the growing emphasis in colonial literature on the rewards earned through labour, rather than god-given rights and wealth. This philosophy of upward mobility through hard work, frugality and intelligence reaches its pinnacle in Benjamin Franklin's *Autobiography* (1794), an excerpt from which is reproduced later in this volume. Further, *Good Order Established* provides a good example of how economics was broadly defined in seventeenth-century America. Budd's piece not only falls under the purview of the themes of the first volume – the transformation from a religious to a commercial society – but it also deals with highly practical economic concerns regarding money, banking and debt.

Good Order Established

IN

Pennfilvania & New-Jerfey

IN

AMERICA,

Being a true Account of the Country ;
With its Produce and Commodities there made.

And the great Improvements that may be made by
means of **Publick Store-houses** for **Hemp**, **Flax** and
Linnen-Cloth ; alſo, the Advantages of a **Publick-
School**, the Profits of a **Publick-Bank**, and the Probability of its ariſing, if thoſe directions here laid down are
followed. With the advantages of publick **Granaries.**

Likewiſe, ſeveral other things needful to be underſtood by
thoſe that are or do intend to be concerned in planting in
the ſaid Countries.

All which is laid down very plain, in this ſmall Treatiſe ; it
being eaſie to be underſtood by any ordinary Capacity. To
which the *Reader* is referred for his further ſatisfaction.

By *Thomas Budd.*

Printed in the Year 1685.

Thofe that have generous Spirits, whofe defires and Endeavours are to bring the Creation into Order, do I dedicate This, the firft Fruits of my Endeavours.

I Taking into confideration the diftreffed Condition that many thoufand Families lie under in my Native Country, by reafon of the deadnefs of Trade, and want of work, and believing that many that have great ftore of Money that lies by them unimploy'd, would be willing and ready to affift and encourage thofe poor diftreffed People, by fupplying them with Monies, in order to bring them out of that Slavery and Poverty they groan under, if they might do it with fafety to themfelves. Thefe Confiderations put me on writing this fmall Treatife, wherein I hope the Reader will have full Satisfaction, that the Rich may help to relieve the Poor, and yet reap great Profit and Advantage to themfelves by their fo doing, which if it fo happen that Rich and Poor are benefitted by following the Advice here given, then will be anfwered the hearty Defires of

Your True and Well-wifhing Friend,
THOMAS BUDD.

It is to be noted, that the Government of thefe Countries is fo fettled by Conceffions, and fuch care taken by the eftablifhment of certain fundamental Laws, by which every Man's Liberty and Property, both as Men and Chriftians, are preferved, fo that none fhall be hurt in his Perfon, Eftate or Liberty for his Religious Perfwafion or Practice in Worfhip towards God.

Ennfylvania and *New-Jerfy* in *America* lieth in about forty & forty two Degrees of North Latitude, and is fevered the one from the other by the River of *Delaware* on the Weft, and feperated from *New-York* Collony by *Sandy-hoock-Bay*, and part of *Hudfons* River on the Eaft. The dayes in the Winter are about two hours longer, and in the Summer two hours fhorter than in *England*, the Summer fomewhat hotter, which caufeth the Fruits and Corn fomewhat to ripen fafter than in *England*, and the Harveft for *Wheat*, *Rye* and *Barley*, being about the latter end of *June*. In the Winter feafon it is cold and freezing Weather, and fometimes Snow, but commonly very clear and Sun-fhine, which foon diffolves it.

The Country is well Watered; the River of *Delaware* being navigable for Ships of great burthen to *Burlington*, which from the *Capes*, or entrance, is accounted an hundred and forty Miles; and for Sloops to the Falls, which is about ten Miles farther.

The Bay of *Sandy-hoock* on *Eaft-Jerfy* is a fafe and excellent Harbour for any Fleet of Ships, which can lie there in all Weathers, and go in and out to Sea in Winter, as well as Summer, and Ships of great Burthen can lie clofe to the Town of *New-Perth*, which renders it a good Scituation for Navigation, from whence in fix Hours time at moft, Ships can go out into the Sea; and clofe by the Town of *Perth* runs up *Rarzton* River. From the Falls of *Delaware* River the *Indians* go in Cannows up the faid River, to an *Indian* Town called *Menifincks*, which is accounted from the Falls about eighty Miles; but this they perform by great Labour in fetting up againft the Stream; but they can come down

with

with eafe and fpeed ; the River from the Falls runs from the
North and North-Weft about twenty Miles, as I my felf
obferved in my Travel fo far by the River, but by the *Indians* Information, it cometh about more Eafterly farther up.
I have been informed, that about *Minifincks*, by the River-
fide, both in *New-Jerfey* and *Pennfylvania* is great quantities
of exceeding rich open Land, which is occafioned by wafh-
ing down of the Leaves and Soil in great Rains from the
Mountains, which Land is exceeding good, for the raifing
of *Hemp* and *Flax*, *Wheat*, or any other forts of Corn, Fruits,
Roots *&c.* Where in time may be conveniently fettled a
Manufacture for the making of *Linnen-Cloth*, *Cordage*, *Twine*,
Sacking, *Fifhing-Nets*, and all other Commodities commonly
made of Hemp or Flax : And after great Rains, we may
bring down great quantities of Goods in flat-bottom-Boats,
built for that purpofe, which will then come down, by reafon of the Land-floods with fpeed.

And into this River, betwixt the Capes and the Falls, run
many navigable Rivers and Cricks, fome of them fifteen
or twenty Miles, and others lefs, which Rivers and Cricks
are made by the plenty of Springs and Brooks, that run out
of the Country, many of which Brooks are fo confiderable,
as to be fit to drive Mills. And above the falls, in travelling
of twenty Miles by the Rivers fide, I went over twenty run-
nings of Water, five or fix of them being fit to build Mills
on.

The Country for the moft part is pretty leavel, until we
come about ten Miles above the Falls, where it is Mounta-
nious for many Miles, but interlaced with fertile Valleys.
The Bay and River of *Delaware*, and the Rivers and Cricks
that runs into it, are plentifully ftored with various forts of
good *Fifh* and *Water-Fowl*, as *Swans*, *Geefe*, *Ducks*, *Wigeons*,
&c. And a confiderable *Whale*-Fifhery may be carried on in
the

the Bay of *Delaware*, and on the Sea-Coasts of *New-Jersey*, there being *Whale*-Fisheries already begun, plenty of *Whales* being by experience found there, and the Winter-time being the time for the catching them, they will not thereby be hindred of raising there Summer-Crops ; and the Oyl and Bone being good Commodities to be sent for *England*, there also being in the Bay of *Delaware* and *Sandy-hoock*, *Drums,Sheeps-heads Bass*, and other sorts of large Fish, which may be fit to salt up in Casks to keep for use, and Transportation also.   There are great plenty of *Oysters*, which may be pickled and put up in small Casks for use.   Likewise, in *Delaware* River are great plenty of *Sturgeon*, which doubtless might be a good Trade, if mannaged by such Persons as are skilful in the boyling and pickling of them, so as to preserve them good to *Barbadoes*, and other adjacent Islands.   There are also in the Spring great quantities of a sort of Fish like *Herrings* ; with plenty of the Fish called *Shads*, but not like the *Shads* in *England*, but of another kind, being a much better sort of Fish ; the Inhabitants usually catch quantities, which they salt up, and pack them in Barrels for Winter's Provision.

The Lands from the Capes, to about six Miles above *New-Castle* (which is by estimation ninety Miles) is for the most part very rich, there being very many navigable Cricks on both sides of the River, and on the River and Cricks are great quantities of rich fat Marsh Land, which causeth those parts, to some fresh People,to be somewhat unhealthful in the latter part of the Summer, at which time some of them have *Agues* : Also in and near these Marshes, are small Flies, called *Musketoes*, which are troublesome to such People as are not used to them ; but were those Marshes banked, and drained, and then plowed and sowed, some Years with Corn, and then with *English* Hay-seed, I do suppose it would

would be healthful, and very little troubled with *Musketoes*: and if Cattel did commonly feed on this Ground, and tread it as in *England*, I suppose it would not be inferior to the rich Meadows on the River of *Thames*; and were quantities of this Land laid dry, and brought into Tillage, I suppose it would bear great Crops of *Wheat*, *Peafe* and *Barley*, *Hemp* and *Flax*, and it would be very fit for *Hop-Gardens*, and for *English* Grafs, which might ferve for rich Paftures or Meadow. Alfo thefe Marfhes are fit for *Rape*, and were *Rape*-Mills built, and the defign mannaged, fo as it would be if it were in *England* or *Holland*, a great Trade might be carried on, and many hundred Tuns of *Rape*-Oyl might be made Yearly, and fent to *England*, to the Planters inrichment; and not only fo, but would be for Merchants advantage, they thereby having Goods to freight their Ships, which would tend to the benefit of the Inhabitants in general.

And if thofe Trades and Defigns are carried on to effect, as are mentioned in this Treatife, there would naturally follow Trade and Imployment for *Ship-wrights*, *Boat-wrights*, *Coopers*, *Carpenters*, *Smiths*, *Ropers*, *Marineis*, *Weavers*, *Butchers*, *Bakers*, *Brewers*; and many other forts of Trades would have full Imployment.

From fix Miles above *New-Caftle* to the Falls of *Delaware* (which is about fixty Miles) and fo to the Head of the faid River, the *Water* is clear, frefh, and fit for Brewing, or any other ufe.

The *Air* clear and good, it being fuppofed to be as healthful as any part of *England*.

The *Land* is in Veins, fome good, and fome bad, but the greateft part will bear good Corn, as *Wheat*, *Rye*, *Barley*, *Oats*, *Indian Corn*, *Buck-Wheat*, *Peafe* and *Indian Beans*, &c.

Fruits that grow natural in the Countries are *Strawberries*, *Cranberries*, *Huckleberries*, *Blackberries*, *Medlers*, *Grapes*, *Plums*,

Plums, Hickery-Nuts, Walnuts, Mulberies, Chestnuts, Hassel-nuts, &c.

Garden Fruits groweth well, as *Cabbage, Colworts, Colli-flowers, Sparagrass, Carrots, Parsneps, Turnups, Oyntons, Cow-cumbers, Pumkins, Water-Mellons, Musk-Mellons, Squasbes, Potatoes, Currants, Goosberries, Roses, Cornations, Tulips,* Garden-Herbs, Flowers, Seeds, Fruits, &c. for such as grow in *England,* certainly will grow here.

Orchards of *Apples,* Pears, *Quinces,* Peaches, *Aprecocks, Plums, Cheries,* and other sorts of the usual Fruits of *England* may be soon raised to good advantage, the Trees growing faster then in *England,* whereof great quantities of *Sider* may be made. And were Glass-houses erected to furnish us with Bottles, we might have a profitable Trade, by sending *Sider* to *Jamaico* and *Barbadoes,* &c. ready bottled, which is commonly so sent from *Herefordsbire* to *London.*

It is supposed that we may make as good Wines as in *France,* (if Vineyards were planted on the sides of Hills or Banks, which are defended from the cold North-West Winds) with such Vines as the *French*-men commonly make those Wines of; for the Climate is as proper as any part of *France,* therefore it is rational to believe, that the Wines will be as rich and good as in *France.* There are some Vine-yards already planted in *Pennsylvania,* and more intended to be planted by some *French-Protestants,* and others, that are gone to settle there.

Several other Commodities may be raised here, as *Rice,* which is known to have been sown for a tryal, and it grew very well, and yielded good encrease.

Also *Annis-Seeds* I have been informed groweth well, and might be a profitable Commodity, there being great Quan-tities used in *England* by Distillers.

Liquorish doubtless would grow very well. And I que-stion

ftion not but that *Mather*, *Wood*, and other Plants and Roots for Dyers ufe might be raifed.   *Shuemack* groweth naturally.   Alfo feveral ufeful Durgs grow naturally, as *Saffafrafs*, *Saffaperella*, *Callamus Aromaticus*, *Snake-Root*, *Jallappa*, &c.

The *Pine-Tree* groweth here, out of which is made *Pitch*, *Tar*, *Rofin* and *Turpentine*:   In *New-England* fome make quantities of *Tar* out of the knots of *Pine Trees*, with which they fupply themfelves and others.

There are many other forts of *Plants*, *Roots* and *Herbs* of great Virtue, which grow here, which are found to cure fuch Diftempers as the People are infident to.

Hops in fome places grow naturally, but were *Hop*-Gardens planted in low rich Land, quantities might be raifed to good advantage.

There is no *Lime Stone* as we yet know of, but we make *Lime* of *Oyfter* Shels, which by the Sea and Bay fide are fo plentiful, that we may load Ships with them.

There are feveral forts of good *Clay*, of which Bricks, Earthen-Ware, and Tobacco-Pipes are made;   and in fome places there are Quaries of a ruf hard Stone, which are good to wall Cellars, and fome Stone fit for Pavement.

The *Trees* grow but thin in moft places, and very little under-Wood.   In the *Woods* groweth plentifully a courfe fort of *Grafs*, which is fo proving, that it foon makes the Cattel and Horfes fat in the Summer, but the *Hay* being courfe, which is chiefly gotten on the frefh Marfhes, the Cattel lofeth their Flefh in the Winter, and become very poor, except we give them Corn: But this may be remydied in time, by draining of low rich Land, and by plowing of it, and fowing it with *English*-Grafs-feed, which here thrives very well

The *Hogs* are fat in the VVoods when it is a good Maft-Year.

The

The Woods are furnished with store of Wild Fowl, as *Turkeys*, *Phesants*, *Heath-Cocks*, *Partridges*, *Pidgeons*, *Black-birds*, &c. And People that will take the pains to raise the various sorts of tame Fowl, may do it with as little trouble, and less charge, then they can in *England*, by reason of what they find in the Woods.

Bees are found by the experience of several that keep them, to thrive very well.

I do not question but that we might make good strong found *Beer*, *Ale* and *Mum*, that would keep well to *Barbadoes* the Water being good, and *Wheat* and *Barley* in a few Years like to be very plentiful: Great quantities of *Beer*, *Ale* and *Mum* is sent yearly from *London*, and other places, to *Barbadoes*, *Jamaica*, and other Islands in *America*, where it sells to good advantage; and if *Beer*, *Ale* and *Mum* hold good from *England* to those places, which 'tis said is above one thousand Leagues; I question not but if it be well brewed in a seasonable time of the Year, and put up in good Casks, but it will keep good to be Transported from *Delaware* River to those Islands aforesaid, which by computation, is not above half so far. If Merchants can gain by sending *Beer*, *Ale* and *Mum* from *England*, where Corn is dear, and Freight dear, by reason of the length of the Voyage, we in all probability must get much more, that buy our Corn cheap, and pay less Freight.

Flower and *Bisket* may be made in great quantities in a few Years, the Wheat being very good, which seldom fails of finding a good Market at *Barbadoes*, *Jamaica*, and the *Carieb* Islands: great quantities are sent yearly from *London*, and other places, which if they can make Profit of it, we much more for the Reasons already given.

Pork is but about half the price as in *England*, therefore the Inhabitants will seldom have their Market spoiled by

any

any that come from *England*, of which Commodity the Inhabitants in a few Years will have Quantities to fell to the Merchant, which is falted, and packed in Barrels, and fo tranfported to *Jamaica*, *Barbadoes*, *Nevis*, and other Iflands. Hams of *Bacon* are alfo made, much after the fame manner as in *Weft-Falia*, and the Bacon eats much like it.

Our *Beef* in the Fall is very fat and good, and we are likely in a few Years to have great Plenty, which will ferve our Families, and furnifh Shipping.

Our *Mutton* is alfo fat, found and good, being only fed with natural Grafs; but if we fprinkle but a little *Englifh* Hay-Seed on the Land without Plowing, and then feed Sheep on it, in a little time it will fo encreafe, that it will cover the Land with *Englifh* Grafs, like unto our Paftures in *England*, provided the Land be good. We find the Profits of Sheep are confiderable.

Our *Butter* is very good, and our *Cheefe* is indifferent good, but when we have Paftures of *Englifh* Gafs, (which many are getting into) then I fuppofe our *Cheefe* will be as good as that of *England*.

Our *Horfes* are good ferviceable Horfes, fit both for Draught and Saddle, the Planters will ride them fifty Miles a day, without Shoes, and fome of them are indifferent good fhapes; of which many Ships are freighted yearly from *New-England* with Horfes to *Barbadoes*, *Nevis*, and other places; and fome Ships have alfo been freighted out of *Pennfylvania* and *New-Jerfey* with Horfes to *Barbadoes*; but if we had fome choice Horfes from *England*, and did get fome of the beft of our Mares, and keep them well in the Winter, and in Paftures inclofed in the Summer, to prevent there going amongft other Horfes, we might then have a choice breed of Horfes, which would tend much to the advantage of the Inhabitants.

The

The Commodities fit to fend to *England*, befides what are already named, are the Skins of the feveral wild Beafts that are in the Country, as *Elks*, *Deer*, *Beaver*, *Fisher*, *Bear*, *Fox*, *Rackoon*, *Marten*, *Otter*, *Woolf*, *Muskquash*, *Mink*, *Cat*, &c.

Potashes may be here made, and *Soap*, not only to the fupply of our felves, but to fell to our Neighbours.

Alfo *Iron* may be here made, there being one *Iron*-Work already in Eaft-*Jerfey*.

Likewife, we may furnifh Merchants with Pipe-Staves, and other Coopers Timber and Hoops.

The *Woolen* Manufacture may be mannaged in *Pennfylvania* and *New-Jerfey*, to good advantage, the upper parts of the Country being very fit for the keeping of Sheep, the Wool being found to be good, and the Sheep not fubject to the *Rot*: The Ewes commonly after the firft time, bring two Lambs at once.

But it may be queried, *How fhall the Sheep be preferved from the Woolf?*

I anfwer; Get fuch a Flock as it may anfwer the charge, for a boy to make it his full Employment to look after them, and let them be pend at Night in a Houfe or Fold provided for that purpofe. If one man have not enough to imploy a Shepherd, then let feveral joyn their Stock together.

But it may be queried, *Where fhall Wool be gotten to carry on the Woollen Manufacture, untill we have of our own raifing?*

I anfwer; in *Road Ifland*, and fome other adjacent Iflands and Places, Wool may be bought at fix Pence a Pound, and confiderable Quantities may be there had, which will fupply until we can raife enough of our own.

Alfo, we may have *Cotton-Wool* from *arbadoes*, and other adjacent Iflands in returns for our Provifions that we fend them. So that the making of Cotton-Cloth and Fuftians

may

may be likewife made to good advantage, the *Cotten-Wool* being purchafed by the growth of our own Country; and the Linnen-Yarn being fpun by our own Families, of *Flax*, of our own growth and ordering.

The *Tanning*-Trade and *Shoemaking* may be here mannaged to good advantage, *Hides* being plenty, and to be had at moderate Prices, and *Lark* to be had for only the charge in getting it.

A *Skinner* that can drefs Skins in Oyl, may do very well; for we have *Elk* skins, and plenty of *Buck* and *Doe* skins, which the Inhabitants give (at *New-York*, where there are fuch Trades) one half for dreffing the other.

There ought to be *publick Store-Houfes* provided for all Perfons to bring their Flax, Hemp and Linnen Cloth to, where it may be preferved clean and dry at a very fmall Charge, and the owner at liberty to take it out at his own will and pleafure, or to fell, transfer or affign it to any other. Now the Hemp, Flax and Linnen Cloth being brought into the publick Store-Houfe, and the Quantity, Quality and Value of it there regiftred in the Book, to be kept for that purpofe; and the Perfon that hath put in the faid Hemp, Flax and Linnen Cloth, taking a Note under the Hand and Seal, from the Store-houfe Regifter, of the quantity, quality and value of the Hemp Flax, and Linnen Cloth brought into the publick Store-Houfe, with the time it was delivered; thefe Notes will pafs from one man to another all one as Money: *As for Example*, Suppofe I am a Merchant, that am furnifhed with divers forts of goods, I fell them to a Planter, and receive their Notes which they had from the Store-houfe *Regiftry*, in pay for my goods, to the value of one hundred Pounds. I buy of the Clothier in Woolen Cloth to the value of fixty pounds, and of the **Roper** in Cordage to the value of forty pounds; I pay them by thefe **Notes** on the Store-houfe; the Clother he buys Woolen Yarn

of

of the Mafter of the Spinning-School, to the value of fixty pounds, and payes him by thefe Notes on the publick Store; the Mafter of the Spinning-School buys of the Farmer in Wool to the value of fixty pounds, and pays him by thefe Notes; the Farmer buyeth of the Merchant in Goods to the value of fixty pounds, and pays him by thefe Notes; the Merchant receiveth on demand, from the publick Store, in Linnen Cloth to the value of fixty pound, at receiving thereof he delivereth up the Notes to the Regifter of the publick Store, which are cancelled, and then filed up as Wafte paper. The Roper, when he pleafeth, receives on demand, in Hemp to the value of forty pounds out of the publick Store, by which he is made capable of imploying his Servants in making of Cordage; but he that hath no cccafion to take out this Hemp or Flax, or Linnen Cloth, may pafs thefe Notes from one man to another, as often they pleafe, which is all one as ready Money at all times.

Were the Flax and Hemp Manufactuaries carried on to that height as it might be, it would greatly advance thefe Countries, for did we make our own Sail-cloth and Cordage, we could make Ships, Sloops and Boats at much eafier Rates than they can build for in *England*, the Timber cofting us nothing but Labour. And were more Saw-Mills made (of which there are divers already) to cut Planks and other Timber, both Ships and Houfes might be built at eafie Rates.

Many Ship Loads of Hemp is brought yearly from the Eaft Countries to *England*, which is afterward there made into Cordage, Twine, Sacking, Fifhing-Nets &c. and then tranfported from thence to *Jamaica*, *Barbadoes*, *Virginia*, *New-England*, and other parts of *America*, fo that doubtlefs materials made of Hemp, muft be fold in *America* by the Retaler, at double the price as it coft where it grew; by which it appears that at thofe prices we fhould have double for our labour

bour, to what they have, and our Provisions as Cheap as theirs, it being raised on Land that cost us little.

1. Now It might be well if a Law were made by the Governours and general Assemblies of *Pennsilvania* and *New-Jersey*, that all Persons inhabiting in the said Provinces, do put their Children seven years to the publick School, or longer, if the Parents please.

2. That Schools be provided in all Towns and Cities, and Persons of known honesty, skill and understanding be yearly chosen by the Governour and General Assembly, to teach and instruct Boys and Girls in all the most useful Arts and Sciences that they in their youthful capacities may be capable to understand, as the learning to *Read* and *Write true English, Latine*, and other useful Speeches and Languages, and *fair Writing, Arithmatick* and *Book-keeping* ; and the Boys to be taught and instructed in some Mystery or Trade, as the making of *Mathematical Instruments*, *Joynery*, *Turnery*, the making of *Clocks* and *Watches*, *Weaving*, *Shoe-making*, or any other useful Trade or Mystery that the School is capable of teaching ; and the Girls to be taught and instructed in *Spinning* of *Flax* and *Wool*, and *Knitting* of *Gloves* and *Stockings*, *Sewing*, and making of all sorts of useful *Needle Work*, and the making of *Straw-Work*, as *Hats*, *Baskets*, *&c.* or any other useful Art or Mystery that the chool is capable of teaching.

3. That the Scholars be kept in the Morning two hours at *Reading*, *Writing*, *Book-keeping &c.* and other two hours at work in that Art, Mystery or Trade that he or she most delighteth in, and then let them have two hours to dine, and for Recreation ; and in the afternoon two hours at *Reading*, *Writing*, *&c.* and the other two hours at work at their several Imployments.

4. The seventh day of the Week the Scholars may come to school only in the fore-noon, and at a certain hour in the
after-

after-noon let a Meeting be kept by the School-masters and
their scholars, where after good instruction and admonition
is given by the Masters, to the Scholars, and thanks returned
to the Lord for his Mercies and Blessings that are daily received from him, then let a strict examination be made by the
Masters, of the Conversation of the scholars in the week past,
and let reproof, admonition and correction be given to the Offendors, according to the quantity and quality of their faults.

5. Let the like Meetings be kept by the School-Mistrisses,
and the Girls apart from the Boys. By strictly observing this
good Order, our Children will be hindred of running into
that Excess of Riot and Wickedness that youth is incident to,
and they will be a comfort to their tender Parents.

6. Let one thousand Acres of Land be given and laid out
in a good place, to every publick School that shall be set up,
and the Rent or incom of it to go towards the defraying of
the charge of the School.

7. And to the end that the Children of poor People, and
the Children of *Indians* may have the like good Learning with
the Children of Rich People, let them be maintained free of
charge to their Parents, out of the Profits of the school, ari-
sing by the Work of the Scholars, by which the Poor and the
Indians, as well as the Rich, will have their Children taught,
and the Remainder of the Profits, if any be, to be disposed of
in the building of School-houses, and Improvements on the
thousand Acres of Land, which belongs to the School.

The manner and Profits of a *Spinning-School* in *Germany,*
as it is laid down by *Andrew Yarenton* in his own words, in a
Book of his, call'd, *England's Improvements by Sea and Land,*
take as followeth.

'In *Germany,* where the Thred is made that makes the fine
'Linnens, in all Towns there are Schools for little Girls, from
'six years old, and upwards, to teach them to spin, and so to
'bring

'bring their tender fingers by degrees to spin very fine ; their
'Wheels go all by the Foot, made to go with much ease,
'whereby the action or motion is very easie and delightful:
'The way, method, rule and order how they are govern'd is,
'*1st*. There is a large Room, and in the middle thereof a little
'Box like a Pulpit : *2dly*, There are Penches built round about
'the Room, as they are in Play-houses, upon the benches sit
' about two hundred Children spinning, and in the box
'in the middle of the Room, sits the grand Mistress with a
'long white Wand in her hand ; if she observe any of them
' idle, she reaches them a tap, but if that will not do, she rings
'a bell, which by a little Cord is fixed to the box, and out
'comes a VVoman, she then points to the Offendor, and she
'is taken away into another Room and chastized ; and all
'this is done without one word speaking : In a little Room
'by the School there is a VVoman that is preparing, and put-
'ting Flax on the Distaffs, and upon the ringing of a Bell, and
'pointing the Rod at the Maid that hath spun off her Flax,
'she hath another Distaff given her, and her Spool of Thred
'taken from her, and put into a box unto others of the same
'size, to make Cloth, all being of equal Threds. *1st*. They
'raise their Children, as they spin finer, to the higher Benches :
'2. They sort and size all the Threds, so that they can apply
'them to make equal Cloths; and after a young Maid hath been
'three years in the *Spinning-School*, that is taken in at six, and
'then continues until nine years, she will get eight pence the
'day, and in these parts I speak of, a man that has most
'Chlidren, lives best

Now were *Spining-Schools* settled in the principal Cities and
Towns in *Pennsyvania* and *New-Jersey*, and a Law made to
oblige the Parents of Children, to put their Children to
School, we should then soon come into such a way of making
Linnen-Cloth, as that we should not only have sufficient fo

ou

our own fupply, but alfo fhould have quantities to fell to the Inhabitants of our own neighbouring Provinces, where it will fell at confiderable Prices, they being ufually fupplied from *England*, where it muft be dear, after Freight, Cuftom, and other charges at Importation, with the Merchants profit confidered; and yet neverthelefs this Cloth, thus dear bought will fell in *New-England*, *Virginia*, and fome other places in *America*, at thirty Pound *per Cent* profit, above the firft coft in *England*, and the Moneys paid by Bills of Exchange, and the Retailer makes commonly on Goods thus bought not lefs then twenty Pounds *per Cent*. profit: So that if all things be confidered, the Cloth is fold in *America*, to the Planter at full double the price as it coft from the maker in *France* or *Germany*, from whence its brought to *England*, by which it doth appear, that if we do get fuch Prices for the Cloth that we make, then we fhall have double for our Labour to what they have; therefore it may be well that a Law were made for the encouragement of the *Linnen Manufacture* by the Governours and General Affemblies, that all Perfons inhabiting in *Pennfylvania*, or *New-Jerfey*, that keep a Plow, do fow one Acre of *Flax*, and two Acres of *Hemp*, which would be a means of fupplying us with *Flax* and *Hemp*, to carry on the Manufacturies of *Linnen-Cloth* and *Cordage*; and alfo would be very profitable to the Planter, by imploying his Family in the Winter feafon, when they would have otherwife but little elfe to do, *viz.* the Men and Boys in Breaking and Dreffing of it, and making it fit for ufe, and the Women and Girls in Spining it, and neverthelefs they may carry on their Husbandry as largely, as if nothing of this was done; the Husbandry-Affairs being chiefly betwixt the Spring and Fall.

Now to that end that a *Bank* of *Monies* and *Credit* may be in *Pennfilvania* and *New Jerfey*, a Law may be made, that all

Monies

Monies lent on Intereſt be at 8 *l. per Cent.* by thé year, and that all Bills and Bonds be entred on the publick Regiſtry, and by Act of Aſſembly be made transferable by Aſſignments,ſo as the Property may go along with the Aſſignment ; thereby a Bond or Bill will go in the nature of *Bills of Exchange* ; and ſo *A.* owing 200 *l.* to *B.* he aſſigns him the Bond of *C.* who owed him 200 *l.* and *C.* owing *D.* 200 *l.* aſſigns him the Bond of *E.* who owed him 200 *l.* and ſo one Bond or Bill would go through twenty hands, and thereby be as ready Monies, and do much to the Benefit of Trade.   Alſo, that all Lands and Houſes be put under a publick Regiſtry, and entred in the Book, with an account of the value of them, and how occupied and tenanted, a particular thereof being given under the Hand and Seal of the Office to the Owners.   We having thus fitted our ſelves with a publick Regiſtry of all our Lands and Houſes, whereby it is made ready Money at all times, without the charge of Law, or the neceſſity of a Lawyer ; and a Law being made for the payment of ſuch large Intereſt for Monies lent, and the ſecurity being ſo undeniably good, a Bank will in time ariſe, and ſuch a Bank as will be for the benefit and advantage of *Pennſilvania* and *New-Jerſey,* and Trade univerſal.

Suppoſe my ſelf, and ſome others have in Houſes and Lands in *Pennſilvania* or *New-Jerſey,* worth 3000 *l.* and are minded to mannage and carry on the Linnen Manufactur·, but cannot do it, without borrowing on Intereſt 2000 *l.* therefore we come to the Bank in *Pennſilvania* or *New Jerſey,* and there tender a particular of our Lands and Houſes, and how occupied or tennanted, being worth 3000 *l.* in *Pennſilvania* or *New-Jerſey,* and deſire them to lend us 2000 *l.* and we will Mortgage our Land & Houſes for it ; the anſwer will be, *We will ſend to the Regiſter's Office your particular, and at the return of the Meſſenger you ſhall have your anſwer :* The
Regiſters

Regifters fend anfwer, it is our Lands and Houfes, and occupied, and tenanted, and valued according to the particular, there needs no more words but to tell us the Money, with which we carry on the Trade briskly, to the great benefit and advantage of fome hundreds of People that we fet to work, and to the fupplying of the Inhabitants with Cloth made of Flax, grown, dreft, fpun and wove in our own Provinces ; which Trade we could not mannage and carry on without this credit, but having this credit, we go on with our Trade comfortably, and the Lender will have his ends anfwered, and his Moneys well fecured.   And its certain, fuch an Anchorage, Fund, and Foundation, will then bring out the Monyes unimployed from all Perfons in thefe Provinces, even People of all degrees will put in their Monyes, which will be put out again into Trade to Merchants, and fuch as ftand in need of ready Monyes ; and thereby Trade is made eafie, and much convenienced.

Suppofe ten Families purchafe in *Pennfilvania* or *New-Jerfey* five thoufand Acres of Land, and they lay out a fmall Townfhip in the middle of it, for the conveniency of neighbourhood, to each Family one hundred Acres for Houfes, Gardens, Orchards, Corn-fields and Paftures of Englifh Grafs, the remainder to lie in common, to feed their Cattel ; and fuppofe that by that time they have built their dwelling Houfes, Cowhoufes, Barnes, and other Out-houfes, and have made Inclofures about their home-lots, that their Monyes is all expended, and without a further fupply to buy Oxen and Horfes to plow their Land, and Cows to find their Families' in Milk, Butter and Cheefe, and Sows to breed a ftock on, they will live but meanly for fome time,   therefore to amend their condition they come to the Bank, and there tender a particular of their Lands, valued to be worth 1500 *l* on which they defire to take up 1000 *l*. to purchafe a Stock of Oxen, Horfes, Cows, Sows, Sheep and Servants, by which they will be enabled ab!ed to carry on their Husbandry to great advantage, and the benefit of the Province in general ; and it may be that in two or three years time, they may be able to pay in this Money, with Intereft, to the owner; and in two or three years more may be able to bring into the Bank, to be lent out to others, one thoufand pounds of their own Eftates.

As to the benefit of **publick Granaries** on *Delaware River*, to keep the Corn for all Merchants, Bakers and Farmers that pleafe to fend it thither, that fo the deftruction and damages occafioned by Rats and Mice, may be prevented. In this Granary, Corn at all times may be taken in, from all Perfons that pleafe to fend it, and the Corn fo fent may be preferved fweet, fafe, and in good Order, at a fmall charge for a whole year, and the owner at liberty to take it out at his own will and pleafure, or to fell, transfer or affign any part of the faid Corn to any Perfon or Perfons for the payment of his Debts, or to furnifh himfelf with Clothing, or other Neceffaries from the Merchant; and the Granary-keepers to give good fecurity that all things fhould be faithfully done & difcharged. Now the Corn being brought into the publick Granary, and there regiftred in the Regifter-Book, to be kept for that purpofe; and the Perfon that hath put in the faid Corn, taking a Note under hand and feal, from the Granary-Regifter, of the quantity of Corn brought into the Granary, with the time it was delivered, and the matter and kind of the Corn, then thefe Advantages will enfue :

Firft, Prefervation from the Rats and Mice, Straw to fupply his Cattel, the Chaff for his Horfes, and the light Corn to feed his Pigs and Poultry ; his Husbandry mannaged with rule and order to his advantage ; no forc'd hafte, but thrafhing and carrying the Corn to the Granary in times wherein his fervants have leifure ; fo in feeding time & harveft all People are freed from that. Befides, there being at all times fufficient quanti-
ties

ties of Corn in the Granaries to load Ships, Merchants from *Barbadoes*, and other places, will come to buy Corn; of one Farmer he may buy one hundred Bushels, of another fifty, and so he may buy the Corn that belongs to sixty or eighty Farmers, and receive their Notes which they had from the Granary-Office, which Corn he letteth lie in the Granary until he have occasion to use it, then he orders his Baker to go with those notes to the Granary-Office, and receive such quantities as he hath a mind shall be made into Flower and Bisket, which the Baker does accordingly, and gets it packt up in Casks, and sent to *Barbadoes*; the remainder, if he please, he may sell to some other Merchant that lives at *Barbadoes*, or some other place, and when sold, may deliver the said Merchant the Notes on the Granary-Office, at sight whereof they may receive their Corn, if they please, or they may pass those Notes from one to another, as often as they please, which is all one as Money, the Corn being lodged safe, and kept in the publick Cranary, will be the occasion of imploying much of the Cash of *Pennsilvania* and *New-Jersey*; most People near these publick Bank-Granaries, will be dealing to have some Corn in Bank-Credit; for that cannot miss of finding an encrease and benefit to them in the rise of Corn.

The best places at present for the building of *Granaries*, are, I suppose, *Burlington* in *West-Jersey*, *Philadelphia* and *New-Castle* in *Pennsilvania*, and *New Perth* in *East Jersey*, which places are excellently situated, there being many Navigable Rivers, whereby Trade is very communicable, and the Corn may be brought in Boats and Sloops from most places now inhabited, by water to these publick Granaries, for small charge, and from the Granaries may be carried to Water-Mills to grind, which are some of them so conveniently situated, that Boats may come to the Mill-Tayl, which is also a great conveniency to those that trade much in Corn.

Now

Now I will demonſtrate, and ſhew you the length, breadth and heighth the *Granaries* ought to be of, to hold this Corn; as alſo the Charge of building one of them, and the way how it ſhould be built for the beſt advantage, with the way of ordering and managing the Corn, that it may keep good, ſweet and clean, eight or ten Years. The *Granaries* muſt be three hundred Foot long, eighten Foot wide betwixt inſide and inſide, ſeven Stories high, each Story ſeven Foot high, all to be built of good well burnt Brick, and laid in Lime and Sand very well; the ends of the *Granaries* muſt be ſet *North* and *South*, ſo the ſides will be *Eaſt* and *Weſt*; and in the ſides of the *Granaries*, there muſt be large Windows to open and ſhut cloſe, that when the Wind blows at *Weſt*, the Windows may be laid open, and then the *Granary* man will be turning and winding the Corn, and all Filth and Droſs will be blown out at the Window. When the Weather is fair, then throw open the VVindows, to let in the Air to the Corn; and in the middle, there muſt be Stoves to be kept with Fire in them in all moiſt or wet times, or at going away of great *Froſts* and *Snows*, to prevent moiſtneſs either in the Brick-walls, Timber, Boards or Corn. There muſt be in each ſide of the *Granaries*, three or four long Troughs or Spouts fixt in the uppermoſt Loft, which muſt run about twenty Foot out of the *Granary*; and in fine VVeather, the *Granary* men muſt be throwing the Corn out of the uppermoſt Loft, and ſo it will fall into another Spout made ten Foot wide at the top, and through that Spout the Corn deſcends into the lowermoſt Loft, and then wound up on the inſide of the *Granary*, by a Crane fixt for that purpoſe, and the Corn receiving the benefit of the Air, falling down thirty Foot before it comes into the ſecond Spout, cleanſeth it from its filth and Chaff; theſe Spouts are to be taken off and on, as occaſion requires, and to be fixt to another of the
Lofts

Lofts, that when Veſſels come to load Corn, they may through theſe Spouts convey the Corn into the Boats or Sloops, without any thing of Labour, by carrying it on the Backs of men.

The charge of one *Granary* three Hundred Foot long, eighteen Foot wide, ſeven Stories high, ſeven Foot betwixt each Story, being built with Brick in *England*, as by the Account of *Andrew Yarenton*, take as followeth; *Six hundred thouſand of Bricks builds a* Granary, *two Bricks and a half thick the two firſt Stories, two Bricks thick the three next Stories, Brick and a half thick the two uppermoſt Stories; and the Brick will be made and delivered on the Place for eight Shillings the Thouſand, the laying of Brick three Shillings the Thouſand, Lime and Sand two Shillings the Thouſand; ſo Brick-laying, Lime and Sand will be thirteen Shillings the Thouſand, one hundred and fifty Tuns of Oak for Summers-Joiſts and Roof,* 170 l. *Boards for the ſix Stories, ſixty thouſand Foot, at* 13 s. 4 d. *The one hundred Foot and ten thouſand Foot for Window-Doors and Spouts at the ſame rate,* 48 l. *Laths and Tiles* 100 l. *Carpenters work* 70 l. *Iron, Nails, and odd things* 60 l. *So the charge of a* Granary *will be* 800 l. *There will be kept in this* Granary *fourteen thouſand Quarters of Corn, which is two thouſand Quarters in every Loft, which will be a thouſand Buſhels in every Bay; ſix labouring men, with one Clerk, will be ſufficient to manage this* Granary, *to turn and wind the Corn, and keep the Books of Accounts; fifteen pounds à piece allowed to the ſix men, and thirty pound a year to the Clark or Regiſter, will be Wages ſufficient, ſo the Servants Wages will be* 120 l. per annum, *allow ten in the hundred for Monies laid out for building the* Granaries, *which is* 80 l. *ſo the charge will be yearly* 200 l. *Now if the Country-man pay ſix pence a Quarter yearly for keeping his Corn ſafe and ſweet in the Granary, fourteen thouſand Quarters will come to* 350 l. *for Granary-Rent yearly.*

Adm't

Admit I have a Propiety of Land in *Pennfilyania* or *New-Jerfey*, either place then alloweth me to take up five thoufand Acres, with Town or City-Lots, upon condition that I fettle ten Families on it, therefore I fend over ten Families of honeft induftrous People, the charge of each Family is 100 *l.* as by the account of particulars appears, as followeth.

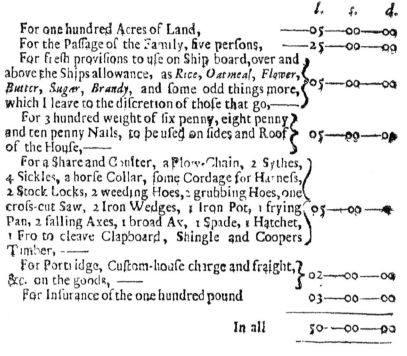

	l.	*f.*	*d.*
For one hundred Acres of Land,	05	00	00
For the Paffage of the Family, five perfons,	25	00	00
For frefh provifions to ufe on Ship board, over and above the Ships allowance, as *Rice, Oatmeal, Flower, Butter, Sugar, Brandy*, and fome odd things more, which I leave to the difcretion of thofe that go, ——	05	00	00
For 3 hundred weight of fix penny, eight penny and ten penny Nails, to be ufed on fides and Roof of the Houfe, ——	05	00	00
For a Share and Coulter, a Plow-Chain, 2 Sythes, 4 Sickles, a horfe Collar, fome Cordage for Harnefs, 2 Stock Locks, 2 weeding Hoes, 2 grubbing Hoes, one crofs-cut Saw, 2 Iron Wedges, 1 Iron Pot, 1 frying Pan, 2 falling Axes, 1 broad Ax, 1 Spade, 1 Hatchet, 1 Fro to cleave Clapboard, Shingle and Coopers Timber, ——	05	00	00
For Portridge, Cuftom-houfe charge and fraight, &c. on the goods, ——	02	00	00
For Infurance of the one hundred pound	03	00	00
In all	50	00	00

The remaing fifty Pounds may do well to lay out in thefe goods, which are the moft vendable in the Country, *viz.*

Ten

	l.	s.	d.
Ten pieces of Serge, at	20	00	00
Six pieces of narrow blew Linnen, containing about seven hundred Yards,	05	00	00
200 Ells of brown Ollembrigs, at about	07	10	00
Half a piece of three quarters Dowlis,	03	10	00
Three pieces of coplered Linnen	02	10	00
Two pieces of Yorkshire Kerseys,	04	00	00
One piece of red Penifton, above 40 yards, at 18 d. per Yard, ———	03	00	00
One piece of Demity,	00	15	00
In Buttons and Silk, Tape and Thred suitable to the Clothes,	03	15	00
In All	50	00	00

And when you come into the Country, you may lay out the above-mentioned goods to purchafe a ftock of Cattel and Provifions, &c. which for goods at the firft coft in *England*, will buy at the prices under-mentioned, *viz.*

	l.	s.	d.
One pair of working Oxen, at	60	00	00
One Mare 3 l. and four Cows and Calves, 12 l.	15	00	00
One Bull 2 l. ten Ewes 3 l. 10 s.	05	10	00
Four breeding Sows, and one Boor,	04	00	00
One fat Ox to kill for winter Provifions,	03	10	00
400 pound of Pork, at 3 half pence *per pound*,	02	10	00
24 pound of Butter, at 4 d. per pound,	00	08	00
One Barrel of falted Fifh,	00	10	00
One Barrel of Malaffas to make Beer,	01	08	00
40 Bufhels of Indian Corn, at 1 s. 8 d. per Bufhel,	03	06	08
20 Bufhels of Rye, at 2 s. per Bufhel,	02	00	00
20 Bufhels of Wheat, at 3 s per Bufhel,	03	00	00
6 Bufhels of Peafe and Indian Beans, per Bufhel,	00	18	00
2 Bufhels of Salt, at 2 s. per Bufhel,	00	04	00
50 pound of Cheefe of the Country-making, at 3 d. per pound,	00	12	06
12 pound of Candles, at 5 d. per pound,	00	05	00
In Sugar, Spice, and other things,	00	17	00
In All	50	00	00

Note, That the above-mentioned Prices is for goods at firſt
coſt in England, which in Country Money would be ſomething above one third higher, *viz.* a Cow and Calf valued
in goods at firſt coſt at 3 *l.* is worth in Country Money 5 *l.*
and other things advance much after the ſame proportion.

My five thouſand Acres of Land coſt me 100 *l.* I had of
the ten Families for the one thouſand Acres diſpoſed of to
them 50 *l.* my Town or City Lots will yield me currant 50 *l.*
by which it appears I am nothing out on the four thouſand
Acres that is left.

I get my five thouſand Acres ſurveyed and laid out to me,
out of which I lay out for the ten Families one thouſand Acres,
which may be ſo divided, as that each family may live near
one to the other ; I intend with them to let the Money lie in
their hands ſix years, for which they to pay me each family,
8 *l* a year, in conſideration of the one hundred pound a family laid out for them , and at the expiration of the ſix years,
they to pay me my 1000 *l.* viz. each family 100 *l.* as by agreement ; my Money being paid me, I am unwilling to let it lie
dead, therefore I lay out in the middle of my Land one thouſand Acres, which I divide into ten lots, in form and manner
as before then I intend, with fifty Servants to ſerve me four
years a piece, I place them on the Land, *viz.* five on each lot.
Their Paſſage, and in goods to purchaſe Cattel and Proviſions,
&c. is to each five ſervants 100 *l.* as before is explained ; Now
I order a Houſe to be built, and Orchards, Gardens and In-
cloſures to be made, and Husbandry affairs to be carried on on
each lot ; ſo that at the four years end as the ſervants time is
expired, I ſhall have ten Farms, each containing four hundred Acres ; for the one thouſand Acres being laid out in the
middle of my Land, the remaining three thouſand Acres
joyns to it.

My

My fervants time being expired, I am willing to fee what charge I am out upon thefe ten Farms and Stock, in order to know what I have gain'd in the ten years paft, over and above 8 *l. per Cent. Intereft*, that is allowed me for the ufe of my Money: I am out by the firft charge 1000 *l*. & the Intereft thereof for four years, at 8 *l. perCent*. is for the four years 320 l. fo that the whole charge on the ten Farms, Principal & Intereft, comes to 1320 l.   Now if I value my ten Farms but at 400 l. each, which is 20 *s. per Acre*, one with another; then the whole will be 4000 l. befides the firft Stock of Cattel and Hogs, &c to each Plantation, with its Increafe for four years, which Stock coft at firft to each Farm 30 *l*. in goods at firft coft, but is worth 40 *l*. fterling, at which rate the Stock on the ten Farms coft 400 *l*. and if we account the four years Increafe to be no more than the firft Stock, yet that is 400 *l*. by which it appears that the ten Farms, and the ftock on them is worth 4800 *l*. out of which deduct the Money laid out, which with Intereft is 1320 *l*. So the the Neat profit, befides 8 *l. per Cent*. allowed for Intereft, is for this ten years improvement, 3480 *l*. and twenty Families fet at liberty from that extream Slavery that attended them, by reafon of great Poverty that they endured in *England*, and muft have fo continued, had not they been thus redeemed by coming into *America*. It may be thought that this is too great an undertaking for one man, which if it be, then I propofe that ten joyn together in this community, and each man fend over five Servants, of which let one of them be an honeft man that underftands Country bufinefs, as an Overfeer, which if we allow him over and above his Paffage and Diet 20 *l*. a year for his four years fervice, this amounts to 80 *l*. which is for the ten farms 800 *l*. which being deducted out of the 3480 *l*. there only remains 2680 *l*. clear profit to the ten men, which is for each man 268 *l*. for his ten years improvement of his 100 *l*. and his 100 *l*. back

again

again with Interest for all the time at 8 *l per Cent. per annum*, the whole producing 448 *l.* for his 100 *l.* first laid out.

Some may object, and say, *They cannot believe the Land of each farm, with its Improvements, will sell at 20 s. an Acre, that is, at twelve years purchase* 1 s. 8 d. per Acre per annum. *because three hundred Acres of it is as it was, viz. Rough Woods.*

I *Answer* ; That although it be so, yet these Woods are made valuable by the twenty Families that are seated near them, the first ten families having been settled ten years, the last four years; for some are willing to have their Children live near them ; and and they having but, one hundred Acres in all, it will not be well to divide that, therefore they will give a good price for one hundred Acres, to settle a Child upon, to live by them, as experience sheweth ; for in *Rhode-Island*, which is not far from us, Land rough in the Woods, not better than ours, will sell at 40 s. an Acre, which is 3 s. 4 d *per Acre per annum* Therefore, Reader, I hope now thou art convinced that there is a probability that what I here inform thee of, will prove true, casualties of Fire, &c. excepted.

The *Indians* are but few in Number, and have been very serviceable to us by selling us Venison, *Indian* Corn, Pease and Beans, Fish and Fowl, *Buck* Skins, *Beaver, Otter,* and other Skins and Furs; the Men hunt, Fish and Fowl, and the Women plant the Corn, and carry Burthens ; they are many of them of a good Understanding, considering their Education ; and in their publick Meetings of Business, they have excellent Order, one speaking after another, and while one is speaking all the rest keep silent, and do not so much as whisper one to the other : We had several Meetings with them, one was in order to put down the sale of *Rum, Brandy,* and other strong Liquors to them, they being a People that have not Government of themselves, so as to drink it in moderation,

ration; at which time there were eight Kings, (& many other *Indians*) one of the was *Ockinickon*, whose dying Words I writ from his Mouth, which you shall have in its order.

The *Indian* Kings sate on a Form, and we sate on another over against them; they had prepared four Belts of *Wampum*, (so their current Money is called, being Black and White *Beads* made of a Fish Shell) to give us as Seals of the Covenant they made with us; one of the Kings by the consent and appointment of the rest stood up and made this following Speech; *The strong Liquors was first sold us by the* Dutch, *and they were blind, they had no Eyes, they did not see that it was for our hurt; and the next People that came amongst us, were the* Sweeds, *who continued the sale of those strong Liquors to us: they were also Blind, they had no Eyes, they did not see it to be hurtful to us to drink it, although we know it to be hurtful to us; but if People will sell it us, we are so in love with it, that we cannot forbear it; when we drink it, it makes us mad; we do not know what we do, we then abuse one another; we throw each other into the Fire, seven Score of our People have been killed, by reason of the drinking of it, since the time it was first sold us: Those People that sell it, they are blind, they have no Eyes, but now there is a People come to live amongst us, that have Eyes, they see it to be for our Hurt, and we know it to be for our Hurt: They are willing to deny themselves of the Profit of it for our good; · these People have Eyes; we are glad such a People are come amongst us. We must put it down by mutual consent; the Cask must be sealed up, it must be made fast, it must not leak by Day nor by Night, in the Light, nor in the Dark, and we give you these four* Belts of Wampam, *which we would have you lay up safe, and keep by you to be Witness of this Agreement that we make with you, and we would have you tell your Children, that these four Belts of* Wampam *are given you to be Witness betwixt us and you of this Agreement.*

A

A Letter from New-Jerfey *in* America *to a Friend in* London.

Dear Friend;

I Having this fhort opportunity, have nothing to prefent thee with, but the Dying Words of an *Indian* King, who died in *Burlington*, and was buried amongft Friends according to his defire; and at his Burial many Tears were fhed both by the *Indians* and *Englifh*; fo in Love, and great hafte, I reft thy Friend, *John Cripps.*

The Dying-Words of Ockaniehon, *fpoken to* Jachkurfoe, *whom he appointed King after him, fpoken in the Prefence of feveral, who were Eye and Ear Witneffes of the Truth thereof.*

I T was my defire, that my Brother's Son, *Jahkurfoe* fhould be fent for to come to me to hear my laft Words, whom I have appointed King after me. My Brother's Son, this day I deliver my Heart into thy Bofom, and would have thee love that which is Good, and to keep good Company, and to refufe that which is Evil; and to avoid bad Company. Now inafmuch as I have delivered my Heart into thy Bofom I alfo deliver my Bofom to keep my Heart therein; therefore alwayes be fure to walk in a good Path, and never depart out of it. And if any *Indians* fhould fpeak any evil of *Indians* or *Chriftians*, do not joyn with it, but to look to that which is Good, and to joyn with the fame alwayes. Look at the Sun from the Rifing of it to the Setting of the fame. In Speeches that fhall be made between the *Indians* and *Chriftians*, if any thing be fpoke that is evil, do not joyn with that, but joyn with that which is good; and when Speeches are made, do not thou fpeak firft, but let all fpeak before thee,

and

and take good notice what each man speaks, and when thou hast heard all, joyn to that which is good. Brother's Son, I would have thee to cleanse thy Ears, and take all Darkness and Foulness out, that thou mayst take notice of that which is Good and Evil, and then to joyn with that which is Good, and refuse the Evil; and also to cleanse thy Eyes, that thou mayest see both Good and Evil; and if thou see any Evil, do not joyn with it, but joyn to that which is Good. Brother's Son, Thou hast heard all that is past; now I would have thee to stand up in time of *Speeches*, and to stand in my *Steps*, and follow my *Speeches* as I have said before thee, then what thou dost desire in Reason will be granted thee. Why shouldst thou not follow my Example, inasmuch as I have had a mind to do that which is Good, and therefore do thou also the same? Whereas *Sehoppy* and *Swanpis* were appointed Kings by me in my stead, and I understanding by my Doctor, that *Seboppy* secretly advised him not to cure me, and they both being with me at *John Hollinshead's* House, there I my self see by them that they were given more to *Drink*, than to take notice of my *last Words*, for I had a mind to make a Speech to them, and to my Brethren the *English Commissioners*, therefore I refused them to be Kings after me in my stead, and have chosen my Brother's Son *Jahkurosoe* in their stead to succeed me.

Brother's Son, I desire thee to be plain and fair with all, both *Indians* and *Christians*, as I have been. I am very weak, otherwise I would have spoken more; and in Testimony of the Truth of this, I have hereunto set my Hand.

The Mark ꝫ of *Ockanickon*, King, now deceased.

Henry Jacob Falekinbery, Intrepreter.

Friendly

Friendly Reader, when *Ockanickon* had given his Brothers Son this good Counſel, I thought meet to ſpeak unto him as followeth ; *There is a great God, who Created all thing, and this God giveth Man an underſtanding of what is Good, and what is Bad, and after this Life rewardeth the Good with Bleſſings, and the Bad according to their Doings ;* to which he anſwered and ſaid, *It is very true, it is ſo, there are two Wayes, a broad Way, and a ſtrait Way ; there be two Paths, a broad Path and a ſtrait Path ; the worſt, and the greateſt Number go in the broad Path, the beſt and feweſt go in the ſtrait Path.*

T. B.

Something in Relation to a **Conference** *had with the* Indians *at* Burlington, *ſhortly after we came into the Country.*

THe *Indians* told us, they were adviſed to make War on us, and cut us off whilſt we were but few, and ſaid, They were told, that we ſold them the *Small-Pox,* with the Mach Coat they had bought of us, which cauſed our People to be in Fears and Jealouſies concerning them ; therefore we ſent for the *Indian* Kings, to ſpeak with them, who with many more *Indians,* came to *Burlington,* where we had Conference with them about the matter, therefore told them, That we came amongſt them by their own conſent, and had bought the Land of them, for which we had honeſtly paid them for, and for vvhat Commodities vve had bought at any time of them, vve had paid them for, and had been juſt to them, and had been from the time of our firſt coming very kind and reſpectful to them, therefore vve knevv no Reaſon that they had to make War on us ; to vvhich one of them, in the behalf of the reſt, made this follovving Speech in anſvver, ſaying, 'Our Young Men may ſpeak ſuch Words as vve do
' not

‘ not like, nor approve of, and vve cannot help that: And
‘ fome of your Young Men may fpeak fuch Words as you
‘ do not like, and you cannot help that. We are your Bro-
‘ thers, and intend to live like Brothers with you : We have
‘ no mind to have War, for when vve have War, vve are on-
‘ ly Skin and Bones; the Meat that vve eat doth not do us
‘ good, vve alvvayes are in fear, vve have not the benefit of
‘ the Sun to fhine on us, vve hide us in Holes and Corners;
‘ vve are minded to live at Peace: If vve intend at any time to
‘ make War upon you, vve vvill let you knovv of it, and the
‘ Reafons vvhy vve make War vvith you; and if you make us
‘ fatisfaction for the Injury done us, for vvhich the War is in-
‘ tended, then vve vvill not make War on you. And if you
‘ intend at any time to make War on us, vve vvould have you
‘ let us knovv of it, and the Reafons for vvhich you make
‘ VVar on us, and then if vve do not make fatisfaction for
‘ the Injury done unto you, then you may make VVar on
‘ us, othervvife you ought not to do it. You are our Bro-
‘ thers, and vve are vvilling to live like Brothers vvith you :
‘ We are willing to have a *broad Path* for you and us to walk
‘ in, and if an *Indian* is afleep in this *Path*, the *Englifh*-man
‘ fhall pafs him by, and do him no harm; and if an *Englifh*-man
‘ is afleep in this *path*, the *Indian* fhall pafs him by, and fay, *He*
‘ *is an Englifh-man, he is afleep, let him alone, he loves to Sleep.* It
‘ fhall be a *plain Path*, there muft not be in this *path* a *ftump* to
‘ hurt our *feet*. And as to the *Small-Pox*, it was once in my
‘ *Grandfathers* time, and it could not be the *Englifh* that could
‘ fend it us then, there being no *Englifh* in the Country and it
‘ was once in my *Fathers* time, they could not fend it us then
‘ neither ; and now it is in my time, I do not believe that they
‘ have fent it us now : I do believe it is the Man above that
‘ hath fent it us,

Some

Some are apt to ask, How we can propose safely to live amongst such a Heathen Poople as the Indians, whose Principles and Practices leads them to War and Bloodshed, and our Principles and Practices leading us to love Enemies, and if reviled, not to revile again ; and if smitten on the one cheek to turn the other, and we being a peaceable People, whose Principles and Practices are against Wars and Fightings ?

I Answer : That we settled by the Indians consent and good liking, and bought the Land of them, that we settle on, which they conveyed to us by Deed under their Hands and Seals, and also submitted to several Articles of agreement with us, viz. 𝕹𝖔𝖙 𝖙𝖔 𝖉𝖔 𝖚𝖘 𝖆𝖓𝖞 𝕴𝖓𝖏𝖚𝖗𝖞; but if it should so happen, that any of their People at any time should injure or do harm to any of us, then they to make us satisfaction for the Injury done ; therefore if they break these Covenants and Agreements, then they may be proceeded against as other Offendors, *viz.* to be kept in subjection to the Magistrates Power, in whose hand the Sword of Justice is committed to be used by him, for the punishment of Evil-doers, and praise of them that do well ; therefore I do believe it to be both lawful and expedient to bring Offendors to Justice by the power of the Magistrates Sword, which is not to be used in vain, but may be used against such as raise Rebellions and Insurrections against the Government of the Country, be they *Indians* or others, otherwise it is in vain for us to pretend to Magistracy or Government, it being that which we own to be lawful both in Principle and Practice.

Q. Whether there be not Bears, Wolves, and other Ravenous Beasts in the Country ?

I Answer : Yes. But I have travell'd alone in the Country some hundreds of Miles, and by missing of my way have lain in the Woods all night, and yet I never saw any of those Creatures, nor have I heard that ever man, woman or child were

hurt

hurt by them, they being afraid of Mankind ; alfo, encouragement is given to both *Indians* and others to kill Wolves,
they being paid for every Wolfs head that they bring to the
Magiftrate, the value of ten Shillings; and the Bears the
Indians kill for the profit of their Skins, and fake of their Flefh,
which they eat, and efteem better than Deers flefh.

Q. Whether there be not Snakes, more efpecially the
Rattle-Snake ?

Anf. Yes, but not many Rattle-Snakes, and they are eafily
difcovered ; for they commonly lie in the Paths for the benefit
of the Sun, & if any Perfon draws nigh them, they fhake their
Tail, on which the Rattles grow, which make a noife like a
childs Rattle ; I never heard of but one Perfon bitten in *Pennfilvania* or *New-Jerfey* with the Rattle-Snake, and he was
helpt of it by live Chickens flit affunder and apply'd to the
place, which drew out the Poyfon ; and as to the other Snake,
the moft plentiful is a black Snake, its bite, 'tis faid, does no
more harm than the prick of a Pin.

I have mentioned before, that there are a fort of troublefom
Flies call'd *Musketoes* (much like the Gnats in *England*) in the
lower parts of the Coun.ry, where the great Marfhes are, but
in the upper parts of the Country feldom one is feen.

There are Crows and Black-birds, which may be accounted
amongft the inconveniences, they being deftructive to the *Indian Corn*, the Crows by picking up the Corn juft as its appearing in the blade above ground, and the Black-birds by eating
it in the Year, before it be full hard, if not prevented by looking after ; but other forts of Corn they feldom hurt.

It is rational to believe, that all confiderate Perfons will fit
down and count the coft before they begin to build ; for they
muft expect to pafs through a Winter before a Summer, but
not fo troublefom a Winter as many have imagined ; for thofe
that come there to fettle now, may purchafe Corn, Cattel,
and

and other things at the prices mentioned, and may have Houses in fome of the Towns of *Pennfilvania* and *New-Jefey* on Rent, until they build for themfelves, and Water-Mills to grind their Corn, which are fuch conveniences that we that went firft partly miffed of.

Thus, Kind Reader, *I have given thee a true Defcription of* Pennfilvania *and* New-Jerfey, *with the* Rivers *and* Springs, Fifh *and* Fowle, Beafts, Fruits, Plants, Corn *and* Commodities *that it doth or may produce, with feveral other things needful for thee to know, as vvell* Inconveniences *as* Conveniences, *by vvhich I keep clear of that juft Reflection of fuch as are more apt to fee faults in others, than to amend them in themfelves.*

T. B.

WHereas I unadvifedly publifhed in Print a *Paper*, dated the 13th of *July*, 1685. entituled, *A true and perfect Account of the difpofal of the one hundred Shares or Proprieties of the Province of Weft* New-Jerfey, *by* Edward Bylling : In which *Paper* I gave an Account of the purchafers Names, and the feveral Proprieties granted to them, part of which I took from the Regifter, the remainder from a Lift given in by *Edward Bylling*, to the Proprioters, as mentioned on the faid *Paper*, which *Paper* I find hath proved Injurious to the aforefaid *Edward Bylling*, although not fo intended by me. Therefore in order to give him Satisfaction, and all others that are concerned, I do acknowledge he hath, fince the publifhing of that *Paper*, fhewed me fome Deeds, wherein he hath feveral Proprieties conveyed back to him again, from the original Purchafers and Judge, he may make good Titles to the fame.

A

A Letter by Thomas Budd, *sent to his Friends in* Pennsilvania *and* New=Jersey.

Dear Friends;

YOu are often in my Remembrance, and at this time I feel the tender Bowels of our heavenly Father's Love flowing in my Heart towards you, in a sence of those great Exercises that many of you have, do and may meet vvithal in your *Spirit al Travel* tovvards the *Land of Promise.*

I am also sensible of the many *Exercises* and invvard *Combats* that many of you met vvithal, after you felt an inclination in your Hearts of Transplanting your selves into *America:* Oh the *Breathings* and fervent *Prayers,* and earnest *Desires* that vvere in your Hearts to the Lord, *That you might not go except it was his good Pleasure to remove you, for a purpose of his own*: This you earnestly desired to be satisfied in, and many of you received satisfaction, that it was your places to leave your Native Country, Trades, and near and dear Relations and Friends to transplant your selves into a Wildernefs, where you expected to meet with many Tryals and Exercises of a differing kind, than what you had met withal in your Native Country ; but this you contentedly gave up to, but not without earnest defire, and fervent Prayers to the Lord for his Wisdom to govern you, and his Fatherly Care to preserve you, and his comfortable presence to be with you, to strengthen and enable you chearfuly to undergo those new and unaccustomed Tryals and Exercises, that you were senfible would attend you in this weighty undertaking, the Lord heard your Prayers, and answered your Desires, inasmuch as that his Fatherly Care was over you, and his living Presence

did

did accompany you over the great Deep; fo that you faw his wonderful Deliverence, and in a fence thereof, you praifed his Name for the fame.

The Lord having thus far anfwered our Souls defire, as to bring us to our defired Port in fafety, and to remain with us, to be a Counfellor of good things unto us, let us now anfwer this Kindnefs unto us by a *righteous Converfation*, and a *pure, holy* and *innocent Life*, that others beholding the fame, may be convinced thereby, and may glorifie our heavenly Father.

The Eyes of many are on us, fome for Good, and fome for Evil; therefore my earneft Prayers are to the Lord, That he would preferve us, and give us *Wifdom*, that we may be governed aright before him, and that he would give a good Underftanding to thofe that are in Authority amongft us, that his Law may go forth of *Sion*, and his Word from *Jerufalem*. Be not backward in difcharging that great Truft committed to you in your refpective Offices and Places, that you may be help-meets in the Reftroration.

And be careful to fupprefs, and keep down all Vice, and diforderly Spirits, and incourage Virtue, not only in the general, but every one in his perticular Family; there is an incumbant Duty lieth on all Mafters of Families over their Family, therefore my defire is, that we may call our Families together at convenient times and Seafons, to wait upon the Lord, and to feek to him for *Wifdom* and *Counfel*, that his Bleffings may attend us and our Families, and our Children may fit about our Table as Olive-branches full of Virtue, then fhall we be full of Joy and Peace, and living Praifes will fpring to the Lord, in that his Bleffings and Fatherly Care hath been thus continued towards us.

Dear Friends; be tender and helpful one towards another, that the Lord may blefs and fill you with his divine Love,

and

and fweet refrefhing Life, which unities our Souls to each other, and makes us as one Family of Love together: Let us not entertain any hard Thoughts one of another, but if difference fhould happen amongft us, let a fpeedy and peaceable end be put unto it; for if Prejudices enter, it will eat out the precious Life, and make us barren and unfruitful to God. We are not without our daily Exercifes, Tryals and Temptations, therefore do defire the Lord may put it into your Hearts, to Pray for our Prefervation, and our fafe return to you, that we may meet together again in the fame overcoming Love of God, in which we parted from you.

My Heart is full of Love to you, and do long to fee your Faces, and to enjoy your Company, that I may more fully exprefs that pure Love of God that fprings in my Heart unto you, then I can do by Writing. Therefore I defire you may reft fatisfied with thefe few Lines, and receive them as a token of unfeigned Love. From

Your dear Friend,

London, the 29th
of the 8th
Month, 1684.

Thomas Budd.

Some

Some material Things omitted in the foregoing part.

IT is to be noted, that the Tide runs to the Falls of *Delavvare*, it being one hundred and fifty Miles from the Capes, or entrance of the said River (which Falls, is a ledge of Rocks lying a cross the River) and also it runs up in some of the Cricks, ten or fifteen Miles, the said River and Cricks being navigable for Ships of great Burthen, there having lain over against *Burlington*, a Ship of about the burthen of four hundred Tuns afloat in four Fathom, at dead low Water, and the Flood riseth six or eight Foot; and there being no Worm that eats the bottoms of the Ships, as is usually done in *Virginia* and *Barbadoes*, &c. which renders the said Countries very fit for Trade and Navigation: And in the said River and Cricks are many other sorts of good *Fish*, not already named, some of which are *Cat-fish, Trout, Eales, Pearch,* &c.

ERRATA.

Page 13. line 16 after *often*, read *as.* Page 25 l. 3 for *seven,* r. *two hundred.* line 19. f. 60 r. 6, l. 31 after *Beans*, r. *at three Shillings.* Pag. 26 l 14 f. *I intend,* r. *I indent.* l. 22 f. *intend,* r. *indent.* pag. 28 l. 11 dele *and.* Pag. 17 f. *ths,* r. *this.* l. 21 after *in,* r. *the.*

THE GREAT BLESSING, OF PRIMITIVE COUNSELLOURS

Increase Mather, *The Great Blessing, of Primitive Counsellours. Discoursed in a Sermon, Preached in the Audience of the Governour, Council, and Representatives, of the Province of the Massachusets Bay, in New England. May 31st. 1693. Being the Day for the Election of Counsellours, in that Province* (Boston, 1693), pp. 1–23.

The father of Cotton Mather, Increase Mather (1639–1723) graduated from Harvard University in 1656 and received his master's degree from Trinity College in Dublin, Ireland, in 1658. Mather held a variety of religious positions in Boston before becoming the acting president of Harvard in 1685, and then president from 1686 to 1701. Mather was chosen to take petitions from the colonists to King James II in 1688, and in 1690 served as an agent for Massachusetts to England. However, Mather is probably best known for his extensive writings on religion, history, politics and science.

One of the themes in Mather's writing was that of the transformation of the religion-based society into a society based on the accumulation of trade and wealth. Mather argues that this transformation undermines society and its religious beliefs. Mather felt that reform was necessary to align Massachusetts more closely with the ideal Puritan society, as delineated in *The Great Blessing, of Primitive Counsellours.* For Mather, the ideal society maintains the stringent Puritan hierarchy of superiors and inferiors that can also be seen in John Winthrop's writings.

THE GREAT

BLESSING,

OF

PRIMITIVE

Counfellours.

Difcourfed in a

SERMON,

Preached in the Audience of the GOVERNOUR, COUNCIL,
and REPRESENTATIVES, of the Province of the *Maffachufets-
Bay*, in *New-England*. *May* 31*ft*. 1693. Being the Day for the
ELECTION of *Counfellours*, in that Province.

By Increafe Mather.

Prefident of **Harvard** Colledge in **Cambridge**, and Teacher of a
Church at **Bofton**, in **New-England**.

Bene agere *&* Male audire Regium eft.

BOSTON,

Printed and Sold, by *Benjamin Harris*, Over-againft the
Old-Meeting-Houfe. 1693.

TO THE

Inhabitants

Of the *Province* of the *Maſſachuſets-Bay,*
In

NEW·ENGLAND.

THAT this Colony was happy as to Civil Government whilſt they Enjoyed their *Former Charter,* is moſt certain. Not that that there where no imperfections attending that Firſt Patent. Our Neighbours in the other Colonies ſaw that there were ſome material Defects therein, which are not in their Charters, that were Granted after *Ours.* But inaſmuch as by Vertue thereof, the Freeman had full Power to Chuſe their own Rulers, they could not be Miſerable, unleſs by unhappy *Elections* they made themſelves ſo.

That ſome great Priviledges contained in the *Old Charter,* are not in that which at Preſent we enjoy, is known to every one : Nevertheleſs there is that in it which calls for great Thankfulneſs to God, whoſe Providence has Smiled as well as Frowned upon us. By Vertue of this Charter every man is Confirmed in the Peaceable Enjoyment of his *Eſtate* and *Property.* Nor can any *Taxes* now be impoſed on you, or *Laws* made, without your own conſent by ſuch *Repreſentatives* as your ſelves ſhall Chuſe. And (which is a greater matter) you are for ever delivered from all Impoſitions on *Conſcience,* which not many years ago you were afraid of. You may ſerve God with all the *freedom* which your hearts can deſire. Nor can there be any *Judge* or *Juſtice of Peace,* but ſuch as the *Counſellors* who are to aſſiſt the Governour ſhall conſent unto. Nor any *Counſellours* Confirmed beſide ſuch as the *Repreſentatives* of the Province ſhall Nominate to the Governour. *Theſe* are things which if you ſleight or undervalue them, the Moſt High will doubtleſs be Offended. Nor is a *Murmuring Spirit* the right way to obtain *more.* When the Children of *Iſrael Murmured* againſt thoſe
that

that had been the Inftruments of their Salvation, what did they get by it? For My own part, If I defire any thing in the World, I Wifh your *Profperity*, and that you were in a Frame fit for, and might enjoy all the Priviledges which your felves can Wifh for, in Order to your own Happinefs. And I thought I had given Demonftrations of my great affection to you, both whilft prefent with you, and abfent from you: which notwithftanding fome ill men (Who they are I know not) have caufed reports to flye about the Country, as tho During my Negotiation for you in *England*, I never opened my mouth for the Vindication of *New England*, and never endeavoured the *Reftoration* of ancient Priviledges, but in taking up with the prefent Charter (when more could not be obtained) followed my own Opinion without the advice of fuch as were your Friends; and acted contrary to Inftructions received from the General Court. But if I never did any thing for the Vindication of the People in this Province, from the Afperfions caft upon them by their Adverfaries, I defire to know who it was that Publifhed the *Narrative of the Miferies of New England*, and that afterwards wrote a *Firft*, *Second*, and *Third*, *Vindication of the People there* ? If I never endeavoured the Reftoration of Old *Charter-Priviledges*, by means of whofe Sollicitations was it, that *Votes* were paffed in the *Honourable Houfe of Commons*, that the *Old Charter* fhould be reftored, and a *Bill* wherin the Judgment againft that Charter was Reverfed, a Copy whereof I can produce ? And who was it that wrote and difperfed, *Reafons for the Confirmation of that Charter* ? Or, that did oftentimes Humbly Addrefs Their Majefties, and Their Principal Minifters of State concerning that affair ? Day and Night have feen, Heaven and Earth have heard, both Worlds are Witneffes, with what Importunities I have Sollicited both God and Man, for all your ancient Priviledges, yea and for Additionals unto them, according to the Inftructions which the General Court fent unto me, about my attendance to every one of which I gave to the General Affembly a Particular and Satisfactory account at my firft Arrival.

That I did not take one ftep without the Advice of the Wifeft and Beft Friends which *New England* has in *England*; there are many in *London* can atteft. My Worthy Dear Friend Mr. *Matthew Mead* in a Letter to a Relation of mine in *Bofton*, is pleafed thus to Write.

Mr. *Mather*, *Has deferved highly of New-England, for the unfainting Dili gence and Indefatigable Endeavours he has fhowed in his Agency for that People And whileft fome with you may perhaps wonder that he has obtained no more, we here, who have the Adva tage of a better Profpect, wonder that he has done fo much. And if men Reward not his great work, and Labour of Love, I am fure God will. What he has done has not been without the Counfel and Advice of the*
beft

beſt Friends that Country has in this, both Parliament Men, Lawyers and Miniſters ; and to be thankful for what you have for the preſent is the way to get what you want hereafter. Theſe are the words of Mr. *Mead.* It were indeed improper for me to produce a tenth part of the Teſtimonies wherewith no inconſiderable perſons have Spontaneouſly favoured and furniſhed me to Juſtify my integrity in this matter ; neverthelefs, the Injuries done me (which I cannnot be ſo Stoical as not at all to reſent) ſince my Return to *New-England,* make it but a reaſonable piece of Juſtice to my ſelf, to bring forth one or two more of them. Not only Mr. *Mead,* but many other Emi-nent Miniſters, with whom I had the Happineſs of a free Converſation in *London,* for the ſpace of Three or Four Years, were ſo kind as to ſend a Letter to the *General Court in Boſton,* Expreſſing their Approbation of my Proceedings. The Letter bears Date, *October 17th.* 1691. And is Subſcribed by, Dr. *Bates,* Dr. *Anneſly,* Mr. *Griffith,* Mr. *Barker,* Mr. *Woodcock,* Mr. *Alſop,* Mr. *How,* Mr. *Mayo,* and ſeveral Other Eminent Divines in that City. Modeſty would reſtrain me from mentioning that reſpectful Charact-er they are pleaſed to impoſe upon me, did not the Suggeſtions of ſome Whiſperers neceſſitate thereunto, that ſo my Friends and Countrymen may be truly informed concerning my tranſactions in their behalf. Their words are as followeth.

We muſt give this true Teſtimony of Our much Eſteemed and Beloved Brother Mr. Increaſe Mather, that with Inviolate Integrity, Excellent Prudence, and Unfainting Diligence, He has managed that great Buſineſs, committed to his truſt. As He is Inſtructed in the School of Heaven to Miniſter in the affairs of the Soul, ſo He is furniſhed with a Talent to tranſact affairs of ſtate. His Proceedings have been with that Caution and Circumſpection as is Correſpondent to the weight of His Commiſſion. He with Courage and Conſtancy has purſued the Noble Scope of his Employment, and underſtanding the true moment of things has preferred the Publick Good to the vain conceits of ſome, that more might be obtained if Peremptorily inſiſted on. Con-ſidering the open oppoſition and ſecret arts that have been uſed to fruſtrate the beſt Endeavours for the Intereſt of New-England, *the happy Iſſue of things is ſupe-riour to our Expectations.*

Your preſent Charter ſecures Liberty and Property, the faireſt Flowers of the Ci-vil State, and which is incomparably more valuable, it ſecures the enjoyment of the Bleſſed Goſpel in it's Purity and Freedom. Altho' there is a reſtraint of your Power in ſome things, that were Granted in the former Charter, yet there are more Ample Priviledges in other things that may be of Perpetual advantage to the Co-lony. We doubt not but your faithfull Agent will receive a Gracious Reward above ; and we hope His ſucceſsful Service will be welcom'd with your entire appro-bation and grateful acceptance. Thus thoſe Reverend and Learned Perſons.

The

The *Whisperers* that have endeavoured to make people believe that the Ministers who Subscribed that Letter did afterwards repent of their so doing, are *Forgers of Lies*. Nor would those Worthy Persons account it any other then a *Calumny* to have such a thing said of them, Four or Five of them having since that Written Letters to some in *Boston* of the same Import with the Former. And so have several Gentlemen in *London*, whose Sentiments and Expressions for the present I forbear to mention.

And whereas that Right Worshipful Gentleman, Sr. *Henry Ashurst*, with whom I had the Honour to be Joyned in the same Agency, in behalf of this Colony, and who did fully concurr with Me in what was done for *New-England*, has bin unworthily reflected on by some *Male-Contents*; for *His* Vindication as well as My own, and that so the Inhabitants of this Province, both such as are now Living, and such as shall come hereafter, may see, to whom they have (under God) bin Beholden, for what Restored *Liberties*, and Confirmed *Properties*, they now do, and are like to possess; I Judge it proper and necessary to publish some passages in his Letter sent to the General Assembly at *Boston*. Dated *December* 28th. 1691. In which He thus Speaks.

I have not for above Twelve Months troubled you with any of my Letters, because I knew my Worthy Friend, Mr. Mather, did not omit any opportunity of acquainting you with every thing wherein your Interest was concerned. I shall not much inlarge upon the Services that Mr. Mather hath done, for you have His True Character sent you by the Reverend Dr. Bates, and other the most Eminent Ministers in and about this Town. But I am sure He has been Faithful to your Interests, and diligent, and unwearyed in your service, with neglect of his Health. He hath lived here for You, and deserveth the greatest Marks of your Favour you can bestow on him. Mr. Mather and My self in Transacting your affairs did not leave any way unattempted that the wisest Friends we could consult with, could direct us to. When the King was Petitioned to make alterations in your Settlement, and to appoint a Governour, and other General Officers, we then joyned all our interests together, and obtained the Naming of every one of them, and other Priviledges that are not granted to any other Plantation. None have been more industrious by all possible means then Mr. Mather, and My self to have obtained your Old Charter. I hope Mr. Mather will do me that justice, to assure you, that I have never omitted any opportunity of serving you to the utmost of my Power. Thus that Worthy Gentleman.

I must now do Him that Right He expects from Me, before all the World And as I have elsewhere said, I say again, it is not in the Power of *New-England* duely to Reward his Endeavours. But to requite him with Censures, will not be only *Vile-Ingratitude* (the *Compendium* of all *Evil*) but great *Folly*

You

You cannot loofe *His* Friendfhip alone : and who will ever make an Intereft for you again, if He muft be rewarded with *Slanders* for all His Care and Pains ? By fuch things you may foon make yourfelves *Friendlefs*, and the moft miferable people in the World. Some Friends of mine in *England* who were very willing I fhould fpend the remainder of My days amongft them, told me, that they had bin informed that the People of *New-England were always ungrateful to their Publick Servants*, & that altho' they knew I had with Induftry & Fidelity ferved them to the utmoft of my Capacity, they doubted, whether they would be fenfible of it or no. My reply to them was, that (with the Divine Permiffion) I would go to *N. Engl*. & fee, and if I found their prognofti-cations true, I fhould fee (the dear people in *Bofton* concurring with me) my Call clear to return to *England* again. And now I cannot underftand but that the Inhabitants of the Province do generally rejoyce in what they at prefent enjoy. And their Reprefentatives did (the laft year) not only thank me, but were fo civil as to propofe a *Reward* for the fervice I had done for them, which I was not free to except, being defirous to convince my Country that (as the Apoftle faid to his *Corinthians*) *I have fought them not theirs.* And that I expect my Reward in another World. Neverthelefs inafmuch as there are *fome* (a few are to many) ill Spirits who make it their defign, by Slanders to difaffect others, I have complyed with the advice of thofe who perfwaded to the Publifhing thefe things that fo Credulous perfons may not be impofed on by the invented ftories of a few Whifperers. I Remember that at My departure from *London*, taking my leave of a Noble Perfonage, and Craving His Lordfhips Advice what might be faid to fatisfy the People of *New-England*, now they were deprived of fo great a Priviledge as that of Chufing their own Governour, His Reply to Me was.

If they will be Diffatisfyed, it is Impoffible that they fhould be Dif-fatisfyed at *You*, for Mankind knows that *You* did all that you could to obtain that and all other Priviledges which themfelves can wifh for. But were I in Your Cafe, at my Return to *New-England*, I would fay to them, *Gentlemen, I have brought to* You, *the Beft* Charter *I could get for you -.* 'Tis in Your Power, *whether you will ac-cept of it or no; If you like it not you may if you pleafe fend it back to the King, and fend over a more Fortunate Agent !* And let them Try (faid my Lord) whether they can find a man in all *New-England* that can get a *better Charter* for them, than you have obtained.

The true and plain State of the Cafe was this : The Colony lay a Bleed-ing for want of a Settlement as to Civil Government. The General Court had in an Adrefs to the King, fignified, *That the former Governour and Affift-ants did not think it fafe, to Enter on the full Exercife of their Old Charter Govern-ment, but did Accept of the Government for the prefent, until by direction from* En-gland

gland, *there should be an Orderly Settlement.* The Agents had no *Instruction* from their Principals not to submit unto whatever Settlement should in *England* be concluded best for them. So that if they had refused what was offered, they could not have answered their so doing. It is an Old Proverb, That *half a Loaf is better than no Bread.* And I must confess I am not of their Opinion, who if they cannot have *every thing* they desire, they will have *nothing*, who prefer their *Late Bondage* to their *present Liberty*; who if they must have a *Governour* Set over them by the King, had rather have a *bad* than a *good* man for such Reasons as I am not willing to mention.

The Lord pardon their Folly. And *O my Soul come not thou into their Secret, unto their Assembly be not thou United.* If after I have done my utmost to Serve you, my Sollicitudes, and the Difficulties that I have gone thro' for your fakes, must have a Requital with that which is known in *New England*, by the Infamous Name of *Country-Pay,* I trust the Grace of God will keep me from being too sensible of it. I am not Conscious to my self of any hurt or wrong I have done, unless four years hard Service, for the preservation of your Liberty and Property, and the procuring of Gifts for you, from Royal and from other Benefactors of greater value than all the Mony I did in that Time Expend on your account, and all this without any the least Recompence be a wrong to you. *Forgive me that wrong.* You are at this day saved from Slavery and Ruine. Whoever has been the Instruments of obtaining such Mercy for you, certainly you will neither please *God* nor Honour *your selves* by abusing them. However you deal with *Me*, be not unkind to *others*, who have deserved well at your Hands. Neither Lessen *Divine* or *Royal* Favours bestowed on you. I pray God it may never be worse with you as to Civil Government then it is at present, and then you will be in that respect, as happy a people as any on the Face of the whole Earth at this Day.

If the *Sermon* herewith Emitted, cause *Praises* to that God who has Restored *Counsellors as at the Beginning*; & Prayers for the continuance of so *great a Blessing*; My Design in granting the *Importunate*Desires of many for its Publication, will be attained. The Lord has Tryed *New-England* with Signal Favours once more, having put them into the hands of Rulers that seeks their Welfare; and He waits to see whether they will be Thankful, and shew themselves fit for the continuance of so great a Blessing, but if instead of that fruit which he expects from such a people, there shall be found amongst them many *Murmurers* against God and his Servants, there is no reason to think otherwise, but that He will very speedily change the Tenour of his Dispensations towards us, which I Implore the Mercy of Heaven to prevent.

𝕻𝖗𝖎𝖒𝖎𝖙𝖎𝖛𝖊

PRIMITIVE
COUNSELLOURS,
A Great
BLESSING.

ISAI. 1. 26.

I will Restore thy Counsellours as at the Beginning.

WHEN *Austin* sent to *Ambrose*, craving his Advice what part of the Scripture he should especially Read, He Commended the Prophet Isaiah to him. He continued Prophesying a very long time; to be sure above Sixty (some think above Fourscore) years. In his Publick Ministry, he never spared any unto whom he was sent to Deliver Messages in the Name of the Lord. His Style is not only Heroick and Majestical, becoming a Magnanimous Spirit, but very Evangelical. Whence some of the Ancients have called him *the Fifth Evangelist*, and the *Apostle of the Old Testament*. His Divine sayings (some or other of them) are Quoted no less than Sixty Times in the New-*Testament*. The usual Method observed by him in his Sermons, is with Awful Severity to threaten Judgments on the Impenitent, and to Predict and Promise mercy to the truly Penitent. And so He does in this Text and Context.

In the preceding Verse the Lord by the Prophet declares that the Judgments inflicted on his People should be Sanctified to their Reformation. He would Turn his Hand upon them, not in Wrath but in Mercy, so as purely to *Purge away their Dross*. This Verse is a farther Confirmation of.

that

that Prediction, wherein there are Two Great Bleſſings promiſed to *Je-rusalem*.

1. That *Judges*, i. e. Chief Magiſtrates *ſhould be Reſtored to them as at the firſt*.

This was neceſſary in Order to their being a Reformed People. For it was by means of the profaneſs of their Princes, that the City and Nation was Corrupted. Nor could a National Reformation be expected until ſuch time as the great ones therein ſhould have their hearts ſett for Religion, and Righteouſneſs.

2. The Lord does here promiſe His People that they ſhall have *Coun-ſellours as at the beginning*. For altho' the Chief Magiſtrate ſhould be for Reformation and Holineſs, if his *Counſellours* be not ſo too, little good can be expected, therefore both are promiſed as a Singular Favour of God unto *Jeruſalem*. The Doctrine before us to be inſiſted on, as ſaitable to the preſent Occaſion. Is,

That Primitive Counſellours are a ſingular Mercy and Bleſſing of God to His Peo-ple.

The Doctrine may be Confirmed in Three *Propoſitions*.

Propoſition. I. *Good Counſellours are the Gift of God.* The Lord ſaith here *I will Reſtore thy Judges and thy Counſellours*. It is not in the Power of all the men in the World to make a good Counſellour, except God firſt make him to be ſuch an one. There are but few men in the World compara-tively who are fit to give Counſel, eſpecially in the difficult affairs of State And they that are, it is God that has furniſhed them with gifts and Qua-lifications for ſuch a ſtation. *Who maketh thee to differ* (ſaith the Apoſtle) *and what haſt thou that thou didſt not Receive*. 1 Cor. 4. 7. * Who is it that makes one man to be greater or better then another ? To be Richer or Wiſer then another. It is the Lord that makes it to be ſo. When *John Baptiſts* Diſciples were troubled that another, (tho' infinitely his Superiour) was preferred before him, He ſaid to them *A man can Receive nothing except it be given him from Heaven*. Joh. 3. 27. If a man has Reputation above ſanother, he has Received it from Heaven, and if he has great accompliſh-ments in more reſpect then one, he is beholden to Heaven for them all. It is ſaid of Solomon, *That God gave him VViſdome and Underſtanding exceed-ing Much, and Largeneſs of Heart even as the Sand that is on the Sea ſhore,* becauſe of the infinite number of Wiſe Conceptions that his Large ſoul was able to Comprehend. 1. King 4. 29. Royal Endowments were confer-red on him, and it was God that did make him fit to be a King. ſo if any man has the underſtanding which is requiſite in a Counſellour, t is God that

has

has given him that **Understanding.** And it is His Proivdence that doe's order who shall be such. There are some in the World who are well accomplished to be in such a Capacity that are not made use of. There are that have this Preeminence belonging to them as their Birth-Right. Noble Men are *Consiliarij Nati.* Others are Chosen and Constituted by the Supream Power. In some Places the People have a Concurrence in the *Election of* Counsellours. This notwithstanding, the God of Heaven determines and over-rules all. Whoever may have an hand in the Choice, their Spirits and all their Actions are disposed of by an Invisible Power. *The Lot is cast into the Lap, but the whole disposing thereof is of the Lord.* Pro. 16. 33.

Moreover when any persons are qualified for, and chosen unto a Service of this Nature, it is God that does incline their hearts, to accept of that Trouble. Indeed the Generality of men (and especially such as are unfit) need no great perswasion to comply with such Offers. But there are some who are as averse to Publick Employments as was *Moses*, when he said *Send I pray thee by the Hand of whom thou wilt send,* only let me be excused. I have had the happiness to be acquainted with a Great and Noble Personage, who was desired by Two Kings Successively to be of Their Council, but declined it. The affairs of a People may be so Perplexed, as that a wise Man may be afraid to meddle, or to be any way interested in their Publick concerns. This we see in what the Prophet Speaks, *Isai.* 3. 6, 7. *Be thou our Ruler, and Let this Ruine be under thy Hand, I will not be an Healer, Make me not a Ruler of the People.* I see (saith He) you are a Ruined People, and I have no mind that your Ruin should be under my Hand, therefore I will not accept of your offer. *Counsellours* (such as are so by their place and office) do *Assist in Government.* Now the Work of Government is no easy Labour. That Celebrated saying of *Melanchthons* has a great deal of Truth in it, that there are there hard Labours *Parturientis* the Labour of Child Birth, *Docentis,* the Labour of one that is a Teacher, *Regentis,* the Labour of one that is a Ruler. They that never did, & were never fit to make trial of it, may think it easy, but others do not find it so. One of the Kings of *England* had in all the Windows of his House a Crown in a Bush of Thorns, to signify what Cares do attend Government. If then Wise men shall be willing to deny themselves as to their own repose, and to encounter with many difficulties in serving the Publick Interest, it is God that has made them so.

Proposition II. Primitive Counsellors are men of singular Qualifications. The Scripture mentions especially four Graces which Rulers and Counsellours should be adorned with ; And they which have them being quailified according

cording to that *Rule which is from the Beginning*, are Primitive Counſellers.

The firſt is P*iety towards God*. Counſellers ought to be, and Counſellers at the Beginning were Godly men. So it was when the Children of *Iſrael* firſt *began* to be a Common-wealth under *Moſes*; and at their *Beginning* to be a Settled Kingdom under *David*. The Judges who were Governours, were Godly, and ſome of the Kings of *Iſrael* were Holy men, and then we may be ſure their Counſellers were ſo too. Pſal. 4.3. *The Lord hath ſet apart him that is Godly for Himſelf*. This was ſpoken concerning *David's* being *ſet apart* to be the chief Ruler over the People of God; ſo they that are *ſet a-part* to aſſiſt him whom God has made Ruler and Governour in Chief ought to be Godly. The firſt Counſeller of State that we read of in the Scripture was *Jethro*, a very pious perſon. He adviſed *Moſes* to chuſe ſome to aſſiſt him in Government, and ſheweth how they ſhould be qualified. *Provide* (ſaith he) *Such as Fear God*. Exod. 18. 31. ſuch as will by their Authority and Example Encourage others to Fear and Serve Him. That will make the Advancement of Gods Intereſt their chief Deſign. That will ſo act & ſo ſpeak as men that really believe they muſt give an Account to the Great and Eternal God. That will often think with themſelves, is this Counſil according to the approving Will of God, and that will not for the World adviſe to any thing which they believe is contrary thereunto.

2. *Fidelity towards men* is another requiſite in a Counſeller. A Primitive Counſeller is qualified with Righteouſneſs as well as Piety. Chooſe *men of Truth* ſaid *Jethro*. *Counſellers are Rulers*. Now he that Ruleth over men muſt be *Juſt, Ruling in the Fear of God*, 2 Sam. 23. 3. They ought to be men, that will give to God the *things that are Gods, and to* Cæſar, *the things that are* Cæſars; yea, that will give to all men their due. *Counſellers* ought to be, and Counſellers at the Beginning were, *Faithful* to him that is the Chief Ruler, in adviſing him for the beſt : Such an one was *Huſhai* the *Ar-chite* unto *David*, 2 Sam. 17. 15. *Thus and thus did Ahitophel Counſel, and thus and thus have I Counſelled*. He Saved the Life of his Prince by giving that Counſel. Men in ſuch a Station ſhould moreover approve themſelves *faith-ful* to the Intereſt of the People, whoſe Welfare as Counſellers they are bound to endeavour. The Prince and the People have not oppoſite Inte-reſts, He that promoves the true Intereſt of the one, does ſo of the other alſo. A great Emperour was wont to ſay, *Non mihi ſed populo*; I am Set in this High Station, not for my ſelf, but for the Nations ſake. So are Counſellers to adviſe unto ſuch things as the People, the Country who are Concerned in them, may have cauſe to Bleſs God for them. Such a Counſeller was *Mordecai* in the Court of *Perſia*. Eſth. 10. 3. *Mordecai the Jew was next unto King Ahaſuerus*; He ws Advanced to be a Right Honourable Privy Coun-ſeller,

feller, *Seeking the Wealth of his* People. It was faid of one of the Kings of *France*, that He was, *Titularis non tutelaris Rex, defuit non præfuit Reipublicæ* So may it be faid of fuch Counfellers, as do not intend and faithfully defign the Good of that people, over whom the Providence of God has placed them, they have only the Name, but not the nature of *Counfellers* in them. True Primitive Counfellers they are not.

3. It is neceffary that *Counfellers fhould be Endued with the Grace of Courage.* The Spirit of Counfel and of *Might*, that is to fay of *Courage*, are conjoyned, becaufe Counfellers fhould be men of Courage, *Ifa.* 11. 2. And this is implied in that of their *Fearing God*, h. e. they muft Fear God and not men. *Mofes* gave it in Charge unto thofe whom he did Commiffion to be Judges, Deut. 1. 17. *You fhall not be afraid of the Face of man.* The like is to be faid unto Counfellers. *Solomons* Throne was fupported by Lions, 2 King. 10. 20. Thus Counfellers who are the Supporters of the Government fhould be of Magnanimous and Undaunted Spirits. The Pillars of a Land muft not Warp either for fear or favour. They may not Fear the Frowns of them that are above them, fo as to neglect their Duty. If they fhould fee the Chief Ruler in danger of falling into any Error, which would be injurious to Himfelf or to his People ; they ought freely tho' humbly to advife Him to defift. It is reported concerning the *Chines*, that the Counfellers of their Prince do with great Freedom admonifh him of dangerous Errors, and that if they do it not, they are not accounted worthy of the Name of Counfellers, or men of Honour. *Joab* did the part of a Faithful Counfeller unto *David*, in diffwading from his ambitious Defign of Numbring the People : *Why* (faid he) *does my Lord the King require this ? Why will he be a caufe of Trefpafs unto Ifrael.* 1 *Chron.* 4. 3. And at another time, when *David* was too much Tranfported with paffion at the Death of his Son *Abfolim*, *Joab* advifed him to refrain himfelf, and to fpeak kindly to the men that had Hazzarded their Lives to Save his ; and *David* had the Wifdom to Hearken to that good Advice. Nor fhould Counfellers in the Difcharge of their Duty, be afraid of the Multitude. *Job* faith, *Did I fear a great Multitude ? or did the Contempt of Families terrify me. Job* 31. 34. He knew that if he did punifh Vice, the Families and Relations of fuch as had fuffered the Law, would reproach him- and a multitude would clamour againft him, but that would not deter him from a Faithful Difcharge of the Duty of his Place ; fuch Courage becomes a Counfeller. Let a man give the beft Counfel in the World, he fhall never pleafe every body : There is fuch variety and Coutrariety in the Opinions of men, that all cannot be pleafed ; fometimes not a few only, but the major part, take in with the wrong fide, and have their unreafonable Diffatisfactions ; now Counfellers

muft

muſt do their Duty, let the World be pleaſed or diſpleaſed. They may not at any time be afraid to own Chriſt and his Cauſe, but if they ſee Deſigns on foot againſt the beſt Intereſt, they ought boldly to interpoſe, and to oppoſe themſelves. It is ſaid of *Joſeph of Arimathea*, that he was an *Honourable Counſeller*, Mark 15. 43 ſome think that he was one of the *Sanedrim*, the great Council of the Nation. Others ſuppoſe him to be one of the Governours Council. Now when there was a *Conſult* about putting Chriſt to Death, this *Joſeph* Entred his Diſſent, and after the Lord was by Forms of Law, and falſe Witneſſes, and an Accuſation of pretended Treaſon, Condemned and Murdered, this *Honourable Counſeller*, went *boldly* unto *Pilate* who had received a Commiſſion to be Governour over the Province of *Judea*, and *Craved the Body of Jeſus*. Thus did He with Exemplary Courage own Chriſt and his Cauſe.

And yet more than all this is required in a Counſeller. A man may be a Pious, a Faithful, a Couragious man, and for all that not fit to be a Counſeller. Therefore 4. *It is neceſſary that a Counſeller be qualified with the Grace of Wiſdom.* The Divine Wiſdom is expreſſed by that of being *Great in Counſel.* Jer. 32. 19. Only God, Angels, and men are Cauſes by Counſel. The more Wiſdom there is in any man, the more able he is to give Counſel : It is noted concerning that Faithful Miniſter of God, *Zachariah*, who was (as Interpreters have noted) an *Eccleſiaſtical Counſeller*, one with whom the King was wont to adviſe in matters of Religion, that He was a *wiſe Counſeller*, 1 Chron. 26. 14. So ſhould all Counſellers be men of Wiſdom. Hence 'tis ſaid by the Prophet. Jer. 49. 7. *Is Wiſdom no more in Teman ? Is Counſel periſhed from the Prudent ? is their Wiſdom vaniſhed.* Imprudent men are unfit to be made Counſellers. *Pharaohs* Counſellers of Old were wiſe men, but his Chief Counſeller *Joſeph* (tho' a young man did Excel them all in Wiſdom. *Pharaoh* ſaid to him, *There is none ſo diſcreet and wiſe as thou art.* Gen. 41. 37. And the Pſalmiſt ſaith of him, that He *Taught* Pharaohs Senators (his Counſellers) *Wiſdom*. Pſ. 105. 22. Courage without Wiſdom, in one that undertakes to be a Counſeller, will do more hurt than good. An Horſe that is full of Metal, if he has no Eyes to ſee his way before him, is a dangerous Creature to make uſe of. If raſh, heady, unthinking men are made uſe of for Counſellers, the Publick Weal of ſuch a People is in danger. The carnal Jews indeed depended too much on this that they had Wiſe men at Helm to be their Counſellers of State Jer. 18. 18. *The Law ſhall not periſh from the Prieſts, nor Counſel from the Wiſe.* We have wiſer men than *Jeremy* (ſay they) to Sit in Council, and therefore what He adviſeth unto is not to be regarded ; but tho' a Nation whoſe Counſellers are great Politicians may poſſibly be ruined (as the Jewiſh
Nation

Nation was) if they have not fuch Counfellers, they are in an ill cafe, as we fhall have occafion anon further to declare.

Propofition III. *Such Counfellers as thefe defcribed are a fingular mercy and Bleffing of God to a People.* I fhall only mention two things that Evince the Truth of this Propofition.

1. *Civil Government is a great and neceffary Bleffing.* Without it the World would foon be Diffolved, and run into Confufion. As one fpeaks, the World would not then be a KOSMOS, a Beautiful Structure, but a *KAOS*, an horrid Heap of Diforder. What would Kingdoms be were it not for Government? but (as *Auftin* expreffes it) *Magna Latrocinia*, great Dens of Thieves. Let a people that have found the benefit of Government be without it for a while, and they will quickly be made fenfible that 'tis a great and a neceffary Bleffing. I have read that it was once a Law amongft the *Perfians*, that after the Death of their King, every man fhould have Liberty to do what he pleafed for five days; and in thefe five days time there was fuch horrid doings, that all the people prized Government the better all their days after. Now Government cannot well be managed by one alone without the Affiftance of Counfellers. Many Eyes fee more than one. 'Tis poffible that one man may difcern that which another does not fee. Befides, the Burden will be too heavy for one alone. Hence *Mofes* faid to the Children of *Ifrael, I am not able to bear you my felf alone. Deut.* 1 9. and again verfe 12. *How can I my felf alone bear your Cumbrances, and your Burdens, and your Strife?* Where there is a great people, the Burden is too heavy for a mortal man, tho' never fo wife and able. *Mofes* was a wife States-man, neverthelefs *Jethro* advifed him to take fome to affift him, in Ruling that numerous people, becaufe elfe the Burden would be fo heavy upon him, as that he muft needs fink and break under the weight of it. Exod 18. 18. The wifeft Ruler in the World needs the affiftance of Counfellers. *Solomon* (the wifeft of men) had his Counfellers about him. The truth is, the Light of Nature has taught men not only to Erect Governments, but that there fhould be Counfellers to affift the Chief Ruler. The Scripture informs us that not only the Kings of *Ifrael*, but the Kings of the Gentiles had their Counfellers, with whom they were wont to take Advice in all arduous Affairs. *Ezra* Bleffeth God, who had extended Mercy to him before *Artaxarxes* the King of *Perfia*, and his *Counfellers. Ezra* 7. 28. And in the 14 verfe *He was fent of the King, and his feven Counfellers* Perhaps there might be Superftition in their fixing on the Number feven, if they did it (as fome Learned Men fuppofe) becaufe they would have their Government to Refemble the Heavens, wherein there are feven Planets : But as to the thing, that there

fhould

should be *Counsellers*, the Light of Nature instructed them; and therefore it is so in all Nations and Governments.

2. *The Intirest and Influence of good Counsellers is great.* They have a great Interest in the Chief Ruler. In Governments, which are more absolute, and much more in those that are more Limited it is so, especially where the principal Ruler cannot Act without their Consent. It cannot be expressed of how great Concernment it is for such a People to be Bless'd with Counsellers *as at the Beginning.* Not only whole *Provinces* but whole *Kingdoms* have Fared the better for the Wise Counsils of one Good man. So did *Egypt*, because there was such a wise Counseller as *Joseph* found amongst them. And the whole Kingdom of *Israel* found the benefit of it, when *David* made the Prophet *Nathan* to be of his Cabinet Council. *Solomon* Owed his Crown, and the People much of their Happiness to the seasonable *Advice of Nathan*, which had a great influence on the Royal Heart of King *David*, in causing him to Nominate *Solomon* to Succeed in Government, whereby great Confusions that otherwise would have happened, were prevented. *Rehoboam* had not lost ten parts in twelve of his Kingdom, if he had followed the wise Advice of his Fathers Counsellers Nor had *Zedekiah* Lost his Kingdom, nor had the City and Temple been Burnt, and the whole Land made Desolate, if the good Counsel of the Prophet *Jeremiah* had been hearkened unto, whom God sent to be a Counseller to them. *If I give thee Counsel (* said the Prophet to the King *) wilt thou not hearken unto me. Jer.* 38. 15. It had been well if he had.

When there are *Counsellers as at the Beginning*, two things usually follow, which make a people happy.

1. *There will be good Judges.* Much of the Welfare of a People does consist in their having Able and Upright Judges, that will endeavour to approve themselves in all things like unto God, the Judge of Judges, with whom there is no Iniquity, nor Respect of persons. Hence *Moses* who Loved the Lords People in the VVilderness more than He Loved his own Life, out of Respect to their VVelfare took of the Chief of the Tribes, VVise Men, and Known, and gave them a *Commission and Instruction*, to Act as Judges, solemnly charging them to acquit themselves as became men in their places Deut. 1. 15,16, 16. Now if there be Counsellers as at the Beginning, there will be Judges as at the First. It cannot but be so in a Government, where no Judges are appointed but with the consent of the Council. Good Counsellers will Advise to good Judges, and good Judges will make the Land happy.

2, *Where*

2. *Where there are good Counsellours, Religion and Reformation will be Encoura-*
ged. Primitive Counsellers will concern themselves to uphold Religion in
the Truth, Purity and Power of it. In King *Joash* his Time, as long as
Jehojadah was his Chief Counseller, *The Service of the House of the Lord*
was duly attended, but when ill Counsellers succeeded and were hearkened
unto, *they Left the House of the Lord God of their Fathers, and Served Groves*
and Idols. There is no great fear or danger of Apostasy in Matters of
Religion, as long as there are *Counsellers as at the Beginning.* It is in their
Power to prevent it, and they will prevent it. For a people to Enjoy the
only true Religion ; to have not only Liberty, but Encouragement to Serve
God in the way and after the manner which Himself in His Holy Word
has Appointed, is a mercy beyond Expression great. And thus it will be
as long as there are such Counsellers as I am speaking of. *Reformers are*
great Blessings to the places where they Live: *Primitive Counsellers* are of
a Reforming Spirit. The Work of Reformation useth to go forward,
when such are in Place. Besides Scripture Examples, we have seen it in
our own Nation. In the Reign of King *Henry* 8. When he had such Counsellers as *Cromwel* and *Cramner*, there was in some things a great Reformation. And in several Reigns since that : Wise Counsellers have made our
Nation happy, and as to many particulars more Reformed than once it
was. There is a Glorious Day a coming, (and I trust in Christ that it is
not far off) when the Church of God throughout the whole World, will
be in a more Reformed State than ever yet was known since the World
began, *When Judges as at the First, and Counsellers as at the Beginning*, will be
the Instruments in the Hands of Christ, by whom it shall be effected.
Wherefore in the next words to my Text, it is said, *afterwards thou shalt be*
called the City of Righteousness, the Faithful City. Jerusalem the Church of
God all the World over shall become a City of Righteousness, but first,
and that it may be so, Primitive Counsellers shall be Restored.

We come now to make some Application of the Doctrine thus far In-
sisted on.

USE I.

Hence the contrary unto this of a Peoples being Blessed with Primitive
Counsellors is a sore Judgment. It is said that *where no Counsel is, the Peo-*
ple fall, but in the multitude of Counsellers there is safety. Prov. 11. 14. Where
there are good Counsellers, and a multitude of them, we may expect
good, and much good, a multitude of Blessings will be on such a People, but where there are none such, nothing but ruine can be hoped
for.

for. The Removal of wife Counfellers is threatned as a fore Judgment. Ifai. 3. 3. When a People is reduced unto that condition, that there are none fit for Counfellors to be found amongft them, their State is deplorable, they are either perfectly undone, or the next door to ruin. Mic. 4. 9. *Why doft thou cry aloud, is the Counfeller perifhed?* There is caufe enough to cry aloud if it be fo. They may well make Loud Outcries of their being an undone people amongft whom the *Counfeller* is perifhed. And thus it is where there are Counfellors of pernicious principles and inclinations: Such an one there was in *Nineveh*, where the King of *Affyria* kept his Court. Neh. 1. 11. *There is one come out of thee that imaginetb Evil againft the Lord, a wicked Counfellor.* Perhaps *Rabfhekeh* might be the Counfellor whom the Prophet there reflects upon. However, one he was that advifed the King to Perfecute the People of God, and to Act Arbitrarily, without any refpect to right or wrong. Such Counfellors there were in *Perfia*, who perfwaded the Emperour to Eftablifh Iniquity by a Law, and then to Perfecute and Murder all fuch as could not with a good Confcience Conform to that Law, Dan. 6. 7,

Politicians have laid it down for a Maxim, and there is a Truth in it, *That a People had better have a bad Prince with a good Council, than a good Prince with a bad Council.* For Evil Counfellors will (as one expreffeth it) *by their poyfonous Whifpers and Inftillations at the Ear, Corrupt the Heart,& Taint the Spirits of the beft Princes.* Kings and Kingdoms have often been Ruined by Evil Counfils. So was King *Ahaziah*, who would needs take fome of the Houfe of *Abab* to be of his Council, and it is noted, that *they were bis Connfellors to his Deftruction.* 2 Chron. 22. 4. The Kingdom of *Ifrael* was divided and fo weakned after the Death of *Solomon*, and unhappy Counfellors were the caufe of it. And thus it has been in our Nation. Not only in former Times, but in our Days. How came the late Abdicated King to be Depofed from his Kingly Throne, and his Glory to be taken from him; but becaufe inftead of hearkening to Counfellers as at the Beginning, he would be Governed by Popifh Counfils.

U S E II.

This Informs and Directs them in whofe power it is to Choofe Counfellers what manner of perfons they are to Elect, namely fuch as were at the Beginning. The VVord of the Lord does Inftruct *this General Affembly*, whom they ought to Chofe or Confirm this Day. What manner of perfons the *Reprefentatives* of this people, who are here before the Lord ought to Nominate, and what manner of Perfons the Governour of this Province is by the VVord of the Lord, obliged to approve of. Unto you that are by the feveral Towns throughout this Government *Deputed* to Act

In their ftead, Let me fay, you have heard from the Word of the Lord, what kind of men Primitive Counfellers were, *viz. God-fearing men, faithful, couragious, prudent,* you have by the *Royal Charter* Granted to you Power to Nominate fuch, and you will pleafe God in fo doing. And let me further add here, that it is very meet that perfons Nominated for Counfellers fhould be men of Eftate, and of fome Port in the VVorld. Ifa. 3. 7. *Thou haft Cloathing be thou our Ruler.* Thou haft an Eftate to Support the place and Dignity of a Ruler, and therefore we Choofe thee. If this be not confidered, Government will be rendred contemptible, and that cannot be without Sin. Let me alfo fay to you who are the Reprefentatives of this People, that it will not be prudence in you (at this time efpecially) to propofe fuch Affiftants to theGovernour as you cannot but know,thatHe cannot Accept of, and fo to neceffitate him to make ufe of his Negative Voice, when He has no defire to do it.And you cannot but know that whoever is Governour, He will judge it neceffary that many of his *Council* fhould have their Habitations near to his, that fo if any fudden Emergency or Danger to the Publick fhould happen, his Council may be at Hand to Advife with. And you cannot but know that no Governour will take thofe into his Council, who are *Malecontents,* and do what in them is to make others to be Difaffected to the Government. No Governour can take fuch men into his Bofome.

And as for your felf Excellent Sir, whom God has made the Captain over his People in this VVildernefs, It is a very great Power which the Divine Providence has put into your Hands, that you fhould have a *Negative* on the *Elections* of this Day. A Power which I confefs, neither you nor any one elfe fhould have had, if any Intereft that I was capable to make, could have prevented it. You know Sir, that I humbly argued againft it to the Kings Majefty, and to many of His chief Minifters of State. But I now fee that God has ordered it to be as it is in Mercy to this his People ; what it may be for the future, when the Ingratitude of an unthankful Murmuring Generation of men, fhall have provoked the Moft High again to fay of *New England,* her Enemies fhall profper, and her Adverfaries fhall be Chief, the Lord knoweth : but at prefent there is more good than hurt in it, and will be fo as long as there fhall be a Governour whofe Heart is Engaged to feek not Himfelf, but the Publick good. You have Sir, at this day good men, and fome of them as wife men as any this Country does afford to be of your Council. And not one of them can be Removed without Your confent, fince the prefent Counfellers muft continue until new Ones are Chofen, and no Election of a New One is valid without your Approbation fignified under Your Hand. And altho' it is neceffary that fome New Ones be Elected, and perhaps convenient that there be fome further Alterations, neverthelefs, no one that is Difaffected to the beft and higheft Intereft, or, to the Government of Their Majefties in *England*, or, that is an Enemy to the Government here, can be impofed on you. So that it is in your power to make this People happy one year longer. And I earneftly pray to God to incline your Heart to do what fhall be pleafing in his fight, and moft conducing to the Welfare of His People.

USE III.

I Conclude, With a Word of Exhortation which Concerns us all.

Let us do what in us Lieth that this fo great a Mercy may be continued to us.

We Read in the Gofpel, that when the Lord Jefus Chrift had taken a Text out of the Prophet *Ifaiah*, He began His Sermon with faying, *This Day is this Scripture fulfilled in your Ears.* Luk. 4. 21. So let me conclude my Difcourfe with faying, This day, is this Scripture fulfilled in your ears, and before your eyes. For God has not only Given but Reftored to *New-England, Counfellors as at the Beginning.* We are all greatly concerned to endeavour the Continuance of fuch a Favour.

You will fay, *What fhall we do that it may be fo. ?*

Anfw. 1. *Let us be careful that thofe fins which provoke the Lord to withhold this Mercy from his People be not found amongft us.* It is fin that does provoke God to take away Good Rulers, and to fend Bad ones. It is Storied that when a very Unworthy Perfon was Advanced to an High Station, a Religious Man Expoftulating with Heaven about it, Received that Anfwer, that it was not becaufe fuch an one was Worthy of that Place, but becaufe that finful people were worthy to bePunifhed with having fo wicked a Ruler fet over them. It was Certainly a True Confeffion which the *Levites* made on a Publick Faft Day. Neh. 9. 37. *The Kings whom thou haft fet over us becaufe of our Sins, have dominion over our Bodys, and over our Cattel, at their pleafure.* They once had Merciful Rulers, and thofe too from amongft themfelves, but they finned them away, and were for a time in the hands of Strangers who did exercife an Arbitrary Power over them, fo that they could not fay that their Cattle, or their Lands, or any thing was their own : all was at the Will and Pleafure of Strangers. *New-Enngland* has had fome experience of this. *Your Land Strangers did devour it in your prefence.* You muft give what they pleafed to demand that fo you might have a pretended Confirmation of your Eftates and Properties.

The

The Counfellours which then carried all were not Counfellours as at the beginning. God has Mercifully delivered you from them. But if the fins which brought that Judgment on the Land are ftil! amongft us unreformed and unrepented of; what can be expected, but that after a clear Sunfhine for a while the Clouds will return again with greater Darknefs than ever? What thofe fins were I need not fay, fo much having been fpoken concerning that, many Years ago. To be fure the great fin of this Generation is their forgetting the Errand on which their Fathers came into this Wildernefs which was not to feek great things for themfelves, but to feek the Kingdom of God and His Righteoufnefs. Let this people recover their Primitive Holinefs, and they need not doubt but God will Blefs them with Primitive Counfellours; and that they fhall fee that promife made to *Jacob* fulfilled, Jer. 30. 8. *Strangers fhall no more ferve themfelves of him.*

2. *Let us be very thankful for what we enjoy.* To be thankful for Mercys, is the way to have them continued What would not *New-England* have given no longer fince then Five Years ago, to have been fure of what they now enjoy? And what, tho' you have not fome Great Priviledges which once you had, and which fhould have been Reftored to you, if He that fpeaketh to you this Day, could have obtained them for you, tho' it be with the Expence of his own Life, and of all that is Dear to him in this World will you be thankful for nothing: becaufe you have not every thing juft as you would have? Do any of you fay, *all that you have is nothing?* I hear there are fome (tho' not many) that fay fo. Let me Reafon with you before the Lord this Day? You have by the Royal Charter granted to you, Property confirmed, fo that every Man may fit under his *own Vine,* and his *own Figtree.* And is this nothing. I am fure you would have thought it fomething, and a great thing too, but a Few years fince. You have all Englifh Liberties Reftored to you, fo that a Governour with a *Juncto* of his Council cannot (as of late they did) make Laws, and impofe Taxes on you, without your own confent, by your Reprefentatives, And is this nothing? No Governour can now caufe you, or your Children or Servants (as not long fince they might) to be fent out of the Province. Your Prefent Charter Secures you againft all fuch Invafions. And do you now account it nothing? You have Peculiar Charter-Priviledges granted to you, which no other Englifh Plantation in the World has. Witnefs your being here this Day. No other Plantation has that Priviledge of Nominating to the Governour, his Council: nor have the Kings Subjects in *England* it felf that Priviledge; and is this nothing? Your Religion is fecured to you. Now you need not fear being fent to Prifon (as fome
of

of you were under a late Government) becaufe you fcruple Swearing by a Book. You may Worfhip God in the greateft Purity, and no one may Difturb you. If you fet apart Daies for Solemn Praier or Praifes, as the Divine Providence may call thereunto, you need not fear being interrupted or Obftructed therein as it was here fix year ago. You may by Laws not only Protect, but encourage that Religion which is the General Profeffion of the Country. And is all this nothing ? You have at prefent a Governour, and a Lievtenant Governour, (and all the Council likewife) from amongft yourfelves, who do unfeignedly feek your welfare. And is this nothing ? Some of you fay it will not be long thus. In which you fpeak more then you know. But Suppofe fo. *Ezra* and the Lords People with him, thought they had great caufe to be thankful to God in that *He had given them a Little reviving in their Bondage,* and extended mercy to them in the fight of the King of *Perfia,* who had by a Charter granted them Liberty to fet up the Houfe of God, and to repair the Defolations thereof, as we may do this Day. But if a Change come, and the Lord be Provoked again to fet Rulers over you that will obftruct what is Good and defireable, you that are the *Murmurers* will be found the Guilty caufe of it before the Lord, in the Name of the Lord be it fpoken to you.

3. *Prayer unto God may be a means to obtain the Continuance of this fo great a mercy.* Be Earneft with God that you may ftill have Counfellours as at the Beginning. And you are on this (as well as on many other) accounts Concerned to pray for the King and Queen ; For as long as Their prefent Majefties fhall hold the *Englifh* Scepter in their Hands, we in *New-England* may hope to fee Good days. God has Bleffed Our Nation with a King in the Prefervation of whom the Fate of *Europe* and of the Church of God is more concerned then it has been in the life of any one Perfon for thefe Thoufand Years. A King that Fights the Battels of the Lord. A King that when a Crown was offered to him, declared, that nothing fhould Oblige him to be a Perfecuter. VVho that has a Spark of Grace in his Heart, will not pray for fuch a King? A King that has more then once or twice in My hearing and to me expreffed a fingular refpect to His Good Subjects in thefe Colonies.

And Pray for the Queen.

For God has bleffed the Nation with a Queen (as well as with a King) the like unto whom (without Reflection on any Predeceffors) never fat on the *Englifh* Throne. A Queen that loveth all people that are good, whatever their perfwafions in matters relating to Confcience may be. A Queen that is a pattern of Vertue to the Nation. A Queen that has

(to

(to my certain knowledge) interceded with the King, that He would be kind to *New-England*. Pray then for the Life and Profperity of fuch a King and fuch a Queen. And I do the rather urge this upon you, be-caufe I have fometimes been favoured with the Liberty humbly to affure Their Majefties, that there are none in the World that Pray for them with more fervency and frequency then do Their Subjects in *New-England*. I befeech you make it appear that I was not miftaken in what I have affirm-ed concerning you.

And pray for them that fhall be Eftablifhed as *Counfellers* and Rulers over you this Day: That the Lord Jefus whofe Name is *Counfeler*, will be with them: That the Lord Jefus who faith, *Counfel is mine aud found Wifdom*, will pleafe to give them of his Spirit, which is the Spirit of Wif-dom and Underftanding, *the Spirit of Counfil and Might, the Spirit of Knowledge and of the Fear of the Lord.*

FINIS.

EXCERPTS FROM
A DISCOURSE CONCERNING THE MAINTENANCE, DUE TO THOSE THAT PREACH THE GOSPEL

Increase Mather, *A Discourse Concerning the Maintenance, Due to those that Preach the Gospel: In which the Question, Whether Tithes are by the Divine Law, the Ministers Due? is Considered: and the Negative Prov'd* (Boston, 1706; reprinted in London, 1709), conclusions 1 and 3, pp. 2–5 and 15–21.

Given Increase Mather's prominent position in Boston's society, his views on religion and politics were very influential in the community. One common theme of his work is the necessity of the subjection of inferiors to their superiors: children to parents, wives to husbands, servants to masters, and society to religious leaders. *A Discourse Concerning the Maintenance, Due to those that Preach* discusses the maintenance of the clergy, and the connection between taxation by the state and state support of religion. Mather concludes that civil magistrates have the responsibility to guarantee support and maintenance to religious leaders. Other topics covered in this piece include the relationship between civil magistrates and religious leaders, the necessity of tithing, and support of those who preach the gospel. The latter was necessary so that preachers did not have to engage in commercial activities, which meant they had less time available for preaching.

A
DISCOURSE

Concerning the

Maintenance,

Due to thofe that

Preach the Gofpel :

In which

The QUESTION, Whether

TITHES

Are by the Divine Law, the Minifters Due ?

IS CONSIDERED:

And the *Negative* Prov'd.

By *J. MATHER*, D. D.

Neh. **13. 10.** *And I perceiv'd that the Portions of the* Levites *had not been given* them, *for the* Levites *and the* Singers *that did the work, were fled every one to His field.*

1 Tim. **5. 18.** *For the Scripture faith, Thou fhalt not muzzle the Ox, that treadeth out the Corn, and the Laborer is worthy of his reward.*

Bofton, N. E. Printed 1706, and Reprinted at *London,* 1709.

CONCLUSION, I.

An Honourable Maintenance is due to the Ministers of the Gospel.

FOR, 1. Their Calling is *Honourable.* It was said of *Samuel, He is a Man of God, He*
1 Sam. 9. 6. *is an* Honourable *Man.* To with-hold from them a suitable Main-tenance, is to make *both* their Persons, *and* their Work *Contemptible.* The light of Nature teach-eth Men to reverence those that are set apart for the especial Service of God. The very *Gentiles* had a great Veneration for their *Priests.* We find in the Scripture (as well as in other

Gen. 47. 22. Writings) that the *Heathen* had an
Ezra 7. 24. *Honour* for such men, and a great regard for their being *Honourably Maintained.*

2. T H E L O R D appointed an *Honoura-ble Maintenance* for his Ministers under the Old *Testament.* For besides the *Tenths,* the First-fruits, and other Offerings, *Thirteen* Cities of Refuge with the Lands belonging to them were theirs. Now, altho' under the Gospel, the *matter* out of which the Stipend of Ministers is to be rais'd, and the *manner* of Payment is not as un-der the Law; Nevertheless, we may from thence

1 Cor. 9. 13. argue by way of Analogy, for so does the Apostle, *Do you not know that they which Minister about holy things, live of the things of the Temple, they which wait at the Altar, are partakers with the Altar?*

3. I N the New *Testament,* the Truth before us is expresly asserted, especially in that place where the Apostle says, *The Lord has ordain'd that*

that they who Preach the Gospel, should live of the Gospel, This he had proved from the Divine Law which appointed, That they who Minister about Holy things, should live of the things of the Temple, as was shew'd.   1 *Cor.* 9. 14.

A N D, from the Law of Nations,   *ver.* 7. *Who goeth a Warfare at his own Charges?* Souldiers do not use to go to War without Pay from the State that employs them. Ministers are engaged in a Warfare, He that has listed them in His Service, will have them Supported therein.

T H E Apostle moreover proveth his Doctrine from the Law of Nature, *Thou shalt not muzzle the Mouth of the Ox that treadeth out the Corn.* To do   *ver.* 9. that is Cruelty and Unmercifulness, which the light of Nature condemns.

N O W can any man suppose, that God will make Laws, to provide that brute Beasts shall be rewarded for their Labour, and that He will not have the Labour, of those that are His own Officers, to be duely acknowledg'd?

B U T besides this Chapter, in which the Apostle does inlarge on this Subject, there are other Scriptures in the New Testament, which command an Honourable Maintenance to be allow'd to the Ministers of the Gospel. What is implyed in that *Double Honour* which they are worthy of?   1 *Tim.* 5. 17. *not* only Reverence, *but* an Honourable Maintenance is doubtless thereby intended. And when its required of them that they should be *given to Hospitality;*   1 *Tim.* 3. 2. This is necessarily implied: for without a Liberal Maintenance

Maintenance it is impoſſible that they ſhould be capable of much Hoſpitality.

4. THERE is in the Scripture an expreſs Rule concerning this matter, ſhewing not only *that* the Miniſters of the Goſpel ſhould beMaintain'd , but *how* this ſhould be done ; the Rule is, *Let him that is taught in the Word communicate to him that teacheth in all good things.* If *not* only ſome, *but* every one that is taught, ſhould communicate to theirTeachers,not only in *Some*, but in *All* good things, they would doubtleſs have a competent Maintenance ; for (as the *Belgick* Annotators have well obſerved) to communicate of *All* good things, is to communicate *Liberally.*

Gal. 6. 6.

BY theſe things it is evident, that the Maintenance of Miniſters is not *Almes* (as ſome would have it) but due *Debt :* They receive it not as an act of *Charity* but of *Juſtice.* They have as much right to it as any *Labourer* has to his *hire.* Therefore when Chriſt ſent forth his Diſciples to Preach the Goſpel, He ſaid, *The Labourer is worthy of his hire.* So do they that Labour in theWord and Doctrine well deſerve the Recompence given to them : *They Work the Work of the Lord,* as the Apoſtle ſaid that *He* and *Timothy* did. The Scripture calls their Maintenance not *Alms* but *Reward* and *Wages.* The Apoſtle tells the Corinthians, that he took *Wages* of other Churches, to do them Service.

Luk. 10. 7.

1 Cor.16.10.
1 Tim. 5.18.
2 Cor. 11. 8.

ONE of the Ancients obſerves, that when the Apoſtle ſaith to theGalatians (who doubtleſs were defective in their duty as to that matter) Let him that is taught communicate to him that teacheth

teacheth; the Greek word is not μεταδιδοτω, which fignifys to' impart, but Κοινωνειτω, which imports a kind *Gal. 6. 6.* of *Commerce*, or Exchange of Spiritual things for Carnal. And whatever People may imagine, the *Wages* which Minifters receive, is not comparable to what they give, if they are diligent and faithful in the difcharge of the Work incumbent on them. *If we* *1 Cor. 9. 11.* *have fown unto Spiritual things, is it a great thing if we fhall not reap your Carnal things?*

T H I S Affertion is deni'd by few that call themfelves *Chriftians.* Some of the firft Reformers (*Bullinger* and others) tell us, that the *Anabaptifts* in thofe days, faid, The Minifters in the Reformed Churches were no true Minifters of Chrift, becaufe they took *Wages* for Preaching the Gofpel. They pretended that Chrift forbad his Difciples to receive any thing for their Labour, becaufe He faid to them, *Freely ye have received, freely give.* *Mat. 10. 8.* But they mifinterpreted, and abufed the Words of our Saviour: Chrift himfelf was Maintain'd by His Followers after He entred on His Publick Miniftry, and fo were the Apoftles. When there- *Luk. 8. 3.* fore the Lord faid, *freely give,* He *Phil. 4. 10,* does not fpeak of Preaching the *15, 16.* Gofpel, but of healing the Sick, and cafting out Devils, raifing the Dead, and the like miraculous Gifts. They might not take any reward for thefe, as the Prophet *Elifha* would not from *Naaman* the Syrian. It was great wickednefs in *Simon Magus*, when he thought to get Mony by the gifts of the Holy Spirit.

CONCLUSION, III.

There is something due to G O D *out of every Mans Estate, and the* Tenth *of his Incomes is the Least that may be supposed.*

THAT every man ought to confecrate a part of his Eftate to pious Ufes is indubitable. Againft this alfo fome pretend their Poverty; but are they poorer than the Widow, that had but two Mites, and yet caft them into the LordsTreafury? Nor do fuch confider, that this is the way to have more. For God will be in no man's debt; *That which he has given, theLord will pay him again. Eccl.* 11.1,2. Such Ventures have a Rich Return. *Caft thy bread on the waters, for thou fhall find it after many days: Give a Portion to feven, and alfo to eight.*

THERE are few that will fay, that nothing is due to God out of their Eftates: but about the *Quota pars*, or how much they ought to give, there are difputes. Some have thought that under the Gofpel a *fifth* part of a man's

yearly

yearly income fhould be devoted to Chrift, *viz.* 200 *l.* out of a Thoufand, which is a *fifth* part; a double portion to *Cant.* 8. 12. the Levitical Tenth. If they whom God has bleffed with great Eftates fhould do thus, they would honour God, and themfelves too.

THE Pious Lord *Harrington*, did not only give the *Tenth* of his Incomes to the Poor, but was other-ways bountiful in many Charities.

Mr. *Gouge* relates concerning that Religious Gentlewoman, Mrs. *Parthenia Lowman*, that in the time of her Widowhood, She devoted above a *fifth* part of her yearly Rents to Charitable Ufes.

Dr. *Walker* reports concerning that Right honourable and religious Lady, the late Countefs of *Warwick*, that fhe enquir'd of a Minifter, What proportion one is obliged to confecrate to God out of his Eftate? Who anfwered, that it was difficult, if not impoffible, to fix a rule that fhould hold univerfally; for that the Families and circumftances of Perfons muft be confidered: but that he fuppofed, That if fhe gave a *feventh* part of her large Incomes, that would be fufficient. She replyed, That was not enough, and that She would not give lefs than a *third* part; which She religioufly performed accordingly: That made fome People fay, That the Earl of *Warwick*, in giving his whole Eftate to his Wife, (as by his Will he had done) had left all his Eftate to Pious Ufes.

THE mentioning of this Noble Example, is a *Satyr* on thofe, who make a Will fo *Sacrilegious*, as out of a great Eftate not to devote one Penny to Pious Ufes. What account will

will fuch Perfons be able to give to God at the Day of Judgment, who would give Him no-thing, that had given much to them !

WHEN we fay that the *Tenth* of a man's Incomes are due to God, we do not intend thereby, That they are due to the *Minifters* of the Gofpel; altho' what is given to them, as fuch, is given to God. But fo alfo is what is laid out in purchafing *Bibles*, and other *Good Books*, defigning thereby to promote the Intereft of Religion in the World: and that which is expended in building Houfes for the Worfhip of God; And that which is given to the Lords Poor, *He that* Prov. 19. 17. *has pity on the Poor, lends to the Lord.* The like is to be faid concerning that which is devoted to *Colleges*, or Schools of Learning, in order to the upholding of Religi-on, which will be loft without good Literature. Well did *Luther* fay, *Si quid Scholafticus confers, Deo ipfi contulifti.* Some Religioufly difpofed Perfons have done great Service for *Chrift*, by Maintaining Poor Scholars in the Univerfities, who have proved *Eminent Inftruments* of Glory to God, and good to His Church.

NOW that at leaft, the *Tenth* of a mans yearly Incomes fhould be thus confecrated to the Lord, feems reafonable,

For,

1. THE Argument infifted on by the profoundly Learned Mr. *Jofeph Mede*, deferves confideration. He reafons thus, God deals very favourably with men if He requires only a *Tenth*, fince that is the leaft part of our Goods, according to the firft divifion. For as Ten is the Periodical number of a fixed and fubftantial na-ture;

nature ; fo when we proceed beyond Ten, we begin to make a new divifion, as eleven is ten and one, twelve is ten and two, &c. Thus as the Number of feven is the Periodical number of Time, God has been favourable to men in commanding only a Seventh part of Time, to be perpetually confecrated to His Service : So in accepting the *Tenth* of our Incomes, Ten beginning the greater number, and including the fmaller, has been efteemed proper for Him who is the firft Caufe, and the laft End of all things. With a *Seventh day* He is acknowledged the Creator, and with a *Tenth part*, the Poffeffor of all things.

2. B E F O R E the Inftitution of the Ceremonial or Judicial Law, the *Tenth* was due to God. *Abraham* gave *Tithe* of all to *Melchizedeck*. Which the Apoftle takes fpecial notice of *four* or *five* Times in one Chapter. Whence it has by Learned and Orthodox Men, been concluded, That this Homage and Tribute is due to Chrift.

Gen. 14. 20.

Heb. 7.

T H E R E never was any Type of Chrift, as a Prieft, but he received *Tithes*, and that not in the right of any thing in himfelf, but meerly in the virtue of his Typical Office ; fo that originally they pertained to that principal Prieft whofe Prieft-hood is Eternal.

A N D we find that *Jacob*, long before the Mofaical Law, Vowed unto God, faying, *Of all that thou givelt me, I will furely give the Tenth unto thee*. We read not, that the Patriarchs did this by virtue of any Pofitive Law : It feems then, that the Light of Nature which taught them

Gen. 28. 22.

them to chufe the Lord to be their God, directed them to confecrate a *Tenth* of their Eftate to their God.

AMONG the *Jews* at this day, many of the Richer fort ufually give away a *Tenth* part of their Eftate to charitable Ufes. Yea, and of old, the *Gentiles* did fo. Hence is that expreffion of *Plautus* ; *Ut decimam folveret Herculi : Pliny* tells us, That the *Arabs* confecrated the *Tenth* unto their god. *Decima quæque veteres dijs fuis offerebant,* fays *Feftus.* Many other Teftimonies concerning this, are cited by Dr. *Spencer,* and by that Learned Reformer, *John Wolphius,* who does from thence conclude, that the Law of Nature has taught Men thus to practife. *de Legib. Hebr. l. 3. c. 10. p. 615.*

I conclude this Argument with Mr. *Baxter*'s words, in his Difcourfe concerning what part of our Eftate we fhould devote to pious Ufes. *I confefs* (fays he,) *page, 97. If we confider how* Decimation *was ufed before the Law, by* Abraham *and* Jacob; *and how commonly it was ufed among the* Gentiles; *and laft of all by the Church of Chrift, it will make a confiderate man imagine, That as there is ftill a Divine direction for One Day in Seven, as a neceffary proportion of Time to be ordinarily confecrated to God, fo that there is fomething of a Divine Canon, or direction for the* Tenth *of our Revenues.* Thus Mr. *Baxter.*

3. A remarkable Bleffing has attended the Eftates of fome who have devoted the *Tenth* of their Incomes to pious Ufes.

Mr. *Mede* (before mentioned) when he was by a fignal Providence chofen a Fellow of Chrifts

Chrifts *College* in *Cambridge*, was fo affected with that Mercy, as that he folemnly Vowed to lay afide every *Tenth* Shilling he fhould receive, and to dedicate it to pious Ufes. This he did religioufly obferve: And altho' his Salery was but fmall, fuch a blefling attended him, as that he not only lived comfortably and and honourably, but was able at his Death, befidesLegacies to his Kindred, to give an 100 *l.* to the Poor, and 300 *l.* to the College, in which he dyed Fellow.

Mr. *Gataker* fpeaks of an eminent Merchant and Citizen of *London* (Mr. *John Parker*) who at his firft Effectual Calling, among other things, then refolved by him, this was one, That he would fet apart every year a *Tenth* of his gain for the relief of the Poor. For three or four years after his doing thus, he did not find that he thrived in his Eftate, yet he was not difcouraged thereby, but ftill gave Liberally and bountifully. And after fome time, God abundantly blefled and increafed his Temporal Eftate, that he would often profefs, that he found thofe Promifes to be true which affirm, That he that Scattereth fhall increafe; and that whoever Lends to the Lord, fhall be repayed.

Mr. *Gouge* fpeaks of one whom he knew, who finding little coming in by his Trade, refolved upon *two* things. 1. To be more careful in Sanctifying the Lords Day. 2. To fet apart the *Tenth* of his Incomes to Charitable Ufes. Whereupon in a few years he gained fo much, as that he gave over his Calling, and Lived upon his Rents.

I fhall mention one Inftance more, and that fhall beMr. *William Whately*, one famous in his
Time

Time, he declared privately to a Friend of his, that he laid afide every *Tenth* Shilling of his Receipts for pious Ufes ; upon which he found a wonderful Blelling on his Temporal Eftate. This Mr. *VVhately* was Minifter at *Banbury* in *Oxfordfhire.*

The Minifter is as much bound to devote the *Tenth* of his Incomes to pious Ufes, as any one of his People.

T H A T excellent Man Mr. *Thomas Gouge,* reports concerning his Father Dr. *Gouge,* who was Paftor of the Congregation at *Black-Friers* in *London,* That from him he firft heard, that men of Eftates, ought to dedicate a *Tenth* part of their yearly Incomes to pious Ufes, and he fays, that his Father did devote a *Seventh* part of his Incomes.

EXCERPT FROM
[AUTOBIOGRAPHY] THE LIFE OF DR. BENJAMIN FRANKLIN. WRITTEN BY HIMSELF

Benjamin Franklin, *[Autobiography] The Life of Dr. Benjamin Franklin. Written by himself*, 2nd edition (Philadelphia, 1794), pp. 111–14.

The self-educated son of a candle-maker, Benjamin Franklin (1706–90), made an early fortune in printing and publishing, including his famous annual, *Poor Richard's Almanac* (1732–58). Franklin's interest in scientific inquiry and travel made him known throughout Europe. In the decades prior to the American Revolution of 1775 to 1782, Franklin operated as the chief colonial ambassador in England and France. He was friends with many of the leading economists of his day, including Richard Price, David Hume, Adam Smith, and the Physiocrats (a school of French thinkers), particularly Du Pont de Nemours, who was a follower of Quesnay. Besides being a prolific writer, Franklin was deeply involved in politics. He served as the Pennsylvania representative to the Albany Conference and drafted the Plan of Union between France and British America in 1754. He held an important part in drafting the Articles of Confederation and the US Constitution. Franklin was a representative to the second Continental Congress (1775), submitting another Plan of Union and worked on the commission to write the Declaration of Independence in 1776. During this time, he became the first Postmaster General, organising the Postal Service through the Continental Congress. Franklin operated as the commissioner negotiating a peace treaty with France, and signed the final commerce and defence treaties between America and France in 1778. Franklin also engaged in negotiations with Great Britain, assuming responsibility for a peace treaty (1781–3). In 1787, he became a member of the Constitutional Convention, and was responsible for the representation compromise incorporated into the American Constitution.

Franklin is also renowned for his characterisation of American economic thought in the eighteenth century. He published on economic topics, ranging from paper money to population theories and free trade, from 1729 until his death. His writings present a synthesis of the best of European economics at the time, including mercantilist theory based on the work of William Petty, Physiocracy, and early English classicism (influenced by Adam Smith and Richard Price). However, Franklin is best known for his philosophy that only frugality and hard work will lead to wealth. These themes are evident in a number of his writings – including *Poor Richard's Almanac* and *Way to Wealth* – but are perhaps best articulated by his own experiences, as recorded in his *Autobiography*.

Nearly at the same period the people demanded a new emission of paper money; the existing and only one that had taken place in the province, and which amounted to fifteen thousand pounds, being soon to expire. The wealthy inhabitants, prejudiced against every sort of paper currency, from the fear of its depreciation, of which there had been an instance in the province of New-England, to the injury of its holders, strongly opposed the measure. We had discussed this affair in our junto, in which I was on the side of the new emission; convinced that the first small sum fabricated in 1723, had done much good in the province, by favouring commerce, industry and population, since all the houses were now inhabited, and many others building, whereas I remembered to have seen, when first I paraded the streets of Philadelphia eating my roll, the majority of those in Walnut-street, Second-street, Fourth-street, as well as a great number in Chesnut and other streets, with papers on them signifying that they were to be let; which made me think at the time that the inhabitants of the town were deserting it one after another.

Our debates made me so fully master of the subject, that I wrote and published an anonymous pamphlet, entitled, An Enquiry into the Nature and Necessity of a Paper Currency. It was very well received by the lower and middling class of people; but it displeased the opulent, as it increased the clamour in favour of the new emission. – Having, however, no writer among them capable of answering it, their opposition became less violent; and there being in the house of Assembly a majority for the measure, it passed. The friends I had acquired in the house, persuaded that I had done the country essential service on this occasion, rewarded me by giving me the printing of the bills. It was a lucrative employment, and proved a very seasonable help to me; another advantage which I derived from having habituated myself to write.

Time and experience so fully demonstrated the utility of paper currency, that it never after experienced any considerable opposition; so that it soon amounted to 55,000l. and in the year 1739 to 80,000l. It has since risen, during the last war, to 350,000l. trade, buildings and population having in the interval continually encreased, but I am now convinced that there are limits beyond which paper money would be prejudicial.

I soon after obtained, by the influence of my friend Hamilton, the printing of the Newcastle paper money, another profitable work, as I then thought it, little things appearing great to persons of moderate fortune; and they were really great to me, as proving great encouragements. He also procured me the printing of the laws and votes of that government which I retained as long as I continued in the business.

I now opened a small stationer's shop. I kept bonds and agreements of all kinds, drawn up in a more accurate form than had yet been seen in that part of the world; a work in which I was assisted by my friend Brientnal. I had also paper, parchment, pasteboard, books, &c. One Whitemash, an excellent compositor, whom I had known in London, came to offer himself. I engaged him, and he continued constantly and diligently to work with me, I also took an apprentice, the son of Aquila Rose.

I began to pay, by degrees, the debt I had contracted; and in order to insure my credit and character as a tradesman. I took care not only to be *really* industrious and frugal, but also to avoid every appearance of the contrary. I was plainly dressed, and never seen in any place of public amusement. I never went a fishing or hunting: A book indeed enticed me sometimes from my work, but it was seldom, by stealth, and occasioned no scandal; and to show that I did not think myself above my profession, I conveyed home sometimes in a wheelbarrow the paper I purchased at the warehouses.

LETTER TO EZRA STILES

Benjamin Franklin, Letter to Ezra Stiles, March 9, 1790, in *The Complete Works of Benjamin Franklin: Including His Private as Well as his Official and Scientific Correspondence, and Numerous Letters and Documents Now for the First Time Printed, with Many Others Not Included in Any Former Collection, Also the Unmutilated and Correct Version of his Autobiography*, ed. John Bigelow (New York, G. P. Putnam's Sons, 1888), vol. x, pp. 192–5.

This collection includes a number of excerpts from Franklin's works and, prior to this piece, an excerpt from his *Autobiography*. This was begun in the 1770s, but published posthumously, originally in French, and then in English in 1793. The excerpt reprinted here is from the second edition in 1794. Franklin's Letter to Ezra Stiles, written later in his life, is also included here as a reflection of Franklin's views near his death on the themes already discussed in his autobiography. These pieces demonstrate Franklin's faith that wealth would be gained through hard work – the Poor Richard philosophy, as demonstrated in his *Poor Richard's Almanac* – independent of a religious, hierarchical society. The excerpt included from Franklin's *Autobiography* illustrates the secularisation of the Puritan or Quaker work ethic, as Franklin chronicled how he gained his own fortune through hard work and intelligence. Reproduced below is his letter to Ezra Stiles, which similarly emphasises the secularisation of economic and social thinking at the close of the eighteenth century.[1]

---

1 A more extensive collection of Franklin's economic writings is available in: Jared Sparks (ed.), *The Works of Benjamin Franklin*, 10 vols (New York: A. M. Kelley, 1971), vol. ii, *Essays on General Politics, Commerce and Political Economy*.

"AS TO JESUS OF NAZARETH"

To Ezra Stiles

REVEREND AND DEAR SIR,   Philadᵃ, March 9. 1790.

I received your kind Letter of Jan'y 28, and am glad you have at length received the portrait of Gov'r Yale from his Family, and deposited it in the College Library. He was a great and good Man, and had the Merit of doing infinite Service to your Country by his Munificence to that Institution. The Honour you propose doing me by placing mine in the same Room with his, is much too great for my Deserts; but you always had a Partiality for me, and to that it must be ascribed. I am however too much obliged to Yale College, the first learned Society that took Notice of me and adorned me with its Honours, to refuse a Request that comes from it thro' so esteemed a Friend. But I do not think any one of the Portraits you mention, as in my Possession, worthy of the Place and Company you propose to place it in. You have an excellent Artist lately arrived. If he will undertake to make one for you, I shall cheerfully pay the Expence; but he must not delay setting about it, or I may slip thro' his fingers, for I am now in my eighty-fifth year, and very infirm.

I send with this a very learned Work, as it seems to me, on the antient Samaritan Coins, lately printed in Spain, and at least curious for the Beauty of the Impression. Please to accept it for your College Library. I have subscribed for the Encyclopædia now printing here, with the Intention of presenting it to the College. I shall probably depart before the Work is finished, but shall leave Directions for its Continuance to the End. With this you will receive some of the first numbers.

You desire to know something of my Religion. It is the first time I have been questioned upon it. But I cannot take your Curiosity amiss, and shall endeavour in a few Words to gratify it. Here is my Creed. I believe in one God, Creator of the Universe. That he governs it by his Providence. That he ought to be worshipped. That the most acceptable Service we render to him is doing good to his other Children. That the soul of Man is immortal, and will be treated with Justice in another Life respecting its Conduct in this. These I take to be the fundamental Principles of all sound Religion, and I regard them as you do in whatever Sect I meet with them.

As to Jesus of Nazareth, my Opinion of whom you particularly desire, I think the System of Morals and his Religion, as he left them to us, the best the World ever saw or is likely to see; but I apprehend it has received various corrupting Changes, and I have, with most of the present Dissenters in England, some Doubts as to his Divinity; tho' it is a question I do not dogmatize upon, having never studied it, and think it needless to busy myself with it now, when I expect soon an Opportunity of knowing the Truth with less Trouble. I see no harm, however, in its being believed, if that Belief has the good Consequence, as probably it has, of making his Doctrines more respected and better observed; especially as I do not perceive, that the Supreme takes it amiss, by distinguishing the Unbelievers in his Government of the World with any peculiar Marks of his Displeasure.

I shall only add, respecting myself, that, having experienced the Goodness of that Being in conducting me prosperously thro' a long life, I have no doubt of its Continuance in the next, though without the smallest Conceit of meriting such Goodness. My Sentiments on this Head you will see in the Copy of an old Letter enclosed, which I wrote in answer to one from a zealous Religionist, whom I had relieved in a paralytic case by electricity, and who, being afraid I should grow proud upon it, sent me his serious though rather impertinent Caution. I send you also the Copy of another Letter, which will shew something of my Disposition relating to Religion. With great and sincere Esteem and Affection, I am, Your obliged old Friend and most obedient humble Servant.

P. S. Had not your College some Present of Books from the King of France? Please to let me know, if you had an Expectation given you of more, and the Nature of that Expectation? I have a Reason for the Enquiry.

I confide, that you will not expose me to Criticism and censure by publishing any part of this Communication to you. I have ever let others enjoy their religious Sentiments, without reflecting on them for those that appeared to me unsupportable and even absurd. All Sects here, and we have a great Variety, have experienced my good will in assisting them with Subscriptions for building their new Places of Worship; and, as I have never opposed any of their Doctrines, I hope to go out of the World in Peace with them all.

For Product Safety Concerns and Information please contact our EU representative GPSR@taylorandfrancis.com Taylor & Francis Verlag GmbH, Kaufingerstraße 24, 80331 München, Germany

Batch number: 08158389

Printed by Printforce, the Netherlands